argentine intimacies

**SUNY SERIES Genders in the Global South**

Debra A. Castillo and Shelley Feldman, editors

# argentine
# intimacies

QUEER KINSHIP IN
AN AGE OF SPLENDOR,
1890–1910

**Joseph M. Pierce**

Cover image: Augusto and Carlos Octavio Bunge, ca. 1880. Bunge Family Archive (Courtesy of Lucía Gálvez).

Published by STATE UNIVERSITY OF NEW YORK PRESS

© 2019 State University of New York Press

All rights reserved

No part of this book may be used or reproduced in any manner whatsoever without written permission. No part of this book may be stored in a retrieval system or transmitted in any form or by any means including electronic, electrostatic, magnetic tape, mechanical, photocopying, recording, or otherwise without the prior permission in writing of the publisher.

For information, contact
STATE UNIVERSITY OF NEW YORK PRESS, ALBANY, NY
www.sunypress.edu

**Library of Congress Cataloging-in-Publication Data**

Names: Pierce, Joseph M., author.
Title: Argentine intimacies : queer kinship in an age of splendor, 1890-1910 / Joseph M. Pierce.
Description: Albany : State University of New York, [2019] | Series: SUNY series, genders in the global south | Includes bibliographical references and index.
Identifiers: LCCN 2018058249| ISBN 9781438476810 (hardcover: alk. paper) | ISBN 9781438476834 (e-book) | ISBN 9781438476827 (pbk.: alk. paper)
Subjects: LCSH: Families—Argentina. | Queer theory—Argentina. | Interpersonal relations—Argentina. | Intimacy (Psychology) | Argentina—History—1860-1910. | Bunge, Carlos O. (Carlos Octavio), 1875-1918—Political and social views.
Classification: LCC HQ590 .P54 2019 | DDC 306.850982—dc23
LC record available at https://lccn.loc.gov/2018058249

10 9 8 7 6 5 4 3 2 1

For **Mable Humble Liles**

CONTENTS

list of illustrations — ix
acknowledgments — xi

INTRODUCTION — 1
The Bunge Family: Queerness, Kinship, and Modernity

CHAPTER ONE — 29
Carlos Octavio Bunge: Queer Desire and Family Fictions

CHAPTER TWO — 91
Sisters Writing, Sisters Reading: The Diaries of Julia and Delfina Bunge

CHAPTER THREE — 137
Spectral Desires: Queering the Family Album

CHAPTER FOUR — 189
Family Pedagogy: The Institutionalization of Kinship

CHAPTER FIVE — 231
National Essays, Home Economics: The Argentine Oligarchy in Decline

EPILOGUE — 267
Toward a Queer Latin American Studies

notes — 283
works cited — 299
index — 313

# ILLUSTRATIONS

FIGURE 2.1 — 102
The diary as palimpsest

FIGURE 3.1 — 148
Carlos Octavio Bunge at Oxford

FIGURE 3.2 — 149
Carlos Octavio Bunge in London

FIGURE 3.3 — 153
Carlos Octavio Bunge and "Nuestra América"

FIGURE 3.4 — 155
Carlos Octavio Bunge in *Caras y Caretas*

FIGURE 3.5 — 158
Carlos Octavio Bunge in casual dress

FIGURE 3.6 — 162
Julia Valentina Bunge as Princesse Lointaine

FIGURE 3.7 — 163
Sarah Bernhardt in *La Princesse Lointaine*

FIGURE 3.8 — 166
Delfina Bunge

FIGURE 3.9 — 167
Delfina Bunge with bouquet

FIGURE 3.10 — 169
Ink drawing of Delfina Bunge by C. Kier

FIGURE 3.11 — 171
Delfina Bunge de Gálvez, 1983, "Escritores argentinos"

FIGURE 3.12 — 173
Hotel Sierras 1

FIGURE 3.13 — 174
Hotel Sierras 2

FIGURE 3.14 — 175
Hotel Sierras 3

FIGURE 3.15 — 177
Walking the grounds of the Hotel Sierras

FIGURE 3.16 — 177
Julia Valentina Bunge, Ignacio Uranga, and Delfina Bunge

FIGURE 3.17 — 179
Delfina and Taita Reading

FIGURE 3.18 — 183
Group of six at the Hotel Sierras

FIGURE 3.19 — 184
Group photo at the Hotel Sierras

FIGURE 3.20 — 186
Excursion in Alta Gracia

FIGURE 3.21 — 188
"Casa en que murió" Carlos Octavio Bunge

## ACKNOWLEDGMENTS

Family is complicated and writing about it has not been easy. But creating, sustaining, and admitting it into my life has been one of the most joyful aspects of this project. This book about families would not have been possible without the support and kindness of my parents, Randall and Catherine Pierce. I don't think I'll ever have the words for what that has meant to me. My brother, Blake, listened like only a sibling can. His partner, Sarah, has brightened many a family gathering and I am so happy that they have brought a new family member, Luke, into the world. My aunt Teena and uncle Bill Liles taught me about family through New Year's Eve parties and lazy afternoon sails. My cousin William and his partner, Natalia, and their daughters Annabelle and Camila, are hilarious and delightful. My cousin Elizabeth and her partner, Lee, amaze me with their exuberance. My late grandmother, Mable Liles, was sharp-witted, elegant, and tirelessly generous, and she would have been so proud to see this book. I dedicate it to her.

At The University of Texas at Austin, I had the great fortune to learn from and with a diverse group of interlocutors in the Department of Spanish and Portuguese and the Lozano Long Institute of Latin American Studies. Héctor Domínguez-Ruvalcaba and Nicolas Shumway provided me with guidance and mentorship and so much more. They taught me how to read better, how to listen, and how to turn my curiosity into questions that matter. My understanding of queer kinship is due in no small part to the space they provided in seminars, coffee shops, and walks around the lake, space that allowed me to think through what has been and what could be. Along the way, I learned a great deal from Lisa Moore, Jossianna Arroyo, Sônia Roncador, and Luis Cárcamo-Huechante. Anne Dibble and Laura Rodríguez made me feel at home. The first stages of research for what would eventually become this book were funded by the Department of Spanish and Portuguese Summer Research Award and the Graduate School Continuing Fellowship.

I want to thank, too, many friends and comrades from graduate school. It was a time of transition in more ways than one, and my life was enriched by the presence of Alejandra Zambrano, Giulianna Zambrano, Rocío del Águila, Enrique Navarro, Marc Amengual, Nicolas Poppe, Brian Price, Jorge García, Danny Méndez, Juancarlos López, Marcelle Beaulieu, and the late Steve Jacobs, whose infectious laugh I miss very much.

At Stony Brook University, my colleagues in the Department of Hispanic Languages and Literature showed enthusiastic support for this work through thick and thin, but more importantly, they fostered an environment for me to grow in all number of personal and professional ways. My sincere appreciation goes out to Adrián Pérez-Melgosa, Daniela Flesler, Kathleen Vernon, Paul Firbas, Lena Burgos-Lafuente, Javier Uriarte, Victoriano Roncero-López, Lilia Ruiz-Debbe, and Lou Charnon-Deutsch. At Stony Brook I have had the privilege to teach graduate seminars and undergraduate courses about queer kinship, (bad) romance, scientific writing, and gender and sexuality in Latin America, and my discussions in those courses with a great many students has improved my thinking, teaching, and engagement with the world. In addition to those students, I would like to thank colleagues from other parts of the university whose encouragement and insight has proven invaluable: Liz Montegary, Lisa Diedrich, Victoria Hesford, Crystal Flemming, Kathleen Wilson, Lori Flores, Tracey Walters, Nancy Hiemstra, Ryan Minor, Nerissa Balce, E. K. Tan, Iona Man-Cheong, Jeffrey Santa Ana, and Sara Lipton.

Writing a book often seems like a lonely enterprise, but now at least I realize that I have been accompanied in thinking and writing by a great many people in and out of the academy. In Argentina, I was accompanied through inside jokes, *asados*, and national archives. My thanks to Mario Pecheny, Daniel Link, María Moreno, Mariano López-Seoane, Silvana Lacarra, Marcelo Plaza, Matías González, Sabrina Frydman, Martín Khabié, María Gabriela Mizraje, and, especially, Lucía Gálvez for opening her home to me and providing access to the Bunge Family Archive. Without her generosity, this book would not exist. In the United States (and elsewhere), I have been supported, challenged, and inspired by a great many people, some of whom agreed to read (or listen to me read) portions of this book, while others helped keep me grounded while writing it: Lawrence La Fountain-Stokes, Ben. Sifuentes-Jáuregui, Yolanda

Martínez-San Miguel, Guillermo de los Reyes, Claudia Salazar Jiménez, Marcos Wasem, Fernando Blanco, Bernardita Llanos, Alejandra Uslenghi, Germán Garrido, Jennifer Tyburczy, Salvador Vidal-Ortiz, Vincent Cervantes, Patricio Simonetto, Rubí Carreño, Paulina Daza, María Amelia Viteri, Elizabeth Freeman, T. J. Tallie, Ramzi Fawaz, Kadji Amin, Matthew Goldmark, Lisa Duggan, Zeb Tortorici, Gabriel Giorgi, Sylvia Molloy, Juana María Rodríguez, J. Kēhaulani Kauanui, Jaskiran Dhillon, Mike Strupp-Levitsky, Lizzie Glaeser, Jeff Kauffman, Ian Hartz, Nick Williams, Matthew Epler, David Román, Jack Halberstam, Macarena Gómez-Barris, Tavia Nyong'o, Nancy LaGreca, Marcia Ochoa, and Diego Falconí. A special note of appreciation goes to James Worsdale, who brings me so much joy, and whose humor and grace have been life sustaining.

Earlier versions of portions of chapter 1 were developed as articles: "'Usted no es hombre para esas cosas': Masculinidad y renegación en la obra de Carlos O. Bunge." *Taller de letras* 58 (September 2016): 127-39; and "Regulating Queer Desire in Carlos O. Bunge's *La novela de la sangre*." *Revista Hispánica Moderna* 69, no. 1 (June 2016): 55-71. The final stages of this book were supported by the Stony Brook University Fine Arts, Humanities, and Social Science Initiative.

Finally, I would like to thank Rebecca Colesworthy, my editor at SUNY Press, who has gone above and beyond, as well as the series editors, Debra A. Castillo and Shelley Feldman, for believing in this project.

IntRoDuctIon

# THE BUNGE FAMILY
## QUEERNESS, KINSHIP, AND MODERNITY

Estuve mirando las fotos de todos nosotros, de mi familia, colgadas en la pared de esta casa y es como si hubiera hablado con ellos y conmigo misma, a lo largo de todos los años pasados, vividos con y a veces sin ellos. Percibí una fuerza rara, única, irremplazable en esos grupos de familia, una energía luminosa y conflictiva si no se atraviesa y se la deja fluir. Por ejemplo, yo iba teniendo caras distintas y no es que fueran cada vez más viejas, más gastadas como temí sino siempre a medias ilusionadas y a medias triste, pero confiando, alegre de estar con ellos, aunque fuera para ese claro momento de la foto.

I was looking at the photos of all of us, of my family, hung on the wall of this house and it is as if I had been speaking with them and with myself, for all these past years, lived sometimes with, sometimes without them. I sensed a force, strange, unique, irreplaceable in those family groups, an energy that is luminous and conflictive if you don't interfere but let it flow. For example, I would take on different faces and it is not that they were getting older, more faded, as I feared but always half hopeful and half sad, but trusting, happy to be with them, even if it were only for that one clear moment of the photo. (Tiscornia 63)[1]

In the scene narrated above family appears implacable, an uncanny feeling of recognition and strangeness. The narrator sees herself reflected in a series of family portraits that look back at her and transform. They take on her expression through a gaze that is at once singular and shared, eternal and ephemeral. Familiar. Subjected to the photograph's queer temporality, she struggles to disentangle the present of her body from its history as part of a family. The photograph makes present other bodies, bodies "that-have-been," historically, materially, as Roland Barthes argues in *Camera Lucida*, and yet which, in this moment of their recognition by the narrator, are not quite here, not quite now. This is a moment in which *queer kinship* is made.

Written by Delfina Tiscornia in late 1988, this intimate text takes another intimate text, the family photograph, as the basis for her own account of how kinship is mediated by the objects that connect family members across time. Delfina Tiscornia (1966-1996) was the great granddaughter of her namesake Delfina Bunge (1881-1952), whose portrait hung on the wall along with other illustrious forebears. Family repeats, as one precocious poet looks back at another.[2] A century apart, kinship is oriented by and around the image of one Delfina who becomes multiple, iterative. In recognizing herself as related, Tiscornia connects to these ancestors through what Marianne Hirsch calls the "familial look." Here, the look projects a futurity that nonetheless depends on the disorientation of historical time. One moment in 1900 is photographed, and then perceived a century later as queerly familiar. Family, like the photograph, emerges through negotiating a sense of self-in-relation, through time rendered historical, through the body as it approximates other bodies, both present and absent. This is the strange, luminous matter of kinship. It lingers. It hides in plain sight and transforms.

*Argentine Intimacies* takes this strange feeling as its point of departure for studying family life in Argentina's fin de siècle (1890-1910). My sense is that we, like Tiscornia, are still under the spell of that turn of the century, that age of splendor in which the matter of kinship was cast anew as something that had been and could be again but different, modern. I begin with the above passage not simply because it dwells on the matter of kinship over time (as memory) and through the body (as experience), or because it was written by one family member about being related to those with whom she shares kinship. Rather, I begin with it because it performs the paradoxical relationship of kinship as simultaneously idealized and enacted. The passage intends to preserve the memory of family members that the author never met, and yet, as a text, it also creates, performs, those very relationships in the present through its writing. Tiscornia's essay was published in the posthumous collection *Ella camina sola* (2006), which was sponsored—and introduced—by Lucía Gálvez, Delfina Tiscornia's mother; Delfina Bunge's granddaughter. The collection reflects on how family is made and is itself the result of the love and loss that so often infuse kinship with a sense of enduring capaciousness.[3] Such intimacy is at once quotidian and extraordinary. I, too, as I was researching this book, would find myself in that same living room, looking at those same portraits, holding a copy of *Ella camina sola* that was given to me by Lucía Gálvez as a parting gift, a remembrance of her daughter. The text is more than a lucid reflection on the qualities that give meaning to family, but an object produced through and by virtue of the logics, the affective charge, of kinship over time. Its sentiment crystallizes how kinship operates as both a structure and as a source of artistic and cultural expression that emerges in the late nineteenth century, when the contradictions of modernity were only beginning to come into focus. I tell the story of how I met Lucía Gálvez below, and of how I came to relate queerly to the family photographs, archives, and histories that Delfina Tiscornia describes with such awe. Before that, however, I want to explain concretely what *Argentine Intimacies* is about and how it contributes to ongoing dialogues about queerness, kinship, and modernity.

At its core, this book is about the paradoxes of kinship. It describes how political, economic, and cultural changes in Argentina at the turn of the century mobilized contradictory responses to what family meant, what it could mean, and for whom. In a broad sense, it is about the power of the family as an ideological framework and contradictory set of relational norms. It deals with the development of nationalism, the fear of social and demographic change, economic promise and decline, the relationship between normativity and queerness, and the intersections of sexuality, gender, race, and class. Each of these issues transverses the kinship imaginary as the significance of the family is made and remade.

In order to approach these issues, I anchor this book in a particular place and time, and on four related individuals. The Bunge siblings, Carlos Octavio (1875-1918), Julia Valentina (1880-1969), Alejandro (1880-1943), and Delfina (1881-1952), were part of a generation of eight.[4] Each of them crafted a distinct authorial voice and body of work. They all had privileged access to power, access that they would exploit and harness to their benefit. They intervened in nationally and internationally significant ways through continued engagement with critical issues (economics, law, culture, literature, art, politics, etc.) as members of the upper class. In short, they were a family of writers who wrote about family. Their father, Octavio Bunge (1844-1910) was a Supreme Court justice, descended from a handsome Prussian adventurer and politician, Karl August Bunge (1804-1849). Their mother, María Luisa Bunge Arteaga (1853-1934), was an accomplished painter and came from a commercially successful Basque family who had immigrated to Uruguay in the eighteenth century. The Bunge-Arteaga family was part of the network of landed elite that consolidated power over the course of the nineteenth century through strategic marriages, political alliances, and business savvy that came to be known as the Argentine *oligarquía*.[5] They were a politically influential, socially respected family that formed an essential part of the intellectual elite in Buenos Aires, as they were also connected to the broader network of wealthy landowners in the province of Buenos Aires.[6] Indeed, the Bunges are one of Argentina's most prolific intellectual families—which is also to say political families—of the late nineteenth and early twentieth century, among the likes of the Mansillas, Guido y Spanos, Villafañes, Ocampos, Borgeses, and Payrós. As a generation of writers who left a vast oeuvre of both public and private texts, the Bunge siblings provide an unparalleled window onto the contradictory period of modernization in Argentina. They enact what Ángel Rama calls the vacillations of power, art, discourse, and signification of "*la ciudad modernizada*" ("the modernized city"; 61).

The two decades that straddle the turn of the twentieth century represent a crucial moment when the state project of normalizing culture demanded specific forms of racial identification, gender performance, and sexuality. The stakes for maintaining the architecture of patriarchal normativity were high at the turn of the century in Latin America, when the concept of family became a battleground for the consolidation of the discourses, institutions, and technologies that shaped modern culture. At the heart of these public debates, the Bunge siblings positioned themselves not only as intellectual leaders of the criollo elite, but as models of a new sociality at the turn of the century that expanded and redefined the family as modern. They intervened in all manner of cultural fields, in society, and in politics, and as such have exerted a tremendous influence over the way that public and private life was understood at that time, an influence that persists to this day. The Bunge siblings wrote lengthy tracts on political economy and education, social psychology and sociology; they wrote school textbooks and literary anthologies; kept diaries and published memoirs; they left family photographs, drawings, and letters. This archive represents a unique opportunity from which to critique the juncture of tradition and modernity, self and other, the normative and the queer.

In seeking to understand what family meant in this particular era, this book engages with queer theory and Latin American studies, interdisciplinary modes of approaching cultural phenomena. In contrast with most queer studies scholarship, however, *Argentine Intimacies* does not seek out alternatives to normative family life as performed by dissident subjects through the channels of minoritarian desire—not new "chosen families"— but rather sees as queer the lived enactment of the orientations that kinship demands, orientations that constantly fail, reshape, and reemerge.[7] It is this queer feeling of a portrait that looks back and smiles your own smile, a portrait as a mirror and a window onto the past-future, that stretches the possibilities of envisioning family as a site of queer scholarship. *Argentine Intimacies* examines the interface of queerness, kinship, and modernity, and argues that the embodiment of what we have come to know as the modern family depends on a constant—often melancholic—negotiation with queerness. By focusing on moments of tension in which the normative family strains to accept its own normativity, rather than on idealized expressions of domestic unity, it broadens the conversation about how cultural and erotic norms are unsettled. It argues that the normativity of kinship is negotiated through its proximity with and desire for the queerness that it takes as constitutive of its own difference.[8] This is not to say that the normative and the queer are irreconcilable, but rather, on the contrary, they are mutually dependent on each other, as a photograph that registers simultaneously identification and estrangement, kinship and queerness, joy and melancholy. This is not a book about queer families, but about how family is queer.

The Bunge family resists easy categorization. They show us how the categories that we tend to use in queer studies often fail to account for the intense negotiation that occurs in establishing what "normative" and "queer" have come to mean. My relationship with this family—mediated, textual—has unfolded over time as a series of disjunctions between theory and text. They have consistently forced me to question assumptions that I did not realize I had made about their lives and desires. The slow process of archival research, the fragile materiality of the objects I have chosen to study, and the difficulty of access have given me time to read and reread, to contradict myself, at times unwittingly. The slowness of this process has also taught me something about how queer studies often seeks a clarity of expression, of difference, that can result in disappointment. We overlook the queerness of the normative family, or perhaps the search for alternatives has drawn the vision of queer studies away from the normative, which becomes flattened out as an object of study, a caricature of normativity. Rather than seek out queerness in its novel forms, in the formations of alternative kinship arrangements, bodily orientations, or becomings, I have learned to focus squarely on the normative family as a productive site of queerness. The question then becomes: what does such a normative family have to say about queerness? It is this question, in fact, that motivates this book. If we can expand what queerness means to include how the normative curves to incorporate ever more dissonance, more bodies, more desires, then we can begin to imagine what might happen to kinship when it no longer materializes relations on its own but rather necessarily through the mediating forces of the strange and the queer.

While the Bunge family played a prominent role in Argentine culture at the turn of the century, they have also been overlooked, for the most part, by its historians and cultural critics. In part, this is due to the politically conservative, white supremacist agenda that was publically espoused by many of the family members. I think, too, that the types of texts they published (and did not publish) have made their work less fashionable, on the one hand, and less accessible, on the other, as a source of literary and cultural criticism. Their creative writing was not avant-garde or formally innovative, while their intimate, private texts have not been made public except in rare instances. One of these instances is the two-volume history of the Bunge family written Eduardo José Cárdenas and Carlos Manuel Payá, which has been an invaluable resource for this project. While Cárdenas and Payá are excellent at weaving historical narrative and primary source materials, they do not question the ideological foundations of kinship, its contradictions, or its fluctuations, as I do in this book. Likewise, intellectual historians such as Oscar Terán, Nicolas Shumway, and Charles A. Hale have flagged Carlos Octavio Bunge, the most prominent figure of this generation, as an exponent of positivist and subsequent eugenic thought in Argentina (and rightly so). But neither he nor the rest of the family has been studied from the perspective of literary and cultural studies, and much less from the lens of queer studies, with one notable exception: Jorge Salessi's *Médicos maleantes y maricas*. Salessi's work is one of the first Latin American studies texts to bring into dialogue queer studies, interdisciplinary archival research, and a critique of foundational national narratives in the Southern Cone. He elucidates how the process of naming deviance has been essential to late nineteenth-century positivism's taxonomical drive to order, contain, and eliminate bodies and desires that contradicted patriarchal heteronormativity and white supremacy. And while I am indebted to Salessi's work for its archival breadth and incisive interpretation of how a new generation of psychologists and social hygienists, as they were called, came to wield positivist science as an extension of state power, my work differs from his in scope and method. On the one hand, I approach relationality as emerging out of the interaction between bodies, affects, and discourses, rather than relying on a Foucaldian approach that privileges discursivity in the creation of taxonomic definitions. On the other hand, I expand on Salessi's historicism by asking how the very elite who defined normativity also sought to question its precepts, rather than advance an intellectual critique of how it came to interpellate nonnormative bodies and desires as ontologically deviant.

While I expand on this below, most literary and cultural criticism of the turn of the century argues that members of the upper class like the Bunge family sought to maintain their claim to cultural relevance by promoting idealized notions of family life bound to domesticity, social hygiene, and patriotism. It would make sense that the lettered elite saw the normative family as a refuge from what positivist scientists described as the threat of gender and class inversion. *Argentine Intimacies* uses the vast corpus of literary and cultural production by the Bunge family as a framework to examine what is left out of this narrative: the range of queer feelings, desires, and gestures by members of just such an elite family. Rather than imagining the family as a conservative space of identity formation, this book asks what the family's queerness—and what queering the familiar—might mean for contemporary understandings of gender, sexuality, kinship, and nationalism. To riff on Judith Butler's provocative phrase, I want to show how kinship is always already queer.[9]

To do so, I examine family members who are related and who write about being related. This is a choice that allows me to critique horizontally, across a particular generation, and transversally, across genres and forms of performing kinship. Here I diverge from Latin American studies scholarship that has privileged certain types of writing, in particular national novels and essays of national identity, by placing understudied forms of expression, such as the diary, the memoir, and the textbook, in dialogue with (and as) national genres. While private writing and the performance of intimacy are not exempt from the cultural and psychological scripts that shape human desires and actions, by looking at these minor genres (and private, intimate cultural production) in tandem with major ones we begin to see that the expression of normativity is only possible as a polyvocal, contradictory suturing of discourses, bodies, and desires. This is why I dwell on the *interface* of writing and kinship, and in turn show how the act of writing becomes a queer performance of self-in-relation. In linking the formal demands of writing (in particular autobiographical writing) to the narrative possibilities of imagining oneself as part of a family, I illustrate how the matter of a text (its structure) acts on and is affected by the desire to relate as kin. This allows me to argue that limitations of form become possibilities of kinship, and that kinship is constituted through the formal qualities of literary and cultural production. In this way, *Argentine Intimacies* brings to bear historical understandings and the lived enactment of kinship on contemporary debates in cultural studies, gender and sexuality studies, and queer theory. Highlighting the tension between individual desires and collective responsibilities, this book demonstrates that the study of national identities must take into account the queer potentials of the modern family.

## REVISING THE FAMILY ROMANCE

As I note above, understanding the ideological alignment between the fictional representation of family and the nation has been one of the central preoccupations of Latin American studies over the past thirty years. However, much of this scholarship has tended to take for granted the role of normative kinship ideologies as a foundational regime in the narration of possible national identities. For example, Doris Sommer's claim that the shape of the modern national community in Latin America was highly influenced by fictional accounts of heterosexual love and marriage, particularly as seen through allegory, is now ubiquitous. Combining insights from Benedict Anderson and Michel Foucault, Sommer links erotic rhetoric and allegorized fiction to propose a foundational "erotics of politics" that is based on at least potentially procreative marital unions, which provide models for nonviolent national consolidation following the wave of independence movements in Latin America (6). The romantic attachments that Sommer highlights posit the only viable outcome of the allegorical romance plot as the ideological imbrication between heteronormative desire and the nation. Learning to love the correct romantic partner and learning to love the nation become one and the same ideological project. While I agree that the channeling of desire to uphold normative sexual, gendered, and racialized formations is central to nation-building projects, as I demonstrate in this book, that desire, that force, must also reckon with queerness in order for it to materialize through the embodied practice of becoming or making kin. The national romance wrestles with a level of anxiety and ambivalence that Sommer does not account for in her work, an instability through which the structurating of desire comes to make sense of the eroticized landscape of modernity in Latin America.

Gabriela Nouzeilles, for her part, shows how the literature of the late nineteenth century can be seen as *"re-escritura escéptica"* ("skeptical rewriting") of the foundational romance novels analyzed by Sommer (15). Nouzeilles shows the continuation of the family model as a vehicle of literary expression as it moves from the Romanticism of the mid-nineteenth century into the Naturalism (in particular) of the turn of the twentieth century. The narrative structure of these turn-of-the-century family romances is quite different from that of their predecessors: rather than utopian unions, we see intrinsic conflict, unavoidable incompatibility, *"familias fallidas"* ("failed families"; 15). Texts such as *Sin rumbo* (1885) and *En la sangre* (1888) by Eugenio Cambaceres, if partially modeled on French naturalism's objective description of reality, were written in a pessimistic tone regarding what the author saw as a national culture lacking a moral (read ethnic) compass. These novels deal specifically with the multiplicity of possible romantic unions in an age of rapid population growth and shifting class and racial categories. In this literature, as Nouzeilles argues, "el casamiento ya no es, como en *Amalia* de Mármol, el final deseable de una historia de amor ideal. (...) En el espacio de la intimidad donde la cópula entre amantes de diferentes clases/razas se consuma, la tragedia (real o probable) casi siempre interviene ("marriage is no longer, as with Mármol's *Amalia*, the desirable ending to a story of ideal love. [...] In the intimate space where copulation between lovers of different classes/races is consummated, tragedy [real or probable] almost always intervenes"; 15-16). If during the mid-nineteenth century the challenges to the union of two idealized protagonists were consistently configured as external to the couple itself, that is, as the product of forces beyond their control (Nature, Destiny, the State, etc.), then after 1880, the year that Buenos Aires became Argentina's federal capital, allegorized romance is no longer immune from internal conflict. Instead, lovers who are identified as biologically incompatible, rather than simply ill-fated, are made examples of what must not be allowed. For naturalist novels the union between different races, classes, or economic interests is no longer situated within a narrative framework that typically leads to reconciliation and the consummation of the ideal pairing; instead, the sexual union of different types of people, read through the biological determinist lens, almost always results in death. At the turn of the century, tragedy operates from the very cellular level of individual characters, who are unable to overcome their own (biological) destiny. Especially for those characters who attempt to forge a union that is not "ideal," the consequences are inevitably harrowing, as in Cambaceres's *En la sangre* or, not coincidentally, in Carlos O. Bunge's *La novela de la sangre*. This naturalist literature reveals a new "somatic epistemology" as Nouzeilles calls it, which seeks to distinguish between healthy and unhealthy bodies, constantly classifying, diagnosing, and treating perceived physical and psychological abnormalities.

The taxonomic ordering of bodies would provide the point of departure for major interventions in Latin American studies by marking an epistemological juncture through which scholars identify a persistent desire to construct an ideal national family, a perfect society based on eugenic principles.[10] This perceived threat of racial and cultural decadence, taking seriously the theory of degeneracy made popular by Max Nordeau, led to a sense of pessimism often referred to as the *mal du siècle*.[11] In this regard, literary scholar J. P. Spicer-Escalante claims that toward the turn-of-the-century authors sought to express the notion of family

> como paradigma de continuidad en relación con los valores nacionales ante la crisis moral de la sociedad argentina finisecular. Es decir, la familia unida—especialmente entre los miembros de la élite—se asocia, más bien, como baluarte de estabilidad ante los cambios sociales y bastión ante la corrupción de los valores sociales tradicionales en un período de transición, producto de los negocios turbios del patriarcado liberal, la oligarquía argentina finisecular.

> as a paradigm of continuity related to national values (when) faced with the moral crisis of turn-of-the-century Argentine society. That is, the united family—especially among members of the elite—is associated, rather, with a bastion of stability in the face of social change and a bastion from the corruption of traditional social values in a period of transition, a product of the shady dealings of the liberal patriarchy, the turn of the century Argentine oligarchy. (116)

This ideological contraction, this introspection, deserves special attention. As Spicer-Escalante puts it, family becomes a closed space, a "bastion of stability," sealed off from the changing times. The ideological construction of family, he claims, becomes perhaps the last unspoiled territory for the elite. I propose, however, that this vision of the family as the only remaining space within which the *oligarquía* would be able to preserve its hegemony may not be as straightforward as Spicer-Escalante suggests. To be sure, in naturalist fictions "appropriate" unions are sanctioned—or violently proscribed. And in this sense, it would seem that there are only two available types of families in turn of the century Argentina: those that uphold the *habitus* of the elite and those that with their very being violate the security and comfort of the symbolic nation. There is no room for ideological dissidence in this formulation, as the primordial goal of the positivist episteme is the scientific division of subjectivities: healthy/unhealthy, civilized/barbaric, productive/unproductive, and so on. My analysis of the complex interplay between intimate, private texts and public demonstrations of nationalism by the Bunge family calls into question the above accounts of a singular ideological contraction by the turn-of-the-century criollo elite. Instead of retreating behind the walls of nuclear patriarchalism, the Bunge siblings open toward a plurality of ideas about kinship and even aim to undermine normative orientations of family. We can see this opening precisely because of the breadth and diversity of the literary corpus that the Bunge family provides; because of how this archive links the public national imaginary with the private expression of sexual, gendered, and historical ambivalence. In summary, rather than consider the family as the last bastion of upper-class stability in the face of new, often radical, modes of political action and social organization, *Argentine Intimacies* demonstrates how the modern family became a space of ambiguity, instability, and fluctuation.

While the allegorical function and pedagogical appeal of the family has been firmly established in Latin American studies, the national family is frequently antimodern, an idealized tribute to family as it must have been before. "Founding fathers," "motherlands," and the "fraternal bonds" of citizenship overlay the language of kinship onto the imagined community of the nation.[12] Family thus engages the intimate proximities of kin and projects them scopically as a mimetic representation for the benefit of the nation imagined as utopian potential. The futurity of kinship becomes indistinguishable from the futurity of the modern nation, which itself returns the image of the ideal family, shaded by political contingencies, colonial histories, racial, and tropic imaginaries, as an expression of their shared utopian promise, and their shared contradictions.[13] Family and nation are better understood as an entanglement of desires, cultural ideologies, and temporalities.

With this in mind, there are two issues that make a revision of the family romance both crucial and possible today. First, Latin American studies has relied on an understanding of erotics, kinship, and subjectivity that emerged in nationalist writing, which itself depends on a presumably stable normative family ideology. In other words, normative kinship is often assumed to have existed precisely because it was normative. What I propose in this book, however, is that familiar normativity emerges through a process of constant negotiation with desires, bodies, and ideologies that resist the very normativity with which the family has been prescriptively characterized in such accounts. This approach to family is made possible by bringing Latin American studies into dialogue with queer studies, whereby the latter provides new tools for understanding how the erotics of kinship is enacted through discursive, corporeal, and performative logics, rather than ideology. Second, what is almost an inversion of my first point, by returning to a moment of prior "crisis" (the turn of the twentieth century) and to the contradictory process by which the taxonomic ordering of bodies and desires became legitimated by discourses derived from positivist science *in Latin America*, we can begin to question the predominance of queer studies as it has been formulated *in the US academe*. Queer studies in the US has consistently sought alternative forms of making kin, but has seldom looked beyond the US to do so. Latin American studies has engaged in extensive cultural critique of the contradictions of modernity, but rarely questions how modernity is based on a supposedly normative understanding of kinship. In bringing these two fields into conversation, I expand what normative kinship can mean to queerness, and at the same time, what the trajectories of Latin American cultures can mean to queer studies.

## QUEER STUDIES AND THE MODERN FAMILY IN LATIN AMERICA

I am not the first to chart an interdisciplinary approach linking Latin American studies and queer studies. My book follows such groundbreaking work as Salessi's *Médicos maleantes y maricas* (1995), David William

Foster's *Sexual Textualities* (1997), José Quiroga's *Tropics of Desire* (2000), Licia Fiol-Matta's *A Queer Mother for the Nation* (2002), and Gabriel Giorgi's *Sueños de exterminio* (2004), among others.[14] Importantly, these interventions have called into question the presumed universal applicability of Anglo-American queer theory and the possibility of its translation to other languages and epistemologies, advocating for a deeper engagement with the particular geopolitical effects of normativity in Latin American contexts, a trend that continues today and which I elaborate on further in the epilogue. What links these early critical texts, in a broad sense, is an insistence on how Latin American societies—in the plural—do not construe particular sexual acts or identities in the same way as North American or European societies by virtue of the particular forms of colonization, and thus racial and sexual political economies, that have been enacted, reinforced, and maintained throughout the modern era. Pursuing research agendas related to patriarchal discrimination, responses to constrictive political and social mores, and the ideological bases of normative embodiment, these early essays tend to frame the study of gender and sexuality in Latin America as a way of eroding the predominance of stigmatized identities. This is to say, much of this pathbreaking scholarship sought to resist the enduring marginalization of LGBT communities in the late twentieth century by historicizing the hegemony of the family in Latin American societies, a move that returned to the mid- and late nineteenth century, when discourses of illness and criminality became attached to nonnormative sexual subjects. Particularly for literary and cultural studies, these interventions dwell on the discursive invention of "sexual deviance" and the subsequent harnessing of its scientific and political utility to maintain regimes of colonial domination. And they often do so by focusing on perversion and deviance as a foil for the normative, or else as activating the processes by which the normative comes to be understood as such. In what follows, however, I propose a revision of this approach, one that interrogates the hegemonic family ideal as harnessing the affective and aesthetic appeal of the deviant, the perverse, and the queer (these are not necessarily synonymous), in order to project itself as modern. By paying attention to the way family emerges as mediated by the structures of kinship and as refracted through the formal possibilities of its expression, I argue, contemporary scholarship can better grapple with the ambiguity of the modern family. Imagining queerness not as anathema to kinship, but rather essential to its modern expression, this book, too, lingers in moments of awkwardness, disciplinary ambivalence, and the fragility of the intimate. Normativity and queerness are not opposed in the modern family, but rather mutually constitutive forms of alignment between bodies, norms, and desires, which shift across time and space.

In both Latin American and US-based scholarship, queerness has been imagined as a destabilizing force that differs from or reshapes the norm, is outside the norm or resists categorization, and is thus pathologized by colonial taxonomies as deviant and disruptive. In most of the aforementioned scholarship, subjectivity is framed as part of a national project in which dissident identities and subversive desires are held up as queer responses to social marginalization. Although I agree with much of the scholarship noted above, for example, Giorgi's claim that the aberrant body of the homosexual paradoxically gives shape to normativity as that which it is not, as that which must be eliminated from the social sphere (*Sueños* 18-19), I still insist that the queer is more than the abject against which the normative gains relief. Rather, by looking closely at the internal negotiations with and through the queer, we glean how the kinship structures that are so often held up as the fundamental building blocks of normative cultural formations are in fact constantly extending beyond the limits of normativity, stretching toward a desire that is at once of the body and that also exceeds it.

Much of my thinking on this matter follows feminist and queer revisions of structuralist anthropology and psychoanalysis. Typically, this line of critique takes as a point of departure the Lévi-Straussian argument that the matter of biology acquires meaning insofar as it is an expression of the demand that men exchange women in marriage, which, according to *The Elementary Structures of Kinship*, is the fundamental basis of human culture. That is, the exogamous marriage tie, which extends the family through a symbolic civic/religious rite, rather than blood relation, becomes the basis for the notion of modern kinship, and thus for recognition of the heteronormative family as the fundamental unit of society. According to Lévi-Strauss, nature becomes culture through this reciprocal exchange. This understanding of culture is coextensive with the division of labor within the domestic sphere and the development of capitalist economies and co-constitutive racial and class distinctions. What Lévi-Strauss would later theorize in anthropology as the structural basis of kinship, late-nineteenth-century Latin American literary and cultural production allegorized as a normative model of social organization that could (and should) be extrapolated to a larger national context.

Feminist scholars such as Gayle Rubin and Eve Sedgwick convincingly argue that this reciprocal exchange leads to the subjugation of women as objects of real and symbolic commerce and to the development of "homosocial" bonds between men. The latter, according to Sedgwick, is an effect of sublimated homoerotic desire that is channeled through the position of women in heteronormative society. In general, poststructuralist critiques of kinship such as these have sought to denaturalize the gender norms undergirding anthropological accounts of belonging—what Rubin describes as the "sex/gender system" through which the dualistic identity positions of woman and man, on the one hand, and the binary opposition of hetero and homo sexuality, on the other, are required for kinship in Western modernity ("Traffic" 169). Likewise, queer critiques of kinship have shed light on how linguistic theories of culture, in particular, those derived from Lacanian psychoanalysis, deepen kinship's reliance on a preconceived, eternal, or "structural" notion of gender within a system of symbolic expression. This symbolic referentiality allows Judith Butler to propose in her influential work *Gender Trouble* (1990) that gender itself is not "natural" but part of the repeated and compulsory enactment of gender within symbolic systems as a *"stylized repetition of acts"* (140), which she would continue to develop in *Bodies that Matter* (1993) as a theory of gender *performativity*.

I am indebted to these feminist and queer interventions, as well as more recent work such as Richard T. Rodríguez's *Next of Kin* (2009) and David L. Eng's *The Feeling of Kinship* (2010), which examines fundamental lacunae in queer theory's early mobilizations of poststructuralist gender and sexuality studies, namely queer theory's silence on racialized, colonial, and globalized embodiments of desire. This being said, it is striking to me how even in these important interventions, queer theory has often eschewed normative kinship as a site of interrogation precisely because of its normativity. In doing so, it often repeats the very primacy of Oedipal socialization that scholars have sought to undermine. While it is no surprise that the Oedipal model has dominated anthropological and psychoanalytic accounts of what kinship means, by seeking out non-Oedipal kinship arrangements queer theory has left little room for expanding what queer kinship could mean as a form of norm erosion and reformulation. The axis of anthropological accounts of kinship, psychoanalytic understandings of desire, as well as queer critiques of those normative regimes is usually Oedipal. This focus on filiation (the vertical lines of heredity) underestimates and often ignores psychic and social relationships established along horizontal planes, in particular the sibling. While it is now common to assert that the cultural demands of kinship depend on the successful negotiation of certain "structural" taboos, in particular regarding incest and patricide, the influence of siblings, sibling rivalry, and the affective demands and possibilities of horizontality remain underappreciated by queer theory.

While I engage in a reading of Oedipal socialization in the fiction of Carlos Octavio Bunge in chapter 1, my aim in subsequent chapters is to show how relational models of sociality can benefit by paying closer attention to how the symbolic and social position of the sibling—what I call horizontality—can offer a new perspective on how kinship negotiates with its own normative precepts. I do this by turning to the work of feminist scholar and psychoanalyst Juliet Mitchell, who provides tools for incorporating the constituent otherness of the sibling as part of the self that is multiple. The sibling need not be neglected by queer theory, and part of what I am attempting to demonstrate in my methodological approach to this archive is that the intimacies that make siblinghood matter often involve queer acts of collusion and conspiracy; collaboration and community.[15] The restrictive psychic and social renderings of kinship through the Oedipal paradigm are well established, and yet, there is a way in which siblinghood can undermine kinship from within, from the very position of normativity on which the family depends.

As a working definition, *queer kinship* is a form of orienting the body and its desires through the structural norms that adhere to kinship over time, and yet also question or eschew those norms in order to gesture toward a different form of relationality that may not yet exist. This queerness is found in kinship's incitement to normativity that nevertheless opens up possibilities for eroding, refashioning, or adapting the norm from within the logics of family. I am trying to advocate for a more capacious understanding of queerness, one that does not tether itself to a particular subject position or disciplinary logic, but rather exists as the reverberating interface between surfaces, forms, and bodies. This is a potentially erotic orientation that is psychic and corporeal, historical and immediate, uncanny and comforting. Thus, in this book I link the expressive demands of performativity, what Foucault calls "technologies of self," to the structural demands of kinship. By bringing to bear these formal mechanisms on the lived experience of relationality, we can better understand how queerness becomes integrated into the possibility of expressing the self as potential.[16] This is why focusing on the particular lived experiences of the Bunge siblings allows me to make the claim that the modernization of kinship is not only about identifying deviance as outside the norm, but rather negotiating what symbolic charge queerness has for the process (as a process) of aligning the norms of the family with the norms of the state. *Argentine Intimacies* proposes a deeply contextualized reading of the technologies, discourses, and symbolic representations that shed light on the contradictions of queerness in normative accounts of kinship relations.

This position takes family as queer in the expression of its own internal logics. I am thinking about this in relation to Butler's theorization of a more recent crisis of normativity, the one posed by the debates around gay marriage in the United States and France in the early 2000s. Thus, once more a century apart, what counts as a cultural demand, a cultural expression of possibility is framed through the family. Butler writes:

> On the one hand, it is important to mark how the field of intelligible and speakable sexuality is circumscribed so that we can see how options outside of marriage are becoming foreclosed as unthinkable, and how the terms of thinkability are enforced by the narrow debates over who and what will be included in the norm. On the other hand, there is always the possibility of savoring the status of unthinkability, if it is a status, as the most critical, the most radical, the most valuable. As the sexually unrepresentable, such sexual possibilities can figure the sublime within the contemporary field of sexuality, a site of pure resistance, a site uncoopted by normativity. ("Kinship" 18)

The two options that Butler offers have to do with possible imaginaries of desire. In the first, she notes that the extension of rights by the state depends on the ability to imagine specific bodies as endowable with a particular legal standing, and consequently what forms of expression (of desire, of politics, of embodiment) those bodies can produce as legally sanctioned subjects. In other words, this option brings previously deviant bodies and desires into the purview of the state through the mechanism of bestowing rights. The second option, then, is the unthinkable outside, the "sublime" that is "pure resistance." But from what source does this resistance draw its energy? How does it activate itself as resistance? Butler figures resistance as an unrepresentable force with no outside—no form—and what already has form—the norm itself—as a totalizing energy that will only diminish through an apocalyptic collision with the equally totalizing force of "pure resistance." My sense here is that Butler overlooks the magnetism of queerness, or perhaps the fuel that queerness provides the normative as that which becomes incorporated in order for the normative to burn so brightly. Butler does not account for the undoing of normativity from within, for the possibility that in the accumulative exercise of norm expansion, certain rifts may emerge, and may even be necessary in order for that expansive process to release the pressure that builds up in the tectonic accommodation of normativity.

This argument marks the radical potential of queerness as existing constitutively outside of culture and thus subjective intelligibility. It asks what is that, there, on the other side of desire? But I want to ask about the this, the here, the inside, for I can only desire something that is within the realm of knowledge—my own realm of knowledge. The desire of the unknown is, in a sense, another way of expressing the desire for myself-as-different-than-I-am. The unknown is not nothing, not emptiness, but a placeholder for what might be and what I might become when I find what I seek. So to desire the queer (or to desire queerly) I need not already know what I seek, but rather sense its movement, its potential. Thus, to incorporate myself into the flow of desire is to become aware of what I thought I knew, what I might have thought, or what happens unexpectedly, to interrupt or reorient my search. This desire is sensational, intuitive. We often think that there is an outside of the norm, a threshold. But if there can be no way of thinking that which is unthinkable, or knowing that which is unknowable, then the queerness that is said to mark the limits of normativity was never actually outside, but always already within, lingering. And yet, *queer kinship* emerges when that imagined outside that is actually inside synchronizes, vibrates the desiring subject who either disavows or accepts that moment in order to maintain the normative or experience its undoing.

The development of queer theory in the US has drawn on alternatives to "the norm," on reimaginings and creative refashionings, on campy and parodic iterations. For queer theory the norm has been a site of pleasurable undoing, appropriation, and *twisting*. Queer theory gets off on queering those norms to which we are beholden for our difference. As Kadji Amin astutely observes, this has put pressure on queer studies to excavate alternative lives and lifeways for its theoretical matter in order to produce knowledge as a field (182). If queer idealization of the nonnormative is an ethically complex and historically variable process, then this is also so for the lives, sexualities, genders, and desires that are held up as ideal advocates of normativity. But this does not mean that these normative enactments of corporal and affective dispositions—normativity itself—is perfect in its execution of such a mandate. The normative constantly fails. Thus, I want to insist on the queerness of the normative family. As I argue in this book, family implies feeling the pressure of queerness and either pushing back against it or becoming part of its flamboyant instability. As a researcher I am not exempt from this feeling, from this form of relating across time to people whose intimacy I seek to understand, or even to disrupt. As I have set out thus far, my approach to queer kinship is informed by the archival materials that I analyze in this book, materials that exist as evidence of this queerness, and which produce the effects that I am theorizing with their very physical presence. Before providing an overview of the chapters that follow, in the next section I describe how I came to relate queerly to this archive and its contradictions. I am not a disinterested surveyor of texts and images, but rather engage the archive in its lingering materiality as part of an ongoing dialogue with its temporalities and desires. The queerness of the archive resides not in its capacity for ideological documentation, but in its continuous repercussion in the field of desire.

## THE BUNGE FAMILY ARCHIVE

As an embodied subject I reach out toward this archive in what can only ever be an incomplete approximation of the attachments that it produces. The texts that I analyze here constitute an intimate archive that records a public presence—desired, staged, performed—that is fading from memory. I, too, am implicated in this process as I construct an archive in hopes of re-membering pieces of the past. As a scholar positioned in the United States academe, having grown up in South Texas and completed my graduate work in the United States, I have often questioned my own investment in researching a family that was so different from my own, and yet, also, recognizable in its very banality. To research the family as a historical structure and lived experience is also to imagine one's own forms of enactment of kinship, one's feelings of likeness and of incommensurability. I relate to these subjects as I imagine what I might have done in their place and time. I open myself to the possibility of becoming entranced by these archives and the secrets they bear. What is more, in writing this book, I invite you, the reader, to do so as well. At times I have felt more than a bit of voyeuristic pleasure, imagining that I am the only person in decades, perhaps ever, to read a confession or to see a gesture, a smile that was meant for someone else. My presence interrupts the intimacy of the archive, as my interpretation orders it in a new way, perhaps betraying the very intimacy that drew me to it in the first place. I have often wondered if the Bunge siblings could have imagined my presence, a century later, an interloper in the field of family secrets. To be clear, I mean that the archive is intimate in three distinct ways: (1) the diaries, photographs, and other materials I study reveal intimate (private) thoughts and gestures; (2) the person who keeps the archive, Lucía Gálvez, does so in the privacy of her home (and is related to the people whose archive she keeps); and (3) as a researcher, I am also implicated in the process of organizing, framing, and interpreting materials that document the conflicting desires of a period distant in time and place, and yet familiar, intimate.

I first came in contact with the Bunge family archive in 2011, when I made an exploratory research trip to Buenos Aires. I had received a grant to consult the collection of Argentina's Biblioteca Nacional, where I hoped to find a novel titled *Mi amigo Luis* that was supposedly written by Carlos Octavio Bunge under a pseudonym (Hernán Prinz) and published in 1895. Cárdenas and Payá mention *Mi amigo Luis* in their work, and in addition to referring to Carlos Octavio directly as "homosexual," claim that the novel presents a transparent reflection of his feelings of isolation and inner torment as a young man (*Familia* 250). My initial research impulse was motivated by a desire to discover just what this angst looked like, and what textual evidence there might be for making such a claim. As I scoured the novel, which is in fact held at Argentina's Biblioteca Nacional, I recognized many themes of Bunge's later writing: class anxiety, a fascination with masculine intimacy, and ambivalence toward the future of the nation.[17] But I did not find any clear evidence of homoeroticism that would satisfy my own (naive) yearning to rewrite literary history.

However, while I was in Buenos Aires, I was also able to contact Lucía Gálvez, and make an appointment to visit her in her home. I explained that I was conducting research on the Bunge family, and that I had read with great interest her edited volume of Delfina's diaries. I think the novelty of my interest was a major factor in her agreeing to see me. I think, too, that her desire that the work of her family members be further studied, understood, and even venerated also played an important role. During that initial meeting we discussed the history of the family, the changing landscape of Argentine politics, and the intellectual partnership forged by her grandparents, Manuel Gálvez and Delfina Bunge. Lucía asked me to help her take out some objects from an antique *arcón*, as she called it, a large chest that was filled with century-old folios. Among them, a family album, sepia photographs glued to black pages that were annotated by Delfina Bunge, bound in vinyl. It had been her archive, I realized, but it had also been updated, modernized. We sat in Lucía's living room and flipped through the pages of an heirloom that would eventually become the object of my analysis in chapter 3. It was the same living room described by Lucía's daughter, Delfina Tiscornia, in a book of poetry that I would take as a parting gift, and which I now use to begin this book.

The act of sharing this intimate space is an important aspect in the queer relationship that I have with this archive and with its archivist. Lucía and I shared in the intimacy of remembering kinship, which is to say, we shared an affinity for making sense of how the matter of kinship comes to bear on the present, as it extends inevitably into the future. We sat for hours flipping through those pages, remembering. I too, shared family stories, telling Lucía about my relationship with family memories that I had and did not have.[18] I narrated how I am Cherokee but that I did not know that when I was growing up. I told her how my Native American father had been adopted by a white family, and that we had recently gone through the process of opening the sealed adoption records and reconnecting with his birth mother, my grandmother. This involved recovering archival traces of an Indigenous past, a family secret, a history before memory.[19] In this way my interest in queer kinship is both academic and personal. I too have experienced the entanglements, the visceral feelings produced by the archive.[20] Thus, part of my interaction with Lucía Gálvez and her (family) archive had to do with how I have also had to grapple with the paradoxes of archival legitimacy, desire, and history. Though we came to appreciate family archives under very different circumstances, we both shared in the feeling (even the awe) of experiencing the identification that can come through time and space by virtue of the material residues of familiar lives.

As our conversation continued, Lucía asked me if I would like to see the textbooks that Delfina and Julia had written together. "Of course," I replied, and she brought out her own copy of *El Arca de Noé*, a book that had been cowritten by the sisters in the early years of the twentieth century. She offered to let me take it with me so that I could make a copy for myself. These types of materials usually do not make it into libraries or official archives, and though I had not envisioned writing about school textbooks, I accepted. As I held this fragile book, I realized that it had been marked up, in fact used by Lucía's children *as a family textbook*. The idea that a national pedagogy could be projected out of the intimacy of the family, which forms the basis of chapter 4, first occurred to me in that moment. There, I take *El Arca de Noé*, as a point of departure for reading the pedagogy of the family as political, which is also to say, reading politics as a family project.

As I was leaving, Lucía offered to provide me with a digital copy of the photo album that we had been perusing and which she was in the process of having scanned. She had already intuited the fragility of the archive, its finite materiality, and, in this digital era, sought to preserve these photographs as data, as a copy of a copy. These are the images that I would ponder over and reorder, archive in my own way, as I sought to discover how the spatiality of kinship became visible through the staging and enactment of intimate proximity. While some of the photographs that I analyze in chapter 3 have been published in other venues, mine is the first attempt to study them as an archive, a collection of images that can speak to the intimate family dynamics that may not be made explicit in writing. Here, to think about pose, gesture, and look, the intimate connection that comes in both staged portraiture and candid family snapshots, has led me to posit the queerness of familial proximity as a method of understanding the connections made evident (or obscured) by the physical remnants of the family photographic archive.

When I returned to the United States, I was satisfied with myself. I had found something precious: a new archive. In the years that followed, however, as I continued to develop an understanding of the intimate relationships between publicity and privacy, the nation and the family, the queer kinship at the heart of the Bunge family archive, I realized that my ability to access this archive, as well as its existence in the first place, is based on institutional and structural privileges that have limited the presence of marginalized subjects—and their archives—in and as history. In a sense, what I began to realize was how the place of the archive enacts a set of power dynamics itself; that it does not simply record them, but rather, is the material evidence, the relic, of those power dynamics. The archive, like the nation, like the photograph and the diary, unfurls toward a future that seemingly precedes the logic of the archive itself.[21] Because of this futurity it is also an intrinsic element in the structuring of white supremacy, upper-class hegemony, and heteropatriarchy. It is not lost on me that this particular archive is produced in order to maintain those structures of power. As I have been residing with these texts, these images, and this counterpoint of voices, I have come to realize that the way in which this normativity was expressed did not quite sound as I thought it would. The documents revealed more than I was expecting, a more nuanced and complicated relationship with those very structures of power than I was prepared to entertain at the beginning of my research. I realized that in order to project themselves as invested with the power of the archive, with acts and lives that were worth archiving, the Bunge siblings also had to construct themselves as and through the technologies of modernity, a process of staging the self vis-à-vis the social. I began to suspect that the archive did not simply register normative relations, but the contradictory desires at the heart of family itself. It is in this sense that my relationship with the archive is queer. I participate in its disruptive temporality as well as its ephemeral nature, attempting to approach its silences as well as what it enounces as presence, as the material residue of past lives, desires, and memories.

In 2015 I took another research trip to Buenos Aires, after having completed my graduate work and begun the appointment that I currently hold at Stony Brook University. On that occasion I wanted to update Lucía about the status of my book project, and to share some of the ideas that I had developed about the archive itself. On this occasion our visit was brief. The archivist/historian was still enthusiastic about sharing stories and discussing the intimate details of the Bunge family, but she was less talkative. I did most of the chatting, once again at her dining room table. This time she asked me to bring out Delfina's diaries from the *arcón*. I had never seen them in person. The occasion made me nervous, as if I were beholding something that I might not have been meant to see, an archival dream come true. We did not spend hours flipping through pages. Instead Lucía invited me to take a few of the notebooks to the United States for my research. I would bring them back, of course, I emphasized. I thanked her and offered to find a way to digitize these archives too. Perhaps my university's library would be willing to help in this capacity. We agreed that that made sense, and parted with the promise of keeping in touch. After all, I did have to return the diaries. As I complete this manuscript, I have yet to find an institutional repository willing to house and/or digitize the manuscript texts, family albums, herbarium, and textbooks, among other various objects. The quantity and variety of materials has made this difficult, as has the very privacy of the archive. Since it is not already housed in an institution, soliciting funding to do so has been complicated by a lack of existing institutional support. The family archive is at once a rich source of understudied materials and a collection that is difficult to make public.

Back in the United States, I understood, upon actually holding the object in my hands, that what I thought was an original manuscript diary was in fact a copy of the original, which, in turn, had been annotated by the diarist at a later date. I describe the palimpsestic nature of this diary practice in chapter 2, but it is important to note here, regarding the archive, that my understanding of the intimacy of the text did not come from reading it, but feeling it, holding it in my hands. The materiality of the diary came to inspire a new way of thinking about the archive as an interface between subjects who read and write, and who reread and exchange the object as a point of contact between readers who relate by textualizing their relationships. As a whole, however, these archives are still not readily accessible to the public. One of the ways that I gained access to this archive was through a shared interest in the Bunge family, but also in family in general—as an affective and cultural field. This is a complicated proposition that involves the overlapping desires of the researcher (me) and the repository (the heir of the Bunge family archive, Lucía Gálvez), for whom family means something very different. What we shared, in the end, was an understanding of the intimacy of the archive itself, and the contradictions that it continues to hold. These contradictions are at the heart of each of the following chapters, which deal with the process by which normative kinship arrangements negotiate with an expansive, and often disruptive, queerness that is key to the modernizing impulse of the turn of the century.

## INTIMATE ROUTES

*Argentine Intimacies* elucidates the seductive force of heteronormativity in the writing of the Bunge family, while also excavating the relational desires, attachments, and identities that emerge as queer in a crucial moment in Latin American history. Rather than taking the family at face value, I question the relationship between literary representation, form, and the potentials of representing and reproducing kinship. I organize the chapters around formal attributes and generic conventions, though I also question the relationship between the familiar and the formal and link chapters by establishing key intertextual dialogues around historical, political, and cultural moments. I move from analyzing the public genre of fiction (chapter 1) to the private archives of the diary (chapter 2) and the family photograph (chapter 3), then the private/public domain of the school textbook (chapter 4), and the stridently public national essay (chapter 5). All of these forms of writing engage the queerness of kinship as it emerges through the representational possibilities of genre. Thus, I argue that the space of the family stages a range of affective possibilities (beyond the "normative" and the "perverse") that speak not only to the desire to maintain upper-class hegemony in the face of shifting social and political terrain, but to the productive position of queerness for rethinking race, class, and kinship.

Chapter 1, "Carlos Octavio Bunge: Queer Desire and Family Fictions" examines the conflicting role that national futurity plays in the fiction of Carlos Octavio Bunge. I read his work as an effort to model cohesive heteroromance, an effort that is constantly frustrated by the emergence of queer desire within narratives of the family. Rather than seek to define Bunge's sexuality itself, this chapter takes up his most widely read novel, *La novela de la sangre* (1903) and his collection of short stories, *Thespis* (1907), which together reveal how turn-of-the-century cultural anxieties intersect with Bunge's particular rendering of family fictions that queer national literature. By focusing on the intersection of national literature and queer desire, I demonstrate that Bunge's fiction is marked not by heteronormative romance but by constitutive ambivalence toward the futurity of the nation.

Chapter 2, "Sisters Writing, Sisters Reading: The Diaries of Julia and Delfina Bunge" focuses on a unique coincidence in Latin American culture: sisters who (1) simultaneously kept a diary for an extended period of time, (2) actually shared, read, and commented on reading each other's diaries, and (3) though under quite different circumstances, published these diaries subsequently. I read the diaries of Delfina and Julia Bunge as an interface through which the textual form of the diary both depends on and creates new understandings of self and other in the early years of the twentieth century. In this chapter I lean on Foucault's "technologies of self" in order to propose that the link between text and body creates queer possibilities of sororal relations. Examining both manuscript notebooks and later published versions, I show how writing and reading the diary plays a crucial role in shaping each sister's ideological positions regarding courtship, marriage, and sisterhood. From this exploration I argue that the cultural anxiety over the division of public and private space, and in particular women's labor, led each sister to stake a claim of individuality that emerges through the process of imagining herself as different from—but potentially the same as—her sister.

Chapter 3, "Spectral Desires: Queering the Family Album" extends the argument from the previous one by shifting from the textual to the visual archive. Here, I take the family album—as a material object—to buoy an epistemic project of defining queer relationality. This chapter makes use of a wide range of photographic documentation, including *cartes de visite*, studio portraiture, and candid photographs of the Bunge family and sees these visual representations not as illustrations of the familiar, but as sites that reveal a constellation of family relationships that are imbued with the specter of queer affect. Drawing on theoretical interventions by Roland Barthes and Marianne Hirsch, I ask what the disciplinary site of the family album fails to account for as an archive of proximities and gestures. By focusing on the possibilities of sibling relatedness, of horizontal kinship relations, as haunted by the erotic charge of filial competition for the visual space of the photograph, this chapter proposes the residual presence of self and other as implicated in the process of technological reproduction.

Chapter 4, "Family Pedagogy: The Institutionalization of Kinship" moves from the intimate to the national. I explore the Bunge family as a self-defined national model as seen through the textbooks written by Carlos Octavio and Julia and Delfina. I demonstrate how nationalism is modeled as familiar in Julia and Delfina's cowritten secondary school textbook, *El Arca de Noé* (1916). I then link this modeling of the familiar to the memory of family life in Carlos Octavio's *Nuestra Patria* (1910), which sets out practical coordinates for assimilationist schooling derived from his earlier treatise *Evolución de la Educación* (1901). This analysis focuses on the role of pedagogy during the period of the Argentine centennial (1910). Here I discuss the methods used to inculcate a sense of *patria* and nationhood in the Argentine youth, a process of institutionalization of culture that had at its core a traditional Catholic notion of family life, which, paradoxically, figures as both a national ideal and a model to challenge.

Chapter 5, "National Essays, Home Economics: The Argentine Oligarchy in Decline" builds on the programmatic rendering of national identity as part of an ongoing effort to maintain cultural relevance in the face of a rapidly shifting population. Focusing on three important essays, Carlos O. Bunge's *Nuestra América: Ensayo de psicología social* (1903), Delfina Bunge's *La mujer y la vocación* (1922), and Alejandro Bunge's *Una nueva Argentina* (1940), I engage with the contradictory place of the Bunge family regarding the politics and economics of modernization in the first half of the twentieth century. Expanding the temporal focus we see the problematic position of women in a shifting labor force exemplified by Delfina's call for the expansion of women's participation in national publics. Her essay represents a counterpoint to, on the one hand, Carlos Octavio's early transhistorical account of Argentina's supposed racial decadence, and on the other, Alejandro's equally pessimistic rendering, forty years later, of the precarious position of Argentine whiteness in the face of declining birth rates for the upper class.

Pointing toward the future of queer studies as a transnational and transhistorical method, I conclude by returning to the ephemeral nature of the family archive and the family as a queer archive. My goal in the epilogue, "Toward a Queer Latin American Studies," is to chart the multiple trajectories and genealogies that are implicated in the study of queerness as an epistemic project. I ask how queer studies can relate the affective tensions, intimacies, and identifications of the current moment to historical accounts of the normative, proposing that the study of kinship and the potential queerness of the family endure as an urgent political and intellectual endeavor.

In mapping the interventions that this book makes in the following chapters, this introduction has described how I approach the Bunge family archive and what my relationship with that archive means. It is my hope that this book provides tools for reimagining what kinship is and what it could be, and for rethinking how queerness attaches itself and transforms the normative, pointing out its instability, its transigent reshaping, in a moment in which the elite sought to project an image of its own splendorous sociality for those others, those deviants and degenerates who populated the dark recesses of the national imaginary. One contradiction that I have yet to address, finally, is this book's subtitle, *Queer Kinship in an Age of Splendor, 1890–1910*. By describing the turn of the century as "an age of splendor" I do not mean to celebrate the nationalism, racism, or patriarchalism that undergird the dominance of the Argentine elite. Rather, I aim to highlight the perspective the elite projected of itself as a living example of a project of cultural nationalism that depended on an expansion of its own vision of authority, grandiosity, and brilliance. Such splendor inspired Julia to imagine her own life as part of a spectacular tradition, as we can see in the subtitle she gives her own published diary, *Época maravillosa, 1903-1911* (*Marvellous Epoch, 1903-1911*). The subtitle that Lucía Gálvez gives to the published edition of Delfina Bunge's diaries also reflects this notion: *Diarios íntimos de una época brillante* (*Intimate Diaries of a Brilliant Epoch*). The "luminosity" that Delfina Tiscornia describes in the portraits of these women was at the heart of the political and social understandings of the intellectual elite. But it is also true that such splendor was a cause of anxiety. It led Carlos Octavio Bunge to accuse his contemporaries, whom he called the *"jeunnesse dorée,"* of becoming "metallized," allowing their desire for fortune, for gold, to blind them to their avarice.[22] It led Alejandro Bunge to lament the end of an era of "maravilloso desarrollo y progreso" ("marvellous development and progress") in which men like him dominated the cultural, political, and economic spheres, an Argentina no longer basking in "las radiaciones de los grandes astros" ("the radiance of the great stars"; *Nueva* 516). This splendor is at once an invitation to believe in the promise of a nation ever destined for greatness—whose very name, Argentina, means that which shines; whose flag bears the radiant Sun of May—and to remember the mercurial nature of power in its ever shifting dynamics. This splendor is neither permanent nor guaranteed, and families such as the Bunges, even as they sought desperately to feel the brightness of their own splendorous reflection, also contributed to the undoing of the hegemony of a family model, at once luminous and clouded by the knowledge of its inevitable decline.

chapter one

# CARLOS OCTAVIO BUNGE
## QUEER DESIRE AND FAMILY FICTIONS

"Usted no es hombre para estas cosas" ("You are not a man for these things"; cited in Cárdenas and Payá *Familia* 214). That is how the presiding medical officer at Argentina's Escuela Naval Militar (Naval Academy) diagnosed Carlos Octavio Bunge, then fifteen years old, when he was interned for suffering a nervous breakdown in 1890. His father, Octavio, had sent him there after being expelled from the prestigious Colegio del Salvador (College of Our Savior) for insubordination.[1] He was supposed to learn discipline, to obey, to calm his rebellious nature. But the rigors of military life proved too much for the young man. He hated having to wake up early and, what is more, the other cadets made fun of him for writing poetry to pass the time. He was not there to scribble verses, but to become a man, and he had failed to prove himself *as a man*. In letters to his mother from those months, he would describe himself in a state of existential crisis. He did not know who he was, or what he was supposed to be. But he did know that he was not like the other cadets, "not a man for these things." More than simply marking him as unfit for military life, it is a diagnosis that marks him as queer.

Perhaps because of this failure, he would dedicate himself to discovering the inner workings of Argentine society, its history, and its psychology over the course of his life. He would go on to become a prolific and celebrated social scientist, even if today he appears a minor figure. The desire to prevent or correct social maladies was a touchstone in Bunge's work, which ranged from the social sciences to jurisprudence to fiction and pedagogy. Along with other positivist intellectuals he was committed to ordering a world in flux. The intense modernization of the turn of the century led to class conflict and political revolutions, new forms of living and loving, new bodies to classify, new (and old) desires to name. He studied law at the Universidad de Buenos Aires (University of Buenos Aires) and upon graduating in 1898 was contracted by the municipal government of Buenos Aires to write a report on European school systems. Crossing the Atlantic for the first time, in 1899 he arrived in Southampton and spent time in both London and Oxford. He relished the dinners in Hyde Park as well as conversations with the students and the tutors, who were celebrities of the British intellectual world. Outside of Argentina, he found an environment that was more open to his interests and perhaps more accepting of his ambivalences. He would write in red ink from Oxford, "varios son los casos en que he tenido aquí lo que llama Thackeray '*a romantical friendship at first sight*' " ("on several occasions I have had here what Thackeray calls '*a romantical friendship at first sight*' "; cited in Cárdenas and Payá *Familia* 328). These friendships were brief but intense, and, as I show in chapter 3, punctuated by a series of self-portraits that he had commissioned—evidence of his desire to belong and to be remembered—and which he distributed as mementos upon his departure. Bunge continued to Germany and later Spain, where he met and sought guidance from Miguel de Unamuno, who had published his important essay on the Spanish national character *En torno al casticismo* only four years earlier (1895).[2]

To Argentina Bunge returned triumphant, brimming with confidence and sporting the latest fashions. He published his findings under the title *El espíritu de la educación* (*The Spirit of Education*) a probing inquiry into the connections between racial mixing, history, and pedagogy, which was well received in his homeland. His contemporaries celebrated his brilliance and his charm. A precocious talent, Bunge was offered a position at the Universidad de Buenos Aires where he taught literature, law, and education. Tireless, in 1903 he would publish two book-length essays, *Nuestra América: Ensayo de psicología social* (*Our America: Essay of Social Psychology*) and *Principios de psicología individual y social* (*Principles of Individual and Social Psychology*), in addition to two novels, *La novela de la sangre* (*The Novel of Blood*) and *Xarcas Silenciario* (*Xarcas the Silent*). By all accounts, he was a new force to be reckoned with among Argentina's elite.[3] The enigmatic young man took the Argentine intellectual world by storm at the turn of the century.

Manuel Gálvez, a prolific novelist and memoirist—who would become Bunge's brother-in-law in 1910 upon marrying Delfina Bunge—narrates this moment as contradictory for Carlos Octavio:

> Su fecundidad, su talento, la originalidad de su espíritu y la novedad de sus ideas, inquietaban en el mundo de la alta sociedad y en el de las letras. Agréguese con todo esto, un singular tipo de hombre del Norte, una distinción aristocrática, cierto dandismo en el vestir y un temperamento rebelde y agresivo, y se comprenderá que, durante algunos años, Carlos Octavio Bunge fuese "un caso."
>
> His fecundity, his talent, the originality of his spirit and the novelty of his ideas, disquieted in the world of high society and in that of literature. Add to all of that, a singular type of Northern man, an aristocratic distinction, a certain dandyism of dress, and a rebellious and aggressive temperament, and one will understand that, for a few years, Carlos Octavio Bunge was "a case." (Gálvez, *Recuerdos* 1: 283)

In this view, it is Bunge's physical presence, in addition to his ideas, that disturbs the Porteño elite.[4] Not only his application of innovative methodologies, but also his "spirit." Gálvez recalls the residual effects of Bunge's "temperament" more than the content of his intellectual production; he seems to have been more struck by Bunge's "dandified" fashion sense and "aggressive" personality than by his writing. Here, Bunge is a mystifying presence to be contemplated, studied, and perhaps avoided. He belongs to the elite by virtue of his family background and his Germanic lineage, but he remains "a case." Many of the central contradictions of Bunge's life are present in this description. He was quite obviously a talented writer, yet there was something indecipherable about him, something felt but impossible to say.

The insinuation present in Gálvez's memoir, as well as in contemporary accounts of Bunge's life, is that of a man tormented by an inner strife.[5] This unrest, as it is often described, served to inspire his copious and often frenetic scholarly production, and prompted his oscillation between patriotic celebrations of *argentinidad* (Argentineness) and a disheartened ambivalence regarding the national project of modernization. For example, contemporary historian Osvaldo Bazán portrays Bunge as "la luz intelectual de principios de siglo XX, el niño mimado que tenía a su disposición los teatros, las revistas y el Estado para difundir su pensamiento, el más bello de los pensadores de la elite" ("the intellectual light of the early twentieth century, the coddled child who had at his disposal the theaters, the magazines, and the State to disseminate his thought, the most beautiful man of the intellectual elite"; 158). The fact that Bunge's position as a member of the elite granted him access and opportunities is not the point, however, as Bazán concludes: "[Bunge] no salió jamás de un armario que él mismo ayudó a construir" ("[Bunge] never came out of a closet that he himself helped to build"; 158). Bazán describes him as a closeted homosexual who could not find the courage to "come out"—who in fact contributed to entrenching homophobic discourses and institutions at the turn of the century. Disappointed, Bazán once more diagnoses Bunge, but this time through the lens of contemporary gay and lesbian studies.

I have no interest in discovering the *truth* of Bunge's sexuality. I am, however, drawn to his queerness because it speaks to the contradictory ways in which gender, sexuality, and kinship were understood and enacted at the turn of the century in Argentina. I mean this in three specific ways. First, Bunge's physical presence, mannerisms, and lifelong bachelorhood, in addition to family lore, have led historians and cultural critics to tether him to the indecipherability, the unstableness, of what we now call queer, at least in the Anglophone academe. He may or may not have been "homosexual" but he was certainly thought of—both in 1900 and the twenty-first century—as *raro* (strange, queer). Second, and more importantly, his work, and in particular his fiction, is rife with narratives that posit, at times favorably, the failure of heteronormative romance. These texts reveal turn-of-the-century anxieties over gender roles, family stability, and sexuality. That is, his creative work questions just what it means to maintain the hegemonic sexual economy on which upper-class society depended. Third, his fiction queers the turn of the century literary canon in Argentina with its refusal to provide normative answers to these cultural anxieties, instead oscillating between a nostalgic yearning for a premodern past and a speculative projection of what modes of gender performance, sexuality, and kinship will emerge in the new century. The queerness of his work is not found in its portrayal of sexual acts or in constructing sexually dissident characters, not in its allegorical renderings of social decline, but in the way it provides a mode of questioning gender norms, how it depends on romantic failure, and is itself a space that yearns for and gestures toward erotic attachments that consistently evade classification.

In this chapter I explore how Bunge's writing, rather than his presumed identity, does not fit normative understandings of sexuality. To grapple with these contradictions, I focus on two of Bunge's most important works of fiction: his most widely read novel, *La novela de la sangre* (1903) and the short story collection, *Thespis* (1907). Both hinge on modeling romantic attachments for a public, in Bunge's view, that needed to be educated in the art of proper romance. And yet, these texts also question the possibility, indeed the desirability, of just such a model. Even though Bunge traffics in narratives of heterosexual romance, his texts, as I demonstrate, actually undermine the viability of normative sexuality. His narratives consistently reject, fail, or disavow their place in this plot of heteronormativity. My central claim in this chapter is that by paying attention to these moments of failure and rejection we can uncover a different Bunge, a man who is not simply a "case" or a "closeted homosexual" but a complex writer whose work allows us to rethink the relationships between queerness, desire, and narratives of national belonging.

## FAMILY ROMANCE AT THE TURN OF THE CENTURY

Before turning to Bunge's fiction, it is important to contextualize the narration of family ties and romantic attachments in the fiction of the turn of the century. As noted in the Introduction, since the colonial period, and especially over the course of the nineteenth century, the patriarchal criollo family has served as the central organizing principle of Latin American societies. Rooted in Catholic doctrine and concerned with the biological reproduction of ideal national subjects, a wide range of social actors began to question the family model starting in the 1870s. This period witnessed the reorganization of urban space as *conventillos* (tenement houses) were carved out of upper-class homes left vacant in the old Colonial center, and the elite began to move toward more "hygienic" neighborhoods of Belgrano and Palermo. Social norms were changing as well, with Socialists and Anarchists proposing radical new ways of living and organizing the economy, threatening the very class structures on which upper-class hegemony was built. And women began to move into the public sphere, asserting the right to education, work, equal treatment under the law, and eventually to vote. Cultural expressions, too, from literature to theater to music harnessed this anxiety over the increasing cosmopolitanism of the turn of the century. In particular, naturalist literature provided a crucial forum for these debates.

By the 1880s authors had begun to question earlier forms of allegorical representation of family unity, and to diagnose, treat, and attempt to eliminate nonreproductive sexualities as modes of feeling and being that did not contribute to the national cause. Novelists from what would come to be known as the Generation of 1880 such as Eugenio Cambaceres, Francisco Sicardi, and Julián Martel narrated nonnormative bodies and desires as aberrations that would debilitate the national stock.[6] It is here that queer practices and dissident sexualities become explicitly treated as a threat to the nation. Creative writers and scientists alike began to see "degenerate" bodies and desires as anathema to the concept of the nation as family. If at mid-century the family model served an allegorical function to model national unity, as Sommer argues, at the turn of the century, it was more frequently used as a metonymical representation of illness. Following Nouzeilles, in the literature of the turn of the century, "la familia fue el espacio en el que convergieron el interés político, la vigilancia higienista y el saber eugenésico. Motor de la reproducción biológica y moral, la institución familiar conectaba el cuerpo individual y el organismo social al mismo tiempo que regulaba las fronteras entre lo privado y lo publico" ("the family was the space in which political interest, hygienic disciplining and eugenic knowledge converged. As a motor of biological and moral reproduction, the family institution connected the individual body and the social organism at the same time as it regulated the borders between public and private"; 41). Here the crisis of modernity is a crisis of family—what family means, how it is to be maintained, what dangers are posed to it both within national boundaries and from abroad. This is a chain of social anxiety that threatened to derail the positivist belief in progress and social advancement through science, and which endangered the reproductive demands of the nation. Particularly salient for Argentina, though not exclusively so, turn-of-the-century narratives supported and were often directly linked to the politics of *blanqueamiento* (racial whitening).[7] As historian Donna Guy has shown, high rates of child abandonment and illegitimate births, in addition to legalized prostitution and the specter of *la trata de blancas* (white slavery) all contributed to the notion—particularly for the elite—that in spite of Argentina's relative economic clout, modernization had come at the expense of the familial stability of its colonial past (*Sex and Danger* 37-44).

It is in this context that the Bunge's novels matter. Members of the upper class sought to maintain hegemony by promoting an idealized notion of family life linked to domesticity, social hygiene, and patriotism. The complicity between medicine, the disciplining of bodies, and the entrenchment of a traditional model of kinship, sheds light on the role of literary representation at the service of the national project. While Bunge's fiction questions how the nation comes to depend on heteronormative romance, it is not politically progressive. He directly participates in the scientific racism of the turn of the century.[8] His novels locate ethnically dubious subjects (such as gauchos and Italians) along a spectrum of racial degeneracy that he saw as contrary to the promise of Argentina's future as a white nation. Bunge's racism is plainly evident in his expository, scientific writing, described in detail in chapter 5, and his fiction also has a decidedly white supremacist basis. In studying it I am by no means condoning this racism. On the contrary, in order to understand the racism that was central not only to Bunge's work, but to turn-of-the-century literature as a whole, we need to be able to examine the interlocking threads of kinship, desire, and the body (as raced, sexed, and gendered) that emerge as they are framed by the family romance. The anxieties of Argentine modernity are essentially played out through the body, and the definitional indeterminacy of Mestizo (mixed-race), queer, and working-class bodies plays a crucial role in the national project and its ideologies. Bunge's white supremacy may be par for the course among the Argentine elite, but by situating these discourses of race, gender, sexuality, and family in context and in dialogue, we can better understand how power is enacted through the corporal imaginaries of the late nineteenth century, imaginaries that still hold sway in contemporary debates on immigration, nationalism, and culture.

Bunge's fiction is a site of conflicting desires and attachments. If we are to consider not simply the representational value of normative kinship in his work, but also the types of desires that emerge in his writing, then the way that his characters *belong* becomes crucial. This is because Bunge's narratives serve as an important archive for rethinking the relationship between blood, intimacy, and the structures of kinship. His fiction is invested in proposing models of filiation and futurity, and yet, these models are vexed by a constant sense of inadequacy and failure. His work dwells on characters who desire to contribute to the successful future of the national project (which is one of racial whitening, capitalist expansion, and cultural homogenization), but who also relate queerly to others, to the state, and to its demand for reproductive futurity. This is not to say that Bunge proposes an alternative queer family to the models of national romance that predominate in the nineteenth century and the first decades of the twentieth. As I make clear in the Introduction, I am not seeking out kinship formations that diverge from the norm, but rather those that reveal how the norm is constantly failing to live up to its own precepts. Bunge's fiction consistently narrates the failure of the family model as the only possible—or even the only desired—outcome of heteroromance. Thus, I read Bunge's fiction as stretching the boundaries of what has typically been considered a corpus of texts that promotes the Argentine imaginary of nationalism, modernity, and normativity. His work responds to the need to imagine the modern family in new ways. *La novela de la sangre* aims to provide a model of national belonging, but never quite manages to uphold the structures of desire that would be necessary for a national family.

## *LA NOVELA DE LA SANGRE*: REWRITING FAMILY FUTURES

"El Doctor Bunge, observador acertado y precavido generalizador, estudioso, inteligente, carece de imaginación y de gusto; no es artista" ("Doctor Bunge, a skilled observer and prudent generalizer, studious, intelligent, lacks imagination and taste; he is not an artist"; Olivera 304–5). The opinion of literary critic Ricardo Olivera is at once deferential to the intellectual capacity of his contemporary, Carlos O. Bunge, and pedantic in its dismissal of his literary ability. Bunge may possess those qualities important for an "observer" but not those of an "artist." In other words, he may be an acceptable social scientist, but he lacks the creative mind of a literary genius. What is more damning still, according to Olivera, Bunge lacks good taste, that contested domain of the cultural elite at the turn of the century for whom class belonging was a performance, a *pose*, of "good taste."[9] Olivera continues: "Es el suyo estilo pretencioso . . . *retorcido*, sin sobriedad y sin belleza" ("His style is pretentious . . . *twisted*, lacking sobriety and beauty"; 305 my emphasis). If Bunge's intellectual acumen—or his belonging to the Porteño elite—cannot be challenged, his literary style, in contrast, is more than simply deficient, but "twisted," unrestrained, *queer*.

I begin with this example to point out that Bunge's first major work of fiction, *La novela de la sangre*, published in Madrid by Daniel Jorro in 1903, was met with skepticism, if not outright hostility in his native Argentina. This is important because Bunge would go on to drastically change the novel before it was published in Buenos Aires the following year by Biblioteca de La Nación, adding a new final chapter in which he completely alters the dénouement. This is a rare textual example of an attempt to "straighten out" a text whose queerness mobilizes turn-of-the-century literary criticism to limit erotic ambiguity.

Similar, though perhaps more spectacular scenes, dot the landscape of *fin de siglo* criticism in Latin America. Sylvia Molloy eloquently illuminates how José Martí censured Oscar Wilde for his supposed aesthetic incongruity and excessive visibility, and how Rubén Darío pathologized the same figure postmortem ("Too Wilde"). Likewise, Oscar Montero has explicated José Enrique Rodó's policing of erotic excess in Latin American *modernismo*. In all of these cases, turn-of-the-century literary criticism reveals a cultural anxiety regarding the expression of homoerotic desire and transgressive gender performance. Particularly acute for the *modernistas*, the issue of stylistic innovation—writing turned sumptuous, rarified, opulent—in a society that both craved and resisted such cosmopolitanism, strangeness (*lo raro*) would indelibly link an aesthetic question to a moral one (Montaldo, *Sensibilidad* 109). As Molloy suggests, such a conjunction of the stylistic and the moral positions the critic in the role of *arbiter elegantarium*, charged with the responsibility of defining the limits of bourgeois respectability even when faced with the contradictory discourses surrounding European decadence, at once the sign of cultural regression and innovation ("Too Wilde" 190). This was equally true for naturalist writers such as Bunge, whose socially conscientious if racially fatalist novels (at times subtitled "studies") were meant to provide moral and spiritual guidance to readers.

What changed in Bunge's novel and what the implications of those changes might be for Argentine culture at the turn of the century are the central questions that guide my reading of his novel. In order to respond to these questions, I examine the differences between the first (1903) and the second (1904) editions of *La novela de la sangre* as an effect of contemporary literary criticism that reveals the critics' anxiety—we might say panic—regarding the type of desire that is modeled in the text. First, I argue that Bunge is criticized for not providing a viable model for citizenship, understood as a heteronormative ethno-cultural model of national futurity.

In this, Bunge's work resonates with contemporary theorist Lee Edelman's call for queer subjects to embrace their indecipherable position within the symbolic order; to inhabit their death-drive tinged abject status as a way of deconstructing the political (3-14). Bunge's first edition operates on this ambiguous plane of the nonnational and the refusal of a symbolic future. Second, I argue that the changes to Bunge's novel respond to a supposed failure of both message and style that evidence the disciplinary effects of literary criticism and outline the contours of the textual closet. This archive allows us to read the author's response to accusations of failing to contribute to the ongoing project of modernization, the shaping of future citizens, and the nationalization of Argentine literature and culture.

### La novela de la sangre

Tellingly, the novel begins with a wedding: Blanca Orellanos and Regis Válcena are married in a modest ceremony on a fragrant spring evening in 1835. That year, however, also marks the beginning of the "Reign of Terror" of Juan Manuel de Rosas, an era of political repression carried out by the notorious and ever-present *Mazorca*, Rosas's strong-arm police force.[10] The wedding guests are eager to discuss the night's events, as they fear that the Orellanos-Válcena nuptials may have caused an unintended backlash. "Se han casado de noche, tarde, en privado, y *a la francesa*.... Los amigos de Manuelita Rosas nos van a criticar. Lo merecemos" ("They have married at night, late, in private, and in the French style.... Manuelita Rosas's friends are going to criticize us. We deserve it."; 21), notes Gabriel Villalta, Regis's first cousin.[11] In addition to having neglected to invite the daughter of the *Restaurador de las Leyes* ("The Restorer of Laws," as Rosas was called) to the wedding, a highly symbolic omission given the authoritarian political climate, the manner in which the ceremony was conducted, its *style*, "a la francesa," is described as potentially offensive. On the one hand, the protagonists have denied Rosas the right to share *intimacy* with the Válcena and Orellanos families, and in this sense they preempt his supposed right to approve the unions that take place under his domain. The marriage reveals the dictator's exclusion from the process of social interaction of which the marriage rite is a public expression. They "deserve" to be criticized not necessarily for having disregarded Catholic religious tradition, but for violating the *habitus* of their class.

It would not be an exaggeration to state that the entire plot of Bunge's novel is based on this breech of social protocol, for the same night of the wedding Regis is called upon by Rosas's aid-de-camp, Manuel Corvalán, who must bring him immediately to the headquarters of the Federation "para confiarle una comisión honrosa" ("to entrust him with an honorable mission"; 33). The mission is anything but honorable, as Regis is dispatched to meet with the caudillo of Santa Fe, Estanislao López, who immediately imprisons him for no apparent reason other than as retribution for the family's perceived irreverence.

Once Rosas has successfully divided the newlyweds, the novel also separates into two main plotlines. The first follows Regis on his journey to see López, his imprisonment there, and his attempt to escape. The second details the frustrations of the Válcena and Orellanos families in their quest for information about Regis, in Blanca's increasing anxiety, and in the violence of the *Mazorca*. The former takes the protagonist into Argentina's interior, further from civilization, and deeper into his own mind. The latter shows the use and abuse of the social system of interrelated family ties. The romantic tension is provided by the erotic triangle formed between Regis, the idealized criollo man, and Pantuci, a provincial Italian who attempts to win over Blanca (the idealized white woman, as her name indicates) once Regis is out of the picture.

Importantly, Bunge's text resonates with José Mármol's *Amalia* (1851–1852), Argentina's foundational novel, in that both texts are structured as sentimental romances set during the fractious years of the Rosas dictatorship. However, while the protagonists of Mármol's *Amalia* serve allegorical functions that point toward the possibility of a conciliatory national politics, as Sommer has shown, in Bunge's novel the nationally significant protagonists are employed to demonstrate the negative psychological effects of the terroristic Rosas regime. Bunge's text is structured as a mid-century allegorical romance, though its aim is aligned with the turn-of-the-century "somatic fictions" described by Nouzeilles. It is a historical text that brings the collective trauma of the Rosas dictatorship to bear on the romantic relationships of the period and thus on the types of romance that were possible at that time. Before moving to a discussion of the novel's failed national romance, however, I want to briefly sketch the circumstances around the publication and subsequent revision of Bunge's novel in order to provide a context for reading the dramatic shift between the 1903 and 1904 editions.

## Between Olivera and Gálvez: Bunge in *Ideas*

For David Viñas, the turn of the century represents a period of transition, not only in terms of culture, demographics, and urban development, but also with respect to the role of the writer in national life. In fact, Ricardo Olivera is one of those signaled by Viñas as exemplary of this shift from the dilettantism of late-century writers to the professionalization of the early twentieth century (100). Indeed, one of the first steps Olivera took on this path from aficionado to professional was to found the literary magazine *Ideas* in 1903, with the man who would go on to champion the cause of the writer-as-professional, Manuel Gálvez.

As Verónica Delgado has documented, *Ideas* was one of the first publications to actively engage with an emerging market of middle-class readers, as well as to focus specifically on the role of literature and literary criticism in shaping new national subjects in the early twentieth century. Delgado explains as follows:

> *Ideas* exhibió su interés por aspectos ligados a un mercado de bienes culturales posible como lo eran la edición, la traducción, la selección y distribución de las obras, y el éxito, que recubierto de propósitos más elevados, como renovar el pensamiento y el arte o llevar adelante la educación literaria e intelectual de un público amplio, podía presentarse ahora como un objetivo a conquistar.
>
> *Ideas* exhibited its interest in aspects linked to a possible market of cultural goods such as editing, translation, the selection and distribution of (literary) works, and success, which, camouflaged by the most elevated purposes, such as renovating thought and art or carrying out the literary and intellectual education of a broad public, could be presented now as an objective to attain. (271)

It is this selectiveness that turns *Ideas* into a source of cultural policy in the early twentieth century. The publication's goal was to (in)form new readers by presenting them with works that served to construct a new cultural identity, a new *argentinidad*. Its editors chose predominantly nationalist texts, literary works and criticism that emphasized the need to renew the spiritual core of the nation, seen as corrupted by materialist tendencies and beset by immigrants.[12] The goal of the magazine was to vindicate nationalist literature and actively reshape the collective consciousness as produced through the matrix of literary and cultural interventions that were made possible by the publication. As with other periodicals at the turn of the century, *Ideas* saw its role not simply as a guide in aesthetic and moral areas of national significance, but also as a producer of the new "alma argentina" ("Argentine soul"; Delgado 189). I am following Viñas and Delgado in positioning *Ideas* as a site where literary production was evaluated as an intervention in national culture. Yet neither scholar asks what the implications of this position might be for a text such as Bunge's novel, which fails to adhere to the cultural nationalist vision of *Ideas*. This is the site of the closet: where the upper-class enforces heteronormativity, buoyed by an alliance between biopolitics and literary criticism. The rewrite of *La novela de la sangre* evidences this connection between the desire for an expanded reading public and the insistence on a mode of representation that privileges ethnic cohesion through idealized heteroromance. Literary criticism thus becomes the matrix through which the social and the biological reinforce each other.

Olivera's review of Bunge's novel was published in the March-April 1904 edition of *Ideas*, though the text is dated December 1903. Gálvez had also published a review in January 1904, the only time in the history of the publication that two critics—its cofounders no less—reviewed the same text.[13] It is plausible, I think, to date the Olivera review as prior to that of Gálvez, even though it was actually published two months later (the Gálvez review is not separately dated). Even though Olivera had stepped down from the direction of the publication by January 1904, he continued to publish in *Ideas* for some time and would have had direct and extensive contact with Gálvez, who remained as sole director until 1905, when the magazine closed. Thus, it is certainly possible that Gálvez preempted Olivera's unfavorable review with one of his own in an effort to maintain a lasting relationship with one of the rising stars of the Argentine intellectual community, and the man who would become—as I note above—Gálvez's brother-in-law in 1910. Finally, in May 1904, Bunge's revised ending was published in *Ideas* as a stand-alone chapter in advance of the 1904 Argentine edition of *La novela de la sangre*. In short, the Olivera review is dated December 1903; the Gálvez review was published in January 1904; the Olivera review came out in the March-April 1904 edition and was immediately followed by Bunge's new ending in May 1904. In my discussion of these reviews I aim to flesh out my argument for a reading of the space of

*Ideas* as a closet. There are two central themes that become salient in this regard: historical verisimilitude in a fictional text and the author's use of psychopathologic discourse to generate interest in the audience.

## On History

As we saw previously, Olivera does not view Bunge as an artist. This would have been particularly unflattering given the overarching proposal of *Ideas* to inaugurate a new wave of nationally significant literature. What is more, as Graciela Montaldo demonstrates, in Argentina at the turn of the century, *mal gusto* (bad taste) was associated with the amorphous and feminized masses, with the cheap goods they consumed, and the developing culture of the public spectacle ("Hombres" 130). This is the opposite of the intellectual that Bunge had hoped to be.

In particular, Olivera takes issue with what he describes as Bunge's lack of historical verisimilitude:

> La Novela de la Sangre transcurre bajo Rozas. Tiempos climatéricos de luchas enconadas, las pasiones en paroxismo y la diaria peripecia deben atraer al artista: la preferencia de Bunge se explica. Pero es el suyo empeño atrevido. La Historia debe ser auxiliar indispensable de la novela histórica. Y la historia del gobierno de Rozas, demasiado cercano para encontrar imparcialidad, no está escrita.

> The Novel of Blood takes place under Rozas. Climatological times of heated fighting, passions at fever pitch and the daily unpleasantries must attract the artist: Bunge's preference is undestandable. But his is a bold endeavor. History should be the indispensable auxiliary of the historical novel. And the history of the Rozas government, too close to find impartiality, has not yet been written. (300–1)

The question of genre is important in that the possibility of appreciating Bunge's contributions to the Argentine intellectual field rests on his (in)ability to follow the precepts of what Olivera calls "the historical novel." Bunge is criticized for failing to achieve "impartiality." Indeed, Olivera implies that *no one* could write an impartial history of the Rosas regime, which ended *only* half a century prior. But historical verisimilitude was not a hallmark of the literary works written about or because of Rosas. It would be hard to imagine Echeverría, Sarmiento, or Mármol taking historical objectivity as the point of departure for their narrations of the Rosas regime. On the contrary, as contemporary literary scholar Lelia Area notes, "la novela histórica—como matriz genérica—ocupó un lugar preferencial en ellos [Sarmiento y Mármol] debido a que habilitó la interrogación resentida y rencorosa del pasado inmediato" ("the historical novel—as a generical matrix—occupied a preferential place in them [Sarmiento and Mármol] since it made possible the resentful and rancorous interrogation of the immediate past"; 238). It is precisely the "resentment and rancor" in narrating the abuse of the Rosas regime—its violence and terrorism—that characterizes mid-century writing. And in this sense, it is political immediacy rather than historical verisimilitude that characterizes earlier accounts of this era. Olivera, in contrast, is more aligned with a strand of conservative historical revisionism, in which the Rosas regime came to stand for nationalist authority in the face of rising cosmopolitanism, for an autochthonous, paternalist ruler opposed to the liberal elite (Rock, *Authoritarian* 13). The use of the original spelling of the dictator's last name, "Rozas," in Olivera's review, suggests not historical verisimilitude, but the propagandistic revisionism of the cultural nationalists in early decades of the twentieth century. I review the development of antiliberal authoritarian thought in chapter 5 in relation to the national essays written by the Bunge siblings. Here, I want to flag how Bunge's attempt to intervene in a discussion of the psychosocial foundations of Argentine identity struck a nerve with members of the elite invested in redefining nationalism according to ideals of a bellicose masculinity that would gain ground in subsequent decades.

In contrast with Olivera, Gálvez does not see the novel as intending to depict a history: "Sin pretensión de pintar la totalidad de una época, ha trazado Bunge diversos cuadros, característicos y exclusivamente propios de ese tiempo, de un colorido intenso" ("Not intending to paint the totality of an era, Bunge has sketched diverse scenes, characteristic and exclusively pertaining to that period, with intense color"; 80). The intensity with which Bunge narrates stands out, while his intent is compared to that of a *costumbrista* novelist. Still, Gálvez notes, "tratándose de una época no vivida, ha recurrido [Bunge] al elemento psicopatológico, para dar una base de robustez al libro" ("since he is dealing with a period he did not live, [Bunge] has turned to a psychopathological element to provide a robust base for the book"; 83). Acknowledging that Bunge's narrative structure depends on the interest generated by the "psychopathological element," Gálvez sees *La novela de la sangre* as akin to the naturalist fictions of the Generation of 1880, which follow the protagonist through a process of diagnosis and treatment, positioning his or her particular pathology as part of a eugenic master narrative moving ever forward toward a hereditary ideal. That is, Bunge deliberately sets his novel during the Rosas dictatorship, returning to a (primal) scene of national trauma and influenced by psychosocial theories of collective behavior, in order to describe the origins of a collectively felt psychological chain reaction culminating in the cultural malaise of the *fin de siglo*. Olivera picks up on this—"la novela se inaugura con un capítulo de psicología mórbida" ("the novel begins with a chapter of morbid psychology"; 304)—though he is too focused on the historical content of the novel to entertain the possibility of a narrative function for this psychological element. The novel's traumatic beginning is the final point of convergence between Gálvez, Olivera, and Bunge, a juncture that, oddly enough, revolves around the role of kissing for the future of the idealized couple.

## Osculum Interruptum

If Olivera takes issue with the style of Bunge's historical rendering of the Rosas period, he is particularly dismayed by the narrative element the author uses to set up the novel's romantic tension: the kiss. Or more precisely, the kiss interrupted (*osculum interruptum*) on the night of the wedding between Blanca and Regis. Paraphrasing Bonnie Honig, the effect of this interruption is to redirect a chain of events (3). What is more, the interruption of the kiss alters both the narrative direction of the novel and its affective expectations. This moment is key to understanding the queerness of Bunge's text and its relationship with the broader circulation of nationalist literature.

This is the "chapter of morbid psychology" referenced by Olivera, who, after describing the scene, exclaims "La confesión ocupa doce páginas, ¡en plena noche de bodas!" ("The confession takes up twelve pages, and on their wedding night!"; 304). The urgency of the moment (having carried out the wedding in secrecy) and the particular erotic charge of this first kiss underlie Olivera's critique. The relationship between Bunge's novel and *Amalia* is made explicit here as well: "Amalia en idéntica situación escucha temblando el sonar del reloj, y antójasele fatídico. El histerismo de Válcena parece tener origen en esta superstición de mujer sensitiva, metamorfoseada en caso clínico" ("Amalia in an identical situation trembles upon hearing the chime of a clock, and gets the feeling that it is fateful. Válcena's hysterism seems to have its origin in this superstition of a sensitive woman, transformed into a clinical case"; 304). Olivera first identifies the function of the kiss interrupted as central to the psychological treatment of the main characters and continues to note that the trope of the hysterical woman is transformed in Bunge's text, transposed to the male protagonist, Regis Válcena. While Olivera refrains from commenting further, this is a particularly interesting point to explore because when the critic likens Regis Válcena to a "sensitive woman," this cross-gendering invites a reading of the protagonist—as a "clinical case"—through what we could call now a queer lens. Thus, in order to understand the function of the kiss interrupted, we need to first consider the role of the hysterical man, as a turn-of-the-century figure that engages the broader field of somatic understandings of the gendered body.

The history of hysteria is a complex one that contends with disciplinary boundaries, art and science, antiquity and modernity, as well as those of mind and body. As Mark S. Micale points out, it was in the latter part of the nineteenth century that medical interventions in the realm of nervous diseases, as they were then called, came to focus on hysteria as part of psychological rather than the physiological ailments (*Approaching* 33-40). To position Regis, the male protagonist and emblem of normative/national masculinity, as a hysteric is to hearken the chaos of the *fin de siglo* regarding immigration, culture, language, gender, and sexuality. This chaos is read through a diagnostic lens that implies both gender instability and sexual excess. When Olivera names this affliction, he is not simply making plain the prevalence of scientific discourses in naturalist prose but questioning the prominent role that Bunge has given hysteria in this novel. What Olivera seems to disapprove of is that this "case" of hysteria is located conspicuously in the figure of the man charged with bringing order to the chaotic world of the Rosas dictatorship. The national novel should not have a hysteric as its protagonist, Olivera implies. The critic's concern revolves around Bunge's decision to locate male hysteria where it should not be, not in immigrants or working-class men, as was the case in most of European and Latin American sexology, but rather in a white man from the upper class (Micale, *Hysterical* 214-16).

As might be expected, Freud's work was central to popularizing the diagnosis of hysteria in Europe as a particular form of psychosomatic illness. As a disease of modernity and a disease of the mind, hysteria plays a crucial role in early-twentieth-century approaches to the links between gender, sexuality, and psychoanalysis. Indeed, according to Micale, "psychoanalysis effectively began as a theory of hysteria" (*Approaching* 56). In addition to Freud, however, Juliet Mitchell describes psychoanalytic renderings of hysteria according to two strands of thought: one, tracing Rivière and Lacan, which focuses on the hysteric's unstable position in Oedipal socialization, oscillating between normative and incestuous desires, and another, proposed by Charcot, focusing on memory and trauma (6–9). In the first case, there is an emptiness, a longing, often enacted theatrically that characterizes hysteria; in the second, it is an unprocessed traumatic experience that, when triggered, reopens a psychic wound that is then constantly reenacted. Both strands of hysteria—as outlined by Mitchell—are evident in Bunge's portrayal of Regis Válcena, whose psychological trauma is linked to Rosas's return from the so-called pacification wars of the southern frontier in 1828, heralded by a cacophony of church bells. The trauma is revived on the night of the wedding by the ringing of a wall clock given to the newlyweds (that is, the clock is their first wedding gift), which precipitates Regis's self-diagnosis: "Las campanas de todas las iglesias saludaban al caudillo.... Su repiqueteo, su sonoro, su continuo, su infernal repiqueteo, *sonaba en mis nervios de enfermo y de ciudadano.... Porque los argentinos estábamos ya enfermos, como ahora, de una dolencia rara, mitad extenuación, mitad terror*" ("The bells of all the churches greeted the caudillo.... Their ringing, their sonorous, their continual, their infernal ringing, *resounded in my nerves as a sick person and a citizen.... Because we Argentines were already sick then, as we are now, with a strange malady, half exhaustion, half terror*"; 12, my emphasis). It is this trauma that makes the groom unable to kiss his bride. What is more, the symbolic rendering of this event connects the kiss interrupted to the inability of the protagonists to consummate their marriage. The *osculum interruptum* stands in for the *ratum tantum*. The context of hysteria, in particular the hysteric's association with femininity itself, plays an important role in both Bunge's novel and Olivera's critique of it. In this regard, Bunge's main character suffers from a psychological affliction linked not only to the debilitating of his being, but also to his inability to fulfill the normative sex/gender role.

It is no coincidence that Rosas is the figure who sets off the episode of hysteria, since Bunge's novel hinges on the dictator not being invited to the Válcena-Orellanos wedding. This positions Rosas as a threat to kinship bonds, and the novel as a whole as an extended family drama. Rosas, as a historical figure, made possible, or perhaps demanded, what Area calls "un canon político-familiar leído como literatura de la nación" ("a political-familiar canon read as national literature"; 18). For this corpus of texts that includes *Facundo* and *Amalia*, but also, arguably, *La novela de la sangre*, "Rosas se instaló en el imaginario nacional desde la perspectiva de un *pater familiae*" ("Rosas installed himself in the national imaginary from the perspective of a *pater familiae*"; 19). A national father figure demanding to be included not only in the social enactment of marriage rites, but also, crucially, serving as an Oedipal pole against which national literature of the mid- and late nineteenth century defined itself. Seen in this way, the trauma that is recalled on the night of the wedding can also be read as instigating the failure of the protagonist to recognize the Law of the Father. In other words, Bunge generates tension through a male protagonist who refuses (for twelve pages!) the symbolic gesture that would consolidate the positions of male and female within the normative logic of the novel.

But if it is Rosas who interrupts the first kiss—and in doing so sets off the chain of dramatic (and traumatic) events that sustain the novel—it is Regis who, when presented with the opportunity, at the end of the text, willfully refuses to kiss Blanca. This disavowal of his role as the idealized male is the ultimate consequence of his hysterical condition, the manifestation of his queerness. This is the hysteria brought on by Rosas, which culminates in the dissolution of the subject at the end of the novel, when Blanca exclaims:

—Un beso, Regis, y la despedida para siempre, siempre.... ¡Nada más que un beso!

Regis la rechazó con las manos, en un ademán inconsciente, y tan intenso, tan intenso, que más trágico parecía hierático....

Volvióse a oír, en la creciente noche, el grillo que lanzaba su triste, su fría, su diabólica disonancia....

Hizo Regis un esfuerzo sobrehumano para levantarse y huir, sintiendo que, como un joven roble que se arranca violentamente del fecundo limo en que ha nacido y crecido, dejaba allá las raíces de su vida.... Y huyó, *por evitar aquel beso supremo*, huyó....

—One kiss, Regis, and farewell forever, forever.... Nothing more than a kiss!

Regis rejected her with his hands, in an unconscious gesture, and so intense, so intense, that more than tragic he seemed hieratic....

> They heard once more, in the growing night, how the cricket announced his sad, his cold, his diabolical dissonance....
>
> Regis made a superhuman effort to get up and flee, feeling that, like a young oak that tears itself violently from the fecund earth in which it was born and grew up, was leaving behind the roots of its life.... And he fled, *to avoid that supreme kiss*, he fled.... (466–67; my emphasis)

In the 1903 edition of Bunge's novel, the kiss remains forever interrupted. And even though Rosas is the force behind the initial separation of Regis and Blanca, he is not ultimately what keeps them apart. That responsibility falls to Regis, who "flees" his former bride in the precise moment in which their reunion (and thus their future) could be salvaged. In comparing Regis to an oak that has left behind its roots, Bunge heavy-handedly connects him to the denial of genealogical succession. Regis does not simply fail to live up to his potential in the ongoing cycle of procreation, but dramatically rejects his place in the future Argentine nation. He flees "to avoid that supreme kiss," not simply unable, but *unwilling* to kiss Blanca. Regis flees precisely in order to avoid the kiss on which the entire novel hinges, the kiss whose promise of a future will remain ever truncated. But what of this kiss?

A kiss is simultaneously the culmination of a process of seduction and the promise of a romantic future. "Más que la mirada, más que el apretón de manos, más que la caricia, más que el abrazo, tiene el beso una secreta inquietud deliciosa, capaz de poner en tensión todo el organismo y de estremecerlo ansiosamente" ("More than the look, more than the handshake, more than the caress, more than the embrace, the kiss has a secret delicious restlessness, capable of tensing up one's entire organism and of making it shudder anxiously"), wrote José Ingenieros, Bunge's contemporary, in an early twentieth-century survey of the juridical implications of kissing (116). That the nascent scientific community of which Bunge and Ingenieros were certainly at the forefront, would consider "the kiss" not only in its romantic dimensions but also its psychological and legal ones is notable. Here, the kiss signifies not simply as a romantic gesture or instance of social protocol, but as a physiological and neurological phenomenon. Ingenieros continues: "estas prácticas [de besar] entran en el terreno de la patología mental y deben considerarse como formas de masoquismo; implican ya cierta anormalidad de la imaginación o de los sentidos, y puede, entre otros daños generales, causar intensos estados neurasténicos o la misma alienación mental" ("these practices [of kissing] enter the terrain of mental pathology and should be considered as forms of masochism; they imply an existing abnormality of the imagination or of the senses, and they can, among other general harms, cause intense neurasthenic states or even insanity"; 117). Though Ingenieros is referring specifically to the "beso *more colombino* [sic]," the prolonged kiss that lasts "horas enteras" ("for hours"; 116), there remains a connection between the fulfillment of the consensual kiss and the possibility of neurasthenia and mental illness that I am interested in developing further.[14] This enactment of desire, defined specifically as a form of masochism, brings us back to classic definitions of sexual deviance.

As Amber Musser notes, the first case of masochism to be documented and analyzed as a sexual disorder appears in Krafft-Ebing's *Psychopathia Sexualis* in 1890. In this case, Musser continues, "Masochism, according to Krafft-Ebing, was about submission. He considered it a feminization of man's sexual *rôle*, a perversion that was characterized by passivity and subjection" (4). In this early theory, masochism is associated with the abdication of the masculine position within normative social and sexual practice—with the feminization of the male subject. Ingenieros, for his part, seems to propose a slightly more open-ended reading of masochism, applicable to both men and women, and describable in the plural—"forms of masochism." His description of the kiss, however, positions him between Krafft-Ebing and Freud, who, as Musser notes, shifts from hereditary explanations of sexual pathologies toward developmental ones, "away from the paradigm of perversion toward that of neurosis" (6). I would like to highlight two issues here: first, Ingenieros construes the enactment of desire through the kiss as bound up with larger theories of sexual deviance, namely inversion and neurasthenia, and second, that this deviance is described as an abnormal fantasy (*imaginación*) or a corruption of the senses. The prolonged kiss for Ingenieros is not an inherent sexual pathology, though it does exist in the "terrain (or field) of mental pathology," but rather a practice that overstimulates the senses, eventually leading to their failure and exhaustion.

In Bunge's first edition of *La novela de la sangre* we see the reverse of this pathological narrative: it is the interruption of the kiss, its withholding, that eventually leads to the psychic trauma of both Regis and Blanca. Regis's gesture of denying the kiss is described, as we have seen, as responding to an Oedipal (read national) trauma. If in Ingenieros the uncontrolled kiss can be seen as the agent of neurasthenia, in Bunge it is the threat of the kiss, its possibility and symbolic resonance, which serves to punctuate the mental instability of the protagonist, and eventually leads to his subjective dissolution.

The kiss becomes the moment when desire is given its first materiality but always as part of a past and future. The kiss, in this sense, is a gesture toward eroticism that is denied in Bunge's novel. What happens when the kiss is too terrifying to go through with? This is what Bunge takes up through his portrayal of the pathologized protagonist: the kiss as a traumatic experience. And it is this trauma that—through Regis, linked both to Rosas as a *pater familiae* and to the willful refusal to kiss Blanca— marks *La novela de la sangre* as a queer text.

Let us not forget, finally, the utility of the kiss in psychoanalytic theories of socialization. Freud's oral stage, for example, figures pregenital sexuality as passing first through oral and then moving to anal eroticism. While I do not want to rehash the literature on Freud's work, I do want to note that, in such "advanced" versions as the *beso more colombino*, kissing equates the penetrative act of the tongue with that of sexual intercourse. To fear the kiss can also be thought of as fearing sex. The gesture of recoil, of refusal, confirms not simply the sexual anxiety of the protagonist in Bunge's novel, but also, in a Freudian sense, his failure to recognize the correct sexual object choice. Regis is not ambivalent about Blanca, rather he is improperly constituted to desire her as he should in heteronormative society.

## Rewriting National Futures

What changed? The May 1904 edition of *Ideas*, in which Bunge would publish the revised ending of his novel, introduces the text with the following editorial note:

> Visitamos últimamente al doctor Bunge, con el objeto de pedirle una colaboración para nuestra revista.... —Por acaso, vimos sobre su mesa revuelta un grueso manojo de originales, titulado "Novela de la Sangre, segunda edición." Preguntamos entonces al joven y laborioso autor argentino si había reformado mucho ese libro, y nos respondió que así era, en efecto, por haber sido harto deficiente la primer [sic] edición, publicada en Barcelona. En vista de ello, rogámosle nos facilitara algún capítulo inédito, a lo que accedió, dándonos el octavo y final del tercer libro y de la novela,

en el cual le altera a ésta, completamente el desenlace, *adaptándolo quizá mejor al gusto del medio.*

We recently visited Doctor Bunge, with the goal of asking him for a contribution to our magazine.... —By chance, we saw on his disheveled desk a thick bunch of original documents, titled "The Novel of Blood, second edition." We then asked the young and hard-working Argentine author if he had much reformed that book, and he responded that that was indeed the case, effectively, because the first edition, published in Barcelona, was quite defective. In light of this, we begged him to provide us with an unpublished chapter, he accepted, giving us the eighth and final of the third book (part) and of the novel, in which he alters, completely, the dénouement, *adapting it perhaps better to the taste of the average reader.* (14–15; my emphasis)[15]

While it may be true that the directors of *Ideas* came across the recently finished second edition of *La novela de la sangre* "by chance," I think it is more likely that they actively sought out Bunge in order to allow him the chance to redeem himself in the eyes of the public. Olivera and Gálvez specifically reference the new dénouement as a positive outcome of their visit to Bunge's office. This change responds to the "taste" of the reading public that they were actively seeking to shape, bringing us back to the intention of the magazine to develop a readership at the turn of the century by promoting texts that would uphold its nationalist aesthetic and cultural program. This is a pedagogical (and disciplinary) project led by the elite in which the emerging middle class would be provided with models not only of literary merit, but also behavior, desire, and national belonging. The first edition of Bunge's novel is yet again labeled in poor *taste*. However, we are assured, the new ending will sit better with the sensibilities of the majority.

Both endings hinge on Regis's inability to bear the reality of his failed marriage to Blanca. Likewise, for both editions, the dénouement is set up by the romantic triangle formed between Regis and Pantuci, who later lies his way into Blanca's favor, telling her first that Regis has died, and subsequently replacing him at her side when they emigrate to Montevideo. Pantuci is portrayed as a deceptive, degenerate Italian immigrant, "bajo y flaco, de enfermizo aspecto y cutis terroso" ("short and skinny, of sickly appearance and ashy skin"; 106).[16] Despite his somatic inferiority, he is persistent and patient, and eventually manages to marry Blanca, who soon becomes pregnant.[17]

In both the first and second editions, after ten years, Regis returns from his imprisonment to find the home occupied by Blanca and Pantuci, where a young child, "*el nene*," who is never named, greets him. Blanca arrives shortly thereafter, and just when she is about to explain herself to Regis, with a heaping dose of melodrama, Pantuci appears in the doorway. As if awakened from a dream, Blanca declares that her real husband (in both a legal and affective sense) has returned. In both cases, Regis confronts his rival, threatening to kill Pantuci, aiming a pistol at his chest, before Blanca, who is visibly shaken, convinces him to holster his weapon.

The editions begin to diverge, however, around the treatment of "*el nene*." In the first case, after hearing a few choice words from Regis, Pantuci leaves the house, and Blanca, "radicalmente trastornada" ("severely deranged"; 467) wants to leave as well. Both editions also include the following insinuation of her doubts regarding the child: "Tal vez sea mejor que acabe también este niño de mala raza" ("Perhaps it would be better for this mutt child to end as well"; 1903, 318; 1904, 418). The implication is clear: this boy, carrying within him Pantuci's contaminated blood, must disappear from her life so that she and Regis can start anew. The boy's *mestizaje* is damning. He is not simply mixed-race, but *of bad race*.

In the first edition, as we have already seen, Regis rejects Blanca and flees "to avoid the supreme kiss." Blanca is described in the novel's last paragraph: "Y la joven, resuelta á morir, se perdió para siempre, con su hijo de la mano, entre las sombras de una noche sin aurora" ("And the young woman, resolved to die, was lost forever, holding her child by the hand, amongst the shadows of a night without dawn"; 468). Mentally altered, she takes her son with her to disappear into the ether, an everlasting darkness contrasting the purity, the whiteness with which she has been characterized throughout. Here, the hysterical wife is charged with eliminating herself and the unwanted child. This ending hinges on a misogynist view of women's role in Porteño society. Blanca is condemned, it seems, for having been tricked by Pantuci and coerced by her own mother into marrying him, and thus failing in her duty as an abnegating and chaste wife. The message is about the spread of a neurosis that hinders the ability of both men and women to successfully perform hegemonic gender roles. It positions state terrorism as an environmental cause of the crisis of the upper class.

In the second edition, however, Blanca and Regis, accompanied by "*el nene*," walk down to a nearby beach. As Regis is trying to console Blanca, ten years after their first kiss as a married couple was interrupted by Rosas's vengeful order, in the moment they are reunited, described by the narrator as "el momento más intensamente feliz" ("the most intensely happy moment") of Blanca's life, another tragedy strikes (1904, 326). The young child is nowhere to be found. After searching the area, Regis comes to a small sinkhole, and there, at the bottom of the darkness, is the boy. "Más muerto que mi agüelo" ("Deader than my grandpa") is how a local fisherman describes him, in a strangely poetic pronouncement also infused with the rhetoric of kinship (1904, 329). The death of the child, symbolically returned to the womb, compels the Regis to ask himself: "Y si la Providencia lo había querido así, ¿no sería eso mejor para el futuro hogar? ..." ("And if Providence had wanted it so, would it not be better for the future home? ..."; 1904, 330). With this rhetorical question we see the insistence of the narrative of a nationally significant kinship pattern, even through the death of the young boy. The Regis-Blanca union is an idealized future one, and in this sense, the temporality of hegemonic kinship, its ever-forward (reproductive) motion, is restored when the child, a remnant of the past and of an undesirable ethnic combination, is eliminated in the second edition. This is an after-the-fact abortion.

Here, Regis posits that the tragedy of the child's death is diminished not just because it was fated, but because without that child Blanca now has the opportunity to begin a new family with him. Regis even imagines that the loss of this child frees Blanca from the traumatic past she experienced in his absence and from the supposedly contaminated blood running through the veins of "*el nene*." The death of the child and the return of the true husband sever any ties that might have linked Pantuci, the impostor, the unfit Italian, to Blanca. Finally, Pantuci claims, "Yo, como nada tengo que hacer aquí, desapareceré también de este sitio maldito" ("I, since there is nothing left for me here, will disappear as well from this cursed place"; 1904, 333). And as if to prove this once and for all, "envolvió [Pantuci] el ya amortajado cuerpecito en su propio poncho, como para preservarlo del frío, y salió con él de la sala" ("[Pantuci] wrapped in his own poncho the already shrouded little body, as if to protect it from the cold, and with it left the room"; 1904, 333). Pantuci not only disappears from their lives, but he takes with him the last vestige of his biological presence. The cadaver, product of an ill-fated and loveless union, whose blood is that of the type of racial mixture that will only lead to degeneracy, is eliminated.[18] Thus, in the second edition Bunge uses the Italian immigrant as an ethnic scapegoat;

the blood of his mixed-race child is removed from the national stock. To riff on José Esteban Muñoz, "the future is only the stuff of some kids" (95).[19] Not "*el nene*," who is rendered national detritus, on the one hand, for his degenerate blood, and on the other, for having no proper place in society, or at least, having no language to describe it, stuck in the pre-Oedipal phase. Meanwhile, Blanca and Regis are positioned to fulfill their promise of nation building by starting anew, finally able to close the gap between them and follow through the stages of reproductive futurity that had been interrupted by the dictator. In this, we see that it is through the death of the mixed-race child that the heteronormative order is restored.

The queerness of the first ending is found in its refusal of the logic of reproductive futurity. In this ending, Regis rejects the kiss, interrupted by Rosas at the beginning of the novel, which would have restored the protagonists to their rightful place in the national imaginary of the reading public sought by *Ideas*. The young man flees his wife in an unconscious reaction that brings into focus the complete reversal of his desire. The "infected citizen," whose neurosis was caused by the interruption of his wedding night by the dictator, is no longer able to love his wife. The distance between Regis and Blanca, produced by the *osculum interruptum*, is never closed. In Edelman's terms, Regis prefers abjection to the possibility of occupying the role of the idealized male citizen. It is here that we see the inadequacy of the first edition for the reading public of *Ideas*: there is no future for the couple that is emblematic of the very type of union on which the desired cultural and ethnic identity of the turn-of-the-century elite was based. On the one hand, the nationalization of literature and expansion of the reading public depends on representations of heteronormative romance that give shape to an explicitly nationalist future. On the other, racial whitening, *blanqueamiento*, becomes a necessary condition for a modern *argentinidad*. Bunge fails to provide a model of either of these cultural imperatives, and it is here, finally, that we see how the revision of his novel evidences the collusion between literary criticism, cultural nationalism, and the notion of racial purity.

Summing up, Bunge's second edition proposes a model for citizenship based on the cohesive ethnic composition of future generations, potential children who represent the future of the idealized national family. The family unit, insofar as it is understood to be the sociocultural guardian of the nation, is placed in the service of conserving desirable hereditary and cultural qualities and eliminating those deemed anathema to the modernizing project of the upper class. The rewrite turns the ambivalent separation of the protagonists into a celebration of their idealized union. If in the first edition Bunge disavows futurity, in the second he restores the possibility of a future racially acceptable child.

To conclude this section, I would like to return to style. At least for Olivera, Bunge's is a *twisted* style that leaves the reader with a sour taste, a lingering sense of displeasure, that the romantic promise of the nation is not kept, but rather disrupted by the protagonist's vigorous denial of his hereditary mandate. For this reason Olivera's review impunes Bunge's novel for not adhering to "the taste of the majority." If in the 1903 edition Bunge had intended to discipline Blanca for failing to wait for Regis, in 1904 it is the author who is corrected in turn, for failing to provide a plausible model of reproductive futurity. Olivera and Gálvez position themselves, in their role as literary critics, as more than arbiters of style—they set themselves up as guardians of Oedipal socialization for the upper class. Bunge's preface to the revised 1904 edition evidences as much: "he creído un deber enmendarla y mejorarla, limpiándola de muchos defectos" ("I believed it was my duty to fix and better it, cleansing it of many defects"; 3). He expresses not a sense of literary perfectionism, but of *duty* to the cultural project, "our incipient national literature."

We see in the first edition that Bunge writes about heterosexual desire as if it were utterly terrifying. The desire to procreate, to form a nationally significant future (and fertile) union, is marred by the protagonists' infection with the neurosis that overran Argentine society under Rosas. Bunge offers a vision of kinship that is highly problematic, laden with psychological tension that actually makes procreative relationships *un*desirable.

The kiss, again, is key. In the 1904 edition, we read the following resolution to the long awaited reunion between Regis and Blanca: "Después de contemplarla largo rato en el abandono del lecho, se inclinó sobre ella y le besó la frente.... Blanca abrió los ojos á aquel beso. Era el beso mágico del príncipe salvador anunciado por el hada madrina: el mágico beso que venía a despertar a la princesa encantada que dormía en su lecho desde un siglo" ("After contemplating her for a long time in the abandonment of her bed, he leaned over her and kissed her forehead.... Blanca opened her eyes with that kiss. It was the magical kiss of the savior prince foretold by the fairy godmother: the magical kiss that had come to awaken the enchanted princess who had been sleeping in her bed for a century"; 441). Despite my insistence on Bunge's conservative response to the novel's dissatisfying conclusion, I think we may be able to see in the revised ending a gesture toward queerness after all. Why would the problematic *osculum interruptum* be rewritten as a fairy tale? Even in this revised dénouement, the kiss is not a consensual romantic kiss, but transferred to the terrain of enchantment, Regis as Prince Charming; Blanca, Snow White. It is not the same type of kiss that was presented in the crucial scene at the beginning of the novel. Its *style* is different. This kiss seems more like an act of obligation than of sexual desire. Perhaps, then, we can read this kiss, even as it restores the ideal pair to their symbolic positions in a heteronormative and ethnically copacetic union, as a gesture toward queerness that speaks back to the criticism of Bunge's novel as "twisted." Perhaps, in the end, this is Bunge's way of allowing the audience to have its national literature, while through a stylistic sleight of hand shifting heteronormative desire to the realm of fantasy.

This is a novel in which procreative sexuality is obstructed by a male protagonist figured as hysterical, on the one hand, and on the other, a vindictive dictator intent on punishing those who would exclude him from the social rites of marriage. While *Novela de la sangre* stages the failure of heterosexual desire as an effect of Argentina's social psychology, which is itself a product of Rosas's reign of terror, it also provides clues as to how the pressures of heteronormativity emerge from a cultural imperative to create national literature that could educate a growing reading public in the art of successful romance. Through this novel Bunge mobilizes the contradictory discourses surrounding gender roles and sexual intimacy at the service of a national project of cultural and biological reproduction. For him, however, the family is both necessary as a literary device and undesirable as an expression of cultural continuity, both required and terrifying.

### *THESPIS*: PUTTING ON THE MASK

The politically volatile decade of 1900-1910 saw increased state surveillance of immigrants and radical political parties, and—from members of the elite—a recrudescent emphasis on social hygiene, racial purity, and cultural homogeneity. Upper-class writers like Bunge viewed the city of Buenos Aires as overrun by immigrants, whose "insalubrious" lifestyles were often diagnosed by criminologists owing to their "inherent" mental deficiency, a mode of thinking that followed positivist discourses of biological determinism. In 1907 Bunge would publish *Thespis*, a collection of short stories that continued his ideological alignment with the upper class, but which also represents a diversification of his thinking on social and affective bonds. Among these narratives, "El último grande de España" ("The Last Great Man in Spain") and "La agonía de Cervantes" (The Agony of Cervantes"), are set in medieval Spain, and reflect a nostalgic desire for colonial nobility. There are several medical sketches, such as "La madrina de Lita" (Lita's Godmother"), which fictionalize the dangers of racial miscegenation. Likewise, the book includes a pair of satirical pieces that consolidate Bunge's disdain for *modernismo*, "Almas y rostros" ("Souls and Faces") and "El canto del cisne" ("The Swan's Song").[20] But curiously, for a man situated in such a cultural milieu—dominated by positivist science and himself a fervent proponent of biological determinism—*Thespis* also explores how queerness emerges from normative fantasies of national coherence.

This short story collection complicates what has typically been seen as the repression of queer desire in Bunge's writing at the service of the national project of modernization. Focusing on three examples, "El Capitán Pérez" ("Captain Pérez"), "El Chucro" ("The Chucro"), and "Pesadilla drolática" ("Droll Nightmare"), I question just what it means to desire, what types of desire are necessary for the national project of modernization, and how this desire mobilizes queerness in Bunge's work. Each text hinges on a particular form of masculinity that operates both as a caution against and incitement to queerness within normative scripts of sociality. Bunge endeavors to position himself, or at least his authorial voice, at the center of these diverse forms of relation—at times in favor, at times against—the normative underpinnings of gendered sociality.

In fact, *Thespis* opens with the following introductory note:

> Pues este libro es un manojo de cuentos y fantasías, escrito en los más varios estados de ánimo. Presenta, puedo decirlo, distintos personajes y diversos estilos. Por mi rostro han pasado también las máscaras de lino, ya trágicas, ya cómicas.... ¿No es acaso todo escritor—poeta, dramaturgo o novelista,—la sucesiva encarnación de sus personajes? Él siente, actúa y habla por ellos, ellos por él.

> Well this book is a handful of stories and fantasies, written in the most varied of moods. It presents, I can admit, distinct characters and diverse styles. The masks of linen, at times tragic, at times comical, have also passed before my face.... Is it not the case that every writer—poet, dramaturge,

or novelist—is also the successive incarnation of his characters? He feels, acts, and speaks for them, and they for him. (7)

Bunge at once identifies with these characters, these *masks*, and distances himself from them. This is a clever way to introduce a text that revolves around desiring and belonging queerly, but it also lays the foundation for understanding the text as a series of gestures toward performative poses of queerness, for considering each of these characters as covering, masking, a particular form of gendered embodiment, sexuality, and desire, that, at least potentially, resonate with the author himself. Each of these masks relates queerly to Bunge. They at once cover and reveal his desires. Even if this is obvious, it is worth restating that the artifice of fictionalization, here, is deliberately undermined by the author. He does not want readers to interpret his work as pure invention, but rather to link him, the author, to those very states, feelings, and desires that his characters express.

### Inciting Queer Desire in "El Capitán Pérez"

At first glance "El Capitán Pérez" offers an amusing account of the perils of small town living, "pueblo chico, infierno grande" (literally "small town, big hell"), as the popular expression goes. The narrative traffics in gossip, intrigue, and melodrama, a comic rendering of the courtship rituals of an upper-class family fallen on hard times. As with much of Bunge's fiction, it would be easy to dismiss. But "El Capitán Pérez" offers more than sensational fluff. Rather, this short story theorizes incitement, and in particular inciting queer desire through sororal conspiracy, as the basis of heteronormative sexual relations. As we will see, in order for heteronormative eroticism to function properly, it has to pass first through queerness. In this, once again, Bunge's fiction exists on an ambivalent plane between normativity and queerness.[21] As with *La novela de la sangre*, "El Capitán Pérez" attempts to intervene in the debates over family organization and upper-class hegemony by relying on allegorical characters that play out a drama of social disorder. It pushes turn-of-the-century ideas about courtship and romance, while it also strives to provide a model for maintaining upper-class dominance.

The narrator paints a grim picture from the start:

> A modo de fiera en un redil, la desgracia se había encarnizado con la familia de Itualde. Primero perdió en especulaciones toda la fortuna el padre y jefe, don Adolfo. Poco después murió, dejando "en la calle" a su viuda, doña Laura, y sus cuatro hijos: Adolfo, Ignacio, Laurita y Rosa, la pequeña, a quien llamaban "Coca."
>
> Like a caged beast, disgrace had fattened itself on the de Itualde family. First, the father and leader, don Adolfo, lost the family fortune in speculations. Shortly thereafter he died, leaving "in the street" his widow doña Laura, and his four children: Adolfo, Ignacio, Laurita and Rosa, the youngest, who they called "Coca." (175)

"El Capitán Pérez" thus opens with the fall of the de Itualde family, with their displacement and loss of patriarchal structure. The family's plight is set in motion by the father's failure in the financial market. Bunge's short story resonates with Argentine narratives of financial ruin and social disorder, in particular Martel's *La Bolsa* (1890), which details the temptation and perdition of the protagonist/patriarch Luis Glow, who loses his family patrimony and his position as head of household, negating a possible future both for him and the nation (Spicer-Escalante 137). "El Capitán Pérez," in contrast, begins with the death of the patriarch of the de Itualde family, and dramatizes the results of upper-class perfidy; the aftermath of this loss of patriarchal structure. What is more, in Bunge's text, doña Laura would soon pass away. This is a family whose kinship pattern has been dislodged—the siblings are now adult orphans—and the plot details the strategies that the de Itualdes employ to return to economic solvency and to regain both their social standing and familial stability. Thus, the narrative is framed not simply as a critique of financial speculation, but as a model of how to stave off social decline and familial disorganization.

Clearly, the text is in dialogue with a vein of Argentine fiction that takes the financial crisis of 1890 as a touchstone in national politics—1890 marks, too, first time that sectors of the small but growing middle class, as well as working-class groups, began to imagine a new type of public representation in national politics. The "Revolución del 90" was the moment when the working class glimpsed the possibility of a new political reality; it is from this brief opening that the Unión Cívica was born (later the Unión Cívica Radical), the political party that would eventually win the elections of 1916, inaugurating the first time in Argentine history when a popular and middle-class political party would ascend to the presidency. That is, 1890 marks the beginning of the end of the upper-class stranglehold on Argentine politics and culture. The heightened visibility of immigrants and working-class families, anarchists and socialists, created a sense of unease for the elite. This is the anxiety that Bunge is tapping into, the fear that animates this narrative of social decline. Indeed, the de Itualde family serves as an example of what could happen to members of the elite should they continue to lose ground, culturally, economically, and politically, to the growing popular classes.

However, this narrative also hinges on mobilizing queerness to produce heteronormative desire. Paradoxically, the text proposes—perhaps against its own design—that it is only by inciting queer desire in members of the upper class that they will react to their own precarious position and attempt to maintain (or in this case, regain) their patrimony through advantageous marriage alliances. Bunge is narrating the dysfunction of what historian Leandro Losada describes as the "mercado matrimonial" ("marriage market") at 1900, in which upper-class "*niñas*" ("eligible young women") were entrusted with upholding social and indeed biological reproduction of the elite (196–205). I will return to the role of "*niñas*" in Porteño society in chapter 2, but for now it may be useful to remind that, following Gayle Rubin, the political economy of sex is predicated on the historically contingent and culturally variable exchange of women, which simultaneously fixes gender into binary categories and normalizes heterosexuality. This is precisely what has come under scrutiny in "El Capitán Pérez," a political economy of sex that, for Bunge, has come under threat. And yet, it is not through overtly advocating for women's submission to patriarchal authority that this is accomplished in the text, but rather through the incitement to queer desire. Here I am thinking about desire as a libidinal force of attraction and repulsion. Queer desire is neither stable nor fixed, but rather used as a tool to restructure the political economy of sex. It is by inciting this queerness, and thus eliciting its rejection and then propulsion toward heteronormative sociality, that the text is able to do so.

The goal of the de Itualde siblings is to regain their place in society. Adolfo attempts to do so by marrying, but his wife and their child die in childbirth. What is more, Adolfo loses what little money they have left, clearly marked as a model of failed masculinity. Falling into a deep depression, it comes to Laura to care for him, and she insists that the remaining members of the de Itualde family—herself, Adolfo, and Coca—move to Tandil, a small town in the Province of Buenos Aires where Adolfo has been offered a position in a local bank.[22] Ignacio, for his part, remains in Buenos Aires to enlist in the military. Instead of market speculation, they are now supported by Adolfo's bureaucratic job, while the military becomes a viable alternative for a young man in need of employment.[23] This is clearly a family in crisis, having lost their home and fortune, having been symbolically exiled from the capital to the province, and, crucially, no longer benefiting from a patriarchal model of familial organization. This is now a sibling-led household: Adolfo, Laura, and Coca must now find a new way to support themselves.

The plot shifts when a wealthy eligible Porteño bachelor named Mariano Vázquez sends word that he has purchased a property in Tandil and will be moving there shortly. The sisters, Laura and Coca, having been shunned from the local social circles and feeling disenchanted with what they see as a dearth of suitors in the town, immediately begin to plot how they might take advantage of this opportunity. Coca chides Laura: "Es preciso que usemos todas nuestras armas . . . para vencerlo y que quede en casa, contigo, y si tú no quieres o no puedes, aunque sea conmigo" ("We must use all of our weapons . . . to defeat him so that he stays at our house, with you, and if you don't want to or can't, even if it is with me"; 179). "Conquering" Vázquez is described as the most direct way to improving the family's economic position. Laura is unimpressed, however, and claims that Coca should not be "coqueta y mentirosa" ("coquettish and deceptive"), but rather "buena y franca" ("good and frank"; 209).[24] This narrative hinges on conquering a man's heart; on whether men respond to goodness (as Laura would have it), or to deception and cunning (as would Coca). Coca proposes the following course of action:

> Hagamos una apuesta. Pongamos en práctica los dos sistemas, el tuyo y el mío, a ver cuál da mejor resultado con Vázquez. Tú harás la niña buena y yo haré la niña mala. . . . La que le trastorne primero el seso se casará con él y . . . como es muy rico . . . dotará a su hermanita, si se queda soltera. ¡Trato hecho! . . . ¡Nada de echarse atrás!

> Let's make a bet. We'll put our two systems in practice, yours and mine, to see which one has the best result with Vázquez. You will be the good girl and I will be the bad girl. . . . Whoever drives him crazy first will marry him and . . . since he is very rich . . . will provide for her little sister, if she stays single. It's a deal! . . . No going back! (211)

This passage fixes the allegorical position of each sister. Femininity may take two forms: good or bad, chaste or coquettish. Each sister stands in for a particular form of erotics. Bunge's formulation is based on sibling difference as channeled through the power of seduction wielded by each woman. The fact that Laura is portrayed as a caretaker, filling in for their deceased mother, only heightenes the contrast between her and Coca, both of whom, as unwed sisters, are in a position to marry Vázquez. At first glance, it would seem that the "bet" frames the relationship between Laura and Coca as a form of competition in which their respective modes of seduction will instruct readers in how to overcome such adversity.

However, if we look carefully at the passage cited above, the bet placed between Laura and Coca is not actually based on competition. Their differing methods of courtship are aimed at a singular result: providing financial stability *for each other*. They are not competing, but *conspiring*. Importantly, their conspiracy at once recognizes their position as units of exchange in the political economy of sex and imagines otherwise just how they will manipulate their own commodification. They conspire to reap the benefits of their own position as bridewealth. Sororal conspiracy provides a model of feminist praxis that undermines the text's normative vision of courtship.[25] Even though the sisters do compete against each other for Vázquez's affections, their competition is from the beginning ironic. They are manipulating Vázquez for their own (shared) benefit.

With this bet, Bunge is dramatizing typical *fin de siglo* attitudes about the "feminine question."[26] He was well aware of the ongoing debates over gender roles, women's education, and early feminism in the Southern Cone. As we might expect, Bunge's ideas about women are informed by his positivist ideology and tendency toward social Darwinism. However, he takes a surprising stance regarding women's sexuality in his sociological work, which is important for our discussion of "El Capitán Pérez." Before returning to the short story, I want to briefly relate how Bunge theorizes sexuality in the third volume of his study *La Educación*.[27] Here, Bunge writes on the psychological differentiation of the sexes that women are not naturally inclined toward sincerity, but rather deception.

> Obsérvase en ella marcada inclinación a la astucia, a la doblez, al disimulo, hasta a la descarada mentira.... Estas cualidades son consecuencia de la morfología, de la conformación de la mujer, y de su debilidad. Su *aptitud para el fraude* no es más que el resultado de su coquetería, de su *aptitud*

*para el amor.* Ella engaña al hombre, se le acerca y se le escapa, con el casi inconsciente propósito de atraerle, de sobreexitar su pasión sexual. El macho ataca y la hembra se defiende para obligarle a reforzar el ataque: Tal es la ley de la sexualidad.

Observe in her a marked inclination toward guile, duplicity, dissimulation, even outright lies.... These qualities are the consequence of the morphology, of the conformation of woman, and of her weakness. Her *aptitude for fraud* is nothing more than the result of her coquettishness, of her *aptitude for love.* She tricks man, she brings him close and she escapes, with the almost unconscious purpose of attracting him, of overexciting his sexual passion. The male attacks and the female defends herself in order to oblige him to attack again: Such is the law of sexuality. (117 emphasis in the original)

These principles of sexuality reinforce Bunge's vision of patriarchy, proposing that women are biologically destined to weakness and submission to men. His misogyny notwithstanding, what I find interesting about this passage is how Bunge describes *coquettishness* as the product of two equivalent traits: fraud and love. This equivalence makes Bunge's theory of sexual attraction hinge on women's ability to incite desire in men. This is its central feature, its pivot. For this law of sexuality to function women must exist in oscillation between fraud and love. Women reverberate. This difference only makes sense, curiously, because a woman's destiny, through her coquettishness, is not just to attract the attention of a man, but to "overexcite his sexual passion." It is almost as if heteronormative sexuality in men lies dormant, hidden, and only when shaken between these poles of fraud and love is his passion awakened. In other words, heterosexual male passion, as a biological feature, does not exist on its own, but must be conjured by women. The only way for a man to feel passion for a woman is for a woman to incite in him the passion that he does not yet feel. In this version of incitement, men do not automatically desire women, but rather must be coerced. To put it bluntly, in Bunge's sexological theory men do not "naturally" desire women. They must be made to do so.

There are three points that I would like to outline here. First, we sense in Bunge's description a sort of Foucauldian repressive hypothesis: incitement to discourse, incitement to sex, incitement to desire what one should, but does not yet. In Bunge's theory, heteronormative desire in men only comes after being incited by women. That is, within this structuring of desire, Vázquez becomes a love-object rather than a lover, and, what is more, his desire for the de Itualde sisters is not presented as his own idea, but rather must be conjured, perhaps rescued, from a latent state through their incitement to homosocial rivalry. In contrast with most turn-of-the-century criminologists, educators, and hygienists, Bunge is arguing in favor of a form of female sexuality that harnesses queerness in order to maintain heteronormativity. The real taboo, the form of sexuality that women should not be performing, is the sincerity that Bunge attributes to men. Thus, the incitement to heteronormative desire comes by prohibiting the queer desire of/as men that a sincere woman would represent. In other words, men such as Vázquez—idealized, upper class, nationally significant men—for Bunge, must feel queerness first and then reject that queerness in order to desire normatively. In the sexual economy that Bunge is narrating, men such as Vázquez are described as not yet trained to love as they should. The process goes something like this: men must be incited to queer desire, which should then inspire a homophobic reaction, the rejection of that queerness, in order for heteronormativity to be reinstated as the norm. Coca's proposition to "trastornar el seso" implies the same type of operation that Bunge describes in *La educación*: a man must not simply be attracted, but his mind should be mentally altered, turned around, incited to desire what he has not previously desired, or perhaps, what he should not desire.

Second, Bunge's work anticipates Freud's writing on jealousy as a precursor to love. While it is not Bunge's intention to provide a comprehensive social critique of desire, in "El Capitán Pérez" he does insist on a particular rendering of courtship, of desire, that deserves further exploration. When Freud writes about the preconditions for love, he describes them fundamentally from a masculine perspective, that is, how men desire, and why. The "neurotics" that Freud describes love women that they should not. They choose to love women who are either unavailable or of ill repute in a serial chain of desire that intends to "rescue" such women from ignominy (387-94). Here, what Freud calls an " 'injured third party' " is most prescient for my analysis of Bunge's short story. When Freud describes the abnormality of sexual object choice in men, he intends to frame the debate, like Ingenieros, in terms of the division between natural and unnatural desire. Freud writes that the preconditions for love "[stipulate] that the person in question shall never choose as his love-object a woman who is disengaged—that is, an unmarried girl or an unattached married woman—but only one to whom another man can claim right of possession as her husband, fiancé or friend" (388). To desire a woman, for the men Freud analyzes, is only possible when that woman is unavailable, already possessed by another man. The desire to possess is heightened by this very impossibility. After all, Freud notes, this desirous impossibility is only natural, a product of the Oedipal complex. The object choice is a "mother surrogate" in series that must be negotiated as an unending chain of abnormal desire (388). As an incitement to queer desire.

Third, Bunge's theory of incitement dialogues with other systems of sexual desire in Argentina at the turn of the century. For example, we see similarities with Ingenieros, whose psychosocial essays, later collected as a book titled *Tratado del amor*, meditate on the underpinnings as well as the eugenic promise, of desire, love, and marriage. There are two essential elements I would like to emphasize about Ingenieros's work as it relates to that of Carlos Octavio Bunge: (1) heterosexual desire is essentially *voluntary*, and (2) it depends on the ability of potential partners to judge each other to the service of achieving a eugenic ideal. For Ingenieros, eugenic perfection can only be achieved when both partners are free to choose who they desire, without the constraints of social protocol or the influence of class. In contrast with Ingenieros, however, both Bunge's fiction and his expository writing take the ability to choose, the voluntary nature of desire, out of the equation. In fact, for Bunge, desire is not voluntary, but must be coerced. If, for Ingenieros, sexual attraction can be corrupted by social demands of upper-class hegemony, the habitus of the elite, for Bunge, desire is always dangerously unpredictable.

The incitement to queer desire is central to what I referred to earlier as sororal conspiracy, which begins when Vázquez is invited over for dinner. Laura "desempeñ[a] su papel" ("plays her part"), while Coca "no olvidó un momento de hacerse la coquetuela, melindrosa y casquivana" ("did not once forget to be the coquettish one, prissy and frivolous"; 184). They stay in character. Moments later, while Vázquez is admiring a porcelain candy bowl, Coca explains that it is "... de un buen amigo y compañero de armas de mi hermano Ignacio ... el capitán Pérez" ("... from a good friend and brother-in-arms of my brother Ignacio ... Captain Pérez"; 184). Perhaps a moment of "fraud," or inspired invention, Coca wants Vázquez to feel that he has a rival. The narrator helps us understand her logic: "Lo importante era inventarse un novio, ya que no lo tenía verdadero, para despertar los celos en Vázquez... ¡Los hombres debían sentir los celos antes del amor!" ("The important thing was to invent a boyfriend for herself, since she didn't have a real one, to inspire jealousy in Vásquez... Men should feel jealousy before love!"; 184). The first step in Coca's plan of seduction is to incite Vázquez to jealousy. She intentionally creates what Sedgwick calls a homosocial rivalry. Even if Pérez is a fabricated rival, a shadow, his presence is meant to elicit a specific type of emotion (jealousy) and reaction (pursuit) by Vázquez. This staging of eroticism between men is reflective of Bunge's psychosocial writing. Here, in order for Vázquez to desire Coca, she must first incite him to feel the rivalry of another suitor. That is, the incitement to queer desire—and let us not forget that Sedgwick describes homosociality as an "unbroke[n] continuum between homosocial and homosexual" desire (*Between* 1)—is precisely what Coca intends when she invents Pérez. The incitement to queer desire is shaped as a homosocial rivalry, and it is the technique by which Coca aims to win the bet. But in fact there are two rivalries at play. Coca has invented Pérez to rival Vázquez, while Vázquez is himself the object of the conspiratorial rivalry between Coca and Laura. This bet queers normative courtship by placing Vázquez as the object to be conquered rather than one of the sisters. That is, their sororal conspiracy is not about sating a maternal thirst to procreate, but rather, and this is highly suggestive, is framed as a manipulation of the typical transactive nature of the heteronormative marriage plot.

Laura, for her part, "miró con asombro á su hermana, y no se atrevió a aclarar el punto, dejando correr la invención del 'capitán Pérez,' el pretendiente fantasma..." ("looked with shock at her sister, and did not dare clarify the point, letting the invention of 'Captain Pérez' go on, the phantasm suitor..."; 184). If at first Laura is unsettled, she restrains herself, following Coca's lead. This initial moment of sororal conspiracy, born of Coca's quick-wittedness, links the sisters to each other in their plot to conquer Vázquez. And indeed, the phantasmagoric qualities of Pérez take immediate effect. As Vázquez grows desperate to discover the identity of his rival, the sisters carefully flesh out this fantasy. Piece by piece we learn about Pérez as Vázquez does, through his questions and Coca's ever-more-outlandish inventions.

El personaje imaginario llegó así a ser familiar en la casa. La misma Laura, que afirmaba haberlo conocido y tratado en casa de la tía Viviana,

> se prestaba a una broma que parecía inocente.... El capitán Pérez era simpático, buen mozo, alegre, en fin, poseía numerosas condiciones que la buena voluntad pudiera suponer en cualquier sujeto militar joven.... Tenía un brillante porvenir ... Se había batido una vez en duelo ... el capitán Pérez esto ... y el capitán Pérez aquello....

> The imaginary character thus became familiar in the house. Even Laura, who claimed to have met and interacted with him in their aunt Viviana's house, played her part in a joke that seemed innocent.... Captain Pérez was nice, handsome, happy, in sum, he possessed numerous qualities that a willing imagination could suppose in any young military man.... He had a brilliant future ... He had once fought a duel ... Captain Pérez this ... and Captain Pérez that.... (217)

Pérez becomes "familiar" not only because of Coca's ability to manipulate Vázquez with her storytelling, but also because of Laura's part in this conspiracy: "se prestaba," she lent herself to the fiction; she played her part in the spinning of this tale. The seeming innocence of the fabrication is part of the narrative's irony. It is not that Laura *wants* to deceive Vázquez—that would contradict her inherent goodness—but rather that she is invested in supporting her sister through conspiracy. As I note above, their conspiracy takes the function of women as units of exchange between men, what Lévi-Strauss argues is the structural basis of culture, as the very demand through which they begin to manipulate Vázquez, and thus their collaborative work is aimed at undermining patriarchal authority. Their collaborative manipulation lays bare the objectification of women, and they aim to use that normative architecture to their own benefit.

Frustrated, Vázquez laments to the town judge that Coca must be in love with someone else, some captain named Pérez. The revelation spreads like wildfire: from the judge to the doctor to the pharmacist, to the *Club Social*. By nightfall Tandil is consumed with intrigue: Coca de Itualde, "la *Beauty del Tandil*" ("the *Beauty* of Tandil") is engaged to Capitán Pérez. This is of course completely false, but once Coca's "engagement" is made public there is no way to stop the flow of information. Here, gossip functions to network the town, but also to divide it. In fact, one of the town's two journalists, Jacinto Luque of *El Correo de las niñas*, actually claims to have met the illustrious gentleman, Pérez, among the high society of Buenos Aires. The narrator explains how other supposed rivals follow his lead.

Habiendo afirmado Jacinto Luque la suma distinción del capitán Pérez, todos los "dandies" del Tandil declararon conocerlo, siquiera de vista. El presunto novio de la beldad local llegó así á tener cierto renombre en el pueblo. Los innumerables pretendientes de Coca excusaban su derrota adornando al vencedor de excepcionales cualidades.

After Jacinto Luque had affirmed the great distinction of Captain Pérez, all of Tandil's "dandies" declared that they knew him, even by sight. The presumed fiancée of the local beauty thus managed to acquire a certain fame in the town. Coca's innumerable suitors excused their defeat by embellishing the exceptional qualities of the victor. (195)

Pérez becomes an apparatus (a Foucauldian *dispositif*) that facilitates the idealization of a masculine subject while he involves the entire male population of Tandil in this plot. This phantasmagoric figure becomes the standard against which all men in Tandil are measured, a mirror reflecting a collective homosocial desire. That is, the incitement to queer desire that was supposed to only affect Vázquez, now spreads, we might say infects, the public sphere. As readers, we enter a voyeuristic field where we know that Pérez is only a figment of Coca's imagination, and yet, we are still titillated by the heightening tension produced by the conspiracy of the de Itualde sisters that spirals out of control.

The story reaches its climax, when, in the interim, Coca and Laura receive a letter from Ignacio, their brother, who had been stationed in a remote military camp, announcing that he would be paying them a visit in Tandil. He will be bringing a friend with him ... a captain ... named Pérez. (Of course!) The sisters are flabbergasted and due to the short notice unable to avoid what was always going to be the spectacular appearance of the real Capitán Pérez. When Ignacio arrives he is unable to understand a word, except for the news that his companion has garnered, inexplicably, tremendous fame in the town. He remarks, baffled, to Pérez, "No he podido entender claramente lo que pensaban mis hermanos, hablando todos al mismo tiempo ... Parece que creen que tú eres un mito ..." ("I haven't been able to understand clearly what my siblings were thinking, speaking all at the same time ... it seems that they think you are a myth ..."; 219–20). Individual family members are speaking over one another in a cacophony of intrigue while the real Capitán Pérez can only exclaim "¡Yo un mito!" ("Me, a myth!"; 220). As a myth he is more than just a sign, but a magnetic receptacle of desire, a focal point for the gaze of those men who want to be him, who yearn to measure up to him, and those women who desire what he represents as masculine ideal. This ideal subject is used as a tool of incitement for the broader public, just as the de Itualde sisters used him to incite jealousy and then love in Vázquez. The function of Capitán Pérez is to make others desire that he be real. He finally does appear only to discover himself, incredulously, a myth. Or perhaps, a negative. Pérez operates as both an ideal and its shadow. He is a figment of the imagination meant to incite desire, but when he actually appears, his materiality lays bare the rhetorical operations of that desire. In a photographic sense, he is revealed, emerging from the dark room of queer desire from which he was born. This emergence is what marks Bunge's text as invested in the symbolic reverberations of queerness. He only becomes real once he is desired as an ideal. In Lacanian terms, this process represents a variation on what Héctor Domínguez-Ruvalcaba describes as *abject modernity*, in which the fragmentary modern subject in Latin American literature can only come about as a fiction written as real: "Al entrar en el plano de lo simbólico, el sujeto es el Otro cuyo deseo el texto se estatuye como una borradura del Yo para dar lugar a un yo imaginado" ("Upon entering the plane of the symbolic, the subject is the Other whose desire the text establishes as an erasure of the Self to give way to an imagined self"; *Modernidad* 26). In contrast, for Bunge, the material appearance of Pérez is only possible when he overcomes his own erasure, a subject whose appearance owes to the incitement to desire queerly in Tandil, an incitement that spreads throughout the social sphere, and produces him as real.

Coca's conspiratorial incitement reveals the work that is required for heteronormative desire to function as it should. We realize not simply that heteronormative desire must be mediated, but that it depends on an incitement to queerness in order for it to exist at all. Coca must actively manipulate Vázquez's desire in order for him to desire her, and even then this desire fails to produce the romantic couple that would have restored the family to the upper class. In this, Coca appropriates her place as an object of exchange between men. She becomes the object over which these two rivals are to compete, and she is also the ultimate prize. A conservative reading of this manipulation might posit the short story as a warning against the dangers of young women being coquettish, contradicting Bunge's psychosocial writing, but in line with turn-of-the-century social mores. This reading would depend on rejecting Coca's manipulation, and in this short story representing a cautionary tale against such schemes. But in conspiring to seduce Vázquez, they enact a version of exchange in which contra Rubin, women are in fact in a position "to realize the benefits of their own circulation" (174), even if it is through marriage that they must do so. Their conspiracy disrupts the normative pattern of the exchange of women that would have positioned either sister as only ever able to operate as an object to be disputed by men. The de Itualde sisters do not simply offer themselves as units of bridal commerce in the homosocial rivalries that they create, but rather appropriate and subvert their own position as commodities. When the sisters conspire to help each other by inventing Pérez, they are demonstrating their own agency in the cultural imperative to marry. Even if they do imagine marriage as the only way to improve their befallen position in society, and thus uphold that particular cultural imperative, they do so by inverting the position of women in the process of bridal commerce and by manipulating the men they target for social ascendancy.

Vázquez had proposed marriage to Coca in an effort to stave off the advance of his mythical competitor, but the engagement is broken when she falls instantly in love with the real version of her fantasy man. Laura feels it her duty to console Vázquez, who, in appreciation gives her first the complete works of Lamartine and then, after a moment of opportune meditation, an engagement ring. Their sororal conspiracy queerly refashions heteronormative courtship, intimacy, and the symbolic. But we still want to know *who won the bet?* Laura ends up marrying Vázquez, while Coca marries the man (literally) of her dreams. But it is Laura who, with characteristic goodness, pledges to support Coca and Pérez in the purchase of their first home in Buenos Aires. The sisters thus fulfill the story's premise of returning to economic solvency and social prestige, but it is only through the queer incitement to desire, shaped by sororal conspiracy and carried out through homosocial rivalries that this comes about. Perhaps, in the end, they both win, but it is as sisters conspiring that they do so.

### Desiring Submission: "El Chucro"

At first glance "El Chucro" would seem another instance of prescriptive disciplining of social deviants. Set on the banks of the Paraná River, a mysterious creature has been stealing cattle in the area and is even been blamed for the disappearance of Pepa la Gallega, a Spanish cook on the local *estancia*. Soon, provincial authorities are summoned to deal with this terrifying beast, referred to by the "popular imagination" as El Chucro. The premise of this short story is the need to restore order to this outlying area, inviting the reader to identify with the state in controlling and disciplining unruly bodies. The police are entrusted the task of eliminating this threat to society and reestablishing the rule of law. More than just a bête noir, El Chucro stands in for that which must be tamed in order for civilization to thrive. Again, Bunge is trafficking in typical *fin de siglo* anxieties about disorder and social conflict. El Chucro becomes an allegory for the disruptive margins of society, a voracious ogre that haunts the collective consciousness. This figuration is typical of Bunge's narrative and a key feature of *Thespis*. But there is more to this story, which, I argue, ultimately questions the viability of the rule of law, gender norms, and submission to order.

While searching the islands of the Paraná, Peñálvez, the police scribe, is captured by El Chucro, who turns out to be a leather-faced gaucho, "alto, nervioso, de cejas espesas, cutis cetrino y nariz aguileña" ("tall, nervous, with thick eyebrows, jaundiced skin and an aquiline nose"; 48). Carrying a rifle and an enormous *facón* (the gaucho's typical knife), with his "Herculean arms" he drags the frightened officer back to his camp and ties him to a tree (48). In this case, Bunge caricatures the gaucho as a hypermasculine outsider. El Chucro's alterity is matched by his occupation of space—the islands of the Paraná represent a no-man's-land outside of the law—and his capacity for violence, which undermines the legitimacy of the state.

Of course the figure of the gaucho has a long, controversial, and well-documented history in Argentina, one that I will not rehearse here.[28] It is important to point out, however, that Bunge was an active voice in the national debates on the symbolic legacy of the gaucho in the years following Argentina's centennial. In fact, when he was invited to join the Academia de Filosofía y Letras (The Academy of Philosophy and Letters) of the Universidad de Buenos Aires in 1913, he gave a rather divisive lecture titled "El Derecho en la literatura gauchesca" ("Law in gauchesque literature"). About José Hernández's *Martín Fierro* and *La vuelta de Martín Fierro*, which had been hailed by Leopoldo Lugones as Argentina's authentic national epic that same year, Bunge does not hold back.

> muy distante estoy de hallarles el exagerado valor literario y la honda significación social y hasta filológica que les atribuye hoy una crítica tal

vez más *chauviniste* que sincera. Crimen de lesa patria y sacrilegio de lesa poesía, si no interesada burla, antójaseme el proclamar las donosas parodias de Hernández altos poemas comparables a los de Homero o de Dante.

I am far from finding in them the exaggerated literary value and profound social and even philological significance that have been attributed to them today by criticism that is perhaps more chauvinist than sincere. I find proclaiming Hernández's amusing parodies to be poems of high culture comparable to those of Homer or of Dante to be a crime against the fatherland and a sacrilege against poetry, if not an intentional mockery. (19)

Accusing Hernández of faulty poetic technique, on the one hand, and on the other, contemporary literary criticism as misguided—and chauvinist—in its exaltation of his work, Bunge derides this mining of the figure of the gaucho for an authentic Argentine heritage as crude and inappropriate.[29] What is more, for Bunge, these critics are capitalizing on the vulgar populism of the gaucho to enhance their status among the lettered elite. He warns:

A fuer de Argentino y de universitario, no puedo menos de alzar mi voz, siquiera sea de paso, contra esas inepcias detonadoras, que so pretexto de nacionalidad y abusando de la ignorancia y patriotería del vulgo, corrompen su sentido de lo bueno y de lo bello tan necesario a la grandeza de los pueblos como la tierra que los sustenta y el sol que los alumbra.

As an Argentine and a university professor, I cannot help but raise my voice, even in passing, against these destructive ineptitudes, which under the pretext of nationality and abusing of the ignorance and patriotism of the masses, corrupt their sense of what is good and what is beautiful that is as necessary to the greatness of peoples as the land that sustains them and the sun that illuminates them. (19)

Bunge takes it as his duty to oppose the "corrupting" of the national literary canon by this pivot toward *Martín Fierro*. Recalling the controversy around his *La novela de la sangre*, though certainly to a lesser degree, he reprises the question of what type of aesthetic treatment, what sense of "goodness" and "beauty" will prove most instructive for the growing reading public. His stance is clear: it is not the gaucho, whose ethnic ambiguity and cultural backwardness should become the (new) basis for Argentine national identity, but the shared Western heritage passed down through Spain and enhanced by Northern European art and philosophy (and blood). Bunge's interest in the gaucho as a historical figure, as a symbol, is not meant to save him from obscurity, but to consign him to Argentina's past.

The thread that unites Bunge's lecture is the gaucho's consuetudinary law, a set of social practices that had developed over time and which constitutes not an absence of law, but a form of justice based on the reciprocal exercise of violence. The gaucho's law is "justicia por su mano" ("justice by his hand"; "El derecho" 23). It is a law of retribution, of proving oneself by the sword, or in this case, the *facón*. Bunge has no interest in rebranding the gaucho as epic. Rather, he is concerned with understanding the relationship between power, law, and history. Indeed, Bunge's principle argument against the classification of the gauchesque as epic has to do with the historical trajectory of law. Referencing Aeschylus's *Oresteia*, he writes that "[e]n la tragedia griega atráese la simpatía del espectador el derecho nuevo, el que vence; en el drama gauchesco, a la inversa, el antiguo, el que es vencido por la fuerza pública" ("[i]n Greek tragedy the spectator's sympathy is drawn to the new law, that which overcomes; in the gauchesque drama, in the inverse, the old, is that which is overcome [defeated] by public force"; 30). In Greek tragedy, patriarchy is this new form of law, "el gobierno absoluto del *pater familias*" ("the absolute governance of the *pater familias*"), which "cimenta el principio de la masculinidad" ("cements the principle of masculinity"; 30). In other words, Bunge argues that in the Greek tradition matriarchy is replaced by patriarchy, the old replaced by the new, ushering in a modern form of sociality that is based on and which sustains the law of the father. On the other hand, in the gauchesque, it is the state's singular appropriation of the use of force (the new) that replaces the gaucho's code of a reciprocal sanguinary ethics (the old). Bunge's analysis of the gaucho hinges on the figure's ability to question the authority of the state to exercise violence. He argues that the state has taken away his right to maintain honor in singular combat. And this particular reading of ethics is what makes the gaucho a threat to the modern state. In "El Chucro," we should keep in mind that the gaucho is precisely the figure that has been destabilizing the order of the state, which must attempt to reassert its claim to legitimacy by apprehending and submitting El Chucro to its laws. This is what *it seems* that "El Chucro" should represent. But there is another disruptive force in this short story that intervenes in the establishment of patriarchal law.

After Peñálvez is captured, El Chucro drags him back to his camp. There, Peñálvez is shocked to find that Pepa, the missing Spanish cook, has in fact been living with El Chucro for the past eight months, and even more so to see how she is acting. When she lived on the *estancia*, Pepa was famous for her audacity: "Respondía a su marido, pegaba á sus hijos, insultaba á los peones, encarábase con el mismo patrón y vociferaba el día entero" ("Talked back to her husband, beat her children, insulted the laborers [peons], she would even face off with the boss and she would shout all day long"; 49). But if she was previously too independent (too masculine), she is now described as a "polluelo friolento" ("scared chicken"), subservient to El Chucro's every demand (60). She is also unmoved by Peñálvez, who, in an effort to elicit sympathy, reminds her of the domestic life that awaits her should she decide to set him free and return with him to the *estancia*: "Todos te recibirán con los brazos abiertos, Pepa, si quieres volver ... Se sabe que el Chucro te robó contra tu voluntad ... ¡Nadie te diría una palabra!" ("Everyone would welcome you with open arms, Pepa, if you want to return ... They know that El Chucro took you against your will ... Nobody would say a thing!"; 51).

In this variation on the captive tale, one of Argentina's foundational tropes, Pepa should occupy the role of nationally significant heroine.[30] But Pepa bears little resemblance to the angelic protagonists of Esteban Echeverría's *La cautiva* (1837) or Eduarda Mansilla's *Lucía Miranda* (1882). Rather, she is figured as what turn-of-the-century *higienistas* referred to as the "tercer sexo" ("third sex") or "mujer fuerte" ("strong woman"), a woman who transgressed gender norms and questioned patriarchal authority (Salessi 205). If El Chucro represents a threat to the social order through his undermining of the state monopoly on violence, Pepa is also subversive for her failure to perform hegemonic femininity. And yet, if she was previously too vociferous, she has now been tamed and silenced. In this, Bunge's narrative would seem to represent a conservative disciplining of feminine autonomy. The woman who used to beat her children, and what is more, questioned her husband and her *patrón*, is now taught a lesson in submitting to authority. If Pepa is depicted as unsavory for her dominating personality while on the *estancia*, she becomes even more transgressive for abandoning—or at least not returning to—her family. Peñálvez implores her: "¿Te has olvidado ya de tus hijos y de tu marido? ... Ellos te han buscado de día y de noche.... Se les ha dicho que has de haber muerto ahogada en el río y te han hecho un funeral.... Te han llorado; todavía andan de luto ... " ("Have you already forgotten about your children and your husband? ... They have been searching for you day and night.... They have been told that you must have died, drowned in the river and they organized a funeral for you.... They have wept for you; they are still in mourning..."; 50-51). Despite this sincere if self-interested plea, Pepa is unmoved.

Bunge's Pepa rejects her role as mother within the normative social paradigm. When she refuses to liberate Peñálvez and flee from El Chucro, it would follow that she deserves her punishment. As I mentioned earlier, this rendering would position Pepa as one of most prominent figures in turn-of-the-century pathology: the emancipated woman or third sex, a woman who must be reeducated, who must submit to patriarchal authority in order for the normative sex/gender system to remain intact. Here, El Chucro would represent the blunt instrument of patriarchy, reprograming her into obedience. But I would like to suggest that this schematic rendering fails to account for the possibility that Pepa might actually want to stay with El Chucro. That is, that she might actually desire to submit to him. In this reading we might speculate that Pepa has entered into a masochistic relationship with El Chucro, and that it is through her own free will that she is able to reject her place within the script of normative motherhood.

Toward the end of the story El Chucro kills Peñálvez, and despite orders to the contrary, Pepa constructs a makeshift cross and places it on the gravesite, one final reminder of her previous life. Infuriated, he bashes her on the head and leaves Pepa for dead. Eventually, though, she regains consciousness and brings herself to her feet. The narrator relates the scene.

> Tomó agua de una vasija, se cerró la bata, se arregló el enmarañado cabello y miró al Chucro con una suprema mirada de amor y de miedo, castañeteándole los dientes. Con grandes precauciones para no despertarlo, metióse bajo su poncho, se acostó á su lado, apoyando la cabeza contra su pecho....

> She drank water from a cup, she arranged her knotted hair and looked at El Chucro with a supreme gaze of love and of fear, chattering her teeth. Taking great care so as not to wake him, she placed herself under his poncho, she laid down by his side, leaning her head upon his chest.... (60)

What type of desire is this mix of love and fear? As I have been suggesting, a normative reading of this story would frame it as a cautionary warning against men who exist outside the law and women who undermine patriarchal authority. But this final gesture speaks to a queerness that intervenes in Bunge's text. This queer reading has to do with Pepa's potential for desiring El Chucro's domination. It has to do with exploring this attraction to violent masculinity, which seems impossible to resist. In this case the conflict is not between civilization and barbarism, as with so many captive tales, but between domination and submission. That is, Pepa's final gesture introduces a masochistic desire to submit to El Chucro. This gesture provides a way of reading "El Chucro" not as insisting on normative gender roles, but rather as questioning the structures of power that underpin them. If Pepa is the type of woman who should be disciplined, this final act reminds us of the liberatory possibilities of submission. It questions the ability to consent to disciplinary power. To choose El Chucro over her normative family is thus to position herself in a relationship in which her agency is tied not to reproduction and motherhood, but to consenting to submit to the violent gaucho.

And yet, we should also ask if the type of agency, and the mutual recognition that that would require, is even possible in this narrative. We should ask if Pepa is truly able to submit. In *Sexual Futures, Queer Gestures, and Other Latina Longings*, Juana María Rodríguez reminds that BDSM practices expose the naturalizing effects power by staging the negotiation and authorization of submission (55). That is, the seemingly natural authority of patriarchy is questioned when one must make explicit the desire to submit to its laws. Even if this is by now a fairly standard line of thinking in queer studies—that BDSM exposes and renegotiates the premises of power—I want to highlight Rodríguez's insightful critique of the possibilities of consent in this context. This is because the key to understanding Pepa's gesture of submission revolves around her ability to consent to submitting to El Chucro.

Expanding on Susan Schmeiser's writing on the "guise of consent," Rodríguez notes, "While sadomasochism is popularly scripted as the erotic performance of uneven power relations (even as it might also perform love, care, and friendship), what rarely gets articulated is how the romantic fantasy of love, marriage, and family likewise depends on uneven power dynamics" (61-62). This is particularly intriguing in the case of Pepa, who in returning to El Chucro, seems to choose his violence over the safety of normative kinship. But even if Pepa does not have a choice, even if she cannot be described as having the agency to choose to submit, Bunge's narrative actually points out the futility of that position. More than proposing a masochistic desire as a way of regaining a sense of autonomy, Bunge's fiction equates Pepa's submission to El Chucro with her submission to the normative family. Pepa is forced to choose between two versions of patriarchal authority, between the violence of civilization (her family) and the violence of barbarism (El Chucro). This amounts to no choice at all, and illustrates what Rodríguez calls the "uneven power dynamics" of normative kinship. The allegorical resonance of this narrative implies that the structural violence of normativity is actually the same as the physical violence of El Chucro. Pepa does remain with El Chucro, perhaps choosing to refuse her place in the normative sex/gender system. But, on the one hand, her refusal also marks the impossibility of resisting violent masculinity; on the other hand, it reveals the perverse coercion inherent in the very structure of kinship that she is compelled to resist. "El Chucro," finally, is a story that narrates the structural binds of patriarchy and the insidious ways in which kinship operates. It is a meditation on the impossibility of choosing between violence and the normative family.

### Generations Undone: Pesadilla Drolática

The queerest story in Bunge's *Thespis* is his "Pesadilla Drolática." Queer in its style, the macabre fantasy represents a notable departure from the collection's realism, and queer in its revision of foundational narratives of filiation. It is a tale that questions the possibility of situating the self within normative kinship patterns; proposing instead, one untethered to theological or anthropological narratives of identity. It revolves around the desire to no longer be, do undo oneself, to dissolve into nothingness. The title makes reference to Balzac's *Les cent contes drolatiques*, a work invested in the bizarre, the extravagant, the droll, and which itself links back to Boccaccio's *The Decameron*.[31] Like Balzac, Bunge seeks to unnerve through the deployment of the nefarious uncertainty of a queer world.

Told in the first person, Bunge's short story recounts twenty-four hours of insomnia, a waking nightmare in which an unnamed diegetic narrator feels compelled to discover the source of his disquiet. At the beginning of the story, the narrator jumps out of bed, exclaiming, "Tucker, ese bribón de Tucker tiene la culpa" ("Tucker, that rascal Tucker is at fault"; 100). The text continues as follows:

> ¿Quién era Tucker? ¿Cómo era Tucker? ¿Qué hacía? ¿Dónde estaba? ...Nada de eso sabía yo; pero sabía bien, ¡ah, muy bien! que él solo, que solo él tenía la culpa... ¿La culpa de *qué*? Yo lo ignoraba asimismo. Comprendía únicamente que *eso* debía ser Algo Terrible, macabramente

terrible, diabólicamente terrible. Sería como una inconmensurable esfera de barro que debía aplastarnos; sería como si todos, hombres y espíritus, me burlasen y me despreciaran; sería, en fin como una cosa que no cupiese en el mundo ni pudiera decirse en lenguaje humano.

Who was Tucker? What was Tucker like? What was he doing? Where was he? ... I knew none of that; but I did know, oh so well! that only he, only he was at fault ... at fault for *what*? I was unaware all the same. I only knew that *it* must be Something Terrible, dreadfully terrible, diabolically terrible. It would be like an incommensurable sphere of mud that had to crush us; it would be as if everyone, men and spirits, were taunting and scorning me; it would be, in the end like something that did not fit in this world and could not be spoken in human language. (101, emphasis in the original)[32]

The framing here, as with much of Bunge's fiction, is of a male protagonist unable to name some deep-seated angst, either the product of environmental factors, as in *La novela de la sangre*, or an inherent biological defect, as with much of his sociological writing. This angst is asphyxiating, crushing, and epistemic. The impossibility to name this affliction reminds us from the outset of the incommensurability of queer desire with the symbolic. The narrator's affliction can neither be said—it has no sign—nor does it have a place in this world—it has no signifier. The unspeakableness of what ails the narrator of "Pesadilla drolática" puts us firmly in the field of naming (or obfuscating) queerness, and is reminiscent of Lacan's *objet petit a* (180). That is, if Bunge's text is staging the search for the source of the narrator's conflict, it is also a text in search of naming the desire that has no name, or that can never have a name. In Lacanian terms, this search is not necessarily a search for self, but rather for the lack that constitutes the subject within the symbolic, the "eternally lacking object" that initiates the subjective drive for completeness (180). In this sense, the search for "*eso*" is an impossible endeavor to satisfy the narrator's thirst for self-knowledge. It is a desire to know, to become constituted as whole, but one that will never be possible in this world. More than hinting at the narrator's queerness, it marks him as a subjective impossibility within this crumbling landscape. But if "*eso*" cannot be named, its source is identified from the beginning: a solicitor named Tucker. What Tucker has done to produce this angst remains a mystery, however, and what follows, akin to other narratives of diagnosis, somatic fictions, is the narrator's obsessive pursuit of the source of his own affliction.

As dawn breaks, the narrator's servant brings him "un desayuno de hirviente sangre humana" ("a breakfast of steaming human blood"; 102). Evidently, the tone of this short story leans heavily on the grotesque, and even if the persnickety narrator does not actually drink the blood, deeming it too hot, the connection to the sanguinary remains an important detail to keep in mind with this text that navigates the impossibilities of kinship. Is the narrator a vampire? Is this his affliction? The association evokes the trope of the vampire as deviant, monstrous, and disruptive of heteronormative sexuality. The fact that Bram Stoker's *Dracula* (1897) opens with a solicitor named Jonathan Harker invites speculation on the relationship between the two works. Is Tucker a cipher for Harker? I cannot say with certainty that Bunge would have read *Dracula*, though it is plausible. He had been to England in 1899, as I note earlier, and spoke and read English, French, and German. It is clear that Bunge is attempting to push the boundaries of the psychological, in particular male paranoia and queer eroticism in this work, which is both his queerest and his most gothic. More suggestive still, this secret, this silent, unnamable anguish, resonates with yet another gothic novel: Oscar Wilde's *The Picture of Dorian Gray* (1891).

The critique of gothic literature, particularly from Britain and the United States, actually served to support the formation of the field of queer studies. George E. Haggerty argues in *Queer Gothic* that "transgressive social-sexual relations are the most basic common denominator of gothic writing" (2). The gothic, with its ruins, the uncanny, the monstrous, takes otherness as a central trope that elicits queer interventions in subjectivity and belonging. Haggerty's work aims to historicize the history of sexuality studies, and he is invested in complicating modern understandings of sexual deviance, in particular those that point to a calcified homo/hetero binary. In this effort, Haggerty situates the perverse pleasures of eighteenth-century gothic literature, incestuous and violent, as not simply predating, but also informing—structuring—nineteenth-century sexology (20).

In the case of Latin America, we should consider, too, the historical specificity of gothic literature. If no canonical tradition of the gothic can be dated to the turn of the nineteenth century, when neoclassical and later pre-Romantic poetry, philosophical, and political writing dominated literary production on the eve of Independence, then it makes sense that Latin America had a different relationship with tropes of the monstrosity, deviance, and the sublime than Britain and the U.S. Recent scholarship has begun to flesh out this difference, to remap this literary and cultural landscape, which has consistently neglected Latin America and the Caribbean as a site of production—rather than simply a source—of gothic texts. Leaning on postcolonial theories prominent in Latin American cultural studies, Gabriel Eljaiek-Rodríguez points to early manifestations of the genre in which the circulation of gothic texts in Latin America in the nineteenth century involves a process of "tropicalization" and "transculturation" of gothic tropes, themes, and imagery, which created "distinctly regional and hybrid variations" of canonical gothic texts (14). Eljaiek-Rodríguez analyzes short stories by Juan Montalvo, Juana Manuela Gorriti, Horacio Ladislao Holmberg, and Rubén Darío in his survey of early Latin American gothic fiction, seminal texts, "semillas," as he calls them, "that demonstrate early interest in the Gothic genre, and the extensive knowledge of writers who, perhaps not consciously constructing a corpus, nevertheless laid the groundwork for future generations of writers and filmmakers" (21). If it is clear that throughout the nineteenth century writers from the Latin American canon were interested in modernizing literary and cultural expression, it is important to note that it is not only through the naturalist use of scientific discourses of disease and abnormality, or modernism's aesthetic renovation, but also through the reworking of narratives of the supernatural, the uncanny, and the gothic.

Bunge's gothic relies on two guiding characteristics: the relationship between the body and its environment, and the narrative restructuring of the symbolic. The former serves to ground the story's intertextuality, its supernatural tone and psychological investment; the latter embeds a critique of relationality—filial, biblical, anthropological—as part of this search to name the narrator's unnamable affliction. I will return to the question of filiation below. Regarding the body, as the narrator sets out in search of Tucker, the world around him comes undone. The sky is falling and the earth is becoming viscous. Human beings have transformed into puppets, and suddenly the narrator begins to lose himself, literally. First an ear, later a foot, a leg, he begins to shed body parts. And yet, he is unfazed by this disembodiment: "Yo tenía el privilegio de la salamandra, de hacer retoñar los muñones para recuperar los órganos perdidos" ("I had the privilege of the salamander, of sprouting again [from] my stumps in order to recuperate my lost organs"; 103). If he may or may not be a vampire, is he also, or perhaps more properly, a zombie? The decay that characterizes his environment is also applied to his body, which, like the salamander, regenerates, oscillating between a desire for and against its own corporeal integrity.

When the narrator finally manages to find Tucker's office, a bolt of red lightning illuminates the sky and the door mysteriously opens. He begins to climb a spiral staircase. After thousands of flights, the narrator finally comes to "el final de aquella nueva escala de Jacob" ("the end of that new Jacob's Ladder"; 103). This is the first of several biblical allusions in "Pesadilla Drolática." In this case, it refers to Genesis 10-22, Jacob's dream of a ladder reaching heaven on which angels ascend and descend, of God announcing Himself as the God of Abraham and Isaac, promising that Jacob will be given the land where he had the dream, and that he will bear many children who will inherit this land, renamed Bethel ("house of God"). In Bunge's fiction, however, the narrator actually ascends the stairs/ladder and rather than the voice of God, finds that a woman, Nanela, is awaiting him. In fact Nanela is the narrator's fiancée, and she has been waiting there for seven years.

> —¡Siete años! ... ¡Pobre Nanela! ... Pero tú sabes ...
> —Sí, yo también sé—me interrumpió ella—que el pérfido de Tucker, mi tío y tutor, tiene la culpa.
> —¡Cómo!—exclamé lleno de asombro.—Yo creía que Tucker era tu padre. Riéndose con sus dientes centellantemente blancos, ella me informó:
> —Algunas veces es mi padre, otras un extraño, otras mi tío y tutor. Eso depende del estado de ánimo.
>
> —Seven years! ... Poor Nanela! ... But you know ...
> —Yes, I also know—she interrupted me—that that perfidious Tucker, my uncle and tutor, is at fault.
> —What!—I exclaimed full of surprise.—I thought that Tucker was your father.
> Smiling with her sparkling white teeth, she informed me:
> —Sometimes he is my father, or a stranger, or my uncle and tutor. That depends on his mood. (106)

Is Tucker Nanela's uncle or her father, her tutor or a complete stranger? It seems this depends not on blood relation or the social making of kinship, but simply his *mood*. That is, Tucker relates to Nanela based on feeling rather than filial or symbolic kinship. If this story is linked to the biblical narrative of Jacob, one of the patriarchs of the Old Testament, then how are we to take this queer retelling? And second, if Tucker's house is positioned as the celestial landing to this new Jacob's ladder, then is Tucker also God? This is clarified by the lines that immediately follow those cited above, in which the narrator states that Tucker "está en el fondo de la casa, mirándonos á través de las paredes con sus ojos de ahorcado o de basilisco" ("is at the back of the house, watching us through the walls with his bulging or basilisk eyes"; 106).[33] Tucker is able to see through walls; his bloated eyes have the power of the (un)dead and the cunning of the basilisk. Here Bunge shifts toward the medieval bestiary. The king of snakes whose look could kill, the basilisk is a symbol not only of queer birth—the unfertilized egg of a cock—but also, according to Cirlot, of the inversion of the Holy Trinity (23). This is a world in which the source of the narrator's unnamable affliction has upended the symbolic position of God, of order, of patriarchy. Tucker is the epitome of evil, and the narrator's search for him is transformed from a journey of self-discovery into one of atonement.

The first part of Bunge's short story, then, revolves around tropes of inversion and symbolic illegibility, disordering kinship relations and reframing traditional interpretations of the divine. The environment, bodies, filial relations, and symbolic intelligibility are all in flux. The second half focuses on the marriage of Nanela to the narrator—their flight from and eventual rejoinder with Tucker. Nanela implores: "Tenemos que irnos lejos, muy lejos. Pues ten por seguro que ese canalla de Tucker nos persigue" ("We have to go far away, very far away. You can be sure that that swine Tucker is after us"; 108). Even after what would ostensibly represent the grounding of heteronormative erotics between Nanela and the narrator—marriage—Tucker (and thus *it*) continues to weigh on their minds. The affliction is not resolved by marriage, and the newlyweds realize that they must confront Tucker in order to be rid of his influence. Thus, their honeymoon—ironically figured as a trip around the world—transforms into their attempt to escape Tucker's gaze. They flee. As they spin into orbit, Tucker remains unshakable, at least in the mind of the narrator. After traversing fantastic and mythological realms, even "La Ciudad de la Muerte" ("The City of Death"), the narrator exclaims: "¡Esposa mía! ... ¿No podría ser Tucker el Fantasma del Remordimiento?" ("My wife! ... Could it not be that Tucker is the Ghost of Regret?"; 110). Even if Nanela quickly dismisses this claim, Tucker takes on an ever more pronounced moral prescience. If at first he was figured as the unnamable source of angst, the repercussions of that psychic debt are increasing in frequency and strength. Tucker may also represent a feeling of inescapable, unstoppable, guilt. This flight begins to take its toll, too, on the physical nature of the protagonists. The narrator loses his eyes—like Oedipus?—but regrows them by blinking. Their bodies continue to waste away, until finally the narrator realizes, "Era yo un simple esqueleto andante" ("I was nothing more than a walking skeleton"; 112). From vampire to zombie to walking corpse, their escape from Tucker culminates with the physical deterioration of both Nanela and the narrator, whose "hilo de vida" ("life line"; 112), they fear, is running out.

The story comes to a dramatic conclusion when the narrator and Nanela remember—they had apparently forgotten—that Tucker is already dead and has been buried in a nearby cemetery. Nanela, who must now be called Eva, underscoring the narrative's biblical grounding, leads the narrator to the cemetery, where the portico is guarded by "¡una viva y rugiente Esfinge de piedra!" ("a living, roaring Sphinx of stone"; 114). Oedipal and Genesis narratives combine though not necessarily as intertext, but rather as a manifestation of symbolic incompatibility. This short story is framed as a self-diagnosis, a search for the truth about the origin of the narrator's affliction. These references to filiation and patriarchal sociality serve as relief to this constant loss of self. Even the sphinx is not as it should be: "En vez de proponernos cuestiones insolubles para devorarnos si no las resolvíamos, como a Edipo y a tantos otros mortales, huyó a nuestra vista arrastrando el rabo" ("Instead of proposing impossible questions to us in order to devour us if we did not answer them, like to Oedipus and so many other mortals, it fled on sight with its tail between its legs"; 114).

Nanela/Eva is constantly renamed: "Rosalinda, Isaura, Dioclecia, Xantippa, Agripina, Isabel de Hungría, Delia, Valentina y María de los Dolores" (115). The rhythm of this naming is vexing, and the significance of these references is unclear.[34] From fictional characters to historical figures and saints, this aggregated femininity positions Nanela as a marker for all women. Nanela, too, is an enigmatic name, probably an anagram for *la nena* ("the young girl"), though it also resonates phonetically with *la nana* ("the nanny"), *anhela* ("yearning"), or *ángela* ("angel"). The narrator, in contrast, remains unnameable, as he admits: "Nunca tuve nombre. O, si lo tuve, ya no lo tengo. Lo he perdido" ("I never had a name. Or, if I did have one, I no longer do. I have lost it"; 115). If the name of the narrator's ailment is unspeakable, and his own name is unknown, the names of his wife are ever-changing, multiple, profligate, and connected to an abstract femininity of unstable mooring.

When the protagonists finally come to Tucker's tomb, they open it to find him alive and well, "hasta sano y de buen color" ("even healthy and of good color"; 117). If it was previously the narrator who was figured as potentially vampiric through his breakfast of steaming blood, Tucker now emerges from a coffin, unaffected by time. The link is suggestive of the type of relationship that may exist between these two men: the narrator may also be the queer progeny of his wife's father/uncle/tutor. In fact, Tucker may actually be the father of both protagonists. The specter of incest, supported by the references to Oedipus, is reinforced by the first interaction between Tucker and the narrator: "me dio [Tucker] un abrazo y me besó paternalmente, diciendo:—¡Oh mi querido sobrino! ¡Oh mi querido hijo!" ("[Tucker] hugged me and kissed me paternally, saying:—Oh my dear nephew! Oh my dear son!"; 117) Tucker now relates as father/uncle to both protagonists. The narrator's search, framed as a redemptive journey to confront the source of his unnamable affliction, Tucker, culminates with the discovery that Tucker may be his father, and that he may have already married his own sister. Even if we take this kinship classification as metaphorical, the implication is that the narrator and Nanela are at least potentially siblings.

If the unnamable affliction that spurs Tucker's journey culminates precisely in the moment in which he should redeem himself by confronting his tormentor, we are let down in the end. Tucker's paternal kiss, underscoring the narrative's queer oedipalization, results in the following reaction in the narrator: "Sus labios de carne de víbora, al posarse en mi frente, me dieron tanto asco y tanta risa, que no me atreví a increpar a Tucker por sus infamias" ("His lips of serpentine flesh, upon touching my forehead, made me feel so sick and caused me so much laughter that I didn't dare confront Tucker for his calumnies"; 117). In yet another kiss that should be avoided— we will recall *La novela de la sangre*'s *osculum interruptum*—this one reminds the narrator of "*eso*," the evil inside of him that cannot be named. What is more, the effect of this kiss is the provocation of an uncanny mix of "*asco*" and "*risa*" that leads to the narrator losing his nerve to confront Tucker. The paradoxical nature of desire is a constant in Bunge's fiction.

One reading of this scene could view the source of the narrator's affliction as paternal angst. Cárdenas and Payá, for example, argue that the narrative stages Carlos Octavio's personal conflict with his own father, Octavio, with whom he had fallen out, presumably over the young man's homosexuality. They write:

Carlos Octavio había construido una alegoría heterodoxa del pecado original. Un dios bifronte, padre del bien y del mal, instilador de culpas en sus hijos, era denunciado como el verdadero responsable del drama vital que motivaba la desesperación de los humanos. En la irreverente teología del joven autor, el hombre y Eva, la mujer, trataban de encontrar las explicaciones últimas. Cuando las hallaban, advertían horrorizados que su padre era una víbora demoníaca y se condenaban a la destrucción, no sin antes advertir que estaban en manos del autor del mal.

Carlos Octavio had constructed a heterodox allegory of original sin. A two-faced god, father of good and of evil, who instilled guilt in his children, was denounced as the one truly responsible for the vital drama that motivated human desperation. In the irreverent theology of the young author, the man and Eve, the woman, sought out final explanations. When they found them, they realized, terrified, that their father was a demonic snake and that they were condemned to destruction, not without first realizing that they were in the hands of the author of that evil. (*Hermanos Bunge* 354)

The historians identify the central characteristic of Bunge's short story as the horror of its ending, which stages the confrontation between Tucker and the narrator as leading inevitably to the latter's destruction. This would seem to represent a normative Oedipal drama in which the son desires to confront his father but fails in the end. This would signal the restoration of patriarchy: the father's law upheld; the son's submission ensured. But the historians sidestep the affective valence of this horror: the potentially incestuous relationship that is at the heart of this narrative.

This reading of "Pesadilla Drolática" takes its plot at face value: the narrator's search for Tucker, the source of his psychological angst, ends with the inevitable failure of that search. The search to confront the narrator's queerness was doomed from the start because there can be no atonement for the type of queerness that he is attempting to resist. But Tucker is not only the source of the narrator's angst. He also represents the possibilities of expressing queerness as both an erotic attachment and a position within a normative structure of kinship. If Tucker relates as father and uncle to both Nanela and the narrator, then he comes to stand in for the expression of queer desires, attachments, and relations; for the queering of normative kinship. Or rather, for what will always be (and what always was) queer about kinship. We should recall that Tucker's position within the kinship system is not biological, or even affective, but depends on his mood. Relating otherwise here comes to be expressed as both homoerotic and incestuous.

Contemporary queer theory in the US has done a great deal of work in situating the cultural imperative of the incest taboo, proposing new ways of being in the world that no longer depend on the cultural scripts of normative kinship that are marked by the slippage between structural anthropology and psychoanalysis. David Eng, for example, outlines the naturalization of "displacement" as the rubric by which normative kinship comes to make the Oedipal drama the only "way of being in the world" (89). Here displacement refers to the normative demands of exogamy at the heart of structural anthropology. Eng's argument echoes Judith Butler's claim that kinship is "always already heterosexual," a claim which, as I note in the Introduction, fails to account for the rippling energy that fuels normativity, its tendency to absorb that which it depends on to define itself as normative.

The question of normativity, of what type of family model would predominate in Argentina at the turn of the twentieth century was a primary preoccupation for Bunge, among other members of the elite. Immigration, radical politics, and cosmopolitanism led many to double down on the form of normative kinship as essential to the modernization of *argentinidad*. And this is what makes Bunge "Pesadilla Drolática" so unique. It does not, in fact, model the type of normative kinship that would have been essential to maintaining the class privilege and cultural legitimacy of the elite. Rather, this text abandons normative kinship in favor of the perverse. The marriage between the narrator and Nanela comes to stand for the rejection of normative kinship, rather than its preservation. The bodies that would have secured reproductive—if incestuous—sexuality fall apart, dissolving into nothing by the end of the text.

The short story closes with the following narration, both pathetic and suggestive of the repercussions of the narrator's queerness:

> Aunque Nanela me exhortara:—¡Adelante! ¡Adelante!—la Fatalidad tiraba para atrás el hilo de mi vida, cada vez con más fuerza.... Y yo avanzaba cada vez con menos fuerza.... Tanto me pesaban las piernas que creía echar raíces en el océano de luz que me rodeaba, que me asfixiaba, que me devoraba como a una gota líquida más.... Dejé de sentir mis pies...mis manos...mis brazos...mi cuerpo.... Ya era solo una cabeza flotante en

aquel océano de luz, ¡una miserable cabeza que se disolvía como un terrón de azúcar! ... Perdí el pensamiento, la vista, el tacto ...

Lo ultimo que debí perder eran los tímpanos.... Porque todavía alcancé a escuchar la furibunda voz con que clamaba Nanela:

—¡Tucker, el demonio de Tucker tiene la culpa!

Even though Nanela exhorted me: Onward! Onward!—Doom kept pulling back on my lifeline, each time with more strength.... And I advanced each time with less strength ... My legs weighed so much that I thought I was putting down roots in the ocean of light that surrounded me, that asphyxiated me, that devoured me like just another drop of liquid.... I could no longer feel my feet ... my hands ... my arms ... my body.... I was now just a floating head in that ocean of light, a miserable head that dissolved like a sugar cube! ... I lost the ability to think, sight, touch ...

The last thing that I must have lost were my eardrums ... because I still managed to hear Nanela's frenzied voice as she cried out:

—Tucker, that devil Tucker is to blame! (119)

Here, Bunge figures the material dissolution of the narrator as the final result of his doomed search for redemption. Both the narrator and Nanela want to escape this world. They plan to achieve this by confronting Tucker, but when they do so they realize (1) that there can be no escape, and (2) that they are possibly siblings. The result is that the narrator dissolves into light, as if his eyes had been opened, dilated, to the reality of his condition: the inevitability of his loss of self. It seems that the framing of the story is as an escape from his own self that results in his loss of body and place. Or, perhaps, in the end, it is precisely his own loss of self that he actually desires.

In contrast with *La novela de la sangre*, in which the normative desire to reproduce fails at the last minute, here that very desire produces the annihilation of the narrator. It is not that the narrator realizes he has committed incest. This is not narrated in the text, and his relationship with Nanela is notably lacking in physicality. Rather, it is the impossibility of his desire, of place, of corporality that turns the normative relationship between the narrator and Nanela into the cause of his dissolution. The pathos of this scene marks as inevitable the failure of normative kinship. Here incest functions to underscore the futility of desiring the normative, which can only lead to disappointment and despair.

It may be illustrative to recall, finally, Foucault's reading of incest as "an object of obsession and attraction, a dreadful secret and an indispensable pivot" of the family (*History*: 1, 109). The focalization of family life as a key site of discipline, in this scenario, means "sexuality is 'incestuous' from the start" (108-9). This magnetism is dramatized in Bunge's short story as the inevitability of kinship's failure. Here, in contrast with Deleuze and Guattari, we do not see a body without organs, but rather a corporeal undoing, the body alienated from itself and from its perverse desire. This is a dis-organ-ization of the body. Not an anomalous body, but the impossibility of recognizing itself in its own skin, as a self. It is more like Leo Bersani's "self-shattering" in which the body fragments continually, negating its own regeneration (101). This fragmentation is crucial not only for the narrative structuring of the text, but also for the formal weight that it deploys in disorienting and dislocating the reader. It is perhaps the other side of what Bersani proposes: not self-shattering as undoing, but precisely, becoming light, antimatter, oblivion. It is here, outside of narrative and of Catholic epistemology that the self is always destined for corporeal extinction; the body, its desire, which has no human language, dissolves in a corporeal horizon that has yet to come. Nanela's words, indeed the final line of the story, "Tucker, that devil Tucker is to blame!," serve to underscore the fact that the narrator has no place in this world, and that she has remained to bear witness to his demise, engulfed in light at the last.

This light, finally, is also modernity's splendor, an unbearable, glorious brilliance that is at once everything and nothing, the full expression of desire and the ultimate consequences of the search for ever more fuel. The narrator loses his body, the ability to touch and be touched, to feel. He desires to not desire as he does. The intensity of this search, this furious journey, is overwhelming. His body loses the ability to relate to itself, to react before this subjective impossibility.[35] For a writer such as Carlos Octavio Bunge, this expression of a self that can no longer bear its own body, or that of another, is extraordinary. The body becomes a dis-assemblage of organs that is consumed in a droll delirium. This is a body become light and shadow, echo and silence.

## CONCLUSION

In this chapter, I have read Carlos Octavio Bunge's fiction for what lingers beneath the surface rather than for what it makes evident. It is not as a social scientist that his work stretches our understanding of desire, love, and family, but rather as a narrator of social conventions that he explores the fissures of normativity. To think about desire in Bunge's writing is to think about what types of objects, and what types of reciprocal, oscillating, queer desires are possible. Much of his work has been read as unwaveringly eugenic, as owing to a cultural nationalist program of racial whitening—and it is. But it is also queerly productive in refashioning what desire means, how it means, and under what circumstances this multifaceted desire becomes legible. I hope that in laying this groundwork, the queerness of Bunge's fiction can open up new forms of reading the uneven process of modernization in Argentina at the turn of the century.

*La novela de la sangre* reminds us of the ways in which historical memory and cultural imperatives to marry can crumble under the weight of their own importance. Reading "El Capitán Pérez" allows us to glimpse Bunge's preoccupation with the decadence of the upper-class family, marked with melodramatic flourishes, sibling rivalry, and homoerotic tension. The desire for an ideal national hero can only come about through the incitement to queerness. "El Chucro" underscores what structural binds women must negotiate between normative kinship and a protofeminist liberation of desire. It is a reminder of what modernity obscures in its ever-expansive fictionalization of liberty. Finally, "Pesadilla Drolática" engages us at our most vulnerable moment of queer unbecoming—a text that asks the reader to desire as and with the salamander, the undoing of self. It is more than simply the nightmare of unnamable queerness, but the nightmare of modernity through which the romance of the nation as that of the family is exposed to the inevitable failure of normative desire.

While the structural binds of normativity are at the center of Carlos Octavio's fiction, they also find expression in the writing of other members of the Bunge family. In the following chapter I turn to the personal diaries of Julia and Delfina Bunge, texts that manifest in both form and function a similar ambivalence for the cultural demands of heteronormativity, publicness, and familiarity. Fictional accounts of courtship and heteroromance find a willing if contradictory narrator in Carlos Octavio Bunge. What we see next is how the lived experience of normativity reflects, responds to, and transforms what family means in the diaries of the Bunge sisters.

CHAPTER TWO

# SISTERS WRITING, SISTERS READING
## THE DIARIES OF JULIA AND DELFINA BUNGE

The diary is a queer genre. It does not require a plot to make sense. It signifies in the moment of—and by virtue of—the very act of writing. What is more, the diary need not even *be* writing. It may include peritexts as well as objects: clippings of hair, pressed flowers, correspondences, sketches. That is, it may function simultaneously as text and archive. Its voice is citational, filled with other voices—both collective and individual; it is characteristically heteroglossic.[1] The diarist can relive previous moments by reading the text, which doubles back and leaps forward in time. This iterative nature relies on the relation between time and the diarist, even if the writing is not necessarily constant (a day, a week, a year may pass between entries). With neither the benefit of hindsight nor the imperative to link particular life moments through a cohesive narrative, the diary is often incomplete, full of gaps, repetitive, nonlinear, and open ended (Lejeune 170). But even if the diary may record the present, as it may reflect on the past, it always retains the possibility of a future. As Phillipe Lejeune notes: "All journal writing assumes the intention to write at least one more time, an entry that will call for yet another one, and so on without end" (188–89). Thus, the mode of the diary is dialogical and diachronic, but it always retains a sense of futurity. Those blank pages left to write point to more days, more writing, more life yet to record. At its core it is an aspirational genre that stages the repeated performance of self through the text, a self-in-process.

In imagining the queerness of the diary, I am most drawn to this unending quality, the gesture it makes toward a future not yet lived. I write this keeping in mind José Esteban Muñoz's work, in particular his push to reinvigorate queer studies with a strand of concrete utopianism taken from Ernst Bloch. This may seem implausible since the diaries I study in this chapter do not speak to queer utopianism per se or invoke the type of dissident aesthetics or politics of otherness that Muñoz analyzes in his work. Quite the opposite, in fact, the archive I study is classist, racist, and politically conservative. And yet, these are texts that have at their heart a project of futurity that questions gender norms, sexual attitudes, and kinship relations. One of my principal goals in this chapter will be to highlight the aspirational qualities of the diary, and the ways in which the diarist yearns for a future that is not yet hers. This futurity is buoyed by the formal qualities of the diary, which enacts what Muñoz describes as "a future in the present" (61). This future harnesses an inclination toward imagining the world as different than it has been or than it is. The future in the present is the central quality of the diary's queerness. A second goal is to explore particular moments of erotic tension, gender nonconformity, and familial instability that are not simply made evident but actually produced by the writing of the diary. Thus, this chapter engages queer studies as a method of critiquing the formal qualities of diary writing as it questions the relations that the diary makes possible.

This chapter focuses on the genre of the diary as a queer form of writing. It takes up two women's diaries—Julia and Delfina Bunge—as a way of intervening in the discussion of patriarchal authority, the division of public and private space, and the cultural assumptions that underlie such a project of life writing as theirs. I imagine this chapter as a way of approaching the genre of the diary in a new way—this is a methodological intervention—and an attempt to uncover the cultural expectations, desires, and potential futures that each sister imagines through the process of writing and reading her diary. In reading the diary as queer, I am extending earlier critiques, which have taken the diary as an example of an intrinsically feminist practice.[2] Cynthia Huff, for example, writes the following:

> Diaries are about community, not hierarchy, about communication, not authority. Hence, their inherent generic qualities are subversive to the literary establishment and to the patriarchal social order that it perpetuates in its privileging of texts and genres, each ranked according to unquestioned standards. (6)

She goes on to argue that the diary, like feminist criticism, is subversive for its lack of boundaries, for its intersubjectivity and its blurring of the personal and the professional. I agree that the diary can be subversive, and also that publishing diaries written by women is indeed an important feminist gesture that questions *what counts* as literature. However, I am more interested in the *practice* of writing a diary, rather than its publication, because it is in the making of a diary, in its ontological engagement of bodies around a text that it may evidence queer undoings of authority. Here, I want to propose that the diary represents a key site of exploration not simply of what the diarist *does*, but of what discourses, what possible modes of feeling and thinking are revealed through the process of diary writing. I am taking the diary as a location where individual desires, embodied practice, and discourse converge in the aspiration for a future self. In this, I am reading the diary as an *interface* through which textual form influences the process by which the self emerges as such. This is not to say that the form confirms the process of self-making that is staged by the diary, but that the diary makes certain relationships imaginable; indeed it conjures them into being. The Bunge sisters write each other and themselves in their mutually defining diaries, which reveal the self to be part of an ongoing historical and familial legacy, but also a relational construct. If the form of the diary—in its structuring of rationality—defines the possibilities and limits of self-knowledge, then it also produces, rather than simply records the self who writes. That is, its form influences the personal, affective, and cognitive relationships that emerge on its pages. This means, finally, that the diary is not simply a record of self, but a technology of self-making.

The Foucaulidan reference should not be overlooked here. Foucault's work on the "technologies of self" in ancient Greek and early Christian texts, pivots away from sites of disciplinary power such as the prison and the barracks, as in the first volume of *The History of Sexuality*, toward the question of how the self constitutes itself as a subject (Martin, Gutman, and Hutton 4). Though Foucault does not address contemporary diary practice, he does focus on the role of confession in staging the process by which self-knowledge becomes an avenue to self-care, what he calls in the Greek *epimelēsthai sautou*. The diary may involve confession, but it is not essentially *about* confession. As I have been arguing, it makes possible the imagination of the self, or rather the construction of a self that reaches toward the future. Crucially, though, as Judith Butler points out, in Foucault's later work, "the subject forms itself in relation to a set of codes, prescriptions, or norms and does so in ways that not only (a) reveal self-constitution to be a kind of *poiesis* but (b) establish self-making as part of the broader operation of critique" (*Giving* 17). The constitution of the self through these discursive arrangements has broad ethical and epistemological implications. This process must be understood not simply in terms of moral philosophy, what Butler refers to as "critique," but also in terms of the formal qualities, the modes of address, the framing of social interactions, and the possibilities of relations that are the vehicles of self-making. The Bunge sisters' diaries allow us to view, from multiple vantage points, the ways in which the self that emerges though the process of writing the diary is mutually constructed by the process of reading as and by the sister. These diaries reveal how the form of the diary as well as its reception influence the subjectification of each sister as simultaneously self and other, as sexual and gendered subjects, and as sisters.

I am proposing that the experience of self is oriented by the formative properties of the family, on the one hand, and the refractive qualities of the diary, on the other. Bodies become individuated by virtue of the relationships that the diary frames and makes possible; Julia and Delfina become sisters not only by blood relation but also by virtue of the relationships that the text allows them to imagine, reproduce, and record. These are not synonymous processes, however. The diary is a type of text that is already populated with multiple versions of self that emerge, as well as affective connections with others that must be addressed. The diary shapes these imaginaries as its form influences what can be recorded as meaningful to both the writer and the future reader(s) of the text. Bodies discover themselves in the flows of the narrative, however fragmentary; gendered sisters find their gender and their individuality through the psychic prism of the diary. Thus, if we can think of the diary not simply as a textual record but a technology of self-making, then we can begin to understand the contradictions between individual desires and the compulsions of family life, class alliance, and national belonging that emerge through this archive. The aggregative dimensions of the diary reveal it to be a genre that makes possible the mutual subjective emplotment of each sister as related, as a sister, as part of an ongoing narrative of family. But before turning to the practice of reading the diary as sister, I want to comment first on the type of archive that I am reading, and second on its queer materiality.

## A QUEER ARCHIVE

The preceding discussion of genre is meant to lay the groundwork for my reading of what represents a unique coincidence in Argentine culture: sisters who (1) simultaneously kept a diary for an extended period of time, (2) shared, read, and commented on reading each other's diaries, and (3) though under quite different circumstances, published them subsequently. Though I detail some of this history in the Introduction, it is worth repeating here. Delfina Bunge kept a diary from age fifteen in 1897 until her death in 1952 at age seventy, a voluminous archive of more than 10,000 handwritten and typed pages. Julia began her own journal in 1903 and wrote consistently until 1911, when, at least for a time, she gave up the practice. This text was eventually published by Emecé in 1965 under the title *Vida: época maravillosa 1903-1911*. Julia would publish a second volume, *Vida: Viajes-Trabajo, 1930-1953*, in 1966, which details her work with the Patronato de Leprosos and other benefit societies in Argentina and abroad. Delfina's diary, in contrast, remained unpublished for decades until Lucía Gálvez, as noted earlier, a historian and Delfina's granddaughter, published a selection with commentary titled *Delfina Bunge: Diarios intimos de una época brillante* with Planeta in 2000.

The publishing history of these texts matters for two important reasons. First, in making this intimate writing public in her own lifetime, Julia enacts a form of self-assertion that at once demands space within the masculine sphere of "literature" and questions what literature means by occupying that space with the story of her youth as part of a collective, a network of other young women. To publish the diary with one of Argentina's most important publishing houses, Emecé, is not a small detail; Julia Bunge's *Vida*, appeared in the same catalog with the works of Jorge Luis Borges and Adolfo Bioy Casares. To publish this text in 1965, as the volatile years following the military coup that had ousted Juan Domingo Perón from power in 1955 and into exile lurched toward yet another coup in 1966, marks a nostalgic desire for a prior social order in which the elite, family, and the romance of Argentina's age of splendor were untroubled by the upheavals of the present. For her part, in publishing her grandmother's diary, Lucía Gálvez marks as intergenerational the labor of writing and publishing a woman's diary. She even notes that her daughter, Delfina Tiscornia, actually performed some of the labor of typing up thousands of Delfina Bunge's manuscript diaries for publication. In the Introduction we catch a glimpse of what Delfina Tiscornia felt about repeating the gestures, the ontological relation to the archive, of her great grandmother, and to family as part of a history of queer recognition. These feminist gestures speak to the changing world of the literary marketplace—publishing with the multinational Planeta is once more, not a small detail—but they also contrast with the conservative image with which the Bunge sisters have often been characterized. If the diary is an inherently feminist genre, as Huff argues, or a queer one, as I suggest, then the act of publishing these intimate texts opens up a broader field of feminist/queer space that stretch both forward and backward in time. The praxis of diary writing in its present engages multiple forms of feminist connectivity, while the act of publishing that work subsequently challenges normative gender roles, temporalities, and modes of self-construction in the early, mid-, and late twentieth century.

The second important issue regarding these publications is they have all been submitted to a process of selection and editing. That is, the versions of life writing that I study in this chapter are not strictly speaking original diary manuscripts. These texts emerge as already edited by a family member, an editor, or by the author herself. It is important to note that both sisters did imagine the possibility of publishing their work, as Julia writes in February 1903, "Tenemos la broma de que algún día podrán publicarse nuestros diarios y me aconseja [Delfina] que empiece directamente—'hoy tal cosa'" ("We have this joke that one day our diaries could be published and she [Delfina] advises that I start directly—'today this thing'"; *Vida* 16). For her part, Delfina writes in 1905: "Al leer el diario de Julia, lo veo escrito en letras de molde, lo veo publicado, y me gusta" ("Upon reading Julia's diary, I see it written in printed letters, I see it published, and I like that"; J. Bunge, *Vida* 10).[3] Delfina attempts to guide her older sister about the form of the diary, about how the diarist should begin to write. But Julia resists her sister's advice: "pero yo he pensado que para que resulte más claro *para mis futuros lectores*, es mejor hacerles conocer a mi familia desde el principio" ("but I think that for it to be clearer *for my future readers*, it is better to introduce them to my family from the beginning"; 16, emphasis mine). Julia resists, she claims, so that an imagined future public named explicitly as such will have a better grasp of her personality by situating herself as part of her family. The diary entry continues to dedicate a paragraph description of each of her closest kin. That is, her diary begins with an explicit narration of self as genealogically linked to her ancestors. Even while Julia's statement is framed as something of an inside joke, we cannot discount the fact that if publishing a version of both sisters' diaries, "our diaries," was not a defined objective, at least it was a possibility. This means that both sisters imagined the texts they were writing not only as a personal, intimate record, but one that could be (and was) shared with others, family, friends, but also, future readers.

I would also like to clarify that even though I rely primarily on these published archives, I have been able to access a portion of Delfina Bunge's manuscript notebooks. In the Introduction I detail how I encountered these materials, but here it is important to note that the journals I reference in this chapter are numbered I, IV, V, and IX, which span from 1897, when Delfina first began her writing practice, to 1903 (with gaps in between); they are paginated, and each is introduced with a brief explanatory note. This adds a layer of complexity to this particular archive because, as I discovered, what is commonly referred to as an original manuscript diary is actually a copy. Delfina copied, by hand and later in typescript, all of her own original diaries—a project of systematizing her notebooks that she began in 1928. As I note in the Introduction, she actually refers to them as her "*cuadernos-copia*" "journal-copies." This was a monumental undertaking, one that Delfina describes in an introductory page, dated October of 1943, which I transcribe in its entirety (yet another transcription).

> Vengo de hacer un recuento de los cuadernos-copia, de mi Diario. Y quedo una vez más, y más que nunca, *aterrada* del papel acumulado. Son 18 volúmenes manuscritos, de unas 200 hojas cada uno, lo cual viene a representar unas 7.200 páginas. Y hay además, en formato grande, a máquina, 5 volúmenes de unas 300 páginas cada uno. Igual: 1.500 paginas grandes. Total: unas 10.000 páginas de este formato, más o menos. ¡Y lo que me queda todavía sin copiar!
>
> Me parece dejar, con toda esta carga, una terrible herencia. ¿Y para quién? ¿Para los hijos? Un poco comprometedora... Pero por otra parte pienso, una vez más también, lo que hubiera sido para mí una cosa así, escrita por mi madre en su juventud ¡o por mi abuela! Hubiera sido *de un enorme interés*. Y pienso entonces en Lucía, en Verónica, en otras nietas que pudieran venir... o nietos. Entre ellos alguno saldrá posiblemente a mí, aficionado a Diarios auténticos y a papeles íntimos.

Y sobre todo ... parece ser mi destino el continuar con estas copias ... por lo que me divierte hacerlas. Y por ser para mí lo más fácil y accesible por el momento. Dios me da tiempo. Aparte de la razón de siempre: Me da grima dejar los viejos cuadernos *así* ... son como legumbres sin pelar. Con esa letra a veces tan mala, y con la mala distribución, *no se ven las cosas* ... Y por milésima vez repito que tirarlas al canasto me parecería una pena. De modo que *para poder conservarlas*, no me queda otro remedio que copiar.

Digo que esto me divierte. Pero por otro lado, me es violento; tengo que hacerme violencia, para copiar las cosas tales cuales están, cuando corrigiéndolas podrían mejorar tanto. Cuando veo que algún término me está haciendo falta—en aquellos años juveniles—para decir mejor lo que quiero, y que ese término no lo encuentro y siéndome ahora tan fácil añadirlo; ¡tener que dejar eso como está! ... El remedio a estos males son las notas que añado en tinta colorada.

¿Quizá tengo demasiado escrúpulo en corregir, cuando sólo se trata de alguna corrección de estilo? ... Ahora tomo un gran mazo de cuadernos, comprendiendo desde Marzo de 1901 (19 años de edad), a Noviembre de 1902. Y créaseme que necesito armarme de *valor* para enfrentar todo eso. ...

Para aligerar el trabajo mío y la "lectura" de los herederos, mi primera tendencia es saltar y saltar las partes menos divertidas. ¿Pero, a lo mejor, esas resultan, después de los años de un interés que ahora no sospecho ...?

I have just finished taking stock of my journal-copies, of my Diary. And I find myself once more, and more than ever, terrified by the accumulated paper. There are 18 manuscript volumes, of more than 200 pages each, what represents some 7,200 pages. And in addition, in large format, by typewriter, there are 5 volumes of some 300 pages each. Equals: 1,500 large pages. Total: some 10,000 pages in this format, more or less. And what I still have yet to copy!

With such a burden, I feel like I am leaving a terrible inheritance. And for whom? For my children? An obligation ... But on the other hand I think, once again, what something like this would have been for me, written by my mother in her youth, or by my grandmother! It would have been *of enormous interest*. And then I think of Lucía, of Verónica, of other granddaughters who could come along ... or grandsons. Among them one of them might turn out like me, a fan of authentic Diaries and intimate papers.

And above all . . . it seems to be my destiny to continue with these copies . . . because I have fun doing so. And because it is the easiest and most accessible thing I have at the moment. God has given me time. Beyond what I always say: It disgusts me to leave those old notebooks *like that* . . . they are like beans left unpeeled. With that handwriting that is so bad sometimes, and poorly spaced, *you don't see things* . . . And for the thousandth time I repeat that to throw them all away would be a shame. So *in order to preserve them*, I have no other option than to continue copying.

I say that it is fun. But on the other hand, it does me violence; I have to hurt myself, in order to copy things just as they are, when correcting them could improve so much. When I see that some term is lacking—in those years of my youth—to better express what I want, and that the term I do not find and since it is so easy for me to add it now; I have to leave it like it is! . . . The remedy to these pains are the notes that I add in red ink.

Maybe I have too many scruples in correcting, when it is only a matter of correcting the style? . . . Now I take a big stack of notebooks, stretching from March of 1901 (19 years of age), to November of 1902. And believe me that I need to arm myself with *courage* to confront all that . . .

To lighten my load and the "reading" for my heirs, my first tendency is to skip and skip the least fun parts. But, perhaps, years later, those might be interesting in a way that I cannot see now . . . ? (Notebook V, pp. 1703-4, emphasis and ellipses original)

This lengthy quote is necessary for several reasons. First, it documents the labor that Delfina invests in organizing, copying, and *not editing* the diaries. This is no small task, and one that, as she points out, seems "violent" precisely because copying the text sparks her desire to perfect the narration of the past, her past. She finds it difficult to relive this past without editing it, that is, without imagining—even creating—a different past. Perhaps she would like to forget some of those episodes, some of those feelings. Perhaps the effect of rewriting, and not simply rereading, the diary adds a layer of affective resonance that she finds painful. Second, this is a project that Delfina carries out explicitly in the name of kinship. The Lucía that she mentions in the text is the same Lucía Gálvez who would, half a century later, actually take up the task of editing these diaries for publication. The diary presages the connection between these two women, seeming to map a future project, or rather the continuation of the project of conserving the notebooks for her family. Even those seemingly banal details that the diary inevitably contains might—in the future—prove important. This is the *what if* of the diary, its gesture toward not only a future self yet to be lived, but also other future selves/readers/family members yet to emerge on the horizon of subjective possibilities. This introductory note is written in one present (1943) about writing a past life lived that also recognizes possible future iterations of self and/as other.

Delfina describes these notebooks as a family legacy that she would have liked to possess, a way of knowing the past, of relating to her family through the textual archive. The diary here functions, again, dialogically, stretching the present of writing to the present of copying, to the future-present of reading, editing, and eventually publishing. Finally, even though Delfina claims to resist the temptation to leave out certain portions of the original manuscript, we have no way of knowing whether she actually did so. In fact, Manuel Gálvez would recall: "Al empezar su trabajo [el de copiar sus cuadernos] decidió respetar su obra, dejando sus frases tal como las escribió. Su labor consistió solo en suprimir párrafos, frases y palabras inútiles, eliminar las repeticiones y, sobre todo, borrar todo lo que pudiera comprometer a quien quiera que fuese, especialmente a personas de su familia" ("Upon beginning her work [that of copying her notebook] she decided to respect her oeuvre, leaving her own phrases just as she wrote them. Her task consisted of only leaving out paragraphs, phrases and useless words, eliminating repetitions and, above all, erasing anything that could compromise whoever it may be, especially family members"; *Recuerdos* 2: 697). Yet again, the diary is a family affair. Gálvez fills in what Delfina leaves out: that the very real possibility of publishing the cuadernos-copia implied exposing an intimate life that, more than simply "interesting," could also be socially compromising for an elite family such as theirs.

I will turn to the materiality, the palimpsest, of the *cuadernos-copia* below. Thus far, I have endeavored to be clear about just what type of archive I am reading, and to underscore the affective and physical labor that was required for it to exist at all. I find myself, too, seduced by these "intimate papers," by their contradictions and their admissions, their subtlety, and the weight that both sisters gave to the process of life writing. I am not interested in discovering "compromising" details of the Bunge family, as Gálvez insinuates. Rather, this chapter aims to engage with this complex archive as a way of better understanding how kinship and self-writing interface at the turn of the century in Argentina.[4]

My analysis of the diaries of the Bunge sisters begins at the turn of the century, a period in which each sister is negotiating the cultural imperatives of the upper class. Marriage, courtship rituals, and school friendships dominate this early writing. Julia describes herself as part of the social life of the Porteño elite, and in particular her relationships with potential suitors. Delfina, for her part, notes her reluctance to participate in these social engagements, preferring her piano lessons and her books. Julia's writing revolves around her place in society, while Delfina's is more introspective and philosophical, filled with imaginary dialogues, thought experiments, and moral contemplation. Issues of privacy and publicity, intimacy, and celebrity come to the fore in this period, which concludes spectacularly in 1910, with the centennial celebrations of Argentina's independence, marking a stark contrast in the social lives of the sisters. Their father, Octavio Bunge, presides over these national celebrations and would pass away shortly thereafter. Perhaps more important for their diary writing, Delfina is married in 1910 and Julia in 1911. Julia moved to Santa Fe and stopped keeping her diary for decades, while Delfina took a yearlong honeymoon with Manuel Gálvez in Europe, returning to Argentina with their first child. These events would dramatically change her perspective on marriage, religion, and Argentine nationalism.[5]

## THE DIARY AS PALIMPSEST

As I mentioned previously, Delfina's *cuadernos-copia* represent a systematic attempt to organize this archive as a cohesive body of work. The process of copying her diary involves not just a level of patience and dedication that I for one can hardly imagine, but also an intimate and ontological relationship with the text. The body of the diarist returns to the page, but the page, too, becomes multiple. Take, for example, the following entry from Delfina's Journal Number IV, which documents the years 1900-1901, in which rather than copy the earlier text, she cuts out and glues a section of the original page to the journal, along with an annotation in red pencil (fig. 2.1). The glued text starts out in Spanish, declaring "Hoy he leído esto que me gusta y en parte me vendrá bien" ("Today I read this, which I like and in part will do me good"), which is followed by a citation, in French, about the daily travails of living a moral life. More precisely, the text is about searching within the self in order to better one's understanding of morality. The citation is in fact taken from *Marguerite à vingt ans* (1861), a novel by

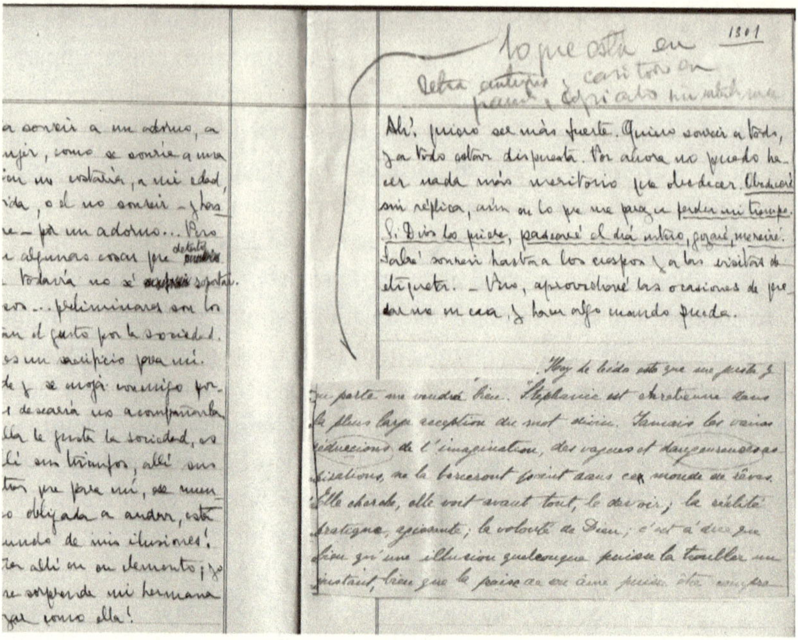

FIGURE 2.1 The diary as palimpsest. Bunge Family Archive (Courtesy of Lucía Gálvez).

Victorine Monniot (1824–1880), which is a sequel to her extremely popular (at least in mid-nineteenth-century France) *Le Journal de Marguerite*.[6] That is, as Delfina is copying, she glues into her *cuaderno-copia* a page of her original journal, which is itself a citation of a novel that takes the form of a young woman's diary, and adds a handwritten annotation indicating the provenance of the text. The text is, in addition to dialogic (even with the author herself), a palimpsest.

This entry brings to the fore several key themes in Delfina Bunge's writing: spirituality, suffering, and introspection. The page illustrated above begins: "Ah! Quiero ser más fuerte. Quiero sonreír a todo, y a todo estar dispuesta. Por ahora no puedo hacer nada más meritorio que obedecer. Obedeceré sin replica, aún en lo que me parezca perder mi tiempo" ("Ah! I want to be stronger. I want to smile at everything, and be up for anything. For now I cannot do anything more merit worthy than obeying. I will obey without responding, even in what seems like a waste of time"; Notebook IV, 1301). Delfina's dissatisfaction stems from what she perceives as an inability to perform in society the role that she imagines she must fulfill. She must smile, even when she does not want to; attend the galas and benefits that her parents and her sister ask her to, even when she views them as a frivolous waste of time. This entry registers a constant debate in Delfina's writing about sacrificing her own desires, her own interests, to others. The issue here is between attending to her inner, spiritual, needs and to the demands placed on a *niña* of the Argentine elite to participate in the elaborate social life of her class. The citation from Monniot engages with a similar sentiment, a question of how to participate in the modern world while at the same time practicing religious faith.[7] Delfina would contemplate entering a convent during these years, something that her family did not encourage, and which her sister Julia found alarming. The fact that Delfina would take up "Marguerite" as a pseudonym only three years later in order to participate in a literary competition sponsored by the Parisian magazine *Femina*, is further evidence of the enduring impact that the work of Monniot held for her. "Marguerite" is not only a young woman struggling between modern society and faith, but a model of how the diary serves as a medium through which that struggle can be expressed and understood.

An admission: I cannot claim to do justice to the volume of writing that these diaries represent in one chapter. As I have already noted, Delfina Bunge's *cuadernos-copia* span more than 10,000 pages of work, some of which has been published, and some of which remains in the family archive. They document, however incompletely, a fascinating moment in Argentine history when the role of women in public was being hotly debated, and in which both sisters reflect on the ambivalence that this period inspired in many women. These diaries come to register these same debates but from the diverging perspectives of two sisters whose class belonging gave them access to economic and social capital that most women did not. These diaries index class privilege and individual desires. In order to approach these texts, I must necessarily be selective, as the diarists themselves were selective when choosing what to record, what to copy, and what to publish. My selections will revolve around key moments in which the diary functions to link the two sisters (to each other and to the broader public) through the practice of writing. In doing so my aim is not to provide an exhaustive study of these diaries, but to show how their production and their function as technologies of self can serve to complicate how we understand gender, sexuality, and kinship in Argentina at the turn of the century.

## SISTERS WRITING, SISTERS READING

It may be illustrative to return to the beginning of Julia's diary: "Me decidí por fin, pero lo que a otros les parece lo más natural, escribir cada día lo que se piensa" ("I have decided at last, what for other people seems so natural, to write down my thoughts each day"; 15). As with most diarists, she starts by describing the origin of her writing practice and her commitment to daily entries, what Lejeune would call opening "a new territory of writing" (187). Almost apologetic, Julia frames the practice of keeping a diary as an individual decision that also responds to "what for other people seems so natural." This individual decision is part of a cultural landscape. This territory may be new, but it is already populated by others. What is more, when Julia likens the practice of diary writing to an archival record, she also reveals the fragmentation of the self who writes the diary. The grammatical shift from the active voice, "me decidí" ("I decided"), to the passive "lo que se piensa" ("what one thinks"), underscores that writing the self is not always a direct transposition of the writer's thoughts. Rather, what we see in this case is a negotiation of different selves. This multiplicity takes shape as Julia continues, "Me he puesto enfrente de mi consciencia y le pregunto: ¿qué sientes?—Necesito saberlo" ("I have put myself before my conscience and I ask it: what do you feel?—I need to know"; 15). Her individual consciousness emerges out of a call and response that is initiated by the self and is carried out through the process of writing. The pages of the journal are imagined as a mirror that reflects back not the physical image of self—not Julia's body—but the consciousness of she who interrogates herself through it. Not a Lacanian mirroring that gives way to subjective identification, but rather a refraction of self through the technology of the diary. The question, "what do you feel?" becomes both the narrative device whereby the diarist is authorized to write and a stimulus that responds to a "need to know" the self.

Writing the diary structures the horizon of cognitive possibilities, as the final lines of Julia's first entry confirm.

> Y por eso escribo, porque me ha llegado el momento de vivir la realidad, de saber lo que pienso y ser dueña de mis sentimientos, y eso espero conseguirlo escribiendo, escribiendo todo lo que pienso y siento, sin pensar lo que escribo, porque si lo pensara aparecerá tal cual yo quiero que aparezca

pero no resultaría el yo íntimo que tengo tan escondido y quiero llegar a conocer.

And that is why I write, because the moment has arrived for me to live [in] reality, to know what I think and to own my feelings, and that is what I hope to get out of writing, writing everything that I think and feel, without thinking about what I write, because if I were to think [to deliberate] about it, it will appear just as I want it to appear but it would not end up being the intimate self that I have hidden so far away and who I want to get to know. (15)

Julia is not content with merely recording her daily life. Indeed, she claims this space will not be filled with sculpted ideas, but rather unmediated feelings and thoughts, a stream of consciousness that will conjure the particular "intimate self" that she "wants to get to know" through the process of writing. Again, the grammar is revealing. It is not only that Julia expresses a desire to know her "intimate self," but that her consciousness is already inhabited by other potential selves. If she were to dwell too long on what she writes in the diary, it is possible that a different self would emerge, one that she may "want to appear," but which is not the "hidden" self that she "wants to get to know," a project of future self-making. Writing the diary raises specters of other selves who must be negotiated with, recorded or not recorded. Even if she wants to record a self that emerges unfiltered onto the pages of her diary, that self is nevertheless one out of many that she willfully sets out to express. The diarist dialogues with other possible selves who jostle for position; her "yo íntimo" ("intimate self") is part of a project of self-making that implies the conscientious crafting of a desired, intimate, interlocutor.

Crucially, her entry reminds us that keeping a diary is not only about writing, but also about reading and imagining a reader. But for whom, we might ask, is the self that Julia "wants to appear"? If the diary is commonly thought of as a private, intimate space, one in which the diarist enjoys the freedom to write those thoughts reserved "for my eyes only," what happens when the writing of the diary is not done exclusively *for yourself* but also for others? What happens when the diary is not private, but shared? I have in mind the following passage from Delfina's *cuaderno-copia*: "Estoy en el espíritu de Julia. En el de su diario. Lo he leído todo el día. [...] Durante su lectura, me imagino—sin quererlo y no sé por qué—que soy un hombre, que soy X, que es él, o cualquier de ellos quien lo lee, y siento lo que ellos deberían sentir si lo leyesen, lo que ellos deberían comprender y amar" ("I am in the spirit of Julia. In that of her diary. I have been reading it all day. [...] When I read it, I imagine—without wanting to and I don't know why—that I am a man, that I am X, that it is he, or any of them who is reading this, and I feel as they must feel if they were to read it, what they should understand and love"; J. Bunge 9-12). This is Delfina Bunge writing about reading the diary of her sister, Julia. Importantly, to be "in the spirit of" her sister, implies an empathetic relation not only to the writer, but also to other potential readers. By reading Julia's diary Delfina contemplates the reactions of others were they also to read it, as she imagines the way that the writer positions herself in relation to them. Here Delfina shows that the diary can also serve to imagine the *self as other*.

This is a queer process enacted not only by the cross-gender identification of the writer with potential male readers, "what they [*ellos*] must feel," but also through the strangeness by which this feeling emerges, "sin quererlo y no sé por qué" ("without wanting to and I don't know why"). This is the seductive power of reading the diary, a moment in which the reader (Delfina) identifies as the object of desire of the writer of the text (Julia). For Delfina, to be "él, o cualquier de ellos" ("he [him], or any of them") is thus to imagine herself as desired by her sister, on the one hand, and on the other, to imagine what it would feel like to be a male reader reading this text. The diary frames the expression of erotic desire between sisters by virtue of its form of address and the particularity of the sisters' practice of both writing and reading each other's diaries. Furthermore, this expression of desire is not written as projection, but the effect of reading. More like an admission than speculation, Delfina describes the link between imagining and feeling as a statement of fact. The diary actually produces this queer feeling between sisters. This is what I call *queer kinship*. Here, to understand oneself as a sister is to feel desired as and by a sister.

The diaries of Julia and Delfina Bunge provide a window onto the ways in which the practice of writing and reading the diary fosters the imagination of self and other through a relational identification *as sister*. The rhetorical contours of their writing, and the form of address that the diary instigates as a genre, are the principal elements that I have drawn on in describing the diary as a technology of self-making. But the gendered dynamic of sisterhood should not be overlooked, nor should the erotic possibilities of discovering sameness/difference through the trope of the sister. The work of feminist critic Helena Michie is useful in this regard. She describes as "sororophobia" the process of negotiation of multiple axes of difference, in particular among sisters. This term, she argues, "attempts to describe the negotiation of sameness and difference, identity and separation, between women of the same generation, and is meant to encompass both the desire for and the recoil from identification with other women. Sororophobia is not so much a single entity as it is a matrix against and through which women work out—or fail to work out—their differences" (9-10). Michie's "matrix" of subjectivity relies on an intragenerational push and pull; sibling rivalry, as well as proximity. Michie signals an architecture of sorority, a usage of "matrix" that implies structure and place, but also development and process, against and through. Sororophobia would be, in this sense, a site, a location, or, as I have noted previously, a stage for the challenging process of becoming "sister." But there is yet another valence to this term that I think is relevant: the etymological root of matrix refers principally to the mother (from the Latin "mater"), and to the womb. Thus, the structure against which and through which sororophobia is worked out (or not) also implicates the mother/the maternal. Michie does comment briefly on this: "Sororophobia also obviously has much in common with, owes its very existence to, is even we might say a daughter of 'matrophobia,'" establishing a connection with feminist psychoanalytic interpretations of maternal love and identification, concluding "[l]ike all daughters, however, 'sororophobia' is always in negotiation with her mother about her separateness" (9). The relationship between the maternal and the sororal is described in terms of filiation. The matrix of sisterly differentiation/identification cannot be separated from the larger structures of kinship that have dominated anthropological and psychoanalytic discussions of culture. But I think, too, the relevance of sorophobia as a "matrix" is more productive if we imagine it as simultaneously a structure of differentiation/identification and a process by which sisters engage with their own origins (as daughters), their potentially sexualized role (as mothers), but also, as lovers.

Michie's understanding of sororophobia is helpful because hints at the way desire functions at the heart of this process of identification and differentiation. It suggests an erotics of the sibling bond is essential to this process. This brings us back to the sister as simultaneously a consanguine and discursive figure, and to the way in which Julia and Delfina Bunge write each other as both. In this vein, Juliet Mitchell's work in clinical psychology provides tools for reading the erotics of sisterhood that Michie notes but does not fully flesh out. Mitchell proposes a shift in psychoanalytic focus from what she calls "vertical taboos," such as the Oedipal complex, to those marking "lateral relations" or siblings (34). In an effort to refine Freud's theory of the death drive, she argues that the sibling bond must be taken into account and that its fundamental properties include similar prohibitions and sublimations: "There is a fundamental desire to murder your sibling. It too meets a prohibition: you must not kill your brother Abel; you must instead love your brother (or neighbour) *as yourself*. The violence must be turned into love—but the possibility of love is already there in the love one has for oneself, what, in psychoanalytic terminology, is called narcissism" (35, emphasis in the original). The relationship between narcissistic love and object-love becomes crucial in that, as Mitchell continues, "Sibling sexuality ranges from sex with someone whom one experiences as the same, to sex with someone whose difference one wants to obliterate" (39). Thus, she claims siblinghood is an originary trauma that introduces lateral competition that must be worked out between members of a generation, a series. Seriality is key to this formulation because it does not hinge on procreative reproduction, but mimesis. The identification of self/other in this scenario is primarily a function of the psychic processes that are enacted by the experience of having/being a sibling; by recognizing the self not as part of a vertical axis of potentially reproductive sexuality, but as part of a series of not-yet-distinguished selves. This is not to say that differently gendered siblings do not have the ability to reproduce, but that their primary point of reference as siblings is iterative rather than procreative. Or rather, the specter of sexual reproduction also imbues sibling competition, not necessarily as competition for the attention of parents, but for each other. The working out of subjective difference corresponds to the negotiation of self-love (Foucauldian self-knowledge) and the conversion of this trauma into acceptable forms of sociality. What Mitchell points out, and what I want to emphasize from the above discussion, is that to experience siblinghood is to negotiate the social and psychological processes by which the self learns not simply that it is different from others, but that it must also negotiate this difference by learning to feel as the self toward others. This is the work that the diary makes possible for the Bunge sisters. The shared diary becomes a space of negotiation of sibling difference, where the trauma of the self/other is textualized as part of an ongoing epistemological project.

Delfina Bunge explicitly describes the social relations between her siblings in an entry dated January 26, 1904.

> Hay familias—y las conozco—en que aparecen todos muy unidos; están siempre en paz; bromean mucho y discuten poco. Y en el fondo, son mucho menos unidos que otros que aparentan discordia. Yo creo que pocos hermanos habrá que tengan más necesidad, unos de otros, que los nuestros—y pocos que discutan más—. Pueden ser aprobados por fuera ... es inútil; sufrirán si no son aprobados en casa. Todos necesitan pensar, discutir y resolver entre ellos.

> There are families—and I know them—in which everyone appears very united; they are always at peace; they joke a lot and argue little. And in the end, they are much less united than other families that seem discordant. I think that there would be few siblings who have more need, for each other, than ours—and few who argue more—. They may be approved of outside ... it's useless; they will suffer if they are not approved of at home. All of us need to think, argue and resolve [issues] among ourselves. (L. Gálvez 142)

Her writing is nuanced and self-reflexive, focused on coming to terms with what it means to be related to her family members. But we also see that she is considering what others, what society, think about her family. It is through the seeming discord of family life that Delfina imagines her own family as more united than others. She astutely observes that family unity is framed by the social pressure to *appear* harmonious. "Aparecer" and "aparentar" are the key verbs. In Delfina's view, family unity is taken as an obligatory *performance* not for the family members themselves, but for outside observers. The facade provided by those families who seem "united" and "at peace" is achieved by joking rather than engaging in serious discussions of politics, art, or social issues. These are gestures of levity that, in Delfina's view, paper over a disingenuous relationship between kin. She has little interest in those families that are approved "*por fuera*" ("outside/by others") precisely because they lack the chaotic intellectual exchanges that she relishes. In contrast, her own family is described as a space of collective debate in which "todos necesitan pensar, discutir y resolver entre ellos" ("we/all of us need to think, argue and resolve [issues] among ourselves"). The difference between "unity" and "discord" is marked by the ability a family has to resolve conflicts though dialogue. This turns family into a space of collective pedagogy that is described in the diary, reinforcing its function as a technology of self-making. That is, Delfina is describing her family (1) as a space in which siblings learn from each other through the repeated staging and resolution of intellectual polemics, and (2) as connected by an affective need rather than blood relation.

Thus far I have endeavored to include the sway of the form of the diary, proposing to read it as an interface between the text and the diarist that produces the category of sister. It is as an interface that the diary implicates its aspirational form in the process of imagining self and other, in imagining the way the self may become other and may propose new ways of being in the world. The diaries represent a collective staging of the social and psychological processes by which the Bunge sisters differentiated themselves from their parents, from each other, and from their peers. In what follows I take three specific moments as examples of the complex interplay between the diary and its effects for the Bunge sisters. These examples have to do with sibling rivalry, publicity, and mutual subjectivity. They point to ways in which the queerness of the diary opens up new possibilities of understanding how familial relations are constituted through the interface of writing as and through the sister.

## EL CASO DELFINA

On June 24, 1904 a letter arrived at the Bunge household addressed to twenty-two-year-old Delfina Bunge congratulating her for being awarded honorable mention in a literary competition held by the Parisian magazine *Femina*.[8] Encouraged by her mother and unbeknownst to her father, she had submitted, in French and under the pseudonym Marguerite, an essay responding to the question: "Is the young woman of today happy?" As I noted earlier, this pseudonym directly links Delfina to Monniot's novelized diary, *Marguerite à vingt ans*, which she quotes at length in her own *cuaderno-copia* in an entry dated October 20, 1900. Soon, however, Marguerite's identity was revealed and, as historians Cárdenas and Payá put it, "La noticia cayó como una bomba en la sociedad" ("The news exploded like a bomb in society"; 173).[9] The news was explosive not necessarily because of *what* was written—a series of character sketches of turn-of-the-century young women—but for *who* was doing the writing. Recollecting the event in his own memoirs, Manuel Gálvez notes, "Antes de que Delfina se iniciara en las letras, una mujer de su elevada condición social, fuese casada o soltera, no podía publicar unas líneas sin caer en el ridículo" ("Before Delfina started out as a writer, a woman of her elevated social condition, whether she were married or single, could not publish a single line without being ridiculed"; *Recuerdos* 1: 115). To write a diary was one thing, but to publish a literary text was quite another for a young woman of the upper class. To become ridiculed, to bring dishonor on the family, to expose oneself to gossip, these are only some of the dangers implied by Gálvez, who hearkens one of the primary dilemmas of nineteenth- and early-twentieth-century women writers: the transgressive publicity of asserting an authorial voice *as a woman*.

Literary scholar María Gabriela Mizraje describes this dilemma as always involving a shift from the traditional private space of the home, and the public, "masculine" space of politics (and writing). The problem, Mizraje asks, is "Cómo moverse entre las sutiles hebras de la discreción y el escándalo, de la intimidad, la difamación y la traición" ("How to move oneself between the subtle threads of discretion and scandal, of intimacy, defamation, and betrayal"; 19). "El caso Delfina," is illustrative of this dilemma in that her essay forces the Bunge family to engage with the turn-of-the-century debate over the role of women in Argentine society; to decide whether their evidently talented daughter should be allowed to expose herself to such scrutiny. In this section, I would like to consider "El caso Delfina" as more than simply a social "bomb," but rather, more suggestively, as a *queer event*. It is a moment in which the threat of queerness engages a range of social actors (family members, friends, literary critics) to grapple with the uncomfortable position of transgressing social norms. The queer event rattles the cage of normativity. It marks a point of divergence from the accepted behavior of a young woman in society and opens a fissure in bourgeois decency.

Importantly, it is not necessarily the act of writing that exposes Delfina to this scandal *in potentia*, but publishing, invading the traditionally masculine space of authorship. In fact, Gálvez played a prominent role in this family drama: as the intrepid founder and director of the literary review *Ideas*, he wanted to be the first to publish Delfina's work in Buenos Aires. His relationship with Delfina reveals how each sister negotiated the scandal of publicness; how the threat of public exposure shaped possibilities of selfhood that is recorded in their respective diaries.

Allow me to narrate the scene: the twenty-three-year-old Gálvez intends to ask permission to reprint Delfina's article in *Ideas*. He arrives at the

Bunge family home on Suipacha, hurried but composed. Delfina answers the door and blurts out, "¿Usted es Gálvez?" ("Are you Galvez?"). A bit confused, he responds affirmatively, and then adds, "Yo quería hablar con su hermana Delfina" ("I wanted to speak with your sister, Delfina"). Quick witted, the young woman retorts: "Mi hermana Delfina soy yo" ("My sister Delfina is me"; L. Gálvez 209). While Delfina correctly identifies the young man, Gálvez, he misidentifies her as the sister of Delfina (that is, Julia). And when she remarks "My sister Delfina is me," she is not simply identifying herself *as herself*, but also as like—if not potentially the same as—her sister. In this case sisterhood is characterized by the folding of one individual subjectivity into another; its origin is the erasure of difference between the two Bunge daughters by a man who sought to strengthen his claim to cultural relevance by publishing Delfina's essay. It is from this erasure that Delfina's subjective "I" stakes a claim of individuality, a claim of difference that emerges from sameness.[10] Gálvez attempts to be the man who first publishes Delfina's work in Argentina, imagining, erroneously that the woman who has greeted him is her sister, Julia. To push this further, it was Gálvez who sought to "initiate" her in the public sphere of writing. The politics of visibility, of women's entrance into the public sphere, is complicated by this failure to distinguish one from the other, just as the erotics of literary novelty is pointed out by Gálvez's objectification of his future wife. This moment reveals how each sister begins to differentiate herself from the other according to the relationship between writing and publicity; how the visibility of each sister becomes another way of understanding how the self is marked by a negotiation with/as a sibling.

*Ideas* was not the only magazine interested in publishing the essay, however, hence the urgency with which Gálvez sought to secure the rights to Delfina's text. In fact the essay was reviewed several times in the Argentine press before it was eventually republished. Literary figures such as Ángel de Estrada in *El Diario*, Emilio Becher in *El Tiempo*, and Juan Pablo Echagüe in *El País* all favorably commented on Delfina/Marguerite's essay (Gálvez, *Recuerdos* 1: 118). In addition, Estanislao Zeballos would respond to the text in the *Revista de Derecho, Historia y Letras* under his own pseudonym, Lady Juana, as an open letter to Marguerite.

This is how the queer event unfolds: Delfina/Marguerite's essay mobilizes a range of social actors to critique the text itself, in addition to the social rupture it represents, but they also want to participate in its queerness. Zeballos, the director of the *Revista de Derecho, Historia y*

*Letras*, crosses gender in order to respond in kind (as Lady Juana). This was not Lady Juana's first article, though it would be her last.[11] In a 1903 social chronicle, "Palermo," she responds to a series of comments that had been sent to her: "Unos creen que Lady Juana no es una mujer, porque dicen que no existe en la *haute* ninguna capaz de escribir" ("Some believe that Lady Juana is not a woman, because they say that there is no woman among the *haute* that is capable of writing"; 87). This is precisely what Delfina's publication brings into question: how can social status be reconciled with the practice of writing. How, Lady Juana implies, could any woman be able to write with the grace and style, with the keen eye that I have? Lady Juana is a figure that seems to fill a void in the publishing landscape in which a new consumer, women, comes to the fore, and is from the outset writing from a queer position. Her gender instability is the product of the stigma attached to women writers. Zeballos has the ability to transgress these gender norms, while Delfina does not. And still, Lady Juana is compelled to comment on Marguerite's essay, whose publication, at least in retrospect, hails a new era in turn of the century writing. The beginning of Marguerite's career seems to presage the end of Lady Juana. And for that matter, the social intrigue caused by Marguerite's publication would also foreshadow the commotion caused by the 1905 publication of *Stella* by César Duáyen, again, a pseudonym used by Emma de la Barra, who wrote Argentina's first ever "best seller."[12] Thus, the covering and uncovering of names, the hiding of identity, this game of masks, was central to the question of how women could write, which women could write, and what circumstances made it possible for their work to be published.

In her open letter to Marguerite, Lady Juana laments the current state of Argentine society in which women, Lady Juana claims, are trained for "la carrera del matrimonio" ("the career of marriage,"), while marriage becomes "un seguro contra los accidentes del cariño" ("an insurance policy against the accidents of affection"; 108). Attempting to sympathize with Marguerite, Lady Juana argues that in general Argentine men lack the moral composition of the women Marguerite describes in her essay. Lady Juana concludes with the following invitation: "si no puedo ser tu alma gemela, porque la tuya está muy altamente colocada, permíteme ser tu alma amiga" ("if I cannot be your soul mate, because yours is very highly placed, allow me to be your soul friend"; 110).[13] Such an invitation at once legitimizes Marguerite's writing as morally correct, and calcifies women's writing as needing to uphold that moral correctness. If Marguerite has transgressed social protocol by publishing, at least she has done so in a manner that seems appropriate to her station in life.

As I mentioned, *Ideas* was not the only suitor for Delfina's text. The editor of the sleek and more popular *Caras y Caretas* also wanted to circulate a selection translated by the author into Spanish and illustrated with a photo of the young woman. Gálvez describes how the family attempted to dissuade the aspiring writer from doing so.

> Carlos Octavio habló en su casa de la proposición de la revista, y todos, padres y hermanos, a pesar de que entre ellos había dos escritores, consideraron absolutamente impropio que una niña distinguida saliera fotografiada en esa forma; y una tía suya, al oír hablar del 'deshonroso' pedido de *Caras y Caretas*, le dijo estas palabras de reproche y de lástima: "Ya ves, hijita, a lo que te expones con escribir...." En esos años el oficio de escritora estaba casi tan mal mirado, en nuestra sociedad aristocrática, como el de actriz o bailarina.

> Carlos Octavio spoke in their home about the magazine's proposal, and everyone, parents and siblings, despite there being among them two writers, considered it absolutely inappropriate that a distinguished young woman would be photographed in that way; and one of her aunts, upon hearing them speak of the "dishonorable" request of *Caras y Caretas*, told her these words of reproach and shame: "Now you see, little one, to what you expose yourself by writing...." In those years to work as a woman writer was almost as poorly viewed, in our aristocratic society, as being an actress or ballerina. (*Recuerdos* 1: 94)

The first distinction Gálvez makes is not related to publishing the text in one magazine or the other, but rather being photographed, that is, visually identified as the author of the text. It seems that what is "dishonorable" to Delfina's aunt is actually the publication of the photograph rather than the text itself. Ironically, this is also an example of the very type of discussion that Delfina referenced earlier, in which "todos necesitan pensar, discutir y resolver entre ellos" ("we need to think, argue and resolve among ourselves.") Despite the prospect of violating the social taboo against the assertion of the female self in public, the decision, taken *as a family*, was to accept the proposal by *Ideas* rather than *Caras y Caretas*. The text could be published, reluctantly, but not Delfina's image. Exposure to scandal, to defamation, and thus to a weakening of the family's stance in Porteño society was at stake. Curiously, this decision contrasts with the visual archive that the family did permit, including several *cartes de visite* taken in professional studios during these very years, in which Julia would pose in the style of European actress Sarah Bernhardt. I analyze these images in chapter 3, but here it is important to note that the venue of publication, *Caras y Caretas*, was too popular, too déclassé, for the family's liking, and the proposition was thus rejected.

What are the conditions that underlie this queer event? When the diary gives way to the essay, Delfina's writing loses the central condition of its own possibility: privacy. Even if, as I have been arguing, the diary praxis of the Bunge sisters is not entirely private but shared, this sharing has its limits. And even if both sisters had contemplated publishing their work from the very beginning of their respective diaries, to actually do so presents the family with a new set of issues, of social mores that must be attended to. One of the issues at stake, then, is the role of the literary marketplace in constructing a woman writer. Galvez's anecdotal recollection conveys the heightened tension between gender and labor, when a woman's right to work was seriously debated in both the public sphere and private homes. Upper-class fears about the inversion of class structures, as we saw in the work of Carlos O. Bunge in chapter 1, were often expressed by appealing to notions of traditional criollo values and linguistic and racial purity. But as historian Donna Guy demonstrates, and as Gálvez's recollection implies, these same fears could also be expressed by linking women's work outside the home to the decadence of the Argentine family.[14] For a woman to write *and get paid for it*, to enter the labor force, brought her dangerously close to other "working women."

Delfina's essay was eventually reprinted in the July 1904 edition of *Ideas*, still in French and signed Marguerite. It indeed caused a sensation. As Gálvez recalls, the magazine sold out in two weeks—the only time it ever sold out—as several Buenos Aires literary critics noted the debut of the country's new *femme de lettres* (*Recuerdos* 1: 93). Her response to the subject of the *Femina* prompt: "The young woman of the next century," is constructed as a collective rendering of contemporary womanhood. The essay was, after all, sourced from her diary and translated to French for the competition. In the essay, Delfina contemplates the relationship between self and other, but also between present and future. The notion of the young woman of the next century, a future self that has yet to become fully realized, links the essay to the diary itself as a diachronic genre: nonlinear, self-reflexive, continually reread. Delfina furthermore imagines the future woman in a range of subject positions that cross gender boundaries: "La jeune fille du *siècle à venir* qui semble emporter avec elle et la fleur du génie et les forces nouvelles de la société. Elle aspire à joindre à ses dons naturels de grâce et d'attrait, les forces viriles, l'indépendance qui seule lui sera donnée par son travail. Elle veut être père, mère, frère, sœur, artiste, ouvrière ... tout!" ("The young lady *of the next century* seems to carry with her the genius's flower and the new forces of society. Her deepest desire is to combine her natural gifts of grace and attractiveness with virile strength, an independence that only her work will give her. She wants to be father, mother, brother, sister, artist, laborer ... everything!"; ellipses in the original 279). The author is attempting to assemble a picture of the possibilities for the young woman of the future by describing qualities that are embodied by a range of characters that closely resemble those around her. She writes, "J'ai essayé d'ébaucher sa structure, ais cette jeune fille peut nous presenter elle-même une grand diversité de caractères" ("I tried to draft its structure, but this young lady can herself appear to us in a great variety of characters"; 288-89). This is yet another example of a multiple subjectivity forming the sense of self, how a young woman sees herself as an index of the qualities she observes in her friends and siblings. That is, the individual is clearly bound to the class with which she associates.

These sketches are meant to portray contemporary society through the personalities of its young women. However, they also contains a kernel of what would decades later become Delfina's feminist position regarding the role of the woman as part of the patriarchal family: "Ne se sentant pas la force ni la vocation pour rompre avec les préjugés de sa famille, avec le milieu ambiant, elle s'aperçoit bientôt que l'intelligence et la bonté se développent partout, et qu'il n'y a pas de temps perdu pour qui sait en profiter" ("She did not feel the strength nor the vocation to break with her family's prejudices, with what surrounded her, she realized soon enough that intelligence and kindness developed everywhere and that no time was lost for she who knew how to enjoy it"; 285). The role of family and culture, in addition to the "milieu ambiant," will remain important touchstones for the woman of the future, according to Delfina. But her "intelligence" and "goodness" will allow her to open up doors previously closed to her.

If Delfina's publication introduces her to the problematic relationship between gender and authorship, it has quite a different effect on Julia. On June 24, 1904, the date of the infamous letter announcing Delfina's award,

Julia describes Delfina's composition as "preciosa" ("precious") and "un gran triunfo" ("a great triumph") (187; 188). However, she also expresses surprise at her sister's accomplishment, claiming "lo que es más notable es que no habiendo aprendido mucho francés pueda escribir tan bien, en un idioma extranjero" ("what is most noteworthy is that not having learned much French she can write so well in a foreign language"; 187).[15] Other than this scant praise, Julia does not remark at all about the content or quality of her sister's essay in this entry. This silence is telling. It marks the subjective difference between one sister and another. It is a silence that frames the limits to what the diary can record. It also marks an affective charge between the two sisters. This silence signals contrast, competition, and difference. While both young women had been studying French for ten years, Julia takes umbrage with the notoriety that her sister was receiving for a talent she deemed insufficient. This seemingly innocuous observation provides a glimpse into the ways in which sibling differentiation follows the contours of literary form, and how it is not only what each sister writes in her diary that signifies as part of an ongoing self-making project, but also what they choose not to record.

Two weeks after this initial episode, after the article appeared reprinted in *Ideas*, Julia's diary writing turns almost exclusively to the notoriety that the publication brings to the family, and, more specifically, to her sister's transgressive publicness. She writes: "La composición de Delfina es siempre el tema. En las visitas, entre niñas, entre jóvenes, no se habla de otra cosa. Y como no le pueden hablar a Delfina porque pone cara de desesperada, todas las ponderaciones y todos los juicios me los hacen a mí" ("Delfina's composition is always the topic. During visits, among young women, among young men, no one talks of anything else. And since they cannot speak with Delfina because she puts on her desperate face, they come to me with all of their praise and all their opinions"; 195). While the topic of conversation may be Delfina's writing, Julia highlights her own role in the queer event and the repercussions of her sister's actions on her. She is frustrated by what she perceives as Delfina's inability to deal with her own newfound fame, and laments the role in which she has been cast, something akin to a shield or modern-day publicity agent. The tone of this section of the diary is notably more aggressive, and Julia, who sees herself as a charming socialite, is forced to revise her role within the family when Delfina becomes suddenly the more public of the two. It is notable that

Julia records Delfina's gesture, her "desperate face," which marks her as unwilling to field questions from others, rather than any discussion that the two might have had about the matter.

The notoriety unnerves Julia, and as part of her ongoing public relations campaign, with the aid of their mother, attempts to mitigate the speculation that has engulfed her sister by sending her to the opera, a staged appearance meant to project a specific type of feminine image. Julia writes,

> Entre Mamá y yo la hemos obligado (así puede decirse) a Delfina a ir esta noche a la Opera. Es ridículo que yo esté yendo todas las noches y ella no vaya nunca. [...] Hoy ha ido doblemente contra su gusto. Dice que es el colmo que la hagamos ir en 9 de Julio, para que todo el mundo la mire como bicho raro, después de su premio de Fémina; que si se tratara de un palco grillé, pase, pero a las tertulias más visibles del teatro...
>
> Es precisamente lo que queremos, que todo el mundo la mire, que vean que aunque sabe escribir, es una niña encantadora y que en su casa no la tratan tan mal.
>
> Between Mother and I we have obligated (one could say) Delfina to go to the Opera tonight. It is ridiculous that I have been going every single night and she never does. [...] Today she has gone doubly against her will. She says that it is the last straw that we make her go on July 9, so that everyone can look at her like a strange creature, after her Femina prize; that if we were talking about a shuttered box seat, fine, but to the more visible galleries in the theater...
>
> That is precisely what we want, for everyone to look at her, to see that even though she knows how to write, she is a charming young woman and we don't treat her badly at home. (189-90)

On this nationally symbolic night, Delfina has been "obligated" to make an appearance, marking a stark contrast between the public resonance of her article and the private movement of her body.[16] It is precisely this physicality that bothers her, to be seen as a "*bicho raro*" ["a strange (or queer) creature"] rather than a woman of letters. Visibility is key. If her family were to have reserved one of the "*palco grillé*," a room enclosed with a removable metal barrier typically used by families in mourning, Julia reports, Delfina would not have put up such a fight. Delfina's foremost concern is being exposed to the gaze of the public in the aristocratic space of the opera, but this is precisely what her family demands. After deciding to prohibit the publication of her image in *Caras y Caretas*, Delfina was required to give her own dramatic performance for an intrigued public.

Rather than a "*bicho raro*," a queer transgressor of social norms, that is, a woman who writes *and publishes*, Julia wants Delfina to be seen as a "charming young woman." The Bunges do not want her literary talent, taken as a statement of fact by the use of the indicative mode ("she knows how to write"), to tarnish her reputation in society. As her final comment reveals, Julia is not primarily concerned with Delfina's reputation, but her own. Here the diary serves to consolidate one sister's normative viewpoint regarding the other as Julia contemplates the effects of public scandal on her privileged place in society and attempts to rehabilitate her sister's image, paradoxically, by exposing her to public view. The friction between the two sisters is palpable here, as it seems that Julia does not want to become the collateral damage of Delfina's sudden notoriety. This conflict is fleshed out through the pages of the diary, which serve to relate how the familial strategy of rehabilitating Delfina's image came about, and what were its aims. Perhaps Delfina would read this later and understand. Perhaps with time she would appreciate what they had "done for her." Perhaps she would read it and never quite forgive them.

The controversy over the publicness of women's writing would not soon die down, however. Delfina Bunge played an important, if undervalued role in calling into question the restrictions placed on women writers in the first years of the twentieth century by class expectations of gendered normativity. Interestingly, the woman who would most dramatically rework the division of public and private literary life in Argentina, Victoria Ocampo (1890-1979), looked up to Delfina Bunge and sought her guidance as an established public writer (if reluctantly so). They were friends from summer months spent in San Isidro, where both the Ocampos and the Bunges had homes. Decades before she would found Argentina's most important literary and cultural review, *Sur* (1931-1970), Delfina and "Victorita" exchanged a series of letters, later published as part of Ocampo's autobiographical oeuvre. In a letter dated August 28, 1908, for example, Ocampo laments the ongoing challenges she sees for both men and women writers.

> *Literato* es una palabra que sólo se toma en sentido peyorativo en nuestro medio. "Es un literato" (o peor aún "es *una* literata") significa un inservible,

un descastado, un atorrante, hasta un maricón (a menos que tenga una cátedra y sea *profesor*. Respetan ese tipo de títulos). Si se trata de una mujer, es indefectiblemente una *bas-bleu*, una *poseuse*, está al borde de la perversión, y en el mejor de los casos es una insoportable marisabidilla, mal entrazada. En cambio la palabra estanciero tiene prestigio. Significa (como en la fábula) veau, vache, cochon, couvée. ¿Es o no verdad?

*Literato* is a word that is only used pejoratively in our culture. "He is a *literato*" (or even worse "she is a *literata*") means a man who is of no use, an ingrate, a lout, even a sissy (unless he has a professorship and the title of *professor*. They respect those types of degrees). If it refers to a woman, she is inevitably a bluestocking, a poser, on the border of perversion, and in the best of cases a raggedy and insufferable know-it-all. In contrast the word landowner has prestige. It means (like in the fables) calf, cow, pig, brood of chickens. Is that not true? (104)[17]

While Ocampo bemoans the fact that the profession of *writer* was universally despised among the elite, her critique revolves around how the practice of writing contradicts gender norms. To be a woman writer is to approach perversion—to be like the early feminists, the "bluestockings," whose transgressive publicness takes them out of the home and into the streets; while to be a man who writes—without a university title—is to approach the category of invert, the useless man, the sissy. Curiously, Ocampo's parenthetical feels almost as if in the moment of writing, she remembers who she is writing to, Delfina Bunge, whose oldest brother, Carlos Octavio, was a writer but also a professor (with a professorship). It feels like a moment of self-correction, or at least an attempt to mitigate the possible implication that Carlos Octavio might be one of those queer men. These points of reference have to do with the value of gendered labor and the purpose of gendered bodies in the early twentieth century. The limitations placed on members of the elite owe to the bourgeois demand for productivity—and reproductivity—within a globalizing economy. Men who write are not "productive" like men who own land; women who write are not quiet enough, not still enough, they "know too much" and speak too loudly for the taste of those men who own land to carry on with their business. In 1908 Ocampo had not yet found the place that she would make her own, the cultural mediary, the *owner* and *producer* of culture in an Argentina that she made cosmopolitan and avant-garde by spending her vast wealth on keeping *Sur* in print. And yet, we see in this early letter a contradiction that would remain constant throughout her life, what Francine Masiello calls a "stance of mediation between public power and private life as expressed through an exacerbated desire for constant self-representation" (157). The representation of self, here a self-constructed and shared as epistolary correspondence, comes to find its way into the *cuadernos-copia* as an extension of the network of women writers that was connected through Delfina Bunge's diary praxis. While in Delfina's diaries her constant, indeed obsessive self-representation would remain circumscribed to the intimate sphere of selected interlocutors, Victoria Ocampo, in contrast, would become a master of the intimate made public, as a public. For Ocampo the intimate became a point of departure for the grandiose role made her own that nevertheless points back to these early anxieties regarding women's writing. It is no coincidence that Ocampo's first editorial project commissioned for *Sur* relates to Virginia Woolf, *A Room of One's Own* (1929) translated by Jorge Luis Borges in 1936 (Mizraje 232).

But if Delfina was already formulating her ideas regarding the frivolity of the social circuit of the aristocratic youth in the early years of the twentieth century, Julia, in contrast, relished the spectacle of her own position. The latter's diary reveals a gradual increase in her time spent "in society" during the period in which Delfina was seriously questioning the utility of such endeavors. As we saw earlier, Julia initially praised Delfina's literary prize, but as the social tension began to rise, and as Delfina was unwilling to face the public's barrage of questions herself, Julia began to see her sister as potentially prejudicial to her own standing in society. The queer event concentrates conflicting desires and interests, stretching the strictures of normativity to their limits. What is more, the queer event is an expression of desire by multiple actors that gives in to the magnetic pull of queerness as a form of life in which the modern and the normative, the dissident and the proper collide and rake against each other, marking a new path for sociality, sexuality, and relationality. Again, this moment is not simply recorded by the diaries, but rather constituted by the formal qualities of reciprocal reading and writing the sister. The event, in so far as it can be considered a critical juncture of ideological and affective contradictions, relies on publicity and privacy, competition and solidarity. The publication of Delfina's *Femina* essay lays bare the work that is required to maintain class privilege, and the lengths to which the family must go to maintain it. Likewise, it hints at a type of freedom, a divergence from social norms, that would be accentuated in the coming years as the family sought alternative arrangements of domesticity, kinship, and labor.

## A QUEER HOME

"Es muy cierto que hay momentos en que tengo deseos de irme de casa, de sentirme libre y de estar sola.... De marchar delante de mí, de llevar mis pasos adonde quiera sin hacer sombra sobre nadie, ni incomodar..." ("It is very true that there are moments in which I have desires to leave home, to feel free and to be alone.... To march on ahead of myself, to take my own path wherever I want without without bothering or casting a shadow over anyone..."; L. Gálvez *Delfina* 74). After the publication of her first literary text, Delfina relates a growing uncertainty about her place within the Bunge home and as part of the normative family. Her desire to "feel free" is related to a growing possibility that she attempt to break from tradition and strike it out on her own, a desire that is contrasted by her interest in following her religious inclinations and joining a monastery. As I discuss in chapter 3, the visualization of Delfina's place in society is dominated by the demand for presence. And yet, she wishes to circulate unnoticed in society, unencumbered by the social demands for recognition, for embodiment. These two poles dominate her writing in the decade between the turn of the century and 1910, a period that includes her first publication and the romantically charged introduction to Manuel Gálvez and which closes with their marriage and honeymoon. In other words, this period starts with Delfina's crisis of identity as part of the upper class, includes the queer event of her first publication, and concludes with her marriage and decision to form a family of her own, thus returning to the fold of normative kinship. Here I focus on the beginning of this arc in which Delfina formulates her desire not to adhere to the normative framework of family life. I turn to Delfina's self-identification as a *solterona* and continue with a more speculative account of the queer living arrangement proposed to her by Carlos Octavio. While Delfina eventually chooses to marry, I highlight the queer possibilities that she imagined for herself, on the one hand, and the fraternal solidarity offered to her so that she could live a life "on her own path," on the other. In this, I reflect on what might have been rather than what actually came to pass. These moments reveal the changing views of gender and sexuality in the early years of the twentieth century in Argentina and serve to highlight the tension between individual desires and responsibilities to family and to class.

In the following entry we learn through Delfina's *cuaderno-copia* that her oldest brother, Carlos Octavio, has invited her to leave the Bunge household and move in with him.

4/6/1904. ¡Pobre Octavio! ¿Quién iba a decir que iba a ser él quien más se preocupase por mí, y el que con más delicadeza supiese insinuarse en mi pensamiento? Puedo casi decir que es el que mejor me comprende. [...] A veces me pinta lo que puede ser la vida de "una mujer sensata, inteligente y distinguida" sin necesidad de que se case. Y me la pinta...con atractivos colores. Me dice cómo, en tales condiciones, se pueden tener nobles goces, y hacer mucho bien. Una vez que salimos a caminar, en San Isidro, a la hora del crepúsculo, y me llevó hasta la famosa chacra de nuestra infancia, me hacía los ofrecimientos más delicados. De vivir con él por supuesto. Sin romanticismo; con cuentas y con todo. "Serás independiente, tendrás tu cuarto, tu piano..."

¡Me ofrecía, como último y más eficaz recurso, un lindo piano de cola! Lo que él no quiere es que...me vaya. Y como único medio de impedírmelo quiere demostrarme el papel de una mujer soltera como natural y bueno: "Una mujer inteligente puede quedarse soltera," me repite.

June 4, 1904. Poor Octavio! Who would have guessed that it would have been him who most worried about me, and who with the most subtlety knew how to reach into my thoughts? I can almost say that he is who best understands me. [...] Sometimes he paints a picture for me of what the life of "a sensible, intelligent, and distinguished woman" could be like without needing to be married. And he paints it for me...with charming colors. He tells me how, under such conditions, one can have noble pleasures, and do much good. One time we went on a walk, in San Isidro, at sunset, and he took me to the famous country house of our infancy, he made the most delicate offers. To live with him of course. Without romanticism; with clear accounts and everything else. "You will be independent, you will have your own room, your piano..."

He offered me, as a last ditch effort and the most effective one, a beautiful grand piano! What he does not want is for me...to go. And as the only way to stop me, he wants to prove the role of a single woman as natural and good: "An intelligent woman can stay single," he keeps telling me. (L. Gálvez, *Delfina* 144)

At the age of twenty-nine Carlos Octavio had been living independently for eight years. By 1904 he was one of the most well-known social scientists and educators in Argentina. Delfina was twenty-three at this time, and, as we have seen from the previous examples, not enthusiastic about what she saw as the ostentation and the falsity characteristic of the upper class in Buenos Aires.

There are two principal characteristics that stand out regarding this diary entry. The first is Delfina's surprise at the fact that Carlos Octavio, rather than one of her other siblings, recognizes her dissatisfaction and proposes an alternative to her current living arrangements. Her question, "Who would have guessed ... ?" may express gratitude toward Carlos Octavio, but it also implies disappointment in Julia, with whom she shared her own diary. We sense similar disappointment from Julia when Delfina published her essay in *Femina* and later in *Ideas*. The second striking characteristic about this passage, and another testament to the queer possibility of sibling relations, is the actual proposal that Delfina's brother makes for her to move in with him, apparently so that she would not feel ostracized by her parents or other siblings and attempt to join a convent. The independence that Delfina craved could have been satisfied by this proposal. The ability to write, to have her own piano, to come and go as she pleased, to be alone. In the context of Argentina at 1904 this arrangement would have been unheard of for members of the upper class.

Carlos Octavio was proposing a queer home. By this I mean that he invites Delfina to reconfigure the habitus of the upper class, rejecting marriage and the patrimonial demands of maintaining or increasing wealth through inheritance. He proposes that they form a home for themselves in which the pressures to marry, to procreate, to perform heteronormativity, would—at least within its walls—be assuaged. What is more, this reconfiguration of intimacy and domesticity, hinges on sibling collaboration, rather than the gendered division of space, labor, and prestige within the home. Even if this arrangement would certainly not have been without its own internal power dynamics, gendered and economic, the notion of sibling cohabitation as an alternative to the hegemonic regime of *patria potestad* suggests that both Carlos Octavio and Delfina were looking to break from tradition and queer their shared domestic space, that is, to make a home based not on patriarchal normativity, but their own desires and interests. The queer home is a space of possibility that privileges the horizontality of the sibling over the verticality of filiation. In short, the proposition involves a break with the normative model of the home as the exclusive locus of family sociability and biological reproduction, indeed, the place within which the family is constituted as such. Instead, Carlos Octavio proposes a sibling partnership, to turn his bachelor residence into a space of sibling collaboration, artistic development, learning, mutuality, and freedom.

But not just any woman could live by herself. According to Carlos Octavio, she has to be "sensible, intelligent, and distinguished." And while these are all qualities that could easily be used to describe Delfina, and this is probably exactly why her brother uses them, they are also clear markers of class. An uneducated, working-class woman would not have the same option, nor, for that matter, would another upper-class "*niña*" without the support of an older, financially independent brother. Carlos Octavio is eager to argue that it is "natural and good" for a woman to live out her life as a "*soltera*" ("single woman"), especially if she is his own sister. In fact, Delfina would contemplate the social standing of a "*soltera*" or "*solterona*" ("spinster") in a diary entry from September 17, 1902.

> ¿Qué es lo que caracteriza la vida de una solterona? ¿Cuándo se empieza a considerar "solterona" a una niña que todavía no es vieja? ¿Cuándo empieza a emplear su vida útilmente? ¿Cuándo busca lo útil para ocuparse de ello? ¡Enhorabuena, empecemos a ser solterona entonces! ¿Qué es ser solterona al fin? Es haberse dado por vencida en la carrera de buscar marido y comenzar a emplear su vida en la otra ocupación. Yo no tengo el trabajo de buscar marido, justo es que trabaje en otra cosa.
>
> What is it that characterizes the life of a spinster? When does "spinster" start to be applied to a *niña* who is not yet old? When does she start to lead a useful life? When does she seek out usefulness in order to apply herself to it? Congratulations! Let us start to be spinsters then! What is a spinster in the end? It is to have given up on the career of husband-seeking and to have begun to use her life in other ways. It is not my job to be a husband-seeker, so it is fair that I work towards something else. (L. Gálvez, *Delfina* 72)

This passage is typical of the way in which the Delfina defines herself in relation to others, or, more prominent here, how she resists societal expectations in favor of a life that she imagines as more fulfilling. Her use of self-directed questions allows us to follow logic by which she justifies her disinterest in participating in the rituals of courtship that defined "*niñas*" at the turn of the century, and self identifies, in contrast, as a "*solterona*." That is, she turns to a queer figure in order to justify her view of the marriage "profession" as disingenuous and unfulfilling. Her sense of sarcasm is notable, while the double valence of this term, "*carrera*," referring both to the speed with which women attempt to find a husband—to courtship as a "race" (a rat race?)—and to the obligation to serve the family in this capacity as a "career," signals what would be a principal theme in Delfina's essay writing in subsequent decades (see chapter 5). In this sense, the entry describes the process of rationalization through which she identifies herself as a woman who is not like the other members of her class.

The "*solterona*" has the potential to relate otherwise (to kin, to friends, to the state). There is an important quality, a queerness, that seems to engulf the figure of the spinster, at once integral to the family, and biologically distant from it; a sister and a daughter but never a wife. She may be marginalized from biological reproduction (within the logic that presumes marriage before pregnancy), but she is frequently integral to family cohesion, functioning as a surrogate in times of need, keeping the peace between quarreling siblings, or serving as an important source of labor within the home.[18] The spinster occupies a liminal space within the hereditary logic of the family, but may play a central role in the quotidian functioning of a home. In fact, Delfina attempts to recast the "*solterona*" in a positive light, specifically by turning to a woman's "utility." But useful in what way and for whom? Just as Delfina defends the figure of the *solterona* in her diary, as we saw above, Carlos Octavio defends the status of the *soltera* in his proposal of a queer home. Though not an outright refusal of marriage, the queer home implies that—at least for a while—both unmarried siblings could continue their intellectual pursuits by sharing a reconfigured domestic space.

Delfina would reject the offer, however, and would continue to live with her parents and Julia until 1910, when she married Manuel Gálvez. We are left, then, with the image of Carlos Octavio attempting to persuade his sister on a picturesque walk through San Isidro, returning to the *chacra* where they first began to collaborate as children through the skits he would write and direct each summer in which his siblings were enlisted as actors (Cárdenas and Payá, *Familia* 185). Perhaps Carlos Octavio sought to rekindle this partnership, seeing in Delfina a kindred spirit, someone who would support his intellectual endeavors and for whom he could provide a temporary respite from the demands of a young woman "in society." It is also possible that Carlos Octavio saw in his sister an individual whose artistic predilections complimented his own, a potential interlocutor, someone who could offer him amenable conversation at home and practical assistance with his own work. Both Julia and Delfina had been enlisted previously to copyedit their oldest brother's work. Delfina could also serve to benefit from his experience, from his connections, and his ability to share with her a world of intellectual growth that she desired.

Ironically, Manuel Gálvez, who in his literary memoirs described Carlos Octavio as "sumamente desordenado, tanto en sus papeles como en sus libros y como en todas sus cosas" ("extremely disorganized, in his papers and his books and in all of his things"), assessed his brother-in-law's domestic needs in the following way: "Le faltaba a su lado una mujer que le apaciguase y le hiciera mucho silencio y mucha calma a su alrededor. Hubiera encontrado más de una que aceptara casarse con él, aunque, tal vez, hubiera sido difícil que, en la vida del matrimonio, ella se aviniese a su carácter" ("He lacked a woman at his side who would calm him down and cultivate much silence and peace around him. He would have found more than one woman who would have accepted marrying him, even though, perhaps, it would have been difficult, in married life, for her to get along with his personality"; *Recuerdos* 1: 287). This passage reveals more about Gálvez's idea of domesticity than that of his brother-in-law. The notion of a woman "appeasing" and "calming" Carlos Octavio in silence is more than a bit misogynist. And more than a bit homophobic: his "*carácter*" is both his personality and his *nature*, that unnameable quality that makes him inherently difficult, unruly, queer. I think, however, that Carlos Octavio might have been looking for something different himself: a partner, a sister with whom he could explore his intellectual endeavors within the space of the home, rather than a wife. The irony, after all, is that it was Manuel Gálvez, rather than Carlos Octavio, who managed to convince Delfina to cohabitate with him, leaving us with yet another homosocial rivalry in which brothers-in-law compete diachronically for the companionship of the same woman.

The queer home eschews normative patterns of time and space. It invites us to speculate about what might have been; what sibling sociality might have developed between Carlos Octavio and Delfina. But it also shines a light on the contradictions of upper-class propriety, pushing the limits of the imperative to marry for women such as Delfina. Was it a missed opportunity? We must imagine the queer home that might have been but never was; the possibilities of sibling cohabitation as an alternative to patriarchal domesticity and the sneaking suspicion that such freedom as was offered by Carlos Octavio was overwhelming in its novelty.

In describing this queer home as an unfulfilled desire, I am struck by the way that such a future-oriented domestic arrangement hinges not on sentimentalism, but parity. "Con cuentas y con todo" ("with clear accounts and everything else"), Delfina quotes her brother as saying. It is not meant as charity, but rather a method of providing a platform for in(ter)dependence. What is more, the queer home is not one in which Delfina would be pressured to marry. Quite the contrary. It is proposed precisely by recalling her desire for an independent life without the tutelage of a husband. While the proposal is aimed at providing the possibility of a future outside of marriage, it does so by harnessing the memory and affective resonance of a bygone moment of youthful intimacy. The queer home may be an impossibility at this point in their lives, but it was not always so. Indeed, the recollection of such queer (im)possibilities is precisely the domain of youth, a moment prior to heteronormative socialization. Faced with the loss of his sister to the convent, on the one hand, and to marriage, on the other, Carlos Octavio imagines a middle ground, a queer third option, in which self-actualization, independence, and the pursuit of individual artistic pursuits would take priority. The queer home represents an unrealized yearning for sibling freedom in the face of the constant pressure to adhere to normative kinship models based on marriage, capital accumulation, and genealogical reproduction. It is a yearning for otherness, a project, a possibility.

## THE CENTENNIAL

So far I have focused on a series of formative moments in which Delfina Bunge expressed the tension between her desire for an alternative to the hegemonic pattern of courtship and marriage and the responsibility she felt to participate in that social milieu. Here, we glimpse the way Julia, in stark contrast, savored her role as integral to that very system. Delfina felt the social pressure to marry as an affront to her personal liberty and argued with her mother and sister about the possibility of a young woman of her class acting independently in society, while Julia saw herself as an essential part of the social fabric of the Argentine elite. And yet, as she approached the centennial, Julia began to question her place "in society":

"Junio 20 - 1910: Y ahora, yo me hago esta pregunta: ¿Voy a seguir andando en Sociedad? ¿Voy a ir a todos los bailes? Sí, voy a seguir yendo a cuanto baile y fiesta pueda. Yo me divierto. A mí me gusta la sociedad. Tengo muchas invitaciones, buenos vestidos, y muchos compañeros" ("June 20 - 1910: And now, I ask myself this question: Am I going to keep going out in Society? Am I going to go to all the dances? Yes, I am going to keep going to as many dances and parties as I can. I have fun. I like society. I have many invitations, good dresses, and many companions"; *Vida* 500). It is not enough for her to admit, without a hint of modesty, that she already has access to the most important social gatherings, and the accouterments necessary for a successful social life. Julia needs to justify her presence in society to herself. The celebrations of the Argentine centennial provide a final example of the way in which the Bunge sisters utilize the space of the diary to enact a form of mutual subjective emplotment. The centennial becomes Julia's last hurrah in public, a final extravagant example of her self-perspective as a Porteño socialite, while, in stark contrast, Delfina is completely absent from the public celebrations (in May), having married Manuel Gálvez in April of 1910 and left the country for their honeymoon. In this sense, 1910 not only marks a political milestone, but also serves as a watershed moment for the Bunge family. In this same year, Octavio Bunge, recently resigned from his post in the Supreme Court, would preside over part of the centennial celebrations, but his health was already poor and he would die later that year, forcing the family to rearrange some of its capital and property. Julia, for her part, would marry Ignacio Uranga, a wealthy *estanciero* from Santa Fe, whom she met on a transatlantic voyage that left Buenos Aires on March 5, 1911. They would take a yearlong honeymoon around the world, and would not return to Buenos Aires until the following year. It also marks the end of Julia's first efforts at diary writing, an end of an era for both sisters, whose relationship would change as they began families of their own.

The political resonance of the centennial celebrations came in a moment of heightened social conflict in Argentina. The Law of Residence (1902) and subsequent the Law of Social Defense (1910) granted wide-ranging powers to local police, who were authorized to detain individuals suspected of fomenting social unrest. These technologies of repression were by and large used against recent immigrants, in particular Italians, anarchists, and socialists, which became almost synonymous during this period. As David Rock describes, "it became routine procedure for the police to break all strikes and demonstrations by force and to arrest and often mistreat and then deport the 'agitators'" (*Authoritarian* 58). It is telling, however, that Julia's diary makes no mention whatsoever of this rising public tension or the development of nationalist ideologies, instead focusing on her family's role in the centennial celebrations, and in particular on her own participation in its most lavish parties.

For example, Julia writes,

> Con motivo del centenario del 25 de mayo de 1910, ha venido la Infanta Isabel, de España, y hay una cantidad de fiestas lindísimas, por el Centenario, y en honor de la infanta. En este momento Papá ejerce la presidencia de la Suprema Corte de Justicia, nombrado expresamente para la circunstancia, y como es natural, lo invitan a todas las fiestas oficiales con su familia. Papá y Mamá van a casi todas las fiestas, y por mi parte yo no me pierdo ni una.

> On the occasion of the centennial of the 25th of May of 1910, the Infanta Isabella, of Spain, has come and there are a number of beautiful parties, because of the Centennial, and in honor of the infanta. At this moment Dad is the president of the Supreme Court of Justice, named expressly for this occasion, and as is natural, he is invited to all the official celebrations along with his family. Dad and Mom go to almost all of the parties, and I myself wouldn't miss a single one. (*Vida* 489)

The occasion is not lost on Julia, whose diary entries for the month of June 1910 are laden with details of the social scene, in particular the splendor of the public celebrations of the Argentine centennial. Notably, these descriptions are cast in a familial light. Since "Papá y Mamá" have been invited to all of the official functions, the balls and galas that were sponsored by various public institutions, Julia's feeling for the resurgent nationalism of the first decade of the twentieth century is heavily influenced by the rhetoric of kinship. She sees herself as a prime example of the refined, gracious Argentine woman, and projects her image as one to emulate and admire. In this way she, as author of her own story, makes a conscious effort to link herself to the process of reaffirming an Argentine national ethos, situating herself as part of an ongoing historical process by which the criollo elite maintained political and social hegemony by adhering to a system of tight-knit social relations, buoyed by strategic marriages and economic ties.

Having secured an invitation to the most desirable ball, as Julia notes, "el de Llavallol (el único importante)" ("the Llavallol [the only important one]"), she also procures a dress imported from Europe by Jacques Doucet, "el primer modisto de París" ("the premier stylist in Paris"; 490, 491). The stage was set for what would be her crowning moment in the Porteño social scene. Julia seemed to be aware of this herself, describing the Llavallol ball as the scene of a rare occurrence: "una cosa, que en mi larga carrera social, lo he visto en Buenos Aires, sólo tres veces" ("a thing, which in my long social career, I have seen in Buenos Aires only three times"; 494). Establishing herself as a veteran of *the scene*, the rare thing that she is about to record features herself as the central figure in the most important social occasion of the Argentine centennial.

> De pronto nos encontramos con que la aglomeración de bailarines había ido desapareciendo y que nosotros éramos los únicos que estábamos bailando. De todas las salas venía gente al hall, hasta que ya no cabía más, la orquesta prolongaba la pieza, y cuando terminó, fue una verdadera ovación. La Infanta Isabel, que también se había trasladado al hall para ver el espectáculo, se adelantó y me dio un beso. "Hijita, eres un amor como bailas, y qué preciosa y elegante estás." Todo el mundo me rodeaba y me felicitaba; querían que bailara de nuevo pero no quise.
>
> Suddenly we found that the throng of dancers had been dispersing and we were the only ones left dancing. People came to the hall from all the other rooms, until it was filled to capacity, the orquestra prolongued the piece, and when it finished there was a real ovation. The Infanta Isabella, who had also relocated to the hall to witness the spectacle, came forward and gave me a kiss. "My little one, it is lovely to see you dance, and how gorgeous and elegant you are." Everyone surrounded me and congratulated me; they wanted me to dance again but I didn't want to. (495)

Not only does Julia describe herself and her dance partner, Tonito Acosta, as magnetically attracting a group of onlookers, but also as eclipsing the attentions paid to the Spanish Infanta, Isabella, Princess of Asturias (1851-1931). The moment is infused with a romantic filigree. Julia narrates this scene telescoping gradually toward herself, the center of attention, the focal point of the group of distinguished guests who come to see the "spectacle." This glowing scene, incredibly, culminates not with the Infanta's royal kiss, but rather with Julia's refusal to prolong the moment, with an awareness of how to occupy the social space and cultural imaginary of the elite—precisely by leaving them wanting more.

This moment marks an extreme contrast with Delfina's stubbornly antipublic stance after the publication of her essay in *Femina* in 1904. Recalling the strategy by which Julia proposed to prove to the world that Delfina was a "*niña encantadora*" in spite of her daring to have published a literary text, we can take the Llavallol ball as the culminating moment in Julia's endeavors to stake out her own space in public. To a certain extent this moment represents the final gesture of subjective differentiation by which Julia's physical presence "*en sociedad*" sharply contrasts that of Delfina, who is conspicuously absent from this event, and also from Julia's retelling of it. At no point does Julia lament the fact that her sister was not there to share in this triumph. Instead, the presence of the Spanish princess serves to heighten the social resonance of this moment, a triumph of (acceptable) feminine publicness, the very type of performance that Delfina would have considered frivolous. The occasion pits the spectacular presence of Julia against the spectral absence of Delfina. It is in this tension, as produced, recorded, on the pages of the diary, that their mutually constituted sisterhood plays out. The diary becomes a technology of subjective differentiation—as witnessed in public—but as described in private, in its pages, for one and the other simultaneously.

## CONCLUSION

"¿Me estoy dirigiendo ya a Mme. Manolo Gálvez? Siempre seguirás siendo Delfina Bunge para mí. He pensado mucho en vos y he sentido no estar en Buenos Aires. ¿Te casaste? Esto me entristece; perdón. ¡El casamiento me parece algo tan temible! Sin embargo, no es por *esa* razón que lo siento en tu caso, sino porque te va a alejar de mí" ("Am I addressing Mrs. Manolo Gálvez already? For me, you will always be Delfina Bunge. I have been thinking about you often and I'm sorry for not being in Buenos Aires. Did you get married? It makes me sad; forgive me. Marriage seems like such a frightening thing! Still, it is not for *that* reason that I'm sad in your case, but because you are going to distance yourself from me"; Ocampo 137, emphasis in the original). This is how Victoria Ocampo begins a letter she sent to Delfina Bunge from Biarritz, France, dated April 24, 1910. Ocampo's two-part reaction is remarkable. On the one hand, she expresses a sense of disappointment in Delfina's news, and on the other, she justifies her sentiment by claiming that the marriage will leave Delfina with less time and interest in maintaining her friendship with Ocampo. This would prove to be the case, as their correspondence would dwindle in the following years and cease in 1912. Ocampo, however, is sensitive to the monumental weight still invested in marriage in the early twentieth century. Her description of it as "frightening" was not an isolated opinion. As we have already seen, Delfina's doubts about marriage focused on the limitations it placed on a woman's independence. Ocampo intuits that Delfina's resistance to marriage has been dropped rather precipitously, and that even for a woman as fervently interested in maintaining her "freedom" as Delfina was, her marriage would quickly alter how she operated socially.

In a diary entry dated April 1912, two years after her marriage to Gálvez, Delfina would write the following:

> Me preguntaba Victorita [Ocampo] si se perdía mucho de su libertad en el matrimonio. Yo le hablé largamente. ¿Bien o mal? No lo sé. El resumen de mi idea era éste:

> Si te refieres a la independencia de tus horas y decisiones, mucho más es la que ganas que la que pierdes. A pesar de las nuevas obligaciones que pueden llegarte tú arreglas tu vida como mejor te parece. Sales sola y mil ataduras que de niña te ataban por todos lados, hasta en tus acciones más insignificantes, se rompen como por encanto. Pero en cambio, créeme Victorita, de la libertad de tu espíritu, de tus alas ... pierdes infinitamente. Se me ocurre una comparación. Si fueras paloma, mientras fueses "niña" las alas te servirían para volar. Una vez casada, y más si tienes hijos, las alas te servirían no ya para volar sino para dar calor. Para abrigar con ellas....

> Little Victoria [Ocampo] asked me if one lost much of one's freedom in marriage. I spoke with her at length. Good or bad? I don't know. The summary of my idea was this:

> If you are referring to the freedom of your time and decisions, you gain much more than you lose. In spite of the new obligations that could come your way you arrange your life as you see best. You go out by yourself and the thousands of bonds that as a child bound you on all sides, even in your most insignificant actions, are broken as if by enchantment. But in contrast, believe me Little Victoria, your freedom of spirit, of your wings ... you lose infinitely. I am thinking of a comparison. If you were a dove, while you were a "child" your wings would serve you to fly. Once married, and

> even more so if you have children, your wings would no longer serve you to fly but rather to provide warmth. To keep others warm.... (L. Gálvez, *Delfina* 253)

It is likely that Victoria Ocampo was asking Delfina for advice regarding her impending marriage to Bernardo de Estrada, a tumultuous relationship that would end in the couple's separation in 1920. The main question, however, remains the same: Can a woman remain independent after marriage? It was a question that seriously affected Delfina's decision to marry Gálvez, and one that Ocampo was also keenly interested in debating. Although Delfina begins her answer somewhat ambivalently, she concludes with a rather predictable metaphor, the dove.

With its resonances in Christian thought, here the dove refers to two specific types of freedom: that of movement through space, and that of the spirit. On the one hand, Delfina argues that the freedom afforded to a married woman to circulate freely is greater than that of a "*niña*"; the binds, "*ataduras*," imposed by parents or by social pressures are undone. On the other hand, however, in this diary entry, written two years after her own marriage, Delfina references a spiritual impasse, or rather an inability to continue to develop her own sense of spirituality. Instead, the wings, formerly the instrument of flight/freedom must be redeployed to provide warmth and to protect children from harm. The same faculties that would have proven indispensable for the intellectual independence and the social development of the young woman are instead used toward the fulfillment of her duties as a mother. In this way marriage, and in particular motherhood, is not equated with the limitation of women's movement through space, but rather with the stunting of her spiritual growth.

While Delfina would continue to contemplate women's freedom and Catholic duty in the pages of her diary and in her public writing, Julia concludes her first published volume with the following lines:

> Dentro de unos días regresaremos a nuestra Patria. Vamos a vivir en Rosario, pasando temporadas en el campo.
>
> Sí, mi marido es estanciero, tal cual yo lo deseaba.
>
> Diré que he podido comprobar, que Ignacio es bueno, generoso, noble, leal, alegre, y que tiene gran entusiasmo por su trabajo.
>
> ¿No es éste un cuento de Hadas?
>
> Un cuento de Hadas, en una "Época maravillosa."

> In a few days we will return home to our Homeland. We are going to live in Rosario, spending periods in the country.
>
> Yes, my husband is a landowner, just as I wanted.
>
> I will say that I have been able to verify, that Ignacio is good, generous, noble, loyal, happy, and that he is enthusiastic about his work.
>
> Is this not a Fairy Tale?
>
> A Fairy Tale in a "Marvellous Epoch." (527)

After their yearlong honeymoon, she and Ignacio return to Argentina in order to establish their home in the city of Rosario, where Ignacio will continue to administer his family's estate. A year on, Julia does not seem to feel the same type of spiritual numbness as Delfina regarding the institution of marriage. Rather, this final question is illustrative not only of Julia's view of herself as part of a romantic "fairy tale," but also of the value placed on marrying someone of Ignacio's particular background and social standing. Although Julia describes herself as having always wanted to marry an *estanciero*, her earlier writing shows her to have been much less sure about the type of man that she would like to marry. Her life as a "niña de sociedad" in this "época maravillosa" ends with a return to the system of complimentary marriages through which the members of the upper class consolidate political and economic capital. It is, in this sense, a retrenchment of the status quo. These questions of publicity and privacy were central to the diaries of Julia and Delfina Bunge, and to their function as technologies of self, but they are not the only venue that the sisters had at their disposal to assert a particular, and peculiar, stance in society. In the following chapter I turn to a second technology, the photograph, through which the Bunge siblings cultivated a desirable public image, and yet, too, a queer familiarity through the pages of the family album.

CHAPTER THRee

# SPECTRAL DESIRES
## QUEERING THE FAMILY ALBUM

Figuras infantiles, en serie. Vestidas, cada una con un determinado traje de fantasía. Cada una ostenta, en una mano, un juguete determinado; en la otra un determinado instrumento de música. El brillo, el prestigio del traje, del instrumento, del juguete, realzando y completando la figura. He ahí cómo se me representa nuestra múltiple infancia: la mía entre la de mis hermanos.

Infantile figures, in series. Dressed, each one with a particular costume. Each one bears, in one hand, a particular toy; in the other hand a particular musical instrument. The shine, the prestige of the costume, of the instrument, of the toy, complementing and completing the figure. This is how our multiple infancy is presented to me: mine among that of my siblings. (D. Bunge *Viaje* 9)

These are the opening lines of Delfina Bunge's memoir, *Viaje alrededor de mi infancia* ("A Trip around My Childhood," 1938). The narrator pauses to contemplate each "infantile figure," each sibling, identified by the objects that mark them as particular: the toy, the instrument, the costume, tokens of individuation that signal the unique personality of each child. The autobiographical narrator, at a distance of more than fifty years, recalls her siblings as different from her and each other, a difference that is produced by their dress and iconography. Delfina's first memory is of herself as part of a generation of siblings presented and described as "serial." And yet, the vignette is also a composite, "our multiple infancy," in which the self is described in relation to others. The individual interfaces the collective.

Memory fixes the location of the narrator, who witnesses and registers each sibling as they pass before her. She dramatizes the idea of experiencing childhood as a place lost in time, a place to which one can travel through memory, "se me representaba" ("as they were presented to me"), shifting to the passive voice, channeling these memories. For Delfina, the genre of the memoir depends on the representational quality that photography provides—or seems to provide. This series of images links the reality of those bodies—their having been there—to the less stable referential quality of the memories and words Delfina has to describe them.

When I first read this passage, I could not help but feel that somehow I recognized it. Perhaps its staging was, like many family memories, recognizable for its formulaic arrangement of bodies in relation. Years later, however, I realized that a photograph of these serial siblings does actually exist as part of the Bunge family archive. I had seen it before. At least I thought I had. The photograph in question was taken around 1885 and depicts Delfina's sister, Julia, as a free-spirited gypsy, couched modestly in the arms of their oldest brother, Carlos Octavio, as a heroically national hussar (the image is labeled "Gitana y húsar" in the family album). In truth, the photograph does not exactly coincide with the memory that Delfina describes in *Viaje alrededor de mi infancia*. But I am still struck by how the two images dialogue, and have often wondered which came first, the photograph or the memory. Or rather, how this imagery of kinship links the fragmentary structure of memoir invariably to the representational and temporal complexity of photography.

In the previous chapter I demonstrated that the diary is a heteroglossic form that stages a process of mutual subjective emplotment and which constructs sisterhood as a recognizable form of relation. In this chapter, I argue that the family album is an archive that does not simply document kinship and class, place and relation, but reveals—in fact depends on—the contradictions of photography as a technology of self. I take the Bunge family album as an archive for interrogating the juncture of privacy and publicity, temporality, and queerness in Argentina at the turn of the century. Put concisely, the Bunge family album records key moments of self-fashioning that mobilize disciplinary logics of representation while simultaneously pushing the limits of display, intimacy, and kinship. Thus, the image of a brother and sister embracing does not simply transpose kinship onto the pages of the family album, but rather constitutes a dynamic site of interrogation, a site where discourses of representation, cultural nationalism, and modernity intersect.

By 1900 the camera had become an indispensable possession for the elite, a tool that served to record familial relations and document the existence of bodies that were related, but also to visually construct relationships between family members in the present and in the future. To this day the camera serves to create a past and to promise a future. Like the diary, the family album entertains an iterative chain of future publics, future viewers, who will also have the ability to relate themselves to their past family members through this archive. It is both a technology of past-making and of iterative futurity.

As a genre, the family album is a cultural artifact that preserves kinship relations for posterity. It reassures the viewer of the continuation of genealogy, a history that is marked by class, nationality, race, and tradition. Typically consumed within the space of the home, among family members or other intimate relations, the viewer of the family album knows that they belong to the history that it represents. For Susan Sontag, the family album is a site of testimony: "Through photographs, each family constructs a portrait-chronicle of itself—a portable kit of images that bears witness to its connectedness" (8). The images of the family album form an architecture of relationality in which the boundaries between public and private, self and other, become constituted, but also blurred. This is particularly salient in moments of crisis, when the family unit is seen as threatened (by immigration, politics, economic decline, etc.). Photography, Sontag continues, "came along to memorialize, to restate symbolically, the imperiled continuity and vanishing extendedness of family life" (9). The family album is not devoid of political value. On the contrary, it evidences the contradictions caused by the shifting terrain of kinship, style, publicity, and modernity in a period of ideological uncertainty. The fear that inspired positivist scientists to analyze and attempt to eliminate sexual deviance and ethnic degeneracy and which led naturalist novelists to warn against class inversion and familial decadence, also found its way onto the pages of the seemingly private family album. As a site of subject formation and a collective archive of kinship regimes, it is an indispensible, though seldom studied, expression of the ideologies of family, class, and nation.[1] The family album is an intimate disciplinary site, as well as a site of disciplining intimacy, gender, race, and class.

Scholars of nineteenth-century photographic history tend to give primacy to the medium's circulation and reproduction.[2] For example, the work of Sontag, Walter Benjamin, and Roland Barthes, while certainly diverse in method and form, has marked the analysis of photography as invested in the image as a sign capable of bearing multiple meanings, many times contradictory. Continuing and condensing this line of thinking for the specific case of the family album, Marianne Hirsch argues that

> [p]hotography's social functions are integrally tied to the ideology of the modern family. The family photo both displays the cohesion of the family and is an instrument of its togetherness; it both chronicles family rituals and constitutes a prime objective of those rituals. Because the photograph gives the illusion of being a simple transcription of the real, a trace touched directly by the event it records, it has the effect of naturalizing cultural practices and of disguising their stereotyped and coded characteristics. As photography immobilizes the flow of family life into a series of snapshots, it perpetuates familial myths while seeming merely to record actual moments in family history. (7)

This interplay between what is seen and what remains unseen, what is expressed by the image and what the image does to codify reality, its relation with mimetic representation, is central to understanding the family album as a site of contradiction. The album itself can collude with hegemonic narratives of family, it can reinstate kinship as always essential to photography, as it can also serve to question what family relations are possible as expression and as memory (and as expressed by memory). The family photograph indexes kinship relations, as it also provides space for individual expression, the divergence from norms, and change over time. Perhaps this is the effect that led Delfina Bunge to narrate her own memories as a photographic series. It is the effect of perpetuating a logic of familial relationality that fixes bodies in time and space, producing rather than simply recording the bonds that constitute the modern family. She sees herself in memory as related, and narrates that relation as if it were photographic. And yet, the album itself—the material object—exposes the constructed nature of kinship as memorialized, and in doing so marks the narration of self (in the third person) as an attempt to reconcile the past with the present, the constitutive temporal gap on which the album depends. The album serves to perpetuate the logic of genealogical relation as constructed while the memoir reveals the process of recognizing the self as related through memory.

Expanding on the work of Barthes and Benjamin, Hirsch defines the familial gaze as an ideological framework, an identifiable set of cultural norms that influence the formal qualities of the photographic archive. It is a projection of idealized relationships that the camera records through the practice of photography. Every culture has its own "familial gaze," Hirsch notes, which "situates human subjects in the ideology, the mythology, of the family as institution and projects a screen of familial myths between camera and subject" (11). The norms of a particular culture intervene in the family photograph—this is what Hirsch calls a screen—which allows the subjects of the photograph to be recognizable as part of a given kinship ideology. A father who oversees his children; a mother who holds her daughter stoically in her lap; children arranged to give the appearance of care and intimacy, or genealogical succession, these stock poses mark the conventions of photographic representation as owing to the ideology of normative kinship. Thus, the familial gaze is not a particular, individual look between subjects, but rather an overarching cultural system that gives the family album meaning. The familial look, on the other hand, does negotiate individual relations. The looks that family members exchange, Hirsch clarifies, "are local and contingent; they are mutual and reversible; they are traversed by desire and defined by lack" (11). In other words, in looking at a family photograph the subject (who looks) is also seen by the object (who looks back from the photograph itself). In fact, I open this book with such a moment: the case of the family photographs that Delfina Tiscornia looks at and also feels herself as being seen by her relatives whose expression she recognizes as like her own. This is the luminous, phantasmatic recognition of kinship that the family look enables. Hirsh notes, "Within the family, as I look I am always also looked at, seen, scrutinized, surveyed, monitored. Familial subjectivity is constructed relationally, and in these relations I am always both self and other(ed), both speaking and looking subject and spoken and looked at object: I am subjected and objectified" (9). This leads Hirsch to conclude that the familial look is "an engagement in a particular form of relationship, mutually constitutive, mediated by the familial gaze, but exceeding it through its subjective contingency" (11). In summary, the familial gaze is an ideological structure that influences the family photograph's repertoire of stock poses and

framing conventions—which can also be challenged or undermined—
while the familial look is where affective relations between family members
are glimpsed as mutual recognition, but also where the eyes can reveal
something that exceeds convention, time, or place. The interplay between
the familial gaze—an ideological construct, and the familial look—an
affective charge, is central to my analysis of the Bunge family album. But
it is important to note, finally, that as an outsider I do not have access to
the familial look as defined by Hirsch. I cannot look as Delfina Tiscornia
looks at a portrait of her great grandmother, and feel as though she, Delfina
Bunge, may also recognize me in return. Rather, I necessarily interpret
these images as holding familial feelings, contradictions, and histories as a
researcher with a particular point of view and context.

In what follows, I explore the dynamics of representation that expose
the familial gaze as a construct that disciplines bodies and affects through
poses that, nevertheless, often exceed, or fail to conform to this normative
ideology. I analyze photographs from the Bunge archive, examples of the
juncture of the gaze and the look, which can serve to elaborate a mode of
reading the family album queerly. By queerness here I am referring to an
excess of representation, a contradictory feeling of belonging, a yearning
for recognition in the eyes of another, which the family album makes possible. As with other chapters in this book, the archive that I study does not
present queerness as a form of epistemological resistance. Likewise, the
queerness of the Bunge family album is not found in a dissident expression
of gender or sexual identity. At times, the pose and the expression of the
subject seem at odds with the context of the photograph, but none of these
images marks a position clearly outside the normative family ideology.
Rather, the album's queerness can be glimpsed in its silences and absences,
in its shadows, in how it frames the contradictory operations of identification and disavowal of kinship relations, dispositions, and feelings. That is,
the queerness of the family album is not found in making evident normative or nonnormative expressions or poses, but rather in the ontological
proximities that it relies on to make sense as a family document, and in the
selective historicity that it demands. This queerness depends on linking the
history accrued by these images to the context in which they are situated;
on framing the family as an ideological construct that simultaneously
exceeds its narrative and temporal boundaries.

I want to be clear on this point. I read the Bunge family album not just
as a documentary object that fixes people in time and space, but as an

archive that at once legitimizes and calls into question normative kinship relations; a technology that reveals glances, looks, and crucially, bodily relations that complicate normative understandings of desire. I am particularly interested in how the staging of intimacy in the family album engages a range of queer affective dispositions that can be mapped onto the cultural function of the image as a material object that circulates at the turn of the century. The family album is not a queer object in and of itself. It is not an artifact that necessarily represents queerness either. On the contrary, as ample scholarship demonstrates, the album is a normative dispositive that aims at disciplining familiar relationships within a conservative bourgeois framework.[3] The family photograph is a modern expression of patriarchal authority and the family album is both its archive and its inspiration. As such, the album serves to maintain patrimony and lineage; it registers hierarchical positions in proximity to and distance from sites of power; it casts women as domestic angels (the *ángel del hogar*) and passive interlocutors; it racializes bodies and partitions spheres of influence and access.[4] However, in my critical reading of the family album, I linger on the details that expose the fractures of this disciplining project. I hone in on the moments when the pose does not quite manage to embody or represent what it should, failures of gesture that leave a residual sense of unresolved or not-yet-mastered normativity. I analyze the interface of the logics of normativity and corporal enactments that lay bare normativity's incompleteness. But in order to speak to the process of regulating bodies and desires that the album enacts, I have to insert myself as a researcher—at a distance and with the advantage of history—into the series of gazes and looks that the album contains. My reading shows that the photographic subjects themselves exceed the system of representation available to them, a system that instantiates the hegemonic value of the image for maintaining class, gender, and ethnic subjectivity. The images are not evidence of a queer subjectivity per se, but rather of the ways in which subjective embodiment strains to adhere to the hegemonic system. The dissident value of the gestural repertoire lies in its exceeding the norm, and this excess is what I interpret as queer.

For example, the image I thought I recognized from Delfina's memoir, "Gitana y húsar," juxtaposes the present of the photograph in which the siblings awkwardly embrace with the historical resonance of the costumes that they wear, on the one hand, and on the other, the future of their embodiment of the gendered norms to which they seem destined in this photograph. Carlos Octavio's costume is an attempt to trap him in (to trap him with?) the cultural value of the military man in Argentina. In fact, the hussar is a key referent in the mimetic process of sexualization with unmistakable resonance for the movements of Latin American independence. A fearsome cavalry soldier prone to reckless and spectacular advances, the hussar is a womanizer and maverick, a man of erotic excess, an unpredictable and debonair swashbuckler. In Argentina, the *Húsares de Pueyrredón* was the country's first official military regiment, formed to combat the British invasion of 1806-1807.[5] But, as I describe in chapter 1, Carlos Octavio would have tortured relationship with the martial masculinity that he is assigned here. That is, this uniform and this photograph presage a queer fascination with the military that Carlos Octavio would not only feel in the flesh—and feel to the point of crisis—but also, as I argue in chapter 4, prescribe as necessary for all young men in his textbook *Nuestra Patria*. The future of Carlos Octavio's masculinity weighs on this image, even if in the present of the photograph, he has no inclination of that future. The masculine prowess of the hussar appears to burden Carlos Octavio from the future, and for her part, the stereotypical exoticism of the gypsy seems to weigh on Julia. The gypsy signifies a nostalgic yearning for a lost, preindustrial, life, but is also a figure of sexual promiscuity, ethnic ambiguity, and often, a fatal attraction for European men (Charnon-Deutsch 239). "Gitana y húsar" is certainly not meant to evoke these semiotic resonances. In this image the familial gaze forecasts these children as destined to a normative enactment of sexuality, gender, and class belonging. But even if the exacerbated sexuality of these figures is mitigated by the children's age, it is important to note how this image codes gender and filial attachment as part of a dialogue with romantic love *that must not be seen* in order for the image to be read as familial. They must not be linked to the salaciousness of the gypsy or the philandering of the hussar so that this image can be read through the familial gaze as one of fraternal, rather than romantic love.

The pairing of masculine and feminine was a common trope in family portraiture, and here should signify their complementarity as siblings according to a familial ideology. The photograph marks both siblings as destined for a normatively gendered future by disavowing an excessive, exoticized past that is tamed through the refined preciousness of their costumes and their age. This is an image of childhood that references erotic excess while simultaneously denying that erotic history. The pose of siblings embracing must necessarily not be read as erotic. This tension is what I am referring to when I argue that the Bunge family archive alternates between normative representations of self that uphold traditional gender roles, and a visual grammar that also calls into question how that normativity comes to exist as such. The queerness of the image lies not in the framing or the subject matter, but rather in the pose of normativity, and in how the photograph itself has both a history and a future that impinges on the present that is recorded.

## THE PORTRAITURE OF THE BUNGE FAMILY

Before continuing, it may be useful to provide a bit of context regarding the introduction and expansion of photography in Argentina. The first daguerreotypes taken in the River Plate region date to 1840. Louis Compte, a French priest, took several landscape images of Montevideo, while American John Elliot opened the first portraiture studio in Buenos Aires in 1843 (Cuarterolo 17-18). While in the mid-nineteenth century these technologies were the exclusive domain of the elite, at the turn of the century, technological advances and cheaper materials made photography available to a wider range of the population. Amateurs, such as the members of the Sociedad Fotográfica Argentina de Aficionados (Argentine Photographic Society of Amateurs), founded in 1889, diversified the subjects of photography, its location, and its circulation (Priamo 277-78). Historian Luis Priamo argues that there are three types of images that have been used to articulate photography and private life in Argentina: (1) "retratos de studio" ("studio portraits"), (2) photographs taken "fuera del studio del fotógrafo" ("outside the photographer's studio"), and (3) "fotos de costumbres" ("photographs of local types and scenes") (270-71). The Bunge family archive that I am concerned with in this chapter is evidence of this expanded use of photography at the turn of the century.[6] In this chapter I focus on two types of images described by Priamo: the studio portrait, specifically the *carte de visite* (*tarjetas de visita* in Spanish) and a series of semistaged photographs taken in and around the Sierras Hotel and Casino in Alta Gracia, Córdoba. The former links the expression of an individual self as part of the social life of the elite, the self among the collective, the self traded, shared, as part of the upper class; the latter represents the collective, in this case the family, in relation and in private. In this, these images starkly contrast with another popular if controversial subject of photography at the turn of the century: the masses. As Graciela Mondaldo has shown, the visualization of the popular classes, the conglomerated, indistinguishable masses, served to heighten upper-class anxieties about shifting power structures in Argentina at the turn of the century. As she writes, "Mass and multitude are consolidated, in the discourse of modernization, as the reprehensible face of the excluded, remnant of a barbarian past that unfortunately persists in modern times and which, as such serves to impede or stem progress" ("Mass and Multitude" 220). If the multitude is a remnant of an unmodern past, the individual is the promise of a prosperous, modern future. Thus, it is worth keeping in mind that the Bunge family album demonstrates a will to individuality that stands in the face of the seeming omnipresence of popular dissent, amalgamation, and indistinguishability. To distinguish oneself through family photography, as I argue below, is also to reject the visual and political economy of the massification of the Argentine public sphere. Thus, once more, the political value of the family album.

As I note in the Introduction, I am referring to digitized images of a physically bound album, part of an archive kept by Delfina Bunge and later Lucía Gálvez. I will only add here that the album contains at least one hundred photographs, typically arranged in pairs or groups of four to a page. I analyze a small portion of these images, and I am rearranging them into thematic groups in order to compare their gestural repertoires. First, I turn to the studio portraits and *cartes de visite* of the Bunge family archive. The composition of these images varies little, upholding, for the most part, the formal demands of the genre. Still, the range of contexts and framing, the diversity of the familial gaze that these images offer, allows for a sustained critique of the self-in-relation. The individual portraits, as part of the family album, come to represent a familial tradition, marking specific moments, personalities, and iconographies, which all serve to position the Bunge family as part of the elite. In the context of the first decade of the twentieth century, these images register the modernity of the Bunge family through their use of pose and style, as they solidify their belonging to the upper class. And yet, many of these images also speak to the impossibility of belonging, to the contradictions of the normative family, to a yearning for a different sense of self than that demanded by the Bunge name.

## CIRCULATING DESIRE: CARLOS OCTAVIO BUNGE

In 1899 Carlos Octavio Bunge traveled to England, where he was researching what would become his monograph, *El espíritu de la educación*, which had been commissioned by the municipal government of Buenos Aires. In addition to experiencing homosocial "romantical friendships" for the first time (see chapter 1), he would write to his mother "Casi me estoy haciendo *fashionable*" ("I am almost becoming *fashionable*"; cited in Cárdenas and Payá *Familia* 329). To document his sartorial success Bunge had two portraits commissioned while in England: one at Oxford (fig. 3.1) and one in London (fig. 3.2). These images function not only as a record of Bunge's physical presence in Europe, but also as an expression of his desire to be remembered by the people he met there. Both images situate Bunge's body in time and space, and at the service of the nation. And yet, they also reveal the burden of his difference as a Latin American traveler abroad. I read these studio portraits in conjunction with contemporary caricatures of Carlos Octavio in order to underscore his problematic *pose* as a public intellectual at the turn of the century. His body becomes a locus through which erotic excess is at once made visible and through which it must be suppressed; his circulation in Europe depends on a performance of class, masculinity, and white superiority. In this, Bunge's body is at the service of the Nation seeking modernity, seeking recognition as modern. But he must maneuver the thin line connecting queerness and modernity, hearkening the excess of homoerotic attachments and the embodied difference of his self-figuration, in order to be seen and remembered. His service to the nation requires his circulation as a queer figure. His queerness, in turn, becomes a feature of the nation that he serves.

The Oxford portrait reveals Carlos Octavio in morning dress. He wears a high starched collar, wide-lapelled waistcoat, ascot tie, pinstriped gray trousers, and black boots with spatterdashes. With black leather gloves, he grasps a walking cane while his top hat sits to the side resting on a stack of books. He is clean-shaven and his short hair is parted slightly off-center. Glancing to the camera's right, his pose is awkward, *almost* casual; his expression, *almost* bewildered. A palm frond extends upward from the cloth backdrop, perhaps an unwitting symbol of his exoticism. *Almost* modern. His eyes affect a vulnerability that marks the occasion: a South American traveler in Europe. In this image we recognize a process

FIGURE 3.1
Carlos Octavio
Bunge at Oxford.
Bunge Family
Archive (Courtesy
of Lucía Gálvez).

of symbolizing the photographic subject as modern through his use of costume and pose. He is dressed formally, but his pose, half-seated, intends to appear informal. In this case, he has styled himself as a turn-of-the-century cosmopolitan gentleman, one familiar with the *almost* disinterested gesture, one comfortable with leisurely nonchalance. In this calculated spontaneity we sense the tension between his dress and his expression. He is recognizably posing in this picture, shoulders too tense, neck too straight, betraying a certain insecurity with himself, and with the role he is aiming to play. *Almost* demure. *Almost* fashionable.

In London, Bunge poses reading a newspaper, seated in a tasseled chair. This portrait is one of iconographic significance. His pinstriped double-breasted suit and matching four-in-hand tie were new purchases

FIGURE 3.2
Carlos Octavio Bunge
in London. Bunge Family
Archive (Courtesy of
Lucía Gálvez).

in England, while the baby's breath boutonniere disrupts the linear motif of the subject's dress. It is *almost* too large for his lapel. Carlos Octavio appears in the center of the frame, angled toward the soft, artificial light. The generic studio backdrop heightens the subject's presence, while his pose has more weight than in the previous image. Here, he is reading the newspaper, connecting himself to European affairs, to the now, to modernity. A noticeable difference in this image is the fact that he has grown a moustache. Less boyish and more in line with the aesthetic of the masculine gentleman, Bunge's London portrait shows a desire to appear more mature that would continue in his later portraiture.

Taken together, these portraits inaugurate a conscientious project of photographic self-representation aimed at connecting Bunge to the interlocutors he met in Europe. As he would write to his mother, upon receiving an invitation from Oxford's New College to attend a banquet held in his honor, Bunge hastily sent for a dozen photographs to be printed in London and delivered to him so that he could distribute them as souvenirs (Cárdenas and Payá *Familia* 330). (He must have had the London portrait made before traveling to Oxford, which might explain some of the stiffness that it reveals.) He realizes that he cannot circulate in Europe's social circles without a *carte de visite*, and endeavors to introduce himself as cosmopolitan, intellectual, and modern. The material resonance of these photographs marks his body as both a public and private good, simultaneously at the service of the Argentine state in 1899—a body to be displayed as representative of that service and that country—and circulating as evidence of those ephemeral "romantical friendships." His photographs are charged with a prefigured nostalgia, perhaps a longing for rejoinder. These *cartes de visite* memorialize the subject as a cosmopolitan traveler, meant to register the presence of a man who is about to be absent. They represent him as having been part of their social milieu, but also as having left it. I am not sure whom Bunge chose to receive these portraits, or into whose archive they came to reside. It is certainly possible that for his "romantical friendships" the images might serve as a reminder of a particular conversation, or a feeling, a sense of shared interest or common understanding. And yet, in both of these images we see a pose of studied distance. Bunge affects a pose that, for some (perhaps) was meant to signify not distance, but proximity. These portraits stage a future longing for his presence by those who receive them as objects, material evidence of his absent presence. In contrast with women's *carte de visite*, in which longing was a central feature and prominent visual trope, Bunge's contradictory presence—at once revealing a studied nonchalance and a yearning to be remembered—speaks to the ways in which his own masculinity was bound to the instability of class and ethnic identification. Bunge's self-figuration in the Oxford and London portraits depends on him performing as "fashionable" for a European audience. He wants to be accepted and remembered by those interlocutors. As a Latin American traveler in Europe, however, he can only approximate modernity. He is only ever *almost* fashionable.

The resonance of Bunge's body in England is contradictory, revealing his desire to be desired and his willingness to extend the reach of Argentina abroad. In subsequent studio portraits Carlos Octavio would strive to maintain the staged dignity initiated by the Oxford and London photographs. For example, a portrait likely taken between 1905 and 1908 is labeled in print at the bottom of the image "Dr. C. O. Bunge," marking it deliberately as *professional*. The subject appears in profile. Soft light illuminates his forehead, accentuating his mustache and dimpled chin. His shoulder and lapel appear out of focus, contrasting the sharp line of sight that leads out of frame. He seems hypnotized in this image, as if transfixed by the performance of his own introspection. Formally, this image resonates with the documentary tradition in Latin America at the turn of the century by which national and regional "types" were classified according to ethnic categories.[7] Here, the profile of a white upper-class man contrasts the profiles of Indians, Blacks, criminals, sexual deviants, and the mentally deranged as types of the modern era. Bunge's profile shot engages the taxonomic drive to register human difference, a form of differentiation that was at the heart of his own ethnocentric social science and which hearkens to mid-century eugenic photography such as that of Louis Agassiz and Francis Galton. In addition, Bunge registers himself as not simply professional, but as a *pensador*, a thinker, a man of intellect, and in doing so he must convert his image into an object of exchange that garners both fascination and respect. From this profile we see that his moustache plays a prominent role in this portrait, a symbol of his age and masculinity. The portrait begs the recipients of this *carte de visite* to hold him in their hands, to study him, his countenance, his race, his thoughts. It asks recipients to imagine along with him that point beyond the frame, that horizon of futurity. To join his gaze toward a yet-to-be perfected Argentina. There is a collective promise in this image, one that positions Bunge as emblematic of the dignified past that the elite should protect and the hopeful future to which they should aspire. It is an image that, even if it circulates within the family (up to the present day) as a record of Bunge's national significance, it is destined, constructed, for use outside of it. It is an image that is meant to circulate as a record of Bunge's value as a public thinker.

In contrast with these commissioned portraits, artist renderings of the public figure offer a different perspective on the circulation of Bunge's presence. As I note in chapter 1, upon his return to Argentina, Carlos Octavio garnered a reputation as a new force in the intellectual community. In September of 1903 to commemorate the publication of his *Nuestra América*, the literary magazine *Ideas* published a caricature of him that was accompanied by the following short biographical caption:

—En la dualidad de las razas,—latino y germano, imaginación y pensamiento. Rico de cultura intelectual, posee las filosofías de los filósofos y la suya. Su obra capital, *El espíritu de la Educación*, ha traspasado las fronteras; y *Nuestra América* le acredita de sociólogo de nota. Leyéndole, piensa uno en los tiempos en que Sarmiento escribía sus libros y Alberdi sus tratados.

—In the duality of the races,—Latin and Germanic, imagination and thought. Rich in intellectual culture, he possesses the philosophies of the philosophers and his own. His principal work, *The Spirit of Education*, has traversed frontiers; and *Our America* proves him a notable sociologist. Reading him, one thinks of the times in which Sarmiento wrote his books and Alberdi his treatises. (54-55)

Here, Bunge is described as having "arrived" as a sociologist. While the comparison to Sarmiento and Alberdi may have been a bit premature, the sentiment of the caption positions Bunge as a man invested in a similar type of probing inquiry into the nature the Argentine people as that undertaken by the aforementioned statesmen. And yet, the text does not actually compare Bunge's work with that of Sarmiento and Alberdi, but rather the moment in which they intervened in the national discussions regarding the political and cultural organization of the country. The reference hearkens back to the bellicose politics that dominated the mid-nineteenth century. This connection paints the turn of the century with an urgent hue, one similar to that in which, as I note previously, national literature (and national essays) responded to the fractious political climate, and in particular the dictatorship of Juan Manuel de Rosas, that dominated mid-century. Bunge's inclusion in this genealogy is not gratuitous, however. He had conscientiously set out to position himself as an intellectual cut from the same cloth as Sarmiento and Alberdi, but one whose updated methods of inquiry—namely social psychology—allowed him greater insight into the shortcomings, challenges, and possibilities facing the population of Argentina and Latin America more broadly. The caption reflects this and marks him as possessing not just philosophical acumen but also, importantly, the ethnic/cultural admixture that was to dominate the intellectual legacy of the Argentine elite in the face of rapid immigration from Southern Europe.

However, the caricature tells a slightly different story than the text that accompanies it (fig. 3.3). The image is part of the series, "Galería de Intelectuales Contemporáneos" ("Gallery of Contemporary Intellectuals"),

FIGURE 3.3
Carlos Octavio Bunge
and "Nuestra América."
*Ideas*, "Galería de
Intelectuales
Contemporáneos,"
F. Barrantes Abascal,
September 1903.

which included figures such as Bartolomé Mitre, Miguel Cané, Ángel de Estrada, and José Ingenieros. The artist F. Barrantes Abascal portrays Bunge towering over an anthropomorphized continent, "Nuestra América," whose upward gaze and darting eyes, whose mouth, part agape, affect an insidiously sensuous relationship. Not unlike turn-of-the-century caricatures of Oscar Wilde, Bunge is marked as a dandy whose physical presence demands attention, too much attention.[8] His oversized bow tie, coifed hair, and punctilious mustache starkly contrast with his half-naked (and half-sized) companion. Bunge, we assume, is leading this orientalized Indian/continent into modernity, to knowledge of his own ethnic and sexual

SPECTRAL DESIRES — 153

backwardness, perhaps to his own extinction. As ever, modernity necessarily implies the extinction of the Indian, permanently fixed in the past. None of this is particularly surprising at the turn of the century in Argentina, where Spencerian eugenics informed both the cultural landscape and state politics. Though I will discuss *Nuestra América* in greater detail in chapter 5, it is worth noting here that Bunge identifies three defining characteristics of Indigenous populations in that work: *resignación* ("resignation"), *pasividad* ("passivity"), and *venganza* ("vengeance"). In Bunge's psychohistorical reading of Latin America, Indians are defined by their status as a fatalistic people destined for extinction or assimilation, yet they may also exhibit an exacerbated tendency toward violent retribution. The history of colonization of the Americas, according to Bunge, has led to the predominance of a eugenically determined psychic configuration in which all Indigenous peoples vacillate between an extreme fatalism and a desire for vengeance (*Nuestra América* 1926, 133).

Even if we consider the stylized satire that is implied by this image, as well as the accompanying text, I am interested in underscoring the curious gaze of this Indian, a gaze that lingers, longing for recognition by the man whose hand he grasps like a child seeking approval. In this caricature, perhaps against its own design, the desire for recognition with which the Indian is portrayed is concentrated in the power of that sensuous gaze. Is Bunge leading this Indian forward into modernity or is the Indian leading him backward to depravity, baseness, and savagery? The crossing glances juxtapose Bunge's gaze out toward an imaginary horizon, a futurity, with the Indian's direct fixation on his companion's body. I want to suggest that Barrantes Abascal invests this Indian with a type of illicit knowledge, his grin not of benign ignorance, but rather lascivious intent. If the viewer is meant to identify with Bunge as the subject of the caricature and the author of the book that it is promoting, then this process is achieved through the recognition of the Indian's gaze as inappropriate. The Indian must be queer, his gaze excessive in its lingering. This gaze must be rejected in order for the viewer to fully identify with the white criollo subject who is unmoved by the Indian's attentions. The Indian's look becomes not one of gratitude, but vengeance. The vengefulness that is at the heart of Bunge's portrayal of indigenous peoples in Latin America is heightened by the insidious subtlety with which the Indian may manipulate such a morally (and here graphically) upright man as Bunge. While it is clear that Barrantes Abascal portrays the Indian as unmodern, undesirable, and childlike, we can also see in his gaze something closer to irony than innocence—a looming, deviant knowledge of where he might take his master. This interpretation is bolstered by the image's portrayal of corporeal mobility. While Bunge's body does tower over the Indian, his feet are firmly planted. In contrast, the Indian, though grasping Bunge's hand, with his right foot slightly arched, appears the likelier of the two to be in motion. This image presents Bunge as oversized and stoic, yet also close, perhaps too close, to the queerness associated with the Indian in Latin America from the colonial period to today. If at first glance this image seems to depict the learned immobility of Bunge's countenance, on closer examination, it also—if not primarily—references the possibility that such a man (that any man) could be drawn perilously backward to degeneracy, lasciviousness, and passivity. It is precisely by insinuating the devious sexual advances of this Indian—the Indian as passive, indeed as a sodomite—that the audience is invited to reject the image, and thus agree with Bunge that they deserve to be eliminated.⁹

In another caricature, Bunge is seated alone smoking a cigarette (fig. 3.4). This drawing appears in the November 21, 1903 edition of *Caras y Caretas*, as part of its series "Caricaturas contemporáneas" ("Contemporary caricatures") and is signed by Cao (José María Cao Luaces [1862-1918]). Rather than visionary nobility, as might describe his portrayal in the previous example, here Cao highlights Bunge's smugness. Again dandified, Bunge is given a languid posture, his left hand folded into his coat pocket; his right, very nearly effete. In contrast with his London studio portrait (fig. 3.2) in which Bunge depicted himself reading, here, he is portrayed as idle. This, combined with an arched eyebrow and rather upturned nose reveals a man unimpressed, perhaps bored. He is drawn as aloof and detached, while his photographic portraiture endeavored to present him as a modern man of intellectual vigor. In this example, the caption is once again revealing: "En un día se escribe un libro entero. Es educacionista, crítico, historiador y novelista *y además es soltero*" ("In one day he writes an entire book. He is an educator, critic, historian and novelist, *and what's more he's single*"; n.p., my emphasis). The rhetorical strategy of this caption is to advertise not just the breadth of Bunge's intellectual production or the speed at which he works, but also his civil status: *single*. Once again, it is not his writing or his ideas that deserve special attention, but rather the way he occupies physical and cultural space at the turn of the century. He is a disruptive figure precisely because of his status as "single." His singleness reverberates, draws attention, glances, *and readers* from across the country. What

FIGURE 3.4
Carlos Octavio Bunge.
*Caras y Caretas*,
"Caricaturas contemporáneas," Cao,
November 21, 1903.

heightened interest does his civil status produce in the readers of *Caras y Caretas*? Curiously, we are once again faced with a Bunge family member stuck between the more popular publication, *Caras y Caretas*, and the literary magazine, *Ideas*. Rather than the "Caso Delfina" that I describe in chapter 2, in which Delfina was forbidden from appearing photographed in print in *Caras y Caretas*, the sensual visualization of Carlos Octavio, and, what is more, his advertisement as "available" for the entire country, is perhaps what the family feared for their precocious daughter. And yet, in this caricature Carlos Octavio is both available and aloof, verified as a *soltero* in the caption, but sensuously distant in the drawing. This tension reflects the contradictory place occupied by Carlos Octavio in the social scene of the elite. He should not be single, but he is.

In both caricatures he is marked as distant, but also excessive. *Ideas* portrays this distance as stoicism, while in *Caras y Caretas*, it appears as smugness. In both, this distance is envisioned by an artist who reflects back onto Bunge's body—the image of Bunge as an image—a way of understanding his circulation in the Argentine *fin de siglo*. I call attention to these depictions because they display (make visible) the ambivalence with which Bunge's body was felt at this time. He embodies an unstable mix of desire and distance, an object of fascination precisely because, at least in the eyes of these artists, he represents a stoic nobility that always verges on coming undone, that risks contamination, excess, queerness. There is a marked difference between these two illustrations and the *cartes de visite* studied earlier. These caricatures reveal how Bunge was perceived, rather than how he portrayed himself, at the turn of the century. These images, which do not find their way into the family album, circulate in public, as artistic representations of a man who wished to control his public image, but could only do so through the studio portraiture that he commissioned of himself. It is in this difference that we find the vulnerability of Bunge's circulation. By 1903 he had already garnered a reputation as larger than life. *Almost* available. *Almost* fashionable. *Almost* normal.

The final portrait of Carlos Octavio that I would like to discuss demonstrates the opposite effect: an image taken in public, but appreciated exclusively in private (fig. 3.5). Of all the images that I have been able to analyze, it is the most casual in pose and in dress. His moustache once again plays a prominent role in the composition, but more importantly, here his normally coiffed hair lets down a casual tendril. In contrast with his studio portraits, in which his hair was rigidly parted, glossy, and fixed with a wax or pomade, here we see his hair slightly out of place, as if he has been playing a sport (perhaps tennis) or riding a horse. This pose reads as real nonchalance, while the earlier portraits aimed at portraying such a disposition, and were not always successful. Despite his folded arms, the loose shape of his right hand suggests an openness, a gesture of comfort that is not seen in any of his staged photographs. His white turtleneck reflects the natural light and illuminates the frame as the wood panels behind him suggest that he is leaning against an outdoor structure or perhaps the deck of a boat. It is not a studio portrait, but a candid snapshot. And as such, it

FIGURE 3.5
Carlos Octavio
Bunge in casual dress.
Bunge Family Archive
(Courtesy of Lucía
Gálvez).

portrays a naturalness that is not found in any of his other photographs. Perhaps it reveals too much of the man whose status as *soltero*, whose dandified style, always marked him as queer. Probably taken between 1913 and 1915, it begs a series of questions, most important among them: who is taking this photograph? While I do not know the answer to that question, I find it important to underscore how this image manages to elicit a response in Bunge that none of his staged portraits could, or, for that matter, were even attempting to portray. Here, he is not posing at comfort, he is comfortable. What I find most striking is the sincerity of Bunge's gaze, which is arresting, magnetic, even tender. He does not address the camera lens, but the person who is taking the photograph. Indeed, I have often asked if the person taking this photograph was Bunge's lover, or partner, or "friend." Or perhaps this is what I, myself, project onto this image as a queer familial look, linking myself to this man who—I want to imagine—expresses affection toward the person taking his photograph.

A brief archival detour: when I was first doing research for this project I had the opportunity to meet and interview Ernesto Cárdenas, one of the foremost historians of the Bunge family. Perhaps in my youthful naivete, I asked him if he possessed or had seen any documentary evidence of

158 — ARGENTINE INTIMACIES

Bunge's purported homosexuality. I was curious—willful—and thought that if anyone had unearthed "concrete proof" it would have been him. Cárdenas replied that there were only rumors, speculation, gossip. *Tell me*, I implored. He had heard from a friend that once on a ferry from Buenos Aires to Montevideo, Carlos Octavio had been caught *in flagrante* with another man. I *gasped*. There was even a love letter improvised on the *boleto*, the boarding ticket, which has since been lost. The story continues that upon arrival in Uruguay, his companion, of lesser means, was arrested, while Carlos Octavio managed to escape the public embarrassment—indeed the criminal proceedings—that surely would have ensued. I have always been curious about this rumor. Curious not because of what it might represent for the history of homosexuality in Argentina, which is beside the point, but rather for what it adds to this particular image of Carlos Octavio Bunge. Did *he* take this photograph? Was this image taken on *that* ferry? I have wondered, too, *why* the photograph has remained in the Bunge family archive. Is it perhaps a subtle acknowledgment of Bunge's queerness? I like to think of this image as material evidence that Bunge's gaze found a recipient who returned the sense of tenderness that is expressed here. In the end, who took this image is not as important as the fact that it still exists in the pages of the family album. The affective register of Bunge's gaze circulates within the space of the family, a reminder not of the public dandy, but of his private candor. This gaze invites a queer identification with the person who inspired such a sincere expression of vulnerability in him. It places the viewer of this image in the position of the unknown photographer, asking us to imagine the affective charge of this particular moment, to sense what it might have been like to inspire in Bunge this quiet intensity.

While it may not be productive to answer definitively *who* took this image, it bears repeating that in the context of the archive of images that exist of Carlos Octavio Bunge, this is him at his most private, gazing softly at another person who captures something found nowhere else. This gesture of vulnerability circulates as part of the family album, perhaps as a memory of what might have been, what love might have existed for Carlos Octavio, a memory shared by the family in the space of the home where, perhaps, he never felt as loved as he did in this photograph. This image captures Bunge at his most intimate, but also records the scarcity of his intimacy. He lets himself be captured, exposed, just this once. His intimate life, revealed, by a photograph. Perhaps this gaze is a mask. Perhaps a closet. Perhaps it allows him to remember himself being gazed at by the photographer. On the one hand, this image reveals the contradictory circulation of Bunge's body, and on the other, evidences a moment of intimacy shared between two people, a moment fixed in time and space, in which this gaze, this longing, perhaps this love, is revealed to have existed. It asks the viewer to imagine the feeling of intimacy that would have been required for this gesture, and this image, to exist at all.

As we have seen, Carlos Octavio Bunge negotiated the demands of heteronormativity with a range of strategies of self-visualization. While the portraits he sat for aim to capture the stateliness required for a public intellectual at the turn of the century, contemporary caricatures express a sense of unease that resonated with the broader public. And yet, in a private portrait, his gaze simultaneously hides and reveals a yearning for intimacy at odds with his public persona.

## CONFLICTING PUBLICS: JULIA AND DELFINA BUNGE

The ambiguous record of intimacy and publicity would also find expression in the personal portraiture of Julia and Delfina Bunge. As daughters—*niñas*—of an elite family, they were pressured to participate in the social life of Buenos Aires at the turn of the century. This social life revolved around the fund-raisers, balls, church functions, *tertulias* (social or literary salons), *corsos* (carriage processions), theaters, and clubs, which constituted the place and sociality of the upper class. And the Bunge siblings were assiduous participants in this social life. As I show in chapter 2, the diaries document not only that the Bunge sisters recognized their place on a stage—through their transcription of the social chronicles of the elite—but also that they were actively engaged in cultivating a public presence in society. This social milieu, while allowing for a certain level of mobility, was ostensibly aimed at continuing the hegemony of the elite through marriage. It was a platform for courtship. To be—or to go out—in society was, if not overtly, implicitly about finding a suitable partner. We see this, too, in the diaries of both sisters. Particularly in the case of Delfina, she feels as if she is being shopped around—and she was not wrong in that. But the fact of the matter remains that both the diaries and, as I argue in this chapter, the family album, offer a counternarrative to this normative sociality, one that depends on reading the staging of self in the studio portraits and the relationality of family in the more spontaneous snapshots. Thus, my aim is not to read these images as transparent representations, but rather to seek out what affect, pose, and expression help us read the familial looks that they express as queer.

Julia, not surprisingly, would grow to appreciate the theatricality of her own public presence. A studio portrait from 1905 evidences her triumph at a benefit gala, where she won the prize for "Most Artistic Hairstyle" (fig. 3.6). The dress and coiffure imitate Sarah Bernhardt's role as Mélissinde in Edmon Rostand's *La Princesse lointaine* (fig. 3.7). Bernhardt: *the celebrity* of the turn of the century, playing an ethereal princess longing for love. Julia: the budding socialite, adopting Bernhardt's splendor. This type of imitation was part of a tradition of young women, *niñas*, who would have their portraits taken as famous actresses in the early part of the twentieth century (Facio 12-13). As we saw in chapter 2, the profession of actress was morally suspect for members of the elite, but this did not prevent young women from posing *in the style of* Bernhardt or other celebrities. In contrast with men's *cartes de visite*, women often posed as objects of adornment or sculptural beauty in keeping with the gendered norms that limited women's mobility. In 1913 Victoria Ocampo would have a portrait made by Leopold Reutlinger, one of the early masters of glamour photography, in his studio in Paris, which is quite similar to Julia's *Princesse Lointaine*. There Ocampo appears in a sumptuous gown, a fur draping over her shoulder, her right foot en pointe, marking a stark contrast with what is probably her most famous portrait, done in 1922 by surrealist Man Ray. It is this earlier tradition, however, of the cosmopolitan woman as identifiably glamorous that calls to Julia Bunge in 1905. This is a tradition based on accessing the iconography of celebrity, on demonstrating a woman's modernity by appealing to her individual artistry, to the splendor of the *fin de siglo*.

Julia's *Princesse Lointaine* is a creole copy of Sarah Bernhardt. By this I mean that she engages in a complex procedure of appropriation and excision that focuses on capturing the allure of the European's queerness (as modern), but also reinforcing the subject's traditional, criollo subjectivity. Julia wears a similarly shaped crown and dress. Bernhardt's diamonds are replaced by bauble pearls. The lilies adorning each side retain the same shape, though Julia's crown is softer, more flexible. Julia's dress is cut with a wider neckline, and includes sleeves be made of tulle. The key elements are all there, and yet Julia's gaze is just a bit off. It is more vulnerable, less sensual than Bernhardt's, whose slightly open mouth and upward gaze

FIGURE 3.6
Julia Valentina Bunge as Princesse Lointaine. Bunge Family Archive. (Courtesy of Lucía Gálvez).

offer a pose more cunningly available Julia's, who gazes rather outward, at a distance, her mouth closed, her chin slightly upturned. She seems somehow too serious, toning down Bernhardt's exuberance.

In fact, Julia would write an incisive diary entry about this portrait:

*Sábado 11* [Noviembre de 1905]: Me he retratado de Princesse Lointaine. Los retratos han salido lindísimos y artísticos. Uno, de frente, tiene la cabeza inclinada, con una expresión sumamente suave, triste, demasiado triste, muy romántico. Hay otro que no me gusta nada. Desgraciadamente es en el que estoy más parecida, esa es mi expresión, entre alegre, franca, vanidosa y arrogante. Me disgusta ese retrato, me hace sufrir. Mamá dice que no es chocante, que es una ridiculez de mi parte decir eso, que es también muy lindo.

Saturday 11 [November of 1905]: I have had my portrait taken as Princesse Lointaine. The pictures turned out very beautiful and artistic. One, face on, has my head inclined, with an expression that is extremely smooth, sad, too

FIGURE 3.7
Sarah Bernhardt in
*La Princesse lointaine.*
(Courtesy of Theatrical
Cabinet Photographs of
Women [TCS 2]. Harvard
Theatre Collection,
Houghton Library,
Harvard University).

sad, very romantic. There is another that I do not like at all. Sadly it is the one in which I am most like myself, that is my expression, between happy, frank, vain and arrogant. I do not like that portrait, it makes me suffer. Mom says that it is not distasteful, that it is ridiculous on my part to say that, that it is also very nice. (268)

Julia's reflection is illustrative not only of her determination to control her own image, but also of her self-reflexive attitude toward that image. Her consternation is not with the picture itself, but with how she wants it to express something that she can no longer control. The version that she prefers, however, she claims, does not quite manage to encapsulate the complexity of self that she is interested in circulating in public. She has an artistic vision of what she should look like, a look that should coincide with what she feels inside. But what can we take in her admission that the portrait and its expression, make her "suffer"? How are we to understand this angst?

Julia is reflecting on an image of her self that does not live up to the expectations of a *niña* in the social circles of the Porteño elite. She reflects on the internalized limits to self-expression. This is a boundary that she seems to be pushing with her arrogance and vanity. And yet, she also expresses an important quality of portraiture: it may reveal something about herself that she would prefer not to display. This tension between self-stylization and an artist's (photographer's) interpretation is crucial to understanding the function of the anxiety recorded by and about this *carte de visite*, which, as a genre demands that the self be displayed according to the conventions of gender, sexuality, class, and taste, but it can also display a self that pushes those boundaries of normative expression. In this, Julia's *Princesse Lointaine* is an example of the tension between harnessing queerness and suppressing its excess. If the genre of the portrait "alludes" to a subject who exists outside of the work itself (Brilliant 7), then the quality of expression that Julia views in herself—that expression that causes her disgust and pain—is the pain of recognition that as a photographic subject, she is no longer in control of her own image. Or perhaps the portrait has revealed something to her about herself that she would prefer not to face. The portrait is an allusion to Bernhardt that itself alludes to the psychic insecurities of the young woman's expression of self.

This creole copy is a form of "posing" at the turn of the century. As Sylvia Molloy describes, "posing in Latin America occurs (and becomes cause for concern) in a diversity of discourses, more precisely, in the intersection of those discourses, where the aesthetic, the political, the legal, and the medical converge" ("Politics" 142). As a cultural gesture of adoption and adaptation, of yearning for modernity in an era of conflicting political and aesthetic proposals, the pose is a bodily orientation that engages both the desire for recognition as modern and the fleeting gestural proximity between modernity and decadence. While Molloy and indeed the majority of Latin American cultural theorists have circumscribed the affects and effects of posing to male *modernista* writers in search of excess, but fearful of its repercussions, it is illustrative to think of Julia Bunge's *Princesse Lointaine* along these lines. In this particular case, it is as a celebrity that Julia is styling herself in Bernhardt's image. The image of herself as a European star is at once essential to her sense of belonging to the Porteño elite, and antithetical to her self-image as a chaste potential wife. She poses as a celebrity in order to imbue her portrait with that alluring quality of the ineffable that Bernhardt represents. As Sharon Marcus argues, "even as celebrity confects a fantasy about peerless, inimitable presence, it turns individuality into a tissue of citations, since not only are stars widely copied, they often present themselves as copies" (1003-4). To imitate the inimitable, in this case, is to confect a sense of uniqueness that heightens Julia's desirability, but not to excess, not in bad taste. To pose as Bernhardt is not simply to copy her style, but to summon from history what illusory resonance she creates with her body, her celebrity, in order that Julia might also approximate such an effect in others.

I should recall that Bernhardt is not just any celebrity. She pushes the boundaries of the feminine. She is essentially, primordially, excessive. William Acree describes Bernhardt's first tour of the River Plate region in 1886 as the spectacular culmination of hemispheric travel by exotic theater troupes, performers, and celebrities, whose function as "cultural intermediaries" served to connect local populations to artistic trends from Europe and the United States (6). It is useful to think of Bernhardt's presence in Argentina along these lines. She is certainly a figure who stands in for European modernity. More pointedly: European modernity *as queerness*. Bernhardt's fame was not based solely on feminine glamour, but gender transgression and sexual adventure. She was luminous in her "breeches roles" in *L'Aiglon* and *Hamlet*, in which she played the male lead (Cobrin 48). Bernhardt's transvestism in theatrical performance could not have been ignored. And this is part of what I imagine that Julia at once wants to embody and suppress. The titillating effect of performing as Bernhardt must have been part of Julia's design. And yet, this Princesse Lointaine seems to escape her grasp, take on a life of her own. The pose creates a fiction that lives on, outside of the subject.

In the context of the family album, this particular image can be indexed to Julia's diary, as we have seen, but it also points to a sharp distinction between the two sisters. Julia's self-imaging is much more bold and sensual. Excessive, yet only to an acceptable limit. She is pushing the boundaries of what can be presented as feminine. And she does so by attempting to contend with both the celebrity and queerness of Sarah Bernhardt, harnessing the actress's glow, while still conforming to the norms of the socialization of the elite. The pose of celebrity creates a new form of presence, an emanating modernity that is at once desirable and terrifying, painful, in the cultural milieu of the turn of the century.

Only a year earlier, in 1904, Delfina had been awarded honorable mention the literary competition sponsored by the Parisian magazine

FIGURE 3.8
Delfina Bunge. Bunge
Family Archive
(Courtesy of Lucía
Gálvez).

*Femina*, which precipitated what I call in chapter 2 "El caso Delfina." Delfina sought a different type of recognition. Not for her public figure, but her intelligence, her writing. In almost all of her portraiture, she recedes from the camera. She fades away (fig. 3.8).

While Julia sought the fantasy of European celebrity, Delfina's visual presence is more realist. Unlike Julia, Delfina's body bears no ornamentation. In this studio portrait she faces the camera, her hair parted, her mouth closed. This is a shy portrait, one accentuated by the photographic technique in which the whiteness of the frame seems to engulf her. Delfina's face almost floats, disembodied. The shadows of her cheeks and her neck, her eyes, give this image a sincerity that borders on sternness. She represents herself as pensive, withholding a part of herself that she seems to want to express, but cannot. In another studio portrait, probably taken at the same session, we see Delfina in an embroidered white dress, standing, grasping a bouquet (fig. 3.9). She gazes longingly downward at the small flowers. Her pose is reflexive, as if lost in thought, in the contemplation of such a fragile object. In Delfina's first portrait she poses in soft focus, and in the second she approaches the *costumbrista* type of elegant but reserved young woman. This introspection stands in stark contrast with Julia's audacious citational practice. Thus, while Julia was engaged

FIGURE 3.9
Delfina Bunge with bouquet. Bunge Family Archive (Courtesy of Lucía Gálvez).

in a deliberately artistic self-presentation, Delfina was much closer to the sincerity of realism in her own self-styling. But perhaps this introspective pose was not the only way Delfina saw herself, or how others saw her.

Delfina's *cuadernos-copia* include several textual representations of herself. However, as a palimpsest of archival material, one object stands out regarding her crafting of a visual presence (fig 3.10). It is an ink drawing of a woman in profile that has been paper-clipped to the diary. The drawing was made by Carlos Kier, son of Valentina Costa Isla and Sabiniano Kier, Argentina's Attorney General from 1892 to 1905. On February 17, 1901 Carlos Kier attended a carnival party organized by Julia Bunge and Stella Achával at the Hotel Edén in La Falda, Córdoba. Delfina would describe him in her diary as "grave, observador y reservado" ("serious, observant and reserved," L. Gálvez *Delfina* 100). The paper on which the drawing was made is in fact the reverse of the hotel letterhead on which the party's program of events is detailed. Festivities included and excursion on horseback, a series of parlor games, various raffles, races for children and adults, among other activities. Curiously, the diary entry on which the drawing is fastened is dated October 26, 1900, and thus precedes the events described on the letterhead and, presumably, the completion of the drawing. The diachronic nature of the diary surfaces again, as it is likely that Delfina had saved the drawing that was made in 1901, and in the process of copying her diary (an effort, as she notes at the end of the journal, which she was undertaking in December 1930), fastened it to this particular page, dated in 1900. This presents a simple question: why did Delfina choose to fasten the drawing there? The entry from October 26, 1900 details a ball that Julia attended with Carlos Octavio and their mother, Maria Luisa. Delfina did not join them, however, and missed a "marvelous" evening during which Julia met several Brazilian dignitaries (Journal IV, 1322). It may be coincidence, but I think it is more likely that this drawing by Carlos Kier illustrates something about Delfina that she would like to have displayed on that particular evening in October of 1900.

This portrait is certainly *of* Delfina, and in characteristic fashion, it is intimate, personal, an ink drawing on the back of a scrap of notebook paper. Its materiality, once more, connects Delfina's cultivation of the diary to her representation as a visual object. This portrait suggests a longing gaze that is so often insinuated but rarely captured by the studio portraits that we have seen. Delfina's self-styling is certainly more melancholic than is Julia's, but this particular illustration, worn, stained, fragile, hearkens a distinguished sense of desire that further points to the public difference between the two sisters. This image reflects back on, though it actually precedes, Julia's portrait as *Princesse Lointaine*. Rather than expose this image to the world, however, Delfina archives it in the pages of her diary. If Julia sought to harness the queerness of European modernity in a gesture of queer celebrity, Delfina in contrast, includes a portrait of herself gazing backward at the pages of her own diary. The contrast between these images is not necessarily one of genre, but of the queer familial look. This drawing reveals a side of Delfina that did not belong in the family album, but rather in her *cuaderno-copia*. And yet it still contributes to the kinship imaginary of the Bunge family; it still hearkens the relationality of bodies, the desire to be seen as and by others, but it also manifests the queerness of sibling publicity as an archival process.

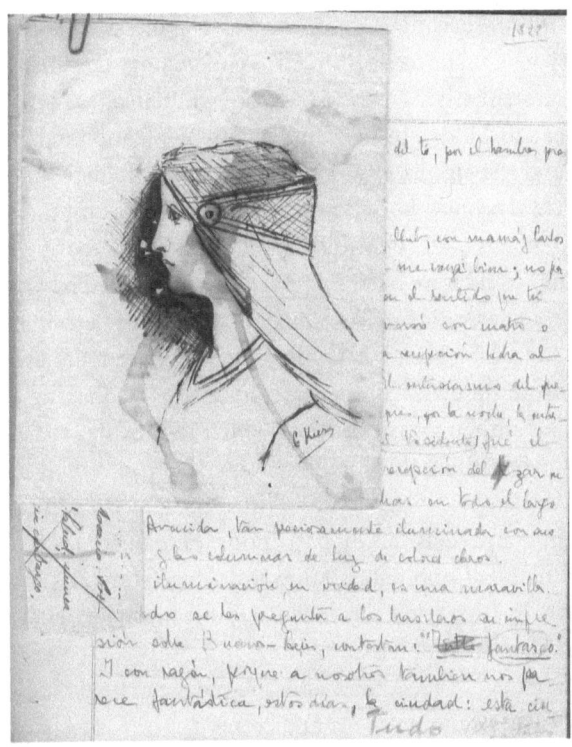

FIGURE 3.10
Ink drawing of
Delfina Bunge by
C. Kier. Bunge Family
Archive (Courtesy of
Lucía Gálvez).

Ironically, it would be Delfina's image that most circulated in the Argentine public sphere, as a commemorative stamp printed by the Casa de Moneda (National Mint) in 1983 (fig. 3.11). Part of a series titled "Escritores argentinos" ("Argentine writers"), the *escritora* would appear alongside her husband, Manuel Gálvez, as well as Pedro B. Palacios (better known by his pseudonym, Almafuerte), Leopoldo Marechal, and Evaristo Carriego.[10] The artist commissioned to produce these drawings, Horacio Álvarez Boero, portrays Delfina gazing at forty-five-degree angle, hair parted on the left ending in loose curls below her ears. Her neck is notably exposed, and her mouth affects a pensive interiority that bears a striking resemblance to her "fading" portrait from decades prior (fig. 3.8). In yet another staging of familiar intimacy, Delfina the writer accompanies her husband, whose value (4,000 pesos) outweighs hers (3,000 pesos). Minted in the year of Argentina's return to democracy, this inclusion in the cultural imagery of the nation implies an appraisal of her spiritual virtuousness, her Catholicism, and her conservative feminism, which spoke to a desire to appeal to a specific type of maternal legitimacy, a conciliatory feminism in the wake of the dictatorship. For a woman whose public image was so carefully guarded, indeed forbidden by her family from publication in her youth, queerly, in the end she circulates as a common stamp, folded back into the nationalist cultural project, herself now an object of consumption, an image commemorated and made quotidian all at once. Prone to introspection, I think Delfina would have been surprised if not appalled by her inclusion in this public orchestration of visual iconography—of herself as a public image of the state. Her past, her family's heritage, her marriage to Gálvez, all come to work on behalf of the state, interested in creating a cohesive literary past, a pantheon of writers, on which to base its return to democratic rule. However, there is something about this contradiction that is in keeping with the lessons of the family album. The cultural capital stored therein, recalled, guarded as family patrimony, here becomes the least common denominator of public life, a lowly postage stamp as the public image of a private life that itself serves to carry the intimate details of other lives from one place to another.

As I note earlier, the images I have been able to access can be divided into two main groups: early studio portraits and *cartes de visite*, and later candid or semistaged images of the family in Alta Gracia. This first group of photographs reveals the self to be a conscientious and deliberate mode of representation in dialogue with the types of photographic technologies available in Argentina at the turn of the century. The studio portraits serve to index not just the body and the presence of the Bunge siblings, but also their fashion choices, their investment in appearing as a particularly styled self. Carlos Octavio yearns to be recognized as fashionable, modern, and professional. He is photographed as distant and refined, even if, in private moments, we glimpse a vulnerability that characterizes his contradictory presence in Porteño society. Delfina almost always appears photographed in white, receding, fading into the backdrop. Julia, in contrast, shines, harnessing the allure of costuming, more elaborate styling, and a wider range of fashion. The siblings use photography and in particular the *carte de visite* as a technology of self that allows each of them to construct a self-image. And yet, this self-image constantly escapes, eludes, or defies their designs. These are images of self that emerge through the contradictory process of cultivating a public image, a process that involves the conscientious negotiation of queerness and modernity, privacy and

FIGURE 3.11 Delfina Bunge de Gálvez, "Escritores argentinos," Horacio Álvarez Boero, Casa de Moneda, 1983.

publicity. The second set of images, to which I turn below, reveals the interconnectedness of the family, its fissures, its limits. These images present the family in less staged, at times spontaneous relation, and that relation, that gestural practice and proximity, reveals much more about the family and the family album as an archive of intimacy and mutuality. Thus far, I have focused on how the photograph intersects with the contradictions of self; in what follows I take the use of photography as a tool of memorializing kinship, narrating time, and orienting family relations.

## FAMILY REUNION:
## SNAPSHOTS FROM ALTA GRACIA

Delfina's health is in decline. She has hypertension and has spent most of 1915 in Alta Gracia, Córdoba, where the air is pure, at least compared to Buenos Aires. She has lost weight but is in good spirits. The family, along with some close friends, has decided to pay her a visit. Among the amenities of the Hotel Sierras is an in-house photographer, Guido, who sets up on the front balcony and takes candid photographs of guests for a modest sum. His purpose is to provide tangible memories of the place, the people, and the good time they are having. Guido's portraiture is documentary and commercial. He capitalizes (on) the confined location and the captive audience/subjects therein. Guido, like many other turn-of-the-century photographers, traffics in the familial gaze, attempting to record for posterity a feeling of relatedness, an intimate moment that would serve to pay the bills.

The Bunge family album contains several photographs of this nature, taken at the Hotel Sierras. Here, I explore the contradictory familial looks that these images record or fail to record. These are candid and semicandid photographs taken during a time of urgent familial relatedness. Delfina's failing health was the occasion for the large reunion of family and friends at the hotel, an occasion that imbues these photographs with a sense of closeness, but also anxiety. This anxiety is laid bare by the familial looks that cross, intersect, collide, or fail to connect. The images taken at the Hotel Sierras constitute an archive of familiarity that is bound together by Delfina's body, by the fear that this might be the last time they could all be together as a family. Thus, the impulse to record owes to a particular familial context, and it exposes some of the underlying tensions of familiarity that are often left out of the public writing of the Bunge family.

## Walk this Way

There is a series of four images that captures small groups or pairs as they traverse the hotel balcony. The photographer positions himself in approximately the same place, and captures an intimate moment, thought to be private, as these small groups pass before him. It is not unlike Delfina's own recollection of a series of individuals—here groups—who passed before the eye of the memoirist—here the lens of the photographer—as discrete and identifiable moments through which sibling difference is not simply recorded, but performed and enacted. These spontaneous photographs represent a procession of kinship relations.

For example, we see Carlos Octavio striding confidently in a white linen suit, buffeted by two men, perhaps hotel employees (fig. 3.12). The backlighting propels these men forward. Carlos Octavio's arms folded behind and weight on the front foot give him a clear sense of motion. He has gravity (and gravitas) in this image. They walk in step but they make an odd group. The man to Bunge's right is dressed formally, is slightly younger than Bunge, and gazes directly ahead at the camera. Carlos Octavio, in

FIGURE 3.12 Hotel Sierras 1. Bunge Family Archive (Courtesy of Lucía Gálvez).

vacation attire angles his face, allowing the lens to capture him in a moment of coyness marked by his slightly arched eyebrow, cigarette dangling from his lips, kerchief spilling out of his breast pocket. The man to Bunge's left, however, is noticeably younger than the other two, wearing a cap (rather than a hat), a coat that is perhaps too big for him, and white pants. He is also noticeably darker, perhaps of mixed-race or African descent. If Carlos Octavio's public thoughts on racial mixing were well known (see chapter 5), this image asks what his private feelings might have been. Here, the image itself actually posits a correspondence, sympathy, between Bunge and the young man to his left. Their bodies share the same pose—hands behind the back—and gait. They walk in step, copacetic. I wonder, then, what Bunge's gaze is meant to imply. The photographer captures a moment in which the physical proximity between bodies of different ages and ethnic backgrounds creates a discordant image, even if the rhythm, the pace, of their movement is congruent. And yet, the lingering question of how these bodies relate seems unresolved, an excess that imbues this image with a strangeness of composition and style.

In another photograph, Carlos Octavio walks alongside his brother, Eduardo (1884-1968) (fig. 3.13). They seem bemused, perhaps by their own conversation or the act of having their picture taken. Their gait is slower than that recorded by the previous photograph. They allow the photographer more time. In contrast with the previous image, here the camera

FIGURE 3.13
Hotel Sierras 2.
Bunge Family
Archive (Courtesy
of Lucía Gálvez).

records a familial relation, one of fraternal contact. Carlos Octavio and Eduardo share an intimate conversation, but also a relationship vis-à-vis the camera itself. They share in the process of being photographed, which is turned into a moment of solidarity or perhaps complicity. This image portrays a sibling look that is reflected by the plane of the camera. In fact, this sibling look is constituted by the camera itself being positioned to record them as they walk. It is the presence of the camera that produces the quality of relation that it then records. Here the camera becomes an actor that solicits a particular form of fraternal relationality. It is as siblings walking, sharing, slowing down just enough, their bodies keeping pace with each other, that they are linked by the moment in which the camera captures their individual looks joined by fraternal complicity. The presence of the camera affects the movement of the bodies that pass before it. It

FIGURE 3.14 Hotel Sierras 3. Bunge Family Archive (Courtesy of Lucía Gálvez).

inspires a desire, perhaps unconscious, to be seen as related, recorded in relation, for the benefit of the family album. The technological imposition of the camera does not simply record these brothers walking, but asks them to walk together for Delfina, for the family album, for posterity. The interjection of the camera frames the corporal relatedness of these siblings, who pass before its lens as a memory, as a projection, as a promise of future sibling bonds.

A third balcony photograph depicts Delfina Bunge with her longtime friend Felisa Areco (fig. 3.14). The contrast in their fashion is remarkable. Delfina's crocheted collar and layered dress flow as she walks, her hands protected by a stole; Felisa, in contrast, is notably butch with a high-waisted belt and blazer, her hands shoved in its pockets. Delfina, whose health was precarious, seems like she is trying to keep up with Felisa, who leads the

SPECTRAL DESIRES — 175

way with authority. Delfina's expression is generous, while Felisa stares directly at the camera, stern, not surrendering to its gaze. This photograph seems like a record not only of Felisa's presence, but also, more poignantly, of her protection. That is, the look that is recorded by that camera defies the photographer's documentary impulse. By occupying the camera's focus and returning its optical fixity, Felisa allows Delfina more space. She prevents Delfina from being captured, from being the focal point of the photographer's gaze.

In an outdoor photograph taken on the same day as the previous example, we see Carlos Octavio, Felisa, and Delfina pausing briefly on a walk of the hotel grounds (fig. 3.15). The cool air has forced Felisa to button up her blazer, with her hand covering up the formerly exposed neckline. Delfina is even more inquisitive in this image, almost perturbed. Though they walk as a trio, Delfina and Felisa are closer to each other, with Carlos Octavio pausing awkwardly as the photograph is taken. If the presence of the photographer was permissible as a novelty within the confines of the Hotel Sierras, outside he seems bothersome. Perhaps the three had something private to discuss. Perhaps they were seeking respite from the sociality of the hotel, only to be interrupted by a prying eye/lens.

There is a notable contrast between this outdoor trio and that comprised of Julia, her husband Ignacio Uranga, and Delfina (fig. 3.16). Back within the confines of the hotel, they stroll leisurely. Here Julia and Ignacio walk arm in arm; Delfina, at arm's length. Delfina is wearing the same dress as in the previous two images (figs. 3.14 and 3.15), though she has changed her hat and wears a light scarf, eschewing the stole. While she and Julia gaze at the camera, Ignacio has turned his head toward Delfina, perhaps reacting to something she said. In this image both sisters smile at the camera. It is in fact the only image I have been able to find in which both sisters appear in the same frame and provide a similar expression. I have not seen an image of the two sisters together, alone. Ignacio, while at the center of this image and separating the two sisters, plays a lesser role in the affective force of the photograph. It is the gaze of each sister—collected by the camera—that connects them, despite Ignacio's presence. Notable, too, is the absence of Delfina's husband, Manuel Gálvez, whose participation at this family gathering was reluctant. In this image, however, the familial look is established by triangulation with the lens of the camera. It is the lens that captures the visages turned slightly toward it, the sisters in relation, as they walk. Here, too, we can see the physical difference between the two

FIGURE 3.15 Walking the grounds of the Hotel Sierras. Bunge Family Archive (Courtesy of Lucía Gálvez).

FIGURE 3.16. Julia Valentina Bunge, Ignacio Uranga, and Delfina Bunge. Bunge Family Archive (Courtesy of Lucía Gálvez).

sisters. Delfina's health has led her to lose weight, while Julia's fitted jacket reveals a busty silhouette. In this, too, Delfina has chosen an outfit that hides her already slim figure, while Julia's full shape is accentuated by her choice of dress.

Taken together, these images recall photographic seriality that is key to both sibling relations and memorializing kinship. As each group passes, they are recorded momentarily, captured in a performance of closeness for the benefit of a future domestic, familial, audience. They create a sense of punctuated continuity. Each interior image depends on the same volume of light at the end of the balcony/arcade, a block that illuminates these figures from behind as they approach the camera, which in turn anticipates the movement of each group. The photographer captures each group in a similar frame but slightly different depth of field. These formal qualities provide this series of images with a clear point of reference, a clear visual grammar, by which each group stands out for the particular gesture that they choose to allow the camera to capture. Because of this similar technique, we can read the four interior and one exterior photographs as a record of affinity and proximity, tandem gazes that constitute fraternal and sororal relations as they join on the lens of the camera. Through this technical framing, the bodies of the subjects become legible as related, but also individual. The familial look in each image is constituted as a momentary, at times reflexive instance in which the personality of each individual exists alongside the feeling of relatedness that the camera channels as a symbol of the photograph's potential to legitimize those feelings. The family album both records and produces familiarity. The plane of the camera lens coordinates the individual familial looks into a constellation of gazes that constitutes the commercial value of the photograph as well as its worth as an archive of systematized collectivity.

### Familial Looks, Crossing Glances

In addition to the images of pairs or trios, the Bunge family album includes a range of larger group photographs also taken at the Hotel Sierras. In these the complexity of familial looks increases, not just because the photographs incorporate more subjects, but also because they reveal (and obscure) interpersonal dynamics, absences, crossed glances, shadows. There is one photograph that serves as a fulcrum between the smaller and larger group images. In it, Delfina sits with Cornelia Groussac (1883-1968)

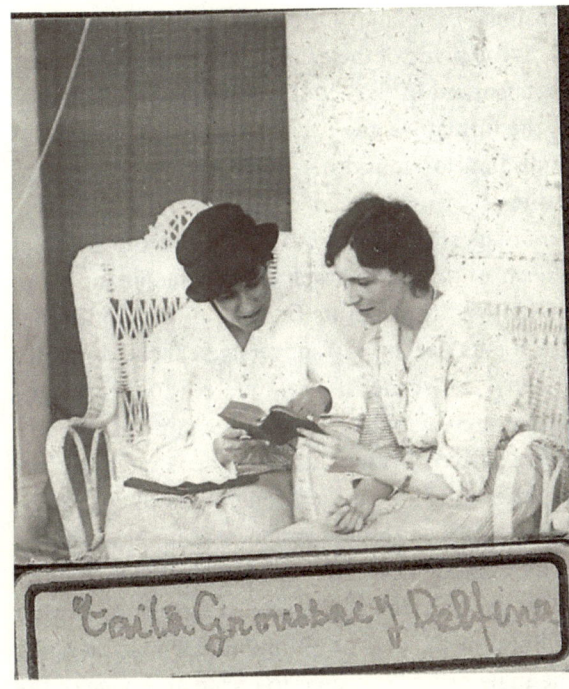

FIGURE 3.17 Delfina and Taita Reading. Bunge Family Archive (Courtesy of Lucía Gálvez).

as they read together (fig. 3.17). The image is accompanied by a caption, written by Delfina, identifying Cornelia by her nickname "Taita," which was given to her by her father, Paul Groussac, whom she would also accompany in reading and writing as his personal secretary when the director of Argentina's National Library began to lose his sight (Benarós 10).

Delfina and Taita shared a dedication to poetry and Catholicism. Eventually they would both become members of the Asociación de Escritoras y Publicistas Católicas ("Association of Catholic Writers and Publicists"), founded in 1939, which sought to develop and promote a Catholic line of thought in the Argentine public sphere. They were prolific lecturers, often speaking to women's groups, Catholic societies, or political parties. This image, however, taken in 1915, shows an intimate moment shared by two women, their hands sustaining a book together. Their fingers graze its pages as they sound out the words together. Together they blend—fade—into a white wicker lounge chair. Their attention focused squarely on the page; they are oblivious to the camera's presence. The lighting of this image presents the book itself as the central organizing feature, while Delfina's dark hair and Taita's black hat are the only other points of contrast against the white background. The plane of the book receives the gaze of the two women readers, as the plane of the camera lens triangulates their relationship as intimate, absorbed in the act of reading. For a woman so prone to introspection, the miniature, the private, this image is remarkable evidence of the quotidian joy found in—and the closeness shared through—the act of reading.

As with many other images of women reading, from the colonial period to today, the subjects of this photograph depict a tactile intimacy, a sensuousness that is achieved through its framing of proximity that is simultaneously feared for its potentially subversive effects. As James Conlon argues, historically, the scene of a woman reading threatens male hegemony by placing her outside of masculine control (39-40). The experience of pleasure derived from reading is independent of male supervision, as is the experience of liberation through knowledge, imagination, or even isolation. Thus, as a trope, women reading has inspired prolific and frequently moralizing artistic representations, in particular by male artists, who often seek to (re)capture and (re)assert dominion over women by highlighting the dangers of uninhibited female pleasure. As Conlon suggests, the male artist "is drawn to create an image of the woman reading primarily as a means of controlling the site and sight of her, of manipulating its meaning to work for him" (40). I underscore the subversive history of the woman with a book in her hand as way of interpreting against the grain what would ostensibly represent an unremarkable moment in the lives of two friends, Delfina Bunge and Taita Groussac. The photograph of these two women reading, as part of the family album, serves to ground their subsequent collaborations as Catholic writers and advocates for Catholic causes. At least for Delfina, this would include the explicit rejection of women's labor outside the home in favor of traditional domestic arrangements, as I discuss in chapter 5. However, visually, this image of women reading also conjures the possibility of an erotic attachment between these two women that is at odds with their published writing on gender norms and sexuality. That is, the image stages a moment of collective pleasure. As the lips of each woman synchronize with the words on the page, together enjoying the pleasure of reading, their hands sustain the weight of the book as their fingers trace and retrace its slick pages. Their minds wander, weave, together, separately, together again, opening up new possibilities for experiencing pleasure even as the photographer's camera clicks in the background.

The intimacy found in the previous image owes to the physical orientation of bodies in relation. It represents a moment in which Delfina and Taita share in the pleasure of reading, their gaze at once collective and individual. This intimacy is captured by the lens of the photographer and archived on the pages of the family album to be viewed, enjoyed, by future family members. The pleasure of this moment becomes a pleasure shared not only in this particular moment, but other future, iterative, moments of relation that are staged by the album. As I have been arguing, the scene of reading is a sensuous one, a moment in which the proximity of bodies in relation constitutes a discrete moment of pleasure. I think, too, we can extend this argument to encompass the pleasure of reading and rereading the family album. If the tactile sensuousness of the book constitutes a liberatory and therefore threatening object for women under patriarchal vigilance, then the archive of the family album not only transfers that moment, that image, onto its pages, but also retains the possibility of transferring the pleasure of that sensuous touch to future viewers, future family members, future fingers and eyes, which possess the pages of the album. This scene of women reading extends to future scenes in which women gather around the pages of the album, reminisce, yearn, touch, delight in the proximity that is generated by the album as an object, which, like the diary, enacts a future in the present.

Sara Ahmed might describe this orientation as *extending* bodies in relation toward each other as a form of relating queerly (115–16). That is, in the photograph of Delfina and Taita reading, the book in hand orients the eyes, the fingers, the bodies of these women toward the pages of the book. It centers their relation on the book, as the framing of the photograph centers their bodily orientation for the subsequent orientation of future family members around the pages of the album. The familial gaze of the family album is oriented through the lens of the camera, while the future familial look of orients toward the pages of the album. The book, like the album, activates the intimacy of familial relationality around particular objects. But these objects also serve to contain, to coalesce, affective dispositions that at once adhere to normative kinship patterns and exceed their limits. Delfina and Taita orient themselves vis-à-vis the book, while the viewer of this photograph in the family album orients herself vis-à-vis the sensual experience of "reading" an image of women reading. This photograph marks bodies in relation as an expression of intimacy in the visual grammar of the family album. It relates relation as an expression of corporal proximity. In the remaining photographs that I study in this chapter, corporal proximity is also crucial, but so too are the ways in which the familial look reflects, refracts, connects, or fails to find the look of another.

There were at least two family portraits made at the Hotel Sierras in 1915. These photographs are less spontaneous than the images studied previously of pairs or groups of three, and they demonstrate a conscientious composition of familial relatedness. They are posed as familial. The family understands that it is being photographed as such. Following Barthes, the family's awareness of the photographer creates a moment in which the bodies that are about to be photographed transform themselves in advance into an image (10). Or, as Hirsch might put it, the familial gaze intervenes in the process of recording a particular moment of relatedness in order to constitute it as familial. While these images can be thought of in terms of a conscientious crafting of familiality, a document that crystallizes kinship relations on the plane of the camera lens, they also record the contradictory looks that emerge in just such a moment. The pose is beholden to the familial gaze, but it also reveals hierarchies of power, proximity, and gesture that are constituted by the familial look.

The first example records a group of six, Manuel Gálvez, Delfina Bunge, Ignacio Uranga, Maria Luisa Arteaga Bunge, Julia Bunge de Uranga, and Jorge Bunge (fig. 3.18). In my own viewing of this image, I am at a loss. I lack the requisite knowledge to decipher what Benjamin would call the "unconscious optics" of this image. And yet, this posed photograph reveals so much about the relations between its subjects. At the center Maria Luisa is dressed in mourning even five years after the death of her husband, Octavio. She would dress in mourning for the rest of her life. Seated, the matriarch anchors this image. Her black dress stands in stark contrast with the two figures in white joining her on the same plane. Her approving smile is reciprocated by all the other subjects of this photograph. Emanating from this center, we can make out four visual reference points: (1) Maria Luisa and Julia look at Delfina; (2) Delfina looks at Jorge; (3) Jorge and Ignacio look at Manuel Gálvez; and (4) Manuel Gálvez looks at the camera. I want to pay close attention to what these looks reveal, as well as what they hide. It seems to me that Gálvez breaks the constellation of familiality in this image. His are the only eyes whose gaze pierces the plane between the camera and its subjects. He alone looks back at the viewer, who is, in turn, forced

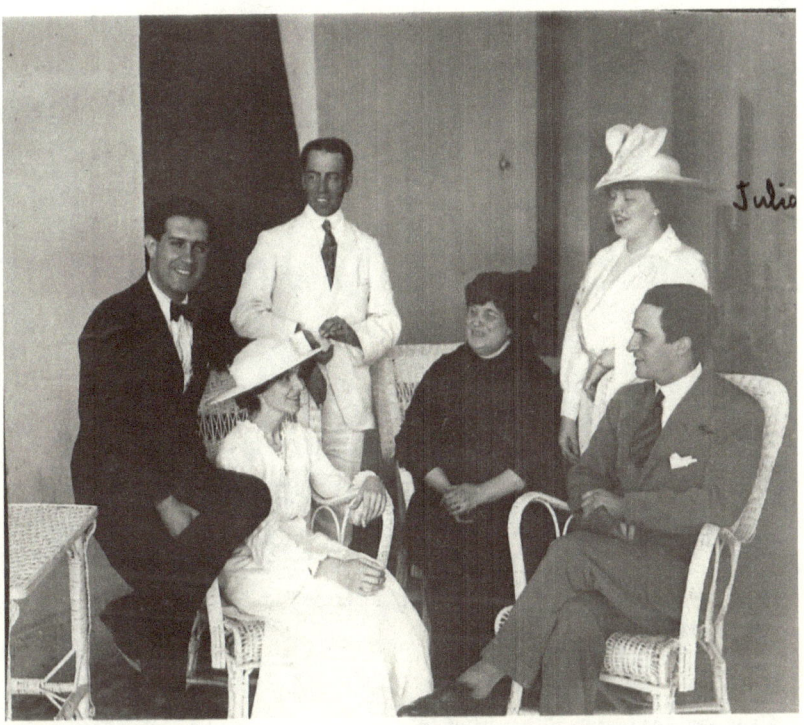

FIGURE 3.18 Group of six at the Hotel Sierras. Bunge Family Archive (Courtesy of Lucía Gálvez).

to negotiate this reciprocal engagement. In looking back at the camera, Gálvez betrays the tacit agreement that is revealed by the remaining looks, which affect ignorance of the camera's presence. He is the only one to break character, so to speak. What is more, when we take these visual reference points as a guide, we can see that Manuel Gálvez and Delfina receive the looks of every other family member. And they are the only exceptions to this visual agreement. While Gálvez looks back at the camera, Delfina looks across at her brother Jorge. Only Gálvez sees the look of the cameraman as he snaps this photograph. Only Gálvez's look escapes the nuclear family structure that connects the remaining subjects of this image. Only he undermines the fantasy of familial contentment by interpellating the gaze of the camera, the viewer, future family members, me, you. Could it be that Gálvez's look belies a slyness that does not fit in this image? Ignacio Uranga, to his left, seems almost surprised. This moment clearly frames familial unity, the family as a nuclear unit, but

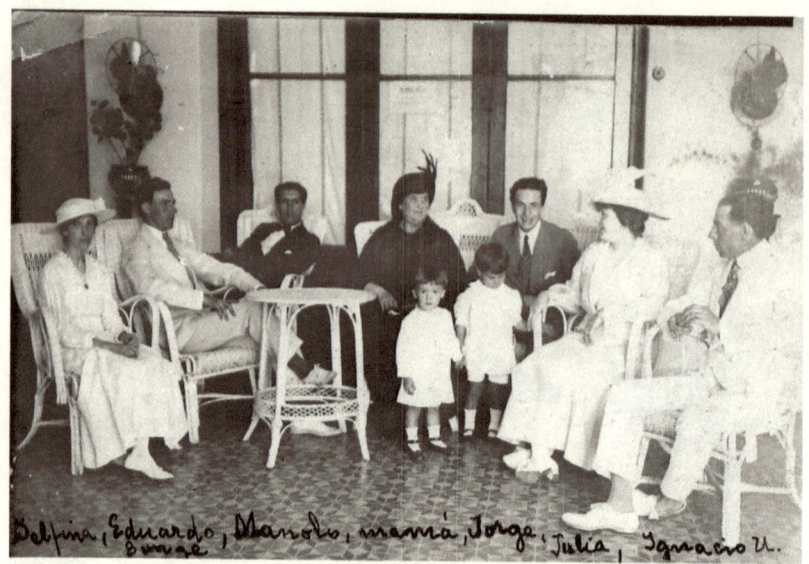

FIGURE 3.19 Group photo at the Hotel Sierras. Bunge Family Archive (Courtesy of Lucía Gálvez).

Gálvez exudes a singularity that is at odds with the photograph's refractive familial gaze. His look veers from the familial toward the individual. There is something he does not want to share with the familial gaze performed here.

The second example is the most populated family portrait taken at the Hotel Sierras (fig. 3.19). Delfina annotates the image, marking it as a record for future family members, so that they too, could identify (with) the subjects of this photograph. María Luisa, "mamá," is once again at the center. This photograph must have been taken on the same day, perhaps only moments after the one studied previously. The family members are wearing the same outfits, though three additional subjects are included: Eduardo Bunge, who is seated next to Delfina; Ignacio Uranga Bunge (1911–1999), looking at the camera, is the oldest son of Julia Valentina Bunge and Ignacio Uranga; and Manuel Gálvez Bunge (1911–1984), the oldest son of Delfina Bunge and Manuel Gálvez, is looking down. The young boys hold hands in a subtle gesture that reminds of the familial gaze that returns in this image. Julia and Delfina are seated opposite each other, posed similarly, legs crossed at the ankles, both in white, both in summer hats. Julia, however is positioned next to her husband, Ignacio, on the right, while Delfina is seated next to her brother Eduardo but quite distant, unrelated, to her husband Manuel Gálvez. Julia expands, arms open, neck raised; Delfina curves inward, hands clasped tentatively on her lap, shoulders rolled slightly forward. She *fades* into the chair. Just as Julia seems to address her, laughing it seems at something Delfina did not catch, or did not appreciate. Delfina seems not to belong to this image. Neither does Manuel Gálvez, whose leisurely pose in the shadows of the corner limits his presence. The most striking look comes from young Ignacio who stares directly at the camera, meeting the viewer's eye. His eyes demand attention, even more so than Delfina or Jorge, who also look toward the photographer. In this portrait the presence of a new generation alters the visual economy of the familial gaze. The precocious directness of Ignacio's look provides a counterpoint to other moments in which a subject returns the gaze of the camera. Does he understand that he is being photographed? Would he remember this moment?

Though we may not be able to answer the question of what Ignacio intends with his look, it is clear that his presence adds a new layer of complexity to the image. This is a multigenerational family portrait. We come full circle. This image presents the continuation of the Bunge family by documenting a moment of familial intimacy. Just as Delfina would write in *Viaje alrededor de mi infancia*, a memory as a photograph serves to connect her to her siblings. It is an image that exists in the family archive, a documentation of presence. The photographic register of this particular moment serves as an intra- and intergenerational point of contact, linking the queer temporality of the photograph—its nostalgia and its futurity bound together—in a moment of intimate display.

The last familial example that I would like to discuss may provide some sense of how integrated photography had become for the Bunge family by 1915. On an excursion in Alta Gracia, a group of at least eight, including Carlos Octavio Bunge, Taila Groussac, and Felisa Areco, pause as another woman takes a photograph (fig. 3.20). The layering of technological proficiency, rural setting, and intimate interaction is palpable in this image. Essentially, it is a photograph of a woman taking a photograph. It documents the process of recording this particular moment of leisure and proximity. The image is dominated by the rural landscape, a foreground that occupies nearly the entire bottom half of the frame, and which reveals

FIGURE 3.20 Excursion in Alta Gracia. Bunge Family Archive (Courtesy of Lucía Gálvez).

the work of time to erode the embankment on which the group stands. In the background, a scraggly bluff juts upward, dividing the image yet again into diagonal quadrants. To the left, a woman manipulates what is likely an Eastman Kodak No. 1 Autographic Camera. To her right, the group pauses, unposed, perhaps awaiting instructions. Out of frame, from the path below, someone snaps a photograph—this image—of the group waiting to be positioned, photographed, registered, remembered. It is an image that precipitates the visualization of connection that the subsequent photograph, the one yet to be taken, was supposed to record, but has not yet. In doing so, this image documents the lingering proximity of a group that is about to be constituted as such. What I find interesting about this image is how it makes literal the process of staging the temporal enactment of the familial gaze. It is, in essence, a deconstruction of a method of positioning bodies in relation for the benefit of the camera's lens. We are able to witness the moment before the photograph, the unawareness that a photograph is being taken and the simultaneous expectation that one is about to be made. One the one hand, this image demonstrates the construction of photographic intimacy, its procedural unfolding, and on the other, it lingers in the family album as a record of both the reality of this moment, and the technological modernity of the subjects that are photographed.

## CONCLUSION

If the previous image demonstrates the procedure of photographic presence, I want to conclude this chapter, in contrast, with one in which the presence of the subject haunts the physical space that is documented. It is a photograph of Carlos Octavio's living room (fig. 3.21), annotated by Delfina: "Sala de C. Octavio (casa en que murió)" ("C. Octavio's living room [house in which he died]"). At first glance, this image registers Carlos Octavio's taste, his choice of fabric, drapery, artwork, his piano. But it also depends on his absence: a room of the house in which he died. Why does Delfina choose this particular point of reference, this parenthetical? While it is possible that this detail is offered as a historical signpost, that is, as an indication to future viewers—who may not be familiar with this place—of what they are looking at. But it is also an image that hearkens the queer home that could have been, the queer domesticity that is only visible in death as unrealized possibility. As I describe in chapter 2, this is the home that was offered to Delfina by Carlos Octavio as an outlet for her artistic pursuits, and as a refuge from the demands to marry that she had stridently rejected in her youth. This is the room she could have inhabited, the piano that she could have played. The spectral presence of her brother is conjured by her handwriting, the physical manifestation of her desire to locate him as belonging to this particular image. She, too, could have belonged to this space, but does so only through absence. But it is only in her brother's death that Delfina is able to insert herself as custodian of a space where she might have resided, but did not, to imagine a life that she could have lived, but did not. Or, perhaps, she does so by *disidentifying* with the life that she actually led.[11] In death her brother casts a queer shadow over the room they might have shared.

I ask myself: what is this legend doing? It is a caption that saves for posterity the absence of the presence of a brother who is no longer there. But without this caption, what would this image be? Without this family inscription, how would I have understood this image? One of the qualities of the family album is that it makes archive out of text, text out of archive. I take the inscription of the fact of a brother's death on the surface of the photograph as meaningful. In concrete terms, the referential quality of the photograph depends on a constitutive lack. Carlos Octavio inhabits this queer space as a spectral presence. A lingering self inscribed by his sister's pen as absent. Finally, we see what Barthes calls the "*Spectrum* of

FIGURE 3.21 "Casa en que murió" Carlos Octavio Bunge. Bunge Family Archive (Courtesy of Lucía Gálvez).

the Photograph," both the spectacle (of opulence, of normative domesticity) and "the return of the dead" (9). Bunge's specular presence returns by virtue of Delfina's inscription on the page of the family album, without which, the referential duration of the image might be lost. We would not know *how to see* this room without the inscription, which thus imbues the space with concrete knowledge of both presence and absence. The lingering embodiment of kinship that is enacted by the technology of the family album is manifest by the inscription on the page, which shapes and reshapes, does and undoes, the private publicness of the Bunge family. While I began this chapter by citing the photographic quality of memory, I conclude with the memorialized quality of photography. It is in this sense that Carlos Octavio's living room constitutes a contested domain of familiality. A living room haunted by death. It is as a memory of a space of familial relationality that this image becomes a photograph, a register of the spectral presence of kinship that is only visible through the imaginary of kinship imagined, projected, lingering as possible.

CHAPTER FOUR

# FAMILY PEDAGOGY
## THE INSTITUTIONALIZATION OF KINSHIP

Throughout the nineteenth century and into the first decades of the twentieth, in Argentina and throughout Latin America, public youth education reflected the interests of the intellectual and political elite—interests such as uniformity and order, morality, technical proficiency, frugality, and patriotism.[1] As the divisive period of national organization transitioned to one of political stability and economic expansion, federal education programs responded to this new social reality by prioritizing the nationalization of young Argentines, a shift that was reflected in the allocation of resources for teacher training (the Escuelas Normales, typically called teachers colleges in English), public school infrastructure, and state sponsorship of research, reports, and textbooks that aligned with directives to instruct students how to feel, act, and thus *become* Argentine.[2] For the elite, the new sociopolitical milieu of the turn of the century demanded new ways of thinking about schooling that could attend to the pressures of immigration, shifting class structures, and changing family dynamics. And yet, pedagogues at the turn of the century feared that the Escuelas Normales were becoming overrun by unmarried, mannish women who, in the absence of patriarchal vigilance, were corrupting new, impressionable teachers—essentially turning them into lesbians—who would in turn corrupt the Argentine youth under their tutelage (Salessi 213-17). The schoolroom was a site of intense debates over the future of the nation, a site in which discourses of gender, sexuality, and nationalism converged around the figure of the child and how best to inculcate in him or her a sense of belonging.

As ever, the Bunge siblings actively participated in the intellectual debates and cultural nationalist programs that were meant to bring young Argentines into the modern era. Carlos Octavio Bunge would publish, among his varied production, a literary anthology for primary school use titled *Nuestra Patria: Libro de lectura para la educación nacional* (*Our Homeland: A Reader for National Education*) in 1910. Only a year earlier, Julia and Delfina Bunge had published, at the behest—and with the support—of their oldest brother, a cowritten primary school textbook, *El Arca de Noé* (*Noah's Ark*), in two volumes (for second- and third-grade students, respectively). While Delfina would continue to write on schooling and national culture over the course of her career—as would Carlos Octavio—their two textbooks represent a fertile if paradoxical juncture of family, pedagogy, and citizenship. Centered on the Argentine centennial (1910) and responsive to its particular ideological contradictions and to the overwhelming desire to inculcate a sense of patriotic duty to the nation in young, impressionable citizens and immigrants, these texts document how kinship and patriotism structured the ideological response to the uncertainty of Argentina's future. The underlying issue of how to relate to those with whom one shares allegiance involves linking the at times abstract responsibilities of citizenship to the intimately felt familiarity of kinship. They invite a simple, but profound question: how does one learn to love one's country? The answer, as unfolds in their pedagogical writing, is not so much about learning *to be* as it is learning *to feel*.

In this chapter I explore the conflicting desires of education, patriotism, and kinship in two interrelated ways. First, I argue that the patriotic aims of childhood instruction need to be understood not only as an expression of the disciplinary authority of the state (which they are), but also as an incitement to feeling queerly toward fellow citizens, family members, and the nation. The relationship between citizens is construed in these pedagogical texts as like—but also as supplanting—the family, while the nation is framed as an extension of the family unit established within the classroom. Thus, to feel Argentine, one had to first feel *related*. I understand this pedagogy as queer because it harnesses the oscillating incitements to attraction and repulsion, identification and disavowal, love and hate, loyalty and disdain, which are at the center of the form of relationality modeled in these texts. Second, I demonstrate how Carlos Octavio, Julia, and Delfina contribute to this queer pedagogy by offering up their own experiences, the memory of their own contradictory desires as children, as the model by which all Argentine children could *and should* relate to others and to the nation. That is, not only do they write textbooks that are modeled on an abstract notion of familiarity and kinship, but they actually offer their experiences as members of their own (exemplary) family to demonstrate the psychological and social processes through which children should pass in order to successfully feel, act, and relate as Argentine. This chapter describes how a particular set of pedagogical texts sheds light on the struggle between a nostalgic yearning for an idyllic (aristocratic) past, and a programmatic future in which queerness holds a central, though seldom recognized, position.

Historians of pedagogy have often viewed primary and secondary school textbooks as an important record of the national culture and patrimony of the nation, and as a record of the horizon of expectations for young citizens.[3] Mark D. Szuchman demonstrates how the figure of the child (and thus of childhood education more broadly) heightened the tensions between private and public spheres after independence in Argentina. As he argues, from the earliest years of the republican period, formal education, on the one hand, was viewed as an avenue to social ascendancy for the growing middle class and, on the other, as a safeguard against the "uninformed" masses that, in the eyes of the elite, could be easily manipulated by *caudillos* and populist demagogues (111). The intellectual elite, fearing this popular gullibility, sought to instill in children a sense of respect for the nation, its history, and its citizens. Early education programs were focused on instilling discipline, with a hierarchical structure that aimed to promote obedience and respect for authority. In the second half of the nineteenth century, however, educational reforms proposed by Sarmiento, then head of the Department of Schools of the State of Buenos Aires, and implemented by Juana Manso, encouraged educators to adopt textbooks and implement pedagogical techniques that eschewed the rote memorization and strict discipline of the early republican years in favor of harnessing children's natural instincts in the process of learning to read and write (Szuchman 130). Nevertheless, these progressivist efforts led by Manso were short-lived, and toward the turn of the century cultural nationalists sought to centralize and standardize the education system in the wake of mass immigration and popular dissent.

The National Law of Education, passed in 1884, established compulsory and secular primary schooling under the direction of federal and provincial authorities. This did little to assuage the anxiety felt by the elite caused by the continued influx of immigrants and fear of their incompatibility with local traditions, culture, and ethnic makeup. Historian Carl Solberg points to the appointment of José María Ramos Mejía to the presidency of Argentina's National Council of Education in 1908 as a turning point in federal attitudes toward pedagogy, and a shift toward cultural nationalism and acculturation as public policy in classrooms (145). Schools were emblazoned with patriotic symbols, students were required to begin each day with a pledge of loyalty to the Argentine flag, and to end each day with a collective song, "Viva la patria" ("Long live the homeland") (Solberg 147). Thus, the decades between 1880 and 1910 mark a period of transition not just in political and cultural terms, but also regarding the pedagogical practices that were meant to shape the future of the *patria*, practices that would shape *how students felt* toward the nation, as an abstract imagined community, and thus toward their fellow citizens. Evidently, education was an essential component in the modernizing project of the elite, but the disciplining of bodies and behaviors, affective ties, and in particular, queerness remains a topic in need of further study.

It may be useful, before turning to *El arca de Noé* and *Nuestra Patria*, to provide an example of what I mean by queerness in this context. In his textbook *El mosaico argentino (Argentine Mosaic)* (1894), J. B. Igon writes: "Amar a la patria es amar la libertad, es amar la ley, es amar el orden, es amar la autoridad, es respetarla, sostenerla, defenderla, es sacrificar las malas pasiones. Amar la patria es detestar y combatir la tiranía, es detestar y combatir la anarquía" ("To love the homeland is to love liberty, it is to love the law, it is to love order, it is to love authority, it is to respect it, to sustain it, to defend it, it is to sacrifice one's bad passions. To love the homeland is to detest and to combat tyranny, it is to detest and to combat anarchy"; cited in Tedesco 85). Love of country is folded into a call to acquiesce to the disciplinary authority of the state, to the national cause, to progress. Igon links a patriotic disposition toward upholding law and order to a moral imperative to "sacrifice one's bad passions." The contrast between love and sacrifice situates primary education as not simply beholden to the politics of cultural nationalism, but as a necessary site of state-sponsored affective indoctrination. We can see here that the implementation of primary and secondary education programs in

Argentina at the turn of the century was directly linked to the centralization of power by the state *and* the channeling of particular feelings toward fellow citizens and immigrants. Crucially, these young students were thought of and indeed addressed as sexual and cultural deviants (at least potentially). Here, to love Argentina is necessarily to combat "tyranny" and "anarchism." These are unambiguous references to those who would contradict state normativity—those who deviate from that norm with their bodies or desires—inaugurating a sentimental framework that requires a singular will to uphold nationalist politics, gestures, and feelings. Love of country depends on hailing and repressing queerness. The manifestation of proper feelings toward fellow Argentines is conditioned by a simultaneous incitement to discover those who would deviate from the norm—those whose "bad passions" cannot be controlled—and to eliminate those "evils" from the national body. Thus, for Igon and many other pedagogues at the turn of the century, the primary goal of classroom instruction was not necessarily to teach facts and figures, but to crystallize the affective dispositions toward the nation and its citizenry that would allow for the purging of queerness from the national body.

The pedagogical writing of Carlos Octavio and Julia and Delfina Bunge is curious for two reasons. First, it encourages a program of behavior that reinforces heteronormativity by mining young students for queer tendencies that must be transformed into acceptable forms of desire and relationality, and second, that program is derived from the erotic instability of the authors themselves. Or, perhaps, from the memory of their own erotic instabilities. That is, only by exposing their own queerness do these books make sense as an extension of the familiar to the national. Illuminating the juncture of family, affect, and nation, their respective textbooks propose a form of patriotic attachment that at once harnesses kinship relations as a metonymy for citizenship and proposes a nostalgic consolidation of normative expressions of gender and sexuality. They inculcate a sense of patriotism by framing classwork and civic participation as an extension of students' duty to the nation—and to the nation *as a family*—while they simultaneously undermine the desirability of immigrant and working-class familial attachments for the national cause. For the textbooks studied in this chapter, the classroom and the relations it fosters are mimetic representations of family and familiarity. Family is both a metonymy of civic participation and locus of affective instability that must be shaped according to the authors' patriotic aims.

## INTER/NATIONAL PEDAGOGY

While this chapter focuses on the familial attachments that imbue the pedagogical texts written by the Bunge siblings in Argentina, it would be a mistake to think that national pedagogy was circumscribed to the nation. Primary and secondary education in Latin America was, like other forms of cultural, political, and economic development, an international phenomenon.[4] While national education policies varied according to economic needs and demographic differences, which were themselves the result of extractivist colonialism, these policies were part of a broader dialogue about modernization and industrialization. Statesmen and educators traveled abroad to attend congresses and to analyze pedagogical practices in Europe and the United States, as well as other Latin American nations. Carlos Octavio Bunge's first trip to Europe in 1899 and subsequent publication of his report, *Espíritu de la educación*, is a case in point. What is more, in many countries a large percentage of schoolrooms were led by recent immigrants or by teachers contracted from Europe or the United States to implement newly created national curricula (Ossenbach 442).

While international trends were adapted and modified according to local circumstances with varying measures of success, the role of women as educators remained a particularly thorny issue across Latin America. An exhaustive treatment of these debates is beyond the scope of this chapter, but it is important to note a few historical trends as they relate to the juncture of family, gender, and nationalism. When distinguished Venezuelan humanist Andres Bello, after more than twenty years abroad, returned to Latin America in 1843 to assume the charge of Rector of the newly formed Universidad de Chile in Santiago, he saw national education as a way of training elite men (and not women) in the art of proper aesthetic values and governance, a model intended to maintain the social and economic dominance of the upper class, who would then provide the masses with an aspirational model (Yeager 79). Bello's vision for Latin America, a vision he attempted to carry out in Chile, was as a hierarchical society in which the education of its brightest (that is most powerful) men aimed at once to validate their primacy and instill a tradition of aristocratic humanism.

Across the Andes, however, Argentina's most important statesman-educator, Sarmiento, aimed to broaden access to basic instruction for rural and working-class citizens by founding normal schools and expanding the pool of capable teachers. This is a view that, while on the surface may seem avant-garde, nevertheless reflected his underlying belief that the state's mission was to develop a literate, moral, and obedient, and thus "civilized" public, a mission to be carried out by supposedly docile women educators.[5] As Sarmiento made clear in his own writing from the 1840s, for him women did indeed have a right to be educated and to educate others, not for altruistic reasons, but rather because it was through the figure of the republican mother/woman that future (male) citizens would be taught the crucial habits, traits, and temperament that was required for civilized modernity.[6]

For his part, José Vasconcelos, the architect of postrevolutionary Mexico's national education policies and the country's first Minister of Education (from 1921 to 1924), while perhaps more famous for having commissioned important murals in public spaces, libraries, and museums, also promoted rural schooling as a way of combining the technological demands of the positivist era with his own spiritual vision for a future-oriented, aesthetically and ethnically cohesive society—fully expressed in his 1925 essay *La raza cósmica* (*The Cosmic Race*). A skilled writer and eccentric politician, Vasconcelos would invite a young Chilean named Gabriela Mistral to Mexico as part of an education platform of indoctrinating Indigenous populations in national ideals as well as gaining proficiency Spanish language and literacy. And it would be Mistral, finally, who actually reinforced the case for a woman's role as not only crucial educators of national citizens, but in the project described by Vasconcelos as "aesthetic eugenics"—a form of state-sponsored miscegenation by which gender and race were bound up in the project of imagining a modern (white or Mestizo) population of the future. As Fiol-Matta puts it, early in her career Mistral "insists that correct [racial] mixing is the foundation of the pedagogical intervention, because the national child is the desired creation of the public-education system" (14).

It is worth repeating that the influence of positivism led sociologists and theorists of pedagogy to seek out environmental causes for the presumed social, political, and cultural backwardness of Latin American nations especially with the rise of the United States as a hemispheric imperial power after the Spanish American War (1898). In the first century of republican Latin America the role of public schooling was central to the vision that each nation sought to project of itself as modern (better yet, to become modern). This modernity was tied to gendered, racial, and sexual dynamics, which positioned women as central yet also dangerous to the future oriented politics of public pedagogy. While most Latin American pedagogues sought to improve economic development through education, that is, to produce more able-bodied workers to advance material gains in the realm of international trade, in Argentina pedagogy was not necessarily focused on developing laborers, but rather on more abstract concepts such as culture and patriotism. Argentine intellectuals imagined their country in a prime position with respect to other Latin American nations, especially those with large Afro-descendant and Indigenous populations; its exceptionalism, and the imaginary associated with it, willfully denied its own multicultural and multiethnic past (and forever *in the past*), as a way of positioning its present as unencumbered by the racial logics of "Mestizo" countries to its north, and Brazil to its east. In contrast with a country like Mexico, whose national pedagogy responded to the postrevolutionary land claims by Indigenous and peasant groups, as well as its proximity to the United States, the Argentine elite saw themselves as having already laid the bases for successful economic development on a global scale. What they sought at the turn of the century was to acculturate those already there into a cohesive national ideology.

As I have been suggesting, a woman's supposedly natural role as mother made her an obvious—though controversial—candidate for educating future participants in civilized modernity, future morally upright fathers and mothers. Women had fewer legal rights and fewer options for earning a stable income in the public sector in the nineteenth and early twentieth century (this trend continues to the present).[7] And yet, while women teachers were charged with promoting the nation's normative interests through education, *maestras* were also active participants in early feminist organizing, a position often at odds with the subservient role imagined for them. To cite just one more example, it was in fact the students and teachers of Costa Rica's first normal school, the Colegio Superior de Señoritas, who, in the wake of the military regime of Federico Tinoco (1917-1919), founded the Liga Feminista Costarricense in 1923, advocating for women's suffrage, improved teachers' salaries, and an end to sex-based employment discrimination (Palmer and Rojas Chaves 45-46). Women were at once necessary to the romantic vision of national motherhood and dangerous to its legitimacy in their assumption of political agency, which began to erode, slowly, the patriarchal domination of men in both public and private spheres. This debate was by no means resolved in the first decades of the twentieth century, when the Bunge siblings published their family-oriented educational texts. While the supposed biological destiny of women to be mothers played into both liberal and Catholic visions of a woman's suitability—indeed patriotic duty—to educate future generations, it was female psychology, a woman's relationship with herself and with her students, that most preoccupied statesmen and politicians.

## QUEER TEACHINGS: FROM THE TEXTBOOK

Pedagogy theorists, particularly from intersectional feminist and queer perspectives, tend to point to the site of the classroom (rather than the textbook) and to the relationship between teacher and student, as key to the contradictory juncture of identification, disavowal, and discipline that shaped the identities of young students in a heteronormative world. This should not be surprising since the classroom is often the primary space of engagement for young people in the psychic, corporeal, and social regimes of normativity. For example, in *The Avowal of Difference*, Ben. Sifuentes-Jáuregui argues that Mario Vargas Llosa's 1967 novel *Los cachorros* demonstrates how upper-class pedagogy instructs in how to recognize and then disavow the queerness that in turn marks the elite social group as cohesive. In this way, the maintenance of upper-class privilege depends on learning normativity through a shared proximity to queerness, but always mediated by the rejection of that which one must not be (queer). When Sifuentes-Jáuregui notes, "more than just a psychic device, disavowal becomes a pedagogical imperative that is performed by the upper-class bourgeoisie in Vargas Llosa's text to outline the limits of their privilege" (153), we sense how whether in the early- mid- or late-twentieth century, class belonging takes shape through a disavowal of queerness, which comes to mark the limits of acceptable sociality. The most prominent example of this contradictory position is the aforementioned Gabriela Mistral, whose public figure has become an important touchstone in Latin American queer studies. In particular, Fiol-Matta illuminates how Mistral inspired (and cultivated) an ambiguous image as national schoolteacher in Chile—and later Mexico—one that harnessed her sexual ambiguity in order to inspire a contradictory process of psychic identification/disavowal, attraction/repulsion in both students and the nation.

Fiol-Matta focuses on the psychic processes by which Mistral as national (as continental) schoolteacher came to supplant the mother in the life of the child. This process requires first disidentification with the mother and second identification with the teacher that would allow for, finally, the successful substitution of both figures by the state. As she reminds, the schoolteacher was "a primary vehicle for the world-making project of the state," which itself becomes "a site of melancholic identification through a construct of national belonging, which depends on the (repudiated) figure of the mother" (39; 47-48). Here, the relationship between schoolteacher, mother, and state, is inevitably marked by a sense of subjective loss. Loss of the figure of the mother who is replaced by the schoolteacher. Loss of the polymorphous sexuality that comes with the subjectification, the psychic "straightening out" that results from the process of affective alignment with the state. This loss of the sense of an individual self allows for the transformation of a child into a citizen. Mistral's queerness is harnessed by the Chilean state to inaugurate a contradictory dis/identification with gender variance and deviant sexuality. In this chapter, I build on Fiol-Matta's theorization by shifting from the space of the classroom to that of the textbook. Both *El Arca de Noé* and *Nuestra Patria* aim to instruct students how to feel and act Argentine by hailing them as part of a familial matrix that is at once a mimetic representation of upper-class sociality and, perhaps inadvertently, an appeal to exploit the queerness that sustained that sociality. These texts shed light on how the Bunge siblings understood the relationship between citizenship and the nation, pedagogy and subjectivity, family and memory, morality and queerness. But they also reveal how the textual structuring of affect depended on harnessing the (Bunge) family's queerness for the benefit of the nation.

This chapter does not deal primarily with the student-teacher relationship, but rather with the textual representation of kinship as a metonymic device meant to produce particular effects and affects. In part, this is because neither Carlos Octavio nor Julia nor Delfina were ever employed as primary or secondary school teachers. While Carlos Octavio did hold several university appointments over the course of his life, his engagement with early education was almost entirely theoretical, as an expert in the history of pedagogy benefiting from the full backing of the Argentine state. Likewise, though Julia and Delfina would go on to publish many textbooks that also aligned with national interests, neither served as a teacher, except—and this is telling—within the space of their own homes (that is, as mothers and grandmothers). In other words, the Bunge siblings never occupied the controversial role of primary school teacher, protected by class privilege and unburdened by the economic need that led many young women and men to join the ranks of "maestras" and "maestros" at the turn of the century. This means that their bodies never felt the contradictory flows of identification, recognition, and substitution that are at the heart of the teacher-student relationship. The texts published by Carlos Octavio and Julia and Delfina do instruct students in proper behavior toward their teacher. However, they do not rely on a process of subjective dissonance, on a rejection of the mother in favor of the teacher, in order to transform students into citizens. Rather, their texts instruct the channeling of affective dispositions toward students and the nation. They focus on developing flows of feeling and on reorienting object relations rather than psychic disavowal.

This leads me to one final methodological consideration. While I draw on both pedagogical theory and queer studies, the texts that I study in this chapter are deeply invested in producing a particular—national—feeling. *El Arca de Noé* and *Nuestra Patria* express a sense of anxiety, a fear of loss, by concretizing a sociality that is no longer viable because of the shifting political dynamics of modernity. The texts then transform that private anxiety into a public project of affective education. The authors' own experiences and family history become a public good to be circulated in a national market meant to convert (potentially delinquent) children into patriots. The melancholy identification noted by Fiol-Matta takes on new meaning in this case: the potential decline—the loss—of upper-class hegemony is transformed into a desirable, indeed a necessary, affect on which successful citizen-making depends. However, in contrast with the redeployment of melancholy in contemporary cultural studies (i.e., Eng, Love, and Cvetkovich), which points to the dynamic potential for radical and queer worldmaking projects that harness melancholy's contradictions, what we see in the Bunge family's pedagogy is the politicization of upper-class nostalgia and fear, molded into programmatic narratives of feeling and eventually overcoming loss. The publicness of these public feelings is what interests me here. In a paradoxical twist, both texts become manuals of public feeling by virtue of their insistence on folding intimate, familial—and thus private—experiences into the hegemonic narrative of national belonging.

Insofar as these texts are based on publicizing the intimate, the reticent but underlying queerness of family attachments comes to form the contradictory well from which springs a conscientious flow of these public feelings. Here, following Cvetkovich, I use the word *feeling* as vernacular, embodied, and intentionally imprecise; as a mode of negotiating beyond, but also through, sensation and affect (*Depression* 4-5). In the end, these textbooks take intimate familial feelings—trauma, desire, love, care—and project them onto the public sphere as essential to the ontological disciplinarity of cultural nationalism at the turn of the century, a strand of political thought which, against its express designs, comes to rely on the family's essential queerness for its own logical substantiation.

I turn first to the two-volume text *El Arca de Noé*, which utilizes a kinship imaginary that draws on the lived experiences of the authors themselves as members of the Bunge family. That is, the text mines the personal memories of Julia and Delfina Bunge as the primary material from which they construct the short stories, parables, and moralistic tales that are meant to instruct students how to feel Argentine. In doing so, this text harnesses kinship relations as a pedagogical tool for young children through which they are taught how to feel toward each other, their school, and the nation. The sisters make explicit the link between family, classroom, and nation, a synecdoche that frames the demand for obedience to the state as a form of familial pleasure. I then approach *Nuestra Patria*, which also makes use of the affective and psychological domain of the family for childhood instruction. Carlos Octavio includes his own childhood memoirs in the text, a nostalgic yearning for a bygone era, which he proffers as a necessary model for young Argentines to emulate. Both *El Arca de Noé* and *Nuestra Patria* utilize the memory of family as a major thematic and structural element. But here the role of family is double: on the one hand, certain sections from both publications are derived from the collective memory of the Bunge family, and, on the other, many chapters deal specifically with teaching familiarity, the affective bonds between siblings, obedience to one's parents, and appropriate gendered behavior, as the logical outcome of the excavation and subsequent rejection of queerness. These are textbooks that draw on intimate family relations, memories, and feelings, in order to produce fealty to the nation in a crucial moment in which the meaning of Argentine citizenship was being contested. What distinguishes these publications from other textbooks of the same era is that the Bunge siblings take their own family as the model for the future of the Argentine people. In doing so, I argue, they conjure the specter of queerness—the queerness inherent in all familial relations—in order to discipline Argentine youth in the art of loving each other. Reminiscent of

Foucualt's rendering of sexuality as a "transfer point for relations of power" (*History* 103), these textbooks do not simply discipline childhood sexuality as an effort to prevent perverse desires. Rather, insofar as the love of country, of fellow citizens, and of the family is understood as a necessary if unpredictable set of affective dispositions, they demand a nationalistic submission to authority that comes as the result of the recognition of those desires and their subsequent transformation into a fraternal linkages. This means that the disciplining of sexuality also requires the routing of desire toward specific institutions, people, and concepts. It means, too, that the school textbook provides a framework through which the family occupies a central—and controversial—role in producing and disciplining queerness. As with the diary and family photograph of previous chapters, the textbook is a technology of self that organizes feeling toward people and concepts, ensuring not just patriotism but heteronormativity and ethnic cohesion.

## *EL ARCA DE NOÉ*:
## FOR LOVE OF FAMILY,
## SCHOOL, AND COUNTRY

*El Arca de Noé* models affective orientations and social belonging through fictionalized dialogue between family members. This operation takes place both in terms of the development of the text and in terms of its narrative framework. That is, in addition to an omniscient narrator that serves as a guide for the student (a ventriloquized voice of the authors), individual characters, Adita, Juan, Jorge, Tito, Mamá (Mom), and Papá (Dad), among others, interject periodically to relate an ethical conundrum or moralistic tale, which is often carried out as dialogue. The text thus alternates between multiple forms of address—dialogue, interior monologue, omniscient narration, poetry, and song—as a way of diversifying its narrative structure and engaging diverse publics in the affective field of the family. All of these voices are related. The organizational impulse is designed to simulate (and stimulate) the feeling of belonging to a medium-sized family whose members participate in the larger world, explore their surroundings, and learn about themselves and each other through their ever more complex experiences (both emotionally and psychologically).

In fact, an idealized domestic scene from the Bunge family household serves as the opening image for the first volume of the textbook.

> Había una vez dos niñas que iban á la escuela, jugaban, y leían sus libros de lectura, lo mismo que vosotros. Tenían muchos hermanitos, y entre todos inventaban los trabajos más interesantes y los juegos más divertidos [...] Era una familia muy alegre. Pero era también una familia estudiosa. Todas las noches podía verse, alrededor de una mesa cubierta de libros y cuadernos, el racimo que formaban las cabezas inclinadas.

> Once upon a time there were two girls who went to school, they played, and they read their schoolbooks, the same as you all. They had many brothers, and together they came up with the most interesting things to do and the most fun games [...] It was a very happy family. But it was also a studious family. Every night you could see, around a table covered with books and notebooks, the cluster that their inclined heads made. (*Arca* 1: 5)[8]

Julia and Delfina integrate themselves and their family history into the text by a narrative device common to fairy tales. The conceit of fictionalizing their own childhood is aimed not at likening them to their readers—they do not present themselves as equals—but rather at distinguishing themselves as models of an ideal affective domestic economy. The young sisters portray themselves as obedient and cheerful, their siblings teaching each other new games. Not unlike Delfina's diary entry from January 26, 1904, discussed in chapter 2, the space of the home stages a collective pedagogy in which closeness is achieved through the repetition of *happy* familial interactions. This "happy family" is at once the Bunge family and the larger national family that Julia and Delfina wish to cultivate in others, a model of domesticity and of sibling collaboration with important resonance in the conflictive political environment of the first decade of the twentieth century. The values of "happiness" and "studiousness" are heightened by the physical orientation of bodies around the family table. This domestic orientation was not lost on Gilberta S. de Kurth, who reviewed the text for *El Monitor de la Educación Común* (*The Monitor of Common Education*) in 1913, and describes it as "lleno de imagines familiares y queridos para los niños" ("full of dear and familiar images for children"; 122). De Kurth continues to emphasize the affective connection between the authors and their young readers: "Y así, insensiblemente, contando cosas agradables y presentando cuadros familiares, fluyen sin esfuerzo las ideas morales: amor, deber, obediencia, justicia, trabajo, caridad" ("And thus, imperceptibly, recounting agreeable things and presenting familiar portraits, moral ideas flow without effort: love, duty, obedience, justice, work, charity"; 123). There are two points that I would like to emphasize here. First, teaching "moral ideas," which is the end goal of primary education, requires effort on the part of the students. That is, morality is not natural but learned. Notably, these ideas range from the immediate to the universal: patriotic notions of justice, duty, obedience, and work ethic are complimented by interpersonal relations of love and charity. Second, such a range of *outcomes* (to use contemporary parlance) is achieved "imperceptibly," unwittingly, by identifying with the "familiar portraits" that structure the text. It follows that at the time of the text's publication the expected audience, children, were assumed *not to be moral*. They had to learn to control their behaviors, indeed their desires, by submitting to the will of the text. In other words, and in line with Foucault's theorization of childhood sexuality, these students were imagined as queer—or as having queer potential—from the outset (*History* 1: 104). Here, all children are presumed queer until proven otherwise, or at least until successfully indoctrinated by the state's curricular apparatus and the teacher's discipline.

It should not be surprising then, that another key site of sexual discipline—the family—became the organizational matrix around which primary and secondary schooling was enacted in Argentina at the turn of the century. Family imagery is linked to the notion of a moral education and conceived of as a collection of affective and ethical relationships that are heavily influenced by Catholic social thought whereby the future citizen becomes like his fellow Argentines. What is more, citizenship is constructed not simply as an abstraction of national belonging, but as intimate, familial. After all, the title, *El Arca de Noé*, serves not only as an intertextual reference to the Bible, but also as the name given to the home occupied by the family that is fictionalized in its pages. The characters live in this "arc," which serves to structure and limit spatially the imaginary of the text. In other words, the family is both the message and the vehicle for educating students in how to approach each other. It is not simply that the Bunge sisters fell back on what they knew most intimately—the family—even though that is probably true—but rather that the familial as an affective and social matrix harnesses better than anything else the experience of (1) repressing queerness, and (2) eliciting feelings of relatedness and care that are not easily achieved through liberal abstractions such as freedom, justice, and patriotism. To expand on this argument, I focus on three key examples from the text for third-grade students.

## Militarism and Productivity

Of all the stories included in *El Arca de Noé*, "Servir a la patria" ("To serve the nation") is the most nationalistic and the most involved in the overarching debate about the future of *argentinidad* around 1910. It is constructed as a dialogue between Max, a student, and his teacher.

> —Estoy deseando que haya una Guerra en mi país, señorita.
> —No digas eso, Max; la Guerra es terrible, cruel.
> —Es que yo quiero pelear para defender a mi patria.
> —Sí, se debe defender a la patria cuando es atacada, pero una Guerra no debe desearse jamás; todo país sufre mucho con ella.
> —Pero usted, señorita, nos ha dicho que debemos servir a la patria. ¿Y cómo la serviremos si no hay guerras?
>
> —I am hoping that there be a War in my country, Miss.
> —Don't say that, Max; War is terrible, cruel.
> —It's just that I want to fight to defend my homeland.
> —Yes, we must defend the homeland when it is attacked, but we should never hope for a War; the whole country suffers a lot in one.
> —And you, Miss, you have told us that we should serve our homeland. And how do we serve her if there are no wars? (*Arca* 2: 58)

Young Max is confused by his teacher's reaction. Having already internalized the need to "serve the homeland," he assumes that the only way to do so *for men* is by defending it in war. He is expressing an idealized masculinity enacted under such circumstances as the crisis of national identity at the turn of the century. His "desire," after all, is not simply that there be a war, but that he be able to defend his "patria" by putting his body to the service of the nation. In this way the security of the nation's identity is conflated with the ability of the nation to defend itself, as masculinity and militarism are directly implicated in restoring what Max perceives as a country in need of rescue.

The link between militarism and masculinity was a key ideological debate at the turn of the century. Indeed, this short story dramatizes a desire, expressed by several Argentine intellectuals, to "masculinize" the public sphere. This story dialogues with the growing trend toward cultural nationalism in the first decade of the twentieth century, a movement whose origin has often been linked to the man Delfina Bunge married in 1910,

Manuel Gálvez. When Max admits naively that he desires there be a war, he is also expressing one of the tenets of early nationalist thought. In particular, the idea that to galvanize opposition to supposed threats to national unity such as communists, anarchists, immigrants, Jews, and *maricones* ("queers"), what Argentina needed was an external enemy, a war with a foreign country. This is precisely what Gálvez would himself write through the voice of the eponymous narrator of his 1910 text *El diario de Gabriel Quiroga* (*The Diary of Gabriel Quiroga*).

> La salvación de la República Argentina está en la guerra con el Brasil. La guerra haría que los pueblos se conociesen, reuniría a los argentinos en un ideal común, y despertaría en el país entero el sentimiento de la nacionalidad. [...] La guerra concretaría en un solo pensamiento los deseos, las esperanzas y los ensueños de todos los ciudadanos.

> The salvation of the Argentine Republic is in war with Brazil. War would force our peoples to get to know each other, it would bring Argentines together through a common ideal, and it would awaken national sentiment (feeling) across the country. [...] War would crystallize in one thought the desires, the hopes, and the dreams of all citizens. (101-2)

Though Gálvez's narrator would eventually admit that such a war would result inevitably in the defeat of Argentina and talk himself out of the idea, he is expressing an important relationship between national sentiment, "el sentimiento de la nacionalidad," and military action. The lack of common identity, of a shared spirituality and sense of nationalism, is what such a war, according to the narrator, would remedy. Gálvez hearkens the fundamental division in Argentine history between city and countryside—populations (peoples) that do not know and rather mistrust each other—suggesting that the only solution to this long-standing division is once and for all to unite the heterogeneous population in one "pensamiento," a shared consciousness of the future and a shared appreciation for Argentina's Spanish heritage. Punctuating his historicist reading, Gabriel Quiroga quips, "En la hora presente, gobernar es argentinizar" ("In the present, to govern is to Argentinize"; 117). Paraphrasing Alberdi's maxim "gobernar es poblar" ("to govern is to populate"), the narrator decries the immigration policies of the mid-nineteenth century that had welcomed immigrants as a way to develop the Argentine economy and, it was hoped, to enrich its culture with their European blood. The implication is particularly damning of cosmopolitan Buenos Aires, where millions of immigrants were especially resistant to cultural assimilation. Rather than more immigrants, Gálvez asserts, it is necessary to turn those already here into Argentines, to become, to make Argentine. In this, *El arca de Noé* intervenes in a key nationalist discussion on masculinity and patriotism, suggesting that in order for young men to serve their homeland, they must recognize first their innate bellicosity and then transform that affect into a productive use of the body.

The story continues.

—No creas, Max, que solo se sirve a la patria con la espada. Se la sirve igualmente con la pluma, con el arado.... Todo hombre que trabaja sirve a la patria. La sirve todo buen ciudadano; y no solo los que pelean son buenos ciudadanos. [...]

Vosotros, niños, que estudiáis en esta escuela, estáis ya sirviendo a la patria, porque la instrucción de los niños aumenta la felicidad y el honor del país.

Un hombre de bien sirve a su patria en todos los actos de su vida.

—Don't you believe, Max, that you can only serve the homeland with the sword. You can also serve with the pen, with the plow.... Every man who works serves the homeland. Every good citizen serves her; and not only those who fight are good citizens. [...]

All of you, children, who study in this school, are already serving the homeland, because the education of children increases the country's happiness and honor.

A good man serves the homeland in all parts of his life. (58–59)

When the narrator responds, "Don't you believe, Max, that you can only serve the homeland with the sword," she prefigures another early-twentieth-century nationalist text, Leopoldo Lugones's 1924 "Discurso de Ayacucho" (also known as "La hora de la espada" ["The hour of the sword"]), which calls for a turn to the armed forces in order to prevent the "demagogy" of popular democracy or socialism. I make this point because Lugones situates the military as the only true agent of nationalism, the force that gave life to the Argentine people by securing their independence. He saw the army as the only institution that could reinstate the hierarchical order that had been lost in the years of democratic liberalism that followed the Revolución de Mayo (Rock, *Authoritarian* 72). This blatantly antidemocratic view was more extreme than many of Lugones's contemporaries. While I will discuss the relationship between nationalist essays and ideologies of kinship in chapter 5, it is important to state here that for Lugones and Gálvez cultural nationalism was based on the idea that the population of Argentina must return to the militaristic masculinity that had predominated during the period of independence. They see the loss of this bravado as a product of the weakening of the Argentine race through immigration and cultural decline.

While Julia and Delfina Bunge do not want the military to be employed to reinstate a prior social order in Argentina, they do recognize that that militarism is socially useful if it can be transformed into a broader, more flexible masculinity that is amenable to capitalist production. In their work, the desire to fight is replaced by the imperative to serve; the young man's seemingly natural bellicose urges are transformed into other forms of productivity. Transformed in this scenario is the apical position of martial masculinity in modern Argentina, replaced by a range of forms of relation to the state. In the end, it is not military service, but capitalist labor that should be the standard by which men are judged: "every man who works serves the homeland." To attend school, to run a farm, to write judicious laws, all are identified as alternatives to the military. They shift this nationalist masculinity from a martial ethos to a capitalistic one in which the new demands of Argentine society—increased production, efficiencies, and modernization—outweigh the desire for a hegemonic manliness rooted in the capacity for physical violence. Thus, the sisters recognize the difficult political climate in which this text was written, proposing to diffuse masculine angst and repurpose it through labor. Not just at school, not just with the sword, but with every act, does an "hombre de bien" ("a good man") prove himself as such. The tale culminates with an exhortation to perform this productive masculinity. This is what Julia and Delfina Bunge propose to the anxious masculine subject, unsure of his role in a society no longer culturally homogenous and which has been infiltrated by "foreign" (read effete) trends in aesthetics and politics. In contrast with Gálvez and Lugones, the Bunge sisters argue that the Argentine man has other avenues, other ways in which to perform masculinity than the purely bellicose. In fact, what they recognize is the constitutive function of melancholia for the angst-ridden masculine subject. They propose to transform that angst, that sense of loss and desire for virile bellicosity, into a public feeling of desire for capitalist production.

"The school"

As I have been arguing, the ideology of *El arca de Noé* is grounded in replicating the family at (and as a) school. In the short story "La escuela" ("The school"), we hear the voice of a young and eager student: "Dice la señorita Elcira que la escuela es como una segunda familia, principalmente para los huerfanitos, a quienes debemos tratar con especial cariño" ("Miss Elcira says that school is like a second family, especially for little orphans, whom we should treat with special kindness"; 12). The link between school and family depends on transferring the feelings typically associated with the bonds of kinship to fellow classmates. Here, the figure of the orphan signifies not only as one in need of special care, but also as one who may not know how to treat others due to his or her lack of parental guidance. It presumes that without this care, those unfortunate orphans will not learn the proper affective dispositions toward fellow citizens, and thus become a nuisance if not a danger to the nation. In this instance the school supplants the home as the site not simply of education, but more importantly, of kindness. This kindness is demonstrated when, in the case of a student who has been repeatedly absent, "la señorita averigua si está enfermo, y, si puede, va a visitarle" ("Miss [the teacher] finds out if he or she is ill, and, if she can, goes to visit him or her"; 12). This line addresses both the teacher and the student, and establishes an ideal protocol for what students can expect in terms of collective care. What is more, the story expands this affective field particularly in moments of failure: "Si alguno comete una falta grave, *todos nos avergonzamos por él*" ("If anyone commits a grave error, *we are all embarrassed for him*"; 13, my emphasis), and success: "si otro es caritativo o lleva a cabo una hermosa acción, nos alegramos y decimos con orgullo: 'es compañero nuestro'" ("if someone else is charitable or does something beautiful, we are all happy and we say with pride: 'he is our classmate'"; 13). To share in both the shame and the pride of others is thus construed as the basis of a collective pedagogy in how to feel in relation (both how to engage with and receive feeling). The classroom expands into the home, as does the intervention of the state in matters of domestic education.

This connection is confirmed, finally, by the synecdoche established between family, school, and nation: "Dice la señorita que el buen nombre de la escuela depende de la conducta de cada uno de nosotros; que en esto, la escuela es también una pequeña patria. Que si aprendemos a cuidar del nombre de nuestra escuela, cuando seamos grandes sabremos cuidar del nombre de nuestras familias, y del nombre de nuestra patria" ("Miss says that the good name of our school depends on the conduct of each of us; that in this, the school is also a little homeland. That if we learn to care for the name of our school, when we are grown we will know how to care for the name of our families, and the name of our homeland"; 13). This symbolic relationship positions the reputation of each (family, school, and nation) as dependent on the good conduct of the students. It is as a member of each group that the individual understands the responsibilities, emotional dispositions, and codes of conduct by which he will be judged. The process of maintaining the reputation of one's name becomes a key element that invokes the preservation of social bonds through a set of learned behaviors, a habitus. By correctly deploying the social bonds that maintain order, one's name comes to be regarded (as patriotic, deviant, worthy, unworthy, etc.). Thus, in order to feel connected to the nation, one must first hold reverence for one's own name—that is, to heredity, patriarchal lineage, to family. As Foucault might say, this process of keeping up one's family name is crucial because it overlays the regime of alliance with the regime of sexuality, and in this sense it is to have successfully been disciplined by both. When the school becomes a "pequeña patria" it frames the love of that institution as a precursor to and model for the love of students' own families and the nation.

Indeed, the representational economy of this lesson depends on the slippage between classroom, family, and nation. It proposes the equivalence of affective dispositions toward each, and gives the state—through its management of public pedagogy—primacy in how feeling develops between individuals and social bodies. To return to the question that I posed at the beginning of this chapter (How does one learn to love one's country?), Julia and Delfina Bunge propose that this happens by learning to love one's school. In this scenario, the public feeling of devotion to the nation comes by modeling love for one's peers in the intimate space of the classroom.

"Another family of emigrants"

A final example of this exhortation to public feeling is found in the short story titled, "Otra familia de emigrantes" ("Another family of emigrants"). "El gallego," José Rodríguez, his wife and three children, represent an immigrant family—a poor, but desirable immigrant family—on their way to Argentina.⁹ The narrator adds, "en su tierra se habían encontrado sin trabajo y por lo tanto sin comida" ("in their country they found themselves out of work and thus without food"; 139). From the outset, Argentina is marked as a land of promise, economic opportunity, and stability. The illustration of this tale shows a vaguely discernible but matronly woman attempting to entertain her young children, huddled together for warmth, while the husband, Rodríguez, stares off into the distance.

The "other" immigrant family referenced by the title of this short story is a family of swallows that undergoes similar hardships on their journey to a new land. The Spanish family is thus anthropomorphically linked to the swallow, a harbinger of spring, but more directly used as a symbol of migration. Like them, the father enjoys the gift of song, which is intercalated throughout the text as a way to set off his doubts: "Dime, dime, golondrina / Que vas cruzando la mar, / ¿es verdad que en la Argentina / todos pueden prosperar?" ("Tell me, tell me, swallow / Who is now crossing the sea, / Is it true that in Argentina / Everyone can prosper?"; 140). The Rodríguez family is one of the thousands who immigrated to Argentina at the peak of the economic boom of the turn of the century. David Rock notes that by 1914 nearly one-third of the Argentine population was foreign-born, and 80 percent were either immigrants themselves or descended from those who had arrived since 1850 (*Argentina* 166). To prosper economically and to escape the hardships of home, were common themes among immigrants, and the Rodríguez family is taken as an example of the type of family that must now be integrated into the Argentine social, political, and economic spheres. It is also notable that this is a Spanish family and not an Italian one, a nod to the cultural nationalist desire to reconnect with Argentina's Hispanic heritage. As we have seen, the connection between Italian immigrants and "anarchism" made them a difficult group to idealize for the elite.¹⁰ In this case, even though many Spaniards were involved in working-class organizing, they were also "salvageable" as living relics of Argentina's colonial past. It is telling that the Bunge sisters would link these Spanish immigrants to the term *golondrina*, which, at least in Argentina, was typically reserved for seasonal Italian farm laborers.¹¹ This conflation marks the Rodríguez family as foreign, but quaint; different, but familiar.

"Al principio él y su familia sufrieron en Buenos Aires muchas privaciones. Pero en su tierra las habían pasado más duras" ("In the beginning he and his family suffered in Buenos Aires for want of many things. But in their land they had been through harder times"), begins the next section

(140). This is a family that suffers its austerity with resignation. Rodríguez may sing of hope, of the future that he might provide for his family, but never laments. The Rodríguez family uses its voice as adornment rather than protest; their hardships are transformed into folkloric melodies sung to pass the time. Finally, their luck begins to change when the family starts to sell *mantillas*, the lacework typical of their homeland, establishing a mode of production within the family, a domestic economy of cultural artifacts for consumption by the Argentine public. Rodríguez and his son venture out to sell what his wife and daughters produce at home. This binary division of labor between does not disturb the association of women with handiwork and of men with the public space of the market. Here the Bunge sisters are hearkening back to a bygone era of female domesticity. As with other parts of Latin America, before industrialization in the mid-nineteenth century, women's labor was generally restricted to traditional handicrafts such as weaving and to cottage industries such as soap and candle manufacturing (Lavrin 56).

At the turn of the century, however, more women became employed in a range of public and private industries, from public administration (clerical work) to education to various service occupations. For example, Lavrin notes that in Buenos Aires from 1904 to 1909 the number of women with a defined occupation doubled from 104,114 to 223,769 (57). In this context, it should come as no surprise that as women entered the public sphere, many nationalist intellectuals saw women's labor as a threat to social cohesion and as a sign of moral decay.[12] Julia and Delfina are careful to position the survival of the Rodríguez family as the result of a cohesive, gender normative domestic economy, rather than owing to a transgressively public femininity.

The Rodríguez family begins to enjoy some success, returning each day with their lot sold, but, importantly, each day singing a new tune. The men are described as being more successful because of their song, while the women are also described as producing better lacework when they sing. The voice of the immigrant, then, is appropriated by the mechanisms of labor, by the imperative to produce as part of the Buenos Aires economy. This model of performing arduous labor with a smile and a song is portrayed as the best way for the Rodríguez family to survive in their new country; they become a model for others who might use their voice for other, less charming, less folkloric pursuits. What is more, and in keeping with the underlying cultural intent of *El Arca de Noé*, this success is attributed to the family's morality: "Como era una familia honrada, trabajadora y amable con los clientes, pronto reunieron, entre padres e hijos, una fortunita, y pudieron, a los pocos años, regresar a su país con trajes y pañoletas nuevas, y con pasaje de segunda" ("Since they were an honorable family, hardworking and pleasant to their clients, soon they saved up, between parents and children, a small fortune, and they could, after a few years, return to their country with new clothes and headscarves, and with a second-class ticket"; 142). We can see the Bunge sisters invest in this cast of characters the ability to succeed in Argentina, as long as they follow certain conditions: an unflagging work ethic, a cheerful disposition, a smoothly functioning domestic economy, an ability to sing, all contribute to their viability. Their labor is consumed by Argentines not simply for its use value, but also as a link to a desirable historical legacy. They are living examples of the Hispanic heritage on which the cultural nationalists of the turn of the century based their historical revisionism and reevaluation of Argentina's link to Spain. Importantly, however, they are not interested in staying in Argentina, but rather, together, "between parents and children," they save enough money to return to Spain not without first purchasing a new wardrobe to debut on their arrival back home. They are caricatures whose past, whose labor, comes to signify in its presence as well as its absence. They are desirable as immigrants because they are honorable, family-oriented, folkloric, because they are a living anachronism, and because their bodies are inoffensive, removable.

It is certainly true that many immigrants did not make a one-way trip across the Atlantic. But, as historian Susana Torrado reports, this was mostly the case for single men, which constituted 71 percent of the immigration between 1880 and 1923 (94-95). That is, the arrival of families like the one described in this short story would not have been common, with only 38 percent of immigrants in this same period arriving as part of a family, and much less as an entire nuclear family unit (95). Still, the conclusion leaves us wondering whether the Rodríguez family is really wanted in Argentina. They migrated in order to better their economic circumstances, only to return to Spain when they had accomplished this goal, thus confirming some of the main complaints of nationalist politicians who claimed that immigrants only came to Argentina to "hacer la América" ("to strike it rich"). What is clearly lacking in this case is a patriotic sentiment toward their new country, that *public feeling* of belonging. Instead, the Rodríguez family uses Argentina as a space for economic survival, not acculturating to local practices, but rather commercially successful by performing, perhaps exaggerating their foreignness for locals.

The authors may have sensed this ambivalence and conclude the tale by offering a solution that again turns to the feeling of citizenship: "Muchos inmigrantes toman tanto cariño a esta tierra que tan buena acogida les hace, que sacan *carta de ciudadanía* para tener los derechos y cumplir los deberes del ciudadano argentino. ¿Y cómo no amar a una patria a la que aman también los extranjeros?" ("Many immigrants become so enamored with this land because of the warm welcome they receive, that they acquire the *citizenship card* in order to have the same rights and fulfill the same obligations as Argentine citizens. And how could you not love a homeland that is so loved even by foreigners"; 142 emphasis in the original). This final quotation brings us back to the relationship between the student and the teacher as a synecdoche for the larger relationship between the individual and the nation. That many immigrants "so love" Argentina is used as an argument to push current citizens to also love their country. A deficit of patriotic sentiment is the starting point from which the Bunge sisters aim to encourage young Argentines, primarily second-generation immigrants—that is, the Rodríguez families who did not return to their home country—to strengthen their ties to fellow citizens. The political difference, however, posits those who would take Argentine citizenship against those who do not. This practice of patriotic sentimentalism is voiced through the rhetorical question that closes this short story: "¿Y cómo no amar a una patria a la que aman también los extranjeros?" ("And how could you not love a homeland that is so loved even by foreigners"). If the foreigners can love Argentina, then you (citizen) can too, the narrator implies, in a gesture that aims to coerce students into loving the *patria*. In fact, I am tempted to read this final gesture as an attempt to guilt Argentines into loving their country. The rhetorical question is not entirely rhetorical. Rather, it lays bare the fragility of Argentine patriotism at the turn of the century, an affective deficit that is exposed by the absence of the Rodríguez family and by the traces they leave behind. Their lacework, their song, their bodies, become the residue of a subjective presence that was never able (or willing) to assimilate into the national population, that never felt clearly enough the flows of patriotic belonging. Yet the residual effect of their departure makes room for those other immigrants whose relationship with the country falls more in line with the cultural nationalist imperative to love Argentina and obey its norms; to become part of its family. Here,

Julia and Delfina Bunge are writing to express, on the one hand, the corporeal incompatibility of some immigrants to Argentina, and on the other, their own critique of the unpatriotic citizen. Their short story reminds us that the school textbook is also a space within which feelings of patriotism are expressed in contrast with the anxieties about shifting class relations, cultural adaptation, and national identity. In the end, the parable of the Rodríguez family amounts to an exhortation to love. To love the country as one loves one's family. To love one's country because others also love it. To love Argentina *as a family*; as if to belong, to exist as a citizen, depended on directing that love toward fellow citizens who in their recognition of that love come to accept and validate the possibilities of belonging to each other and the nation.

To sum up, by turning the private feeling of loss into a public expression of culture that is harnessed by capitalist production, the Rodríguez family comes to represent a successful immigrant story. In the same way, the Bunge sisters turn their cultural privilege as members of the upper class, into a public deficit. The public feeling of loss may not be explicit in the narrative organization of *El Arca de Noé*, but it remains the underlying premise that must be resolved, transformed into a collective sense of love. In this sense, the Bunge sisters are negotiating what is *owed* to the patria. On the one hand, students are imagined as owing loyalty and obedience to their school, and thus to the nation. On the other hand, they owe love to each other *as citizens*, a love that must be learned by transforming certain private feelings (militarism, loss) into public expressions of confraternity, and, indeed, love. This feeling of citizenship depends on harnessing the trope of kinship, or rather, the love that kinship assumes as inherent to its social organization. As such, the text incites students to make public the love they feel in private (for their own families). Patriotic sentiment is only achieved by transferring the love of oneself and one's family to the school and the nation.

## *NUESTRA PATRIA*: PEDAGOGY, MEMORY, AND MASCULINE ANGST

I argue above that Julia and Delfina Bunge's *El Arca de Noé* is a text that embraces the ambiguity of familial attachments in order to propose a model of belonging that construes the nation as a structural replacement for the nuclear family whereby the textual representation of kinship harnesses the intimacy of the family to do the work of creating public feelings of relatedness. Likewise, Carlos Octavio Bunge was explicit in his desire to contribute to the nationalization of Argentine citizens and to consolidating their collective feeling of devotion to each other, the nation, and the ideals of modernity. In what follows, I examine the process by which he transforms private feelings, memories, and queer dispositions into a public good for Argentine citizens. While his textbook participates in the overarching project of instructing young Argentines in moral, civic, historical, and cultural nationalism, it does so by harnessing the erotic ambivalences of his own childhood, transformed into a national model. I explore the contradictory maneuvers that Bunge deploys in order to advocate for a disciplinary model of family life in Argentina, while also narrating his own youth obsessions as a generalizable example of what all Argentine children must experience, including a fascination with martial masculinity that links back to Bunge's fiction (analyzed in chapter 1) and photographic presence (analyzed in chapter 3). For Carlos Octavio, the anxious masculine subject becomes a key site of exploring the juncture of private and public pedagogy, a site that explores the image, the memory, of himself as a child and projects that image for the nation.

In advance of the publication of *Nuestra Patria*, Bunge published a prologue to his textbook as a separate article in *El Monitor de la educación común*. There, he describes the influence of social psychology on his pedagogical vision: "la Patria según se infiere de la sociología, es ante todo y esencialmente el resultado de los sentimientos e ideas sociales de cada pueblo. Si esos sentimientos e ideas no se cultivan y florecen, la Patria se disgrega y corrompe" ("the homeland as we infer from sociology, is above all and essentially the result of the sentiments [feelings] and social ideas of each people. If those sentiments and ideas are not cultivated and they flower, the Homeland disintegrates and becomes corrupted"; "Teoría" 572). The premise his argument lies in an understanding of the nation as accumulating both feelings and cultural practices that must in turn be nurtured, "cultivated," lest they become "corrupted" through neglect. The botanical metaphor is unoriginal, but powerful. Who is tending this garden—that is, who is in charge of this pedagogical praxis? Likewise, which of the flowering plants are weeds? Bunge asks who belongs to this "*pueblo*" ("people") and who does not. We can infer that not all feelings, not all people, should be cultivated, but rather only those who serve the overarching goals of the intellectual elite to foment national unity. The author makes explicit, however, that defending the *patria* demands not only care and patience, but also an understanding of social difference.

On the surface, *Nuestra Patria* implies an inclusive "we," a "*nosotros*," that includes all Argentine citizens, and yet it is deeply skeptical of the ability recent immigrants and their children have to form part of the national body, and more precisely the national feeling. We see how expanding access to education leads to an anxiety about what that education will actually do. Nicolas Shumway describes this contradiction as inherent to Latin American liberal democracies: "de ahí el doble discurso de todos los gobiernos liberales en algún momento de su historia: son democráticos en teoría pero, en mayor o menor grado, demofóbicos en la práctica" ("hence the double discourse of all liberal governments at some point in their history: they are democratic in theory but, to some degree, demophobic in practice"; *Historia personal* 137). What Shumway calls demophobia, the fear of popular rule, has a long history in Argentina and across Latin America, and was justified by positivist scientists in league with elite politicians at the turn of the century. Argentine intellectuals such as Gálvez—as I note above—Ramos Mejía, de Veyga, Ingenieros, and Carlos Octavio Bunge, cultivated this "double discourse," which saw the education of the masses as essential to mitigating their supposed cultural inferiority for the better functioning of democratic institutions, but at the same time, feared the transformation of the public sphere by a group of people (the masses), those lacking the requisite intellect, culture, or bloodline, whose interests did not align with those of the elite. "To argentinize" was really shorthand for establishing the systems and institutions that would maintain upper-class hegemony.

The most concise articulation of this mistrust appears in Ramos Mejías's *Las multitudes argentinas* ("The Argentine Multitudes") (1899). Ramos Mejía, as I note above, served as the president of Argentina's National Council of Education from 1908 to 1912, and thus was responsible for overseeing the nation's primary and secondary schooling when Bunge published *Nuestra Patria*. For its part, *Las multitudes argentinas* describes the popular classes (the multitude) as impressionable, sensitive, neurotic, passionate, and reactive. "No raciocina, siente" ("It does not reason, it feels"), he writes, of the impulses driving the uneducated masses (33), a view that puts him in line with contemporaneous psychosociological writing from Europe, namely Gustave LeBon's *Psychologie des Foules* (1895). For Ramos Mejía, criollo men have reason, while the largely foreign masses have feelings. Burdened with their linguistic and cultural difference, immigrants were sent to Argentine public schools in order to learn not just reading, writing, and arithmetic, but also how to belong and how become productive (efficient) members of society. Intellectual historian Oscar Terán describes the function of federal school system, under the influence of Ramos Mejía, as a "resorte de nacionalización de las masas que obrara como barrera ante la penetración de ideas subversivas del orden conservador" ("springboard of nationalization of the masses that would function as a barrier faced with the penetration of ideas considered subversive of the conservative order"; *Historia* 139). Thus, cultivating traits such as loyalty, obedience, and discipline was not necessarily meant to provide citizens with the tools to participate in the public sphere, but to set young men and women on a path to recognizing their place in a hierarchical society, particularly for members of recent immigrant groups and the working class. Positivist educators saw the uneducated masses as primal and underdeveloped, and education, insofar as it was the primary location for the state's intervention in popular culture, was tasked with instructing not simply how to master certain basic subjects, but rather, and more urgently, how to *feel*.

*Nuestra Patria* is designed for fifth- and sixth-grade primary school students and also for teachers being trained in Argentina's Normal Schools. From this broad scope (and nearly 500 pages) it is divided into four units: (1) "La tradición y la historia del pueblo argentino" ("Tradition and History of the Argentine People"), (2) "La poesía argentina" ("Argentine Poetry"), (3) "En el país argentino" ("In the Argentine Nation"), and (4) "Cuadros y fases de la vida argentina" ("Portraits and Phases of Argentine Life"). A nationalist literary anthology, the text canonizes writers of diverse ideological backgrounds as it teaches history, geography, and popular and lyric poetry, and describes the cultural tendencies and psychological development of a range of Argentine populations, respectively. In doing so the volume follows a methodological trend at the turn of the century that regarded reading (as opposed to recitation or rote memorization) as the most advanced form of pedagogy for a large and heterogeneous population. From Sarmiento onward literacy not only formed the basis of a modern society, but also one that could make judicious political decisions in the best interest of the nation (de Miguel 110). But a literary anthology is more than just a selection of texts. It is also an ideological *and affective* guide through the history, politics, geography, and domestic economy of the nation. As such, *Nuestra Patria* highlights a broader movement in Argentine intellectual thought to revalue native-born criollos, at the expense of foreigners or recent immigrants. Bunge coincides with other nationalists at the turn of the century such as Ricardo Rojas, Juan Alsina, and Emilio Becher in proclaiming that the most important cultural contributions to Argentina were attributed to men from traditional, landowning families such as his own (Soler 153). To center the role of Argentine criollos was also to propose that their ethnic, cultural, and artistic contributions—as well as their feelings—should become the model for future generations to emulate. In this regard, Carlos Octavio opens his work with the following dedication: "A nuestra Patria, en su primer centenario, tributo el modesto homenaje de este libro, cuyo fin es contribuir a su amor y conocimiento, en las nuevas generaciones de argentinos" ("To our Homeland, on its first centenary, I tribute the modest homage of this book, whose goal is to contribute to its love and understanding, in new generations of Argentines"; n.p.). Love and knowledge are intertwined, indissoluble, in this vision of futurity that links the past (the foundation of the republic in 1810) to the present (the centennial celebrations of 1910), and beyond. From the outset, *Nuestra Patria* is the textual representation of a future-oriented vision of what feelings must be felt in order to produce the type of nation that will be successful in the modern era.

## Images of a Queer Youth

The most direct engagement with teaching love of country appears in the final unit of Bunge's text, "Cuadros y fases de la vida argentina" ("Portraits and Phases of Argentine Life"), which is divided into ten chapters.[13] This section directly links the patriotic pedagogy meant to assuage upper-class anxiety over cultural degeneracy and class inversion with allegorical representations of family, gender, and sociality. In addition to fostering canon formation and cultural standardization, it attempts to predicate a method of psychological development for Argentine youth that takes the author's own childhood as a model. As *the* model. Bunge includes his own childhood memoir as part of this nationalist project, exposing, indeed depending on his own feelings, anxieties, fears, and desires, in order to extrapolate a general rule for how all Argentine children should feel toward each other and toward the nation. The past returns to the space of the textbook as a nostalgic take on what is proposed as the typical Argentine childhood. Bunge's youth becomes the example offered to the nation as what all Argentine youth should feel, become, and desire.

Much like his nationalist precursor Miguel Cané, Carlos Octavio Bunge turned to childhood memories and the family as a space from which to narrate the threat of decadence of the upper class.[14] In the case of Cané, whose *Juvenilia* was published in 1882 when the author was thirty-one years old, Bunge's *Nuestra Patria* was published at the age of thirty-five. The texts are similar in their exaggerated *ubi sunt* posture, but also in their engagement with education and collective identity. Regarding Cané's narrative stance, Sylvia Molloy offers a description that could apply equally to Bunge's in *Nuestra Patria*:

> Written during a time of threatening social change—xenophobia directed towards immigrants was, overtly or covertly, one of the great themes of the period—Cané's book may be read, and indeed should be read, as a rallying cry to the successful happy few; to the elegant, intelligent boys from "civilized" Buenos Aires, who, throughout the pages of *Juvenilia*, outwit their dullard provincial schoolmates, make fun of their ignorant Italian or Spanish servants, and seduce dark-skinned *chinitas* on their clandestine outings. Not so much an elegiac musing over lost youth, *Juvenilia* is a paean to future growth. (105-6)

Xenophobia, racism, and classism connect these two texts, though Bunge's style is quite different from that of Cané, instead favoring a psychological tone that invites the reader to take his text as an example of self-observation and analysis. However, it is the deployment of a civilized, collective "we," that most directly links the nostalgic pedagogy of Cané and Bunge. Neither is interested in valorizing difference; both in marking as exemplary the refined culture, the desirable criollo heritage, which they both fear is under threat.

I want to emphasize that one of the central phenomena described by Bunge in this section is the imprinting of memory on the body. The yearnings that he describes as natural in all children are represented as images that resurface, inspiring a series of associations with that past, and inspiring affective reactions in the present. The relationship between memory as image and the spatial orientation of the body is key. We see Bunge develop these ideas in an article first published in 1909 in *El monitor de la educación común* titled "Recuerdos de infancia" ("Childhood Memories"). This text would later be included in *Nuestra Patria* as lesson 143, still called

"Recuerdos de infancia," and forming part of unit IV, "Cuadros y fases de la vida argentina," chapter III. "El niño" ("The Child"). In it Bunge recounts his first sense of longing ("*añoranza*") from when he was four or five years old, in which he believes he has fallen from a boat in the Paraná River. Drowning, he is about to be swallowed up by a diabolical whale, but at the last minute is saved by his parents. "¿Soné la aventura?" ("Did I dream the adventure?"), he asks ("Memorias" 6; *Nuestra Patria* 356).[15] The example allows Bunge to posit that early childhood memories are the product of a mixture of lived experiences, repressed desires, and suggestion. In describing this episode as a "longing" rather than a "memory" or a "dream," he asks the audience to feel along with him the nostalgia inherent to such a visceral moment. He draws attention to the pliable mind of the child in order to propose that such "longings" not only persist in adulthood, but actually form the basis of an image-based associative subjectivity. Bunge's recollection is thus necessarily imbued with a sense of lack that must be psychically filled over the course of his life. Childhood education plays an essential role for Bunge's present in that it establishes memories, images, desires, that evoke visceral reactions later in life. If we are to take his own self-analysis as representative of all children (as he does), then we can see that crafting, or even implanting, particular associations between image and feeling, can have important effects in the way students feel toward a teacher, an object, even the state as adults. To return to childhood memories, and, what is more, to craft through public education images that elicit nationalist associations and patriotic *feelings*, is a key if implicit goal of Bunge's pedagogical writing.

These memories are like scars: "El frío del agua, mi terror, las marcas de la malla en la carne" ("The cold of the water, my terror, the marks of the net on my flesh"; "Recuerdos" 6; *Nuestra Patria* 356).[16] Bunge seems to feel this moment more than remember it. A Freudian reading might consider this dream of a drowning child as representative of Bunge's fear of separation from his parents and an inability to control his own locomotion; a fear of death and a wish to be protected. For Freud, such "bewildering" dreams deal with "wish fulfillment" (150), that is, they owe to a certain lack or desire that is sought through the dream. I note this Freudian connection because Carlos Octavio would comment about his own dream/memory, "Háceme esto pensar que nuestras reminiscencias dimanan, en puridad, de otras anteriores. Más que de las sensaciones iniciales, nos acordamos de habernos acordado otras veces, de modo que un recuerdo no es más que el ultimo de una larga serie de recuerdos repetidos y encadenados" ("This makes me think that our reminiscences emanate, in truth, from earlier ones. More than the initial sensations, we remember having remembered them at other times, such that a memory is nothing more than the last in a long series of memories repeated and linked"; "Memorias" 6; *Nuestra Patria* 357). This proposal turns adult associations into the product of a serial chain of memories whose verisimilitude is not as important as the affective work that they do *in the present*. That is, Bunge's vision of adult psychology depends on evaluating the feelings that attach to certain objects, images, and people. This chain turns the initial feeling (*sensación*) into a memory of having remembered. Thus, the psychic present becomes an accumulation of memories derived from earlier moments of suggestion or fear, an image felt in the flesh that solidifies as memory through its repeated iteration.

I do not want to linger on the multiple psychoanalytic readings that could be drawn from this scenario. However, as I note in the Introduction, I am interested in questioning the Oedipal primacy afforded to kinship in both poststructural and queer accounts of relationality, so a brief reflection on the psychic posture set out by Bunge is warranted here. He is intervening in the overarching discussion present in Ramos Mejía and earlier in Le Bon, of the (then) new ways in which social bonds were being theorized at the turn of the century as a symbolic and specifically a visual phenomenon. Ramos Mejía goes to great lengths to describe what he claims to be the susceptibility of the masses to visual stimuli (this as opposed to the rational criollo who discerns through reading and contemplation). This irrational, associative stimulation marks the uneducated man as feared by the elite because, they claim, he is prone to manipulation by a charismatic leader—the legacy of Juan Manuel de Rosas once again surfaces as the mid-century's most adept visual propagandist—whose power derived from his ability to inculcate in the masses a trust born of their ignorance and his ability to excite their emotions. Regarding the psychoanalytic tradition, Ramos Mejía and Bunge are describing what Melanie Klein would put forward as a revision of Freudian theory under the rubric of object relations. At the risk of a gross oversimplification, object relations theory posits that the first emotional relationships that infants establish are with the things, the objects, that they first come into contact with—typically the mothers' breast—and those relationships can take on either positive or negative associations. Thus, the objects—and here I will add the images or memories of those objects—that the infant imbues with meaning, rather than the fixed poles of the Freudian Oedipal complex, mark psychological development not as structural, but associative. In "A Study of Envy and Gratitude" (1956), Klein describes asking patients from her clinical practice to revive what she calls "memories in feelings" as a way of hearkening early frustrations in order to revise them, to mold them, with the help of the analyst into good object relations (228). I suggest that these memories in feelings, the associations established between subject and object, filtered through memory are precisely what Bunge *feels* as fundamental to his own version of self-analysis, an analysis that he then recommends to all young Argentines.

About the chain of memories that I cite above, Bunge would continue to admit that he struggles to articulate the difference between memory and reality, between self and other, subject and object. He writes: "todas mis primeras añoranzas son fantásticas. No se distingue en ellas la línea que separa la imaginación de la realidad; lo ficticio y lo histórico forman compacto y homogéneo conjunto" ("all of my first longings are fantastic. In them it is impossible to discern the line that separates imagination from reality; the fictitious from the historical form a compact and homogenous ensemble"; "Memorias" 6-7; *Nuestra Patria* 357). The desires that an adult remembers having had as a child are thus presented not necessarily as responding to actual lived experiences, but rather yearnings of what might have been, echoes of desires that persist in the present. The bulk of this chapter, "Recuerdos de infancia," revolves around the psychological mysteries of Carlos Octavio's first memories and the effects that those memories have for himself as an adult. In order to position himself as a model citizen in the present, Bunge must describe his own contradictory desires as expressed through his childhood memories, and thus the affective attachments derived from those memories that persist in adulthood. Crucially, those memories in the present are often the result of queer associations between objects, feelings, places, and people in the past. "Cada uno tiene en su alma las más disparatadas asociaciones de ideas" ("Everyone has in his soul the most disparate associations of ideas"; 361), which, Bunge notes, might explain the "inauditas expresiones literarias y hasta actos extravagantes" ("unprecedented literary expressions and even acts of extravagance"; 360-61) of the author (and thus of anyone else) in the present. To be clear, Bunge is suggesting that his own literary imagination, as well as his strange behavior as an adult, owe to the queer association between disparate objects that he developed as a child. This is to say that the adult has an associative memory that may include inexplicable relationships—a queer un-correspondence between object and feeling—that manifests in adulthood. Following our discussion of Klein, here objects accrue a queer charge. The root of this queerness is to be found in the formative, nebulous period of childhood creativity in which object-images become invested with queer feelings.

In the second section of the chapter "El niño," titled "Los primeros entusiasmos" ("The first delights,") Bunge describes his three principal obsessions as a child: stories, the military, and the clergy. His passion for storytelling overshadows all the desires that "normal" young boys exhibit, according to him: toys, candies, and excursions (*paseos*). Rather, he is captivated by fairy tales; moved to tears by realistic accounts of thievery, arson, and murder; and overcome with laughter at certain animal stories (361). The reception of these narratives is always linked to pleasure—specifically to pleasure that overwhelms the senses. For young Carlos Octavio to be told and eventually to tell a story is linked to the pleasure of fantasy and to the ability to create new worlds for himself and others. His greatest pleasure in this period is found in experiencing the affective charge of bringing subjects and objects together, to the limit of intelligibility.

Bunge's passions become more psychologically complex throughout the chapter, and begin to focus on how the male subject is formed through a mixture of violent masculinity and religious devotion. In a line eliminated from *Nuestra Patria* but included in the 1909 essay, Bunge writes: "Viene entonces el culto de lo militar y lo religioso, el respeto al soldado y el amor al sacerdote" ("Next comes devotion to the military and religion, respect for the soldier and love for the priest"; "Recuerdos" 29). Positioning the formation of masculinity at the juncture of the violent and the sacred, Bunge explains,

> Entusiasmábame el desfile de tropas, marchando los soldados en escuadras tan simétricas que parecían de juguete, al son del tambor y del clarín. Según se me había dicho, desafiaban al enemigo y defendían a la patria. Yo los admiraba de todo corazón, aunque también los temía. En mi alma infantil, temía todo lo que admiraba, no concibiendo otra forma de admiración que la impuesta por el poder y la fuerza.
>
> I was delighted by a parade of troops, soldiers marching in squadrons so symmetrical they seemed like toys, to the sound of the drum and the bugle.

> I had been told that they defied the enemy and defended the nation. I admired them with all my heart, though I also feared them. In my infantile soul, I feared everything that I admired, unable to conceive of another type of admiration than that imposed by power and force. ("Recuerdos" 14; *Nuestra Patria* 364)

While the organization of these troops, their symmetrical order, appeals aesthetically to the young man, what truly excites him is the complex affective interplay between admiration and fear. The source of his admiration for them is their ability to inspire dread in him. This phase in Bunge's obsessive youth is characterized by the queer juncture of power, force, and fear. This fear is emblazoned on Bunge's memory.

> Jamás olvidaré un batallón que pasó una vez por la puerta de mi casa; oficiales y soldados me miraban ceñudos al pasar, amenazándome con sus sables y bayonetas ... ¿Cómo pudo ocurrírseme semejante cosa? Probablemente la criada, pretendiendo yo correr detrás de la tropa, me dijo: "Mira como te miran; si te mueves, te van a matar." Y yo, ¡pobre de mí! aterrado miré, sí, como me miraban, temiendo fueran a matarme de un momento a otro....

> I will never forget a battalion that passed one time before the front door of my house; officials and soldiers looked at me scowling as they passed, threatening me with their sables and bayonettes ... How could I have thought such a thing? The maid probably told me, as I was aiming to run after the troop, "Look at how they look at you; if you move, they'll kill you." And I looked, poor me! yes, terrified at how they looked at me, fearing that they would kill me at any moment.... ("Recuerdos" 14-15; *Nuestra Patria* 364-65, ellipses in the original)

As in his short stories, "El Capitán Pérez" and "El Chucro," an indescribable, magnetic pull draws him toward these violent men. Embedded within this gaze is the ever-present possibility of bodily harm. The memory is predicated on the terrifying gaze of these military officers and soldiers, a gaze that threatens to kill, but which also seduces the young man. He is fascinated by the troop and, almost entranced, wants to join their ranks. The staging of this scene suggests that the young man desires to form part of a collective body to which he knows he does not belong. However, the nameless, likely Afro-descendant *"criada"* suggests that doing so—that moving at all—could prove fatal. This is the power of suggestion. Her intervention is aimed at inspiring fear in the young man so that he remain at home, rather than joining the troop. It does not reduce Bunge's desire for these men, but substitutes it with a fear of death by their hands. The body of the young man is addressed by their threatening gaze, drawn into their field of vision and thus constituted as a subject worthy of elimination.

Bunge's queer identification with the military is one of longing and of failure. He was never cut out for military service, and yet, this same fascination remains a constitutive element to be felt and overcome in order for him to see himself as a productive adult. He first describes a fixation with the military, feeling the power and the danger that they inspire, as a psychologically transformational moment in his life, a moment that must be felt, assimilated, and overcome in order to for him to evolve from a rambunctious and petulant child into a citizen capable of contributing to the nation. Indeed, this crisis of queer identification is precisely what Bunge recommends *for all young men* in this textbook, as I explain below.

Bunge is clear about the psychic resonance of these memories in the constitution of the adult self. For him, these memories are a fundamental iterative chain that leads to successful socialization. But these memories hinge primarily on the relationship between the masculine body and its orientation toward psychic objects, and on the social relationships that the body must feel in order for it to become normalized. These early memories are examples of the body's queer longings, only possible as part of an ongoing, future-oriented, path to normativity. Thus, the sexual perversity and gender instability of youth—these indescribable fascinations, longings, desires—become imprinted on the body, indeed constitute the masculine body as in need of constant discipline. Shifting from psychoanalysis to sociology, we see in this memory an example of what Bourdieu calls the "*somatization of the social relations of domination*" (*Masculine* 23; emphasis in the original). Through the evolutionary process "somatization," what Bourdieu calls the "formidable collective labour of diffuse and continuous socialization" (23) the gendered body begins to make sense in the onto-social narratives of childhood development. The body of the young man, Bunge implies, needs this somatic disciplining, lest that very materiality, that proximity to other bodies, escape the grasp of normativity.

From this moment of crisis in which the fascination for martial masculinity imprints on the body a sense of dread, Bunge describes a third obsession, marked by yet another image of men in formation "chicos de un seminario, en larguísimas hileras, de dos en dos y de menores a mayores" ("young men from a seminary, in very long lines, two by two and from youngest to oldest"; "Recuerdos" 15; *Nuestra Patria* 365). In a blunt statement he notes, "Después de los militares, impresionábanme los curas" ("After military men, I was fascinated by priests"; "Recuerdos" 15; *Nuestra Patria* 365). Again, this fascination is marked by an ambivalent orientation toward masculine bodies. Notably, it is not the older, ordained priests that draw Bunge's eye, but rather the seminary students. Their elegant dress and orderly gait, the symmetry with which they traverse both physical and mental space, all serve to enhance Bunge's desire for them. He notes, "Era yo entonces, no sólo crédulo, sino creyente y hasta devoto" ("Then I was not just gullible, but a believer and even devout"), marking a contrast between this past moment and his present ("Recuerdos" 15; *Nuestra Patria* 365). Bunge's fascination is heightened by the visual pleasure that these young men produce in him. The fact that his faith waned over the years—his agnosticism was a source of tension in the Bunge family—only serves to demonstrate the desirability of an initial phase of religious devotion, one in which elegant men occupy a central role in his childhood imaginary. In summary, the three stages Bunge describes include an infancy marked by "barbarous" and fetishistic obsessions that transitions to an erotically charged adolescence in which he is fixated on militarism and then his desires are tempered by religion, and finally, moves to an altruistic state of philosophic understanding that is fostered by the structure of primary education. Attending school provides the young man an outlet for his active imagination, and the discipline that he both craved and abhorred.

As I have been suggesting, Bunge does not conceive of this evolutionary trajectory as unique to his own history, but rather as a generalizable pattern for the psychological development of the ideal student. He makes this clear in the conclusion to his memoir, in which we note a considerable difference between the 1909 and 1910 published versions. In order to show this I first cite from the 1910 edition of *Nuestra Patria*: "Pues bien, estos recuerdos, ¿no compendian y reproducen, paso a paso, el origen de la cultura, el pretérito de los pueblos, la natural evolución de las edades?" ("Now then, is it not true that these memories comprise and reproduce, step by step, the origen of culture, the past of peoples [nations], the natural evolution of the ages?"; 378). In the 1909 article published in *El monitor de la educación común*, however, Bunge is more robust in the scope of his conclusions: "Pues bien, esos recuerdos, *ahora, cuando los evoco*, ¿no compendian y reproducen, paso a paso, *la historia* de los pueblos, el origen de *toda* cultura, la natural evolución *del pensamiento humano a través* de las edades?" ("Now then, is it not true that these memories, *now that I evoke them*, comprise and reproduce, step by step, *the history* of peoples [nations], the origin of *all* culture, the natural evolution *of human thought* through the ages?"; 29 emphasis mine). In the 1909 text Bunge fixes his act of writing in the present, his evocation of these memories as part of an identifiable point of departure from which these reminiscences accumulate—or rather, toward which they have always been accumulating. The central idea remains the same: that Bunge's individual evolution as a child should be understood not as particular, but rather as exemplary of the process of evolution that all children undergo across time. What Bunge leaves out of the 1910 text, however, is revealing: it is not simply the past (*pretérito*), but the history (*historia*) of all peoples (*el pueblo*) that he claims to represent in the flesh. What is more, in the earlier text, he claims that his own memories represent not just the evolution of the ages, but of all human thought—that is, as a generalizable psychic phenomenon. He imagines himself as part of a public in which his affirmation, *this is what I felt*, leads to an affirmative response: *me too*. Thus, in the 1909 text—addressed to the intellectual community, to his peers—Bunge emphasizes the material continuity of this process of evolution, while in the 1910 text—addressed to students—he fixes those memories, those desires, those longings, as part of a past that has already ended. What changed in the 1910 version, then, is the continuity between these queer desires in the past, and the present of writing, learning, and educating.

Bunge validates his own position in the present as the culmination of a process of psychological evolution. To make this clear to students, he adds to *Nuestra Patria* a concluding section that summarizes his analysis.

> Generalizando mi caso con tantos otros que he observado, podría formular así mi conclusión: el niño es un salvaje, que, poquito a poco y a modo de un pueblo, va transformándose en un hombre civilizado. [...] [L]a infancia representa la época del salvajismo originario; la adolescencia, la época de la barbarie; la edad adulta, los tiempos de la civilización y, por fin, la madurez, el último estado cultural, el siglo presente.

> Generalizing my case along with so many others that I have observed, I could put my conclusion thus: the child is a savage, who, little by little and in the same way as a people [nation], transforms himself into a civilized man. [...] [I]nfancy represents the period of originary savagery; adolescence, the period of barbarism; adulthood, the times of civilization; and

finally, maturity, the ultimate cultural state, the current century. (*Nuestra Patria* 380)

The impressionable mind of the young child, according to Bunge, allows him to exist in a liminal space between fiction and reality, but also situates him, on an anthropological level, at an earlier stage in development. The "savagery" of this remote epoch is due to the child's inability to think logically, but also, crucially, to his propensity to feel in the flesh the queer desires that are conjured by his unformed mind, unchecked by rational thought. It is not surprising that Bunge would position "savagery" at a formational position on an evolutionary scale. What is surprising, however, is that the queer desires that accompany this state are not rejected outright. Instead they are necessary so that the "barbarous" adolescent and eventually the "civilized" adult can come into being. Thus, all civilized adults become civilized by experiencing the queer longings of youth *and then rejecting them*.

This process of subjective development clearly follows a Spencerian view of racial evolution. Confirming the relationship between infancy and barbarism (read indigeneity); adulthood with civilization (read whiteness), it is only through a robust program of socialization, education, and discipline that the child (who is like an Indian) learns to channel those longings into appropriate (normative) forms of behavior, that is to become an adult (and thus like a civilized, white man). In a deceptively simple logical association, Bunge likens the history of Latin America's "civilization" of Native peoples to the pedagogical process by which a child becomes an adult. Obfuscating the genocidal campaign against Native populations (known as the *Conquista del desierto* ("The Conquest of the Desert"), he proposes that the acculturation of Indians is akin to the teaching of children, a move made possible only by the elimination of Native peoples from the national imaginary. The Indian, who is always already marked as queer, his savagery, which demands disciplining, makes it possible for the state to oblige in the disciplining of erotic and racial ambiguities in the context of positivist modernity. Not unlike the caricature of Bunge holding hands with an anthropomorphized "Nuestra America" (analyzed in chapter 3), the juncture of eroticism, race, and modernity provokes uncertain feelings toward the matter of history as a guide to present and future.

In *Nuestra Patria* Bunge demonstrates not only how to feel queerly, but how to repress those queer feelings, how to limit the excesses of youth, and how to negate the originary queerness that is the basis of successful adulthood. For turn of the century Argentina this is a remarkable proposal because it unwittingly (or perhaps not) positions queerness at the center—at least at the origin—of successful white citizenship. The queer longings that characterize the child's savagery are in fact the basis of the ongoing process of socialization by which cultural nationalism produces successful citizens. For Bunge, the project of state normalization begins with a private queer feeling that becomes a public good, only for it to be repressed through the psychic process of reorienting object relations, a process he calls *civilization*. The state, in this sense, must simultaneously foster and repress queerness; it must provide a framework within which the child's natural tendencies toward obsession, longing, and queerness can be captured and transformed into a productive and public form of sociality.

## CONCLUSION

In the context of the positivist turn of the century, the pedagogical writing of Carlos Octavio Bunge is distinctive because it takes the author's own subjective experience as an example from which to draw larger conclusions about youth psychology and individual personality development. Bunge's memoir, embedded within *Nuestra Patria*, reveals a contradictory fascination with and fear of violent masculinity, as it claims that this fascination is inherent, indeed necessary in all young men. Bunge, who had no easy relationship with the military, describes his paralysis under the influence of the martial gaze as precisely what the youth of 1910 must revive, conjuring the queerness of homoeroticism to be subsequently reoriented through education. Young Argentines must be willing to submit to the gaze and the authority of the military in order to become fully realized as citizen-subjects. The politics of this pedagogy depends on deepening the psychic processes by which youth are inculcated with patriotic ideals, which themselves depend on the making sense of the unstable desires that mark the passage from youth to adulthood.

In a similar way, *El Arca de Noé* takes the feeling of family as a method for inculcating young men and women in the art of loving self, other, and nation. Julia and Delfina Bunge register this metonymy in their pedagogical writing as one that is essential for the future social cohesion of Argentina. The familiar love they propose is not dialectic but ontological; the proximity of fellow classmates becomes the avenue through which the student (as future citizen) learns to react, share, and indeed, love. In imagining the classroom as a space of patriotic pedagogy, and the teacher as a guide in learning to love the classmate *as family*, the Julia and Delfina equate the familiar affective charge of kinship with the possibility of cultivating a cohesive nation. In both cases family narratives are used to provide a model for young men and women who are assumed to lack the cultural skills (or the desire) to understand what it means to feel and, in the end, *be* Argentine.

The central pedagogical issue posed by Argentine intellectuals at the turn of the century was not how to educate future workers, as it was in other national contexts, but rather how to convince the existing population of the wisdom, the culture, and the capacity of the elite to maintain hegemony. These educational policies were constructed on the basis of a nation imagined as homogeneous (ethnically), but diverse culturally. Thus, the question of standardizing a national curriculum and thus a national culture built in the image of the very elite charged with constructing those images, finds a curious expression in the writing of the Bunge family, who once more, searches its own family archive, its memories and affective ambiguities and mines them for public value. In exposing themselves in this way, they bring to the fore unmentioned traumas, secret desires, and dysfunctional relationships, harnessed into normative affective channels and transformed into productive citizenship. These are textbooks for the nation, but also psychological records of the conflictive process of individuation as a member of the Bunge family, the Argentine upper class, and the nation itself.

CHAPTER FIVE

# NATIONAL ESSAYS, HOME ECONOMICS
## THE ARGENTINE OLIGARCHY IN DECLINE

The nation is a seemingly inexhaustible source of cultural criticism. Few topics are more pervasive and yet so impossible to define with real specificity. Nationalisms ebb and flow with the histories of local cultures, the demands of globalization, and the winds of political change. While it is now ubiquitous to call the nation an "imagined community," postcolonial, feminist, and queer theorists continue to revise what counts as "imagined" and what constitutes "community."[1] However, one quality of nationalism does seem ubiquitous: it is not "natural" but must be learned. While Ernst Renan's 1882 lecture, "Qu'est-ce qu'une nation?" ("What is a nation?"), may be more often quoted for describing the nation as a "daily plebiscite," we should not forget that the consent to governance is predicated on what Renan calls "a soul, a spiritual principle" (19) that is the history of shared pain and glory, and the projection of a shared future. This collective will is variable, and it comes about through the feeling of relatedness, of commonality, that depends on what stories get told, what history remembered, what past glories and pains enshrined, as it does on what future is delineated as possible. For as ever present as a sense of nationhood might seem, it remains a feeling that must be taught in schools, read about in newspapers or literature, felt in song, or displayed through bodily enactments of fealty, sacrifice, pride, and love. And while the nation is often imagined through the contours of kinship, at the intersection of nationalism and the family we find a constitutive uncertainty about the naturalness of both. The nation, like the family, like gender and race, are at once seemingly innate and yet carefully taught, policed, and cultivated by and through modern culture.

The rise of nationalism in Argentina has garnered significant scholarly attention from across disciplines and perspectives. The enduring effects of its fascist ideological orientation, the material legacy of its militarism and authoritarianism, and its historical malleability have made nationalist thought a cornerstone of modern understandings of the social. The Argentine case is not unique, but the degree to which nationalist thought influenced the politics, economics, and culture of Argentina over the course of the twentieth century can hardly be overstated. From today's historical perspective, we see a chain of military interventions inaugurated by the 1930 coup d'état led by General José F. Uriburu, passing through Peronist national populism, which sought to identify the nation with formerly marginalized groups (i.e., the "*descamisados*" and "*cabecitas negras*"), and culminating in the reactionary military dictatorship of 1976 to 1983 (self-described as the Process of National Reorganization).[2] These are ideological strands of a nationalist fabric that weave together such contradictions as the fear of social disorder and the affirmation of traditional family values with socialist utopianism, economic and social (neo)liberalism with labor rights and xenophobia. Simply put, any attempt to understand modern Argentine social life without taking into account the origins and effects of nationalist thought is incomplete.

By most accounts, the Bunge family is a prime example of the conservative shift toward authoritarianism that undergirded nationalist thought in the first decades of the twentieth century. But this is not one of those accounts. It may be tempting to dismiss their writing on racial harmony, family values, and economic development as a straightforward reflection of the elite's conservative response to the fear of social decline. However, as I have been arguing throughout this book, the modernization of kinship represents an uneven, contradictory, and at times paradoxical process that does more than demonstrate fear. If we are attentive to the contours of desire, the intimate proximities and unresolved, speculative, yearning for *something else*, we see that within each of their respective proposals for Argentine nationalism lies the possibility that their own conservative responses rely on the undermining of normative sexuality, on the impossible desire for a past-future family. For them, if the elite was to have a future, the family had to become what it once was, its values returned to a past in which it maintained uncontested hegemony over the direction of the nation.

This chapter addresses the shifting terrain of the nation and the family by focusing on three essays, Carlos O. Bunge's *Nuestra América: Ensayo de psicología social* (*Our America: Essay of Social Psychology*) (1903), Delfina Bunge's *Las mujeres y la vocación* (*Women and Vocation*) (1922), and Alejandro Bunge's *Una nueva Argentina* (*A New Argentina*) (1940). Each text aims to shape the national spirit that seemed under threat. As I have shown in previous chapters, the shifting terrain of kinship depends on incorporating ideological strands that are at times contradictory and queer. In these essays we see how the Carlos Octavio Bunge imagines Argentina's national dysfunction as the result of its history of racial miscegenation, a vision that is fully developed by Alejandro Bunge's equally pessimistic rendering, forty years later, of the precarious position of Argentine whiteness in the face of declining birth rates for the upper class. In between, Delfina Bunge offers a counterpoint by calling for a tentative expansion of women's participation in national politics, a conservative feminist reaction to the growing demand for women's rights. In the first half of the twentieth century, cultural nationalists began to reject positivist science and liberal democracy in favor of a nativist reaction that offered a conservative, spiritual solution to the heightened threat of social disorder. The Bunge family played a key role in defining the bases of this nationalist debate. They were attuned to the ways in which family life, domesticity, and gender were changing during this period, and yet proposed a normative solution to the problem of the modern family that nevertheless expanded and reshaped its meanings for the future.

## THE NATION AS PAST-FUTURE FAMILY

Historian David Rock describes the Argentine Nationalist movement as "a futurism of the past" (*Authoritarian* 1). Such a description underscores the rehabilitation of mid-nineteenth-century discourses such as "order" and "tradition," figures such as the gaucho, and colonial spiritual ideologies based in Catholicism. Though not all nationalists shared the same sociopolitical perspective, this rehabilitation of a lost past, a nostalgic yearning for an ethnically, spiritually, and culturally cohesive population served as the centerpiece for the broader move away from economic and political liberalism and toward authoritarian rule. Navarro Gerassi puts these shared basic principles in the following terms:

> un intenso antiliberalismo; el rechazo del parlamentarismo y de cualquier sistema político que actuara a través de partidos políticos; la necesidad de destruir la democracia mediante un golpe militar; la organización de "jerarquía y orden" mediante una forma vaga de representación corporativa; y una estrecha alianza entre la Iglesia y el Estado.

> An intense antiliberalism; a rejection of parliamentary governance and of any political system that would act through political parties; the need to destroy democracy through a military coup; a vague form of corporative representation that would establish "hierarchy and order"; and a close alliance between Church and State. (16)

Focusing on the political organization proposed by right-wing nationalists, Navarro Gerassi nevertheless points out that in order for this to be accomplished, the historical mythology of Argentina needed to be reshaped, and thus "revisionismo histórico" ("historical revisionism") became the principle outlet for transforming the present and its relationship to the past. Barbero and Devoto, for their part, despite dividing Argentine nationalism into five distinct ideological threads, affirm that all of them share

> una serie de actitudes y principios: cierta posición crítica y disconformidad hacia el sistema imperante; una revisión no uniforme de los valores históricos aceptados como producto de este cuestionamiento del presente; una manifiesta hostilidad hacia el positivismo, relacionada con una crítica a diversos aspectos del liberalismo; una exaltación de la nacionalidad y, por último, una actitud de oposición hacia las filosofías y las organizaciones internacionalistas.

> a series of attitudes and principles: a certain critical position and disconformity toward the dominant system; a nonuniform revision of accepted historical values as the product of this questioning of the present; a manifest hostility toward positivism, related to a critique of diverse aspects of liberalism; an exaltation of nationality and, lastly, an oppositional attitude toward internationalist philosophies and organizations. (10)

The core of these strands of conservative thought is at once temporal and affective: the feeling of the past emerges, disrupting the present. Nationalism is an emergence of past affect in the present that points to the future. In the particular case of Argentina in the first decades of the twentieth century, the nationalist reaction responds to the fear of social disintegration, the loss of class hierarchy, the erosion of cultural and moral values in the wake of mass immigration, uneven modernization, and political activism from socialists, anarchists, and feminists, at times seen as interchangeable foes in a battle for the spirit of the Argentine nation. Finally, tracing the romantic underpinnings of Argentine cultural nationalism, Jeane H. DeLaney argues "it should be understood not simply as a right-wing response to massive immigration and rapid change, but as an intellectual movement driven by the vision of Argentina as an organic, ethnocultural community and a philosophy of history that rejected unilinear notions of historical development" (656). The historical revisionism of the cultural nationalists sought to supplant positivist notions of progress through the rehabilitation of folk traditions, a turn to Spain as the spiritual (Catholic) core of Argentine culture, and an effort to privilege the telluric singularity of the nation and its people. A second, perhaps contradictory, development of this period led to a reimagining of the political sphere as circumscribed to the well-educated few who could interpret this vision of history for the benefit of the nation. While the rhetoric of cultural nationalism was populist, the enactment of political reforms was elitist. Men such as Gálvez and Rojas, but also Carlos Octavio and Alejandro Bunge, drew on the feelings of the masses (such as dissatisfaction, fear, and pride) as an expression of a national ideal that only they could transform into a cohesive public policy. Cultural nationalism responds to a crisis felt by the elite and is theorized by drawing on bygone populist cultural figures in order to interpret those figures as a new national essence. While I agree with DeLaney's historical assessment of the influence of the Romantic tradition in early twentieth-century cultural nationalist thought in Argentina, by paying attention to the role of the kinship imaginary (as co-constitutively raced and sexed) in this process, we glean a slightly different perspective on how the politics of nostalgia were enacted at this time. The essays of Carlos Octavio, Alejandro, and Delfina Bunge reveal that the spiritual malaise of the early twentieth century was also expressed as a drama of family structure, played out in the present but always hearkening back to a past ideal. The family had to be reimagined if this age of splendor was to continue for the elite.

This chapter proposes that the past-future family is marked by a queer yearning for what might be and what could have been, rather than what is. The temporality of historical revisionism asserts the possibility of reinscribing the past on the present in a longing for the future. The community that cultural nationalists propose is necessarily familiar and familial, but one that does not depend on the temporal logics of normativity, but rather the queer feeling of reenactment and reinscription, the uncanny sense that what might have been could still be. The central contradiction of this process is that in Argentina at the turn of the century, the modern family was constituted through productive, industrial time, and reproductive, heteronormative sex, but this temporality was only accessible through a queer irruption of the past in the present.[3] The time of nationalism is now and then, ever reaching toward what was and what could be, positioned at a constitutive impasse of its futurity. One of the most forceful examples of this ambivalent posture is Carlos Octavio Bunge's *Nuestra América: Ensayo de psicología social*. The text diagnoses the social ills of the present by returning to the historical past in order to revise the meaning of cultural and ethnic miscegenation. In doing so, Bunge proposes a nationalist future that attempts to assuage the racial mixing of the past by appealing to geographical determinism and education. He aims to resolve the emergence of fatalistic character flaws in a present that must be different. He denies the future of the present only to reinscribe the past as future.

## MISCEGENATION: BETWEEN PROMISCUITY AND STERILITY IN CARLOS OCTAVIO BUNGE'S *NUESTRA AMÉRICA*

Following the determinist precepts of Gustave Le Bon, Carlos Octavio Bunge proposes that the behaviors, attitudes, and culture (what he calls "social psychology") of Spanish America depend on—and are fatally flawed by—its history of racial miscegenation (*mestizaje*). In his pessimistic view, the political dysfunction of the present is the product of immutable racial characteristics, combined with a particular geographical environment and economic history, which confer on contemporary Spanish Americans essential personality traits that have prevented them from thriving in the modern era. In his words: "La organización política de un pueblo es producto de su psicología. Su psicología resulta de los factores étnicos y del ambiente físico y económico" ("The political organization of a people is the product of its psychology. Its psychology is the result of ethnic factors and the physical and economic environment"; 51).[4] As with most positivists, Bunge looked to scientific racism to explain the realities of his present, the real or desired domination of a white elite over Black, Indigenous, and Mestizo masses, and the persistent failure of political institutions to unify such hybrid societies. The logic goes something like this: if racial characteristics are immutable, and Spanish America is predominantly a Mestizo population, then how can the continent overcome the inherent backwardness of its Indigenous and Black ancestry? If Spanish America is to become prosperous and to overcome its history of racial mixing, then, paradoxically, race both is and cannot be immutable. Differing from European eugenicists, Bunge suggests that over time, and given propitious environmental conditions, certain Spanish American peoples could evolve, but only those who enjoy the moderating effects of temperate (and not tropical) climates. That is, nations like Argentina could overcome their (only slightly) "tainted" blood, while tropical environs with large Afro-descendant populations such as Brazil and the Caribbean, were condemned to degeneracy in the long term.[5]

As I note in chapter 1, Bunge's rendering of Spanish America's past-future has often been flagged for its white supremacist ideology. *Nuestra América* is indeed a racist text that advocates (gleefully at times) for the elimination of Black and Indigenous blood from the continent. Without minimizing this violence, I want to propose that by honing in on the intersection of race, sexuality, and temporality in Bunge's writing, we can better understand the corporeal logics at stake in the early years of Argentina's nationalist resurgence. Bunge sees himself in a moment in which whiteness is running out of time. And yet, he depends on the queer history of race in order to posit a sexual futurity in which the nation overcomes its hybrid past.

Much of my thinking here is influenced by Tavia Nyong'o's elaboration of the "miscegenation of time" (11-13). Nyong'o approaches miscegenation and its counterpoint, amalgamation, by exploring the temporal logics—which are always also racial and sexual logics—through which material bodies became intelligible as racialized in the United States over the course of the nineteenth century. The racial logics of temporality of the United States and those of Latin America vary significantly, though clearly the contradictions of racial mixing have been crucial to both. Indeed, Latin American writers such as Sarmiento in *Conflictos y armonías de las razas en América* (1883) and José Martí in his own *Nuestra América* (1891), though presenting opposing stances, both identified "race" as a key point of nationalist distinction that could propel Latin American nations into a productive and independent future. These texts laid the foundation for nationalist and pan-Latin Americanist revisions of racial mixing, ideological stances that would lead to later essays such as José Vasconcelos's aforementioned *La Raza Cósmica*, but also José Carlos Mariátegui's *Siete ensayos de interpretación de la realidad peruana* (1928), Gilberto Freyre's *Casa-Grande e Senzala* (1933), and Fernando Ortiz's *Contrapunteo cubano del tabaco y el azúcar* (1940). The history of racial mixing has led to countless essays of interpretation of the Latin American reality, a reality that is, nevertheless always marked by the fact of the ongoing material presence of the bodies, histories, and cultures of its diverse population. The sexual politics of hybridity, transculturation, and miscegenation in these national essays deserves a more in depth engagement than I can provide here, though they are an important point of departure. In imagining the future of the Argentine nation, Bunge seeks to assuage fears of racial decadence paradoxically, by sexualizing the present by virtue of a past amalgamation.

Two key ideas spring from Bunge's theory of miscegenation in *Nuestra America*: promiscuity and sterility. On the one hand, Bunge argues that some mixed-race populations are prone to polygamy, and that this sexual profligacy, this undermining of modern, civilized coupledom can lead not only to a less "virtuous" population, but to an excess of mixed-race people (157). On the other, he argues that in certain cases racial hybridity can also diminish the reproductive capacity of the nation, and that sterility is a threat brought by an incompatible racial admixture. If the national stock depends on a past racial miscegenation as it projects a white future, sterility becomes a threat not only to the future of the nation, but the histories embodied by mixed-race people in the Americas.

Bunge argues that promiscuity is a sexual inclination that originates in and because of the tropics. Contradicting the Spencerian division between race and environment, Bunge's argument depends on collapsing the two. Sexual behavior adheres to blood, and tropical blood inevitably leads to promiscuity. He writes,

> En cuanto a la moral sexual, la sangre africana, y aun la indígena, como originarias de los trópicos, de regiones poligámicas, son mucho más "frecuentes" que la europea, procedente de climas fríos, propicios a la monogamia. La plebe de color es, pues, en América, forzosamente, por razones etnográfico-climatéricas, menos casta, menos "virtuosa," que la blanca.

> Regarding sexual morality, African blood, and even Indigenous [blood], as originary of the tropics, of polygamic regions, are much more "frequent" than the European, coming from cold climates, prone to monogamy. The mass of color is, well, in the Americas, forcibly, for ethnographic-climatological reasons, less chaste, less "virtuous," than the white. (157)

In the tropics, even the clergy runs the risk of falling into bad habits, in particular those who, "llevan en abundancia cosquillante sangre africana o indígena en sus venas de célibes..." ("carry in abundance prickly African or Indigenous blood in their celibate veins..."; 157). That is, the sexualized abundance of the tropics seeps into the bodies of people of color, infusing their blood with an unrelentingly promiscuous nature. The unfortunate carriers of this "prickly" tropical blood that remain in the tropics are thus doubly condemned, constitutionally incapable of "virtue," even through faith.

If the place of polygamy is the tropics, then in contrast with European sexologists, Bunge did not have an external location, a "there" in which to deposit the supposed cultural backwardness of sexual promiscuity. As Angela Willey has shown in the case of Krafft-Ebing's *Psychopathia Sexualis*, European superiority was inscribed in nineteenth-century scientific writing because of the naturalness attributed to the supposedly universal practice sexual monogamy among Christian nations. This is particularly salient regarding the English translation of Krafft-Ebing's influential text, which Willey traces as a tool of British empire-building. Referencing the link between European monogamy and barbaric polygamy (for Krafft-Ebing associated with Islam), Willey notes: "The juxtaposition of the categories 'Christian nations' and 'polygamic races' designates polygamy as a naturalized racial characteristic and situates the Christian nation as a stand-in for monogamy and racelessness, or whiteness" (32). Krafft-Ebing can comfortably distance himself from polygamy by naturalizing it as a racial quality that is characteristic of his portrayal of Orientalized Muslims. As Willey makes clear, the predominance of Christian monogamy over (supposedly) Muslim polygamy is a work of biological determinism. But it is also an expression of a British interest, in the late nineteenth century, in crafting a vision of itself as modern and culturally refined, which found a foil in the caricature of Islam as always licentious, and thus, in need of colonial tutelage.

But Bunge had neither the promise of imperialism to justify the caricature of polygamy abroad nor the racialized religious otherness of a foreign community in which to place it. On the contrary, for Bunge, the threat of polygamy is very much "here." And if this promiscuous behavior is already "here," it is also uncomfortably "now." Despite his ethnohistorical approach to *mestizaje*, which Bunge treats as both an empirical fact and problem to overcome, he cannot separate the political dysfunction of his present from the racial mixing of the past. For Bunge, the Spanish colonists were themselves hybrid subjects, the product a geography that had invited extensive invasions by Mediterranean populations (Romans, Arabs, and Jews), and thus is also characterized by intermarriages and ethnic mixing, what he calls the "latinafricanización" ("Latinafricanization") of Spain (118). A geographic crossroads, Spain is a site of conquest and revenge, impressing on its people, according to Bunge, a cultural backwardness and arrogance that remain present in all Spanish Americans. However, Bunge also describes the common African origin of Spanish masters and Black slaves as one reason for the relative "success" of this racial mixture (the Mulatto) in Spanish America (141). The history of African migration to the Iberian Peninsula makes the cross of Spanish and African blood less pernicious than that of the Spanish and American Indian. If the Spanish are characterized by their "arrogance and indolence," American Indians, for Bunge, are "Oriental" in origin, and thus singularly prone to "fatalism," which paradoxically both explains and caused the seemingly effortless conquest of the Americas (132). Thus, Bunge concludes that the cross of Spanish and African heritage is "simple mestizaje" ("simple miscegenation"), while that of Spanish and Indian or African and Indian is "verdadera hibridación" ("true hybridization") (156).

Bunge blames this history for the failure of liberal political institutions to provide cultural and economic stability in the present. He sees the enduring threat of racial degeneracy as a problem that can only be "solved" through a rigorous education program and a greater influx of European immigrants (and thus their "blood"). The temporality of promiscuity thus depends on the prior influence of the tropics on African and Indigenous blood and presumes the greater frequency of polygamy in these hotter climates (and monogamy in colder ones). However, even though the influence of environmental factors occurs before the consolidation of what counts as blood, these factors also exacerbate the effects of that blood for Black, Indigenous, Mulatto, and Mestizo people in the present. That blood and that climate are still the context of Bunge's intervention, and it is blood he wishes to change.

The second characteristic that Bunge attributes to incompatible racial mixtures is sterility. He begins, however, by claiming that in general Spanish Americans are extremely sexually prolific. It is only when racial mixing between similar types, such as Mestizos with Mestizos (rather than Mestizos with Europeans), occurs, that the results become catastrophic. The continual reproduction of similar types, that is, of racial hybrids of themselves, leads to a sterile future: "es aterradora la proporción que dan los híbridos hispanoamericanos de degenerados relativamente ineptos para la propagación de la especie; de mestizos que, del mandato inicial de Jehová— 'creced y multiplicaos'—sólo cumplen la primera parte" ("the proportion of relatively inept degenerates that Hispanoamerican hybrids give for the propagation of the species is terrifying; of Mestizos who, of the initial mandate of Jehovah—'go forth and multiply'—, only fulfill the first part"; 153-54). Recalling the divine mandate of Genesis 1:28 not just to procreate, but to dominate the earth and its creatures, Bunge positions the horror of hybridity alongside mankind's existential purpose of reproduction. If this seems disingenuous for Bunge, a man who had a difficult relationship with the Catholic Church and was described (quietly) as agnostic, it remains a position that aligns with the majority of state-sponsored social science. As both a religious and cultural demand, the legitimate purpose of sex for the elite in the early twentieth century remained the propagation of the species and the transmission of property.[6] It is thus as a foil against the idealized conjugal union that Bunge describes the following forms of degeneracy:

> Entre ellos, el afeminado mulato músico, pianista de nudosas manos, talle virginal, voz de flauta y coqueterías de romántica; el político mestizo de indio, de cutis lampiño y gelatinoso vientre de eunuco ... Entre ellas, la mulata solterona, tan simpática cuando es intelectual y hace de excelente maestra de escuela, produciendo la engañosa sensación de que su raza, si la tuviera firme, sería normalmente apta para el feminismo; y tan repulsiva cuando, inintelectual, simple modistilla, llena su corazón vacío con un fanatismo cualquiera, los iconos del templo o los espíritus parlantes de la mesita de tres pies...
>
> Llamaría yo al fenómeno la semiesterilidad degenerativa del híbrido humano.
>
> Among the men, the effete Mulatto musician, a nubby fingered pianist, virginal figure, fluty voice and coquetry of a romantic woman; the Indian Mestizo politician, with beardless skin and the gelatinous belly of a eunuch

> . . . Among the women, the spinster Mulattress, so nice when she is intellectual and she makes an excellent school mistress, producing the deceptive sensation that her race, if she had a solid one, would normally be apt for feminism; and so repulsive when, not intellectual, a simple little stylist, fills her empty heart with whichever fanaticism, the icons of the temple or the talking spirits of the three-legged table . . .
>
> I would call this phenomenon degenerative semisterility of the hybrid human. (154 ellipses in the original)

For Bunge these figures reside at the intersection of racial and gendered ambiguity. All three of his examples disrupt the normative disciplining of bodies that is the self-proclaimed project of the state. The effete Mulatto musician transgresses masculine decency with his fluty voice, "virginal" figure, and feminine coquettishness. Likewise, the Mestizo politician is unattractive because of his "gelatinous" shape and lack of facial hair, linking him to the queer figure of the eunuch. Finally, the spinster Mulatta is acceptable as a (desexualized) schoolmarm, but repulsive for her choices in fashion and lack of principles, which makes her prone to the spiritism associated with racialized and illogical subjects.[7] These portrayals exacerbate the physical presence of deviant subjects in order to establish them as a threat to normativity. Bunge decries fluidity and softness in men and bemoans stiffness in women. These bodies all display physical qualities that he finds offensive. However, in the case of the Mulatta, Bunge first acknowledges her intellectual ability—even her usefulness as to the pedagogy of the nation—only to later dismiss this figure as spiritually unfit, her racial admixture leading inevitably to her moral corruption. This racist interpretation curiously holds out hope for the Mulatta who manages to carve a place for herself in Bunge's ideology outside of the purely somatic. Her irrationality is actually proof of her potential to move beyond the limits of positivism, and yet, she will never overcome her supposedly innate drives toward the occult—"the talking spirits." Her place is disputed not just as corporal territory, but as one with a spiritual history linked to an antipositivist desire for meaning in a world that desperately sought new ways to make sense of modernity.

While Bunge claims that "degenerative semisterility" is the product of repeated sexual encounters between incompatible human types, hybrids, and not miscegenation (*mestizaje*) writ large, the political ramifications of this racist perspective are clear. Particularly significant is how Bunge's vision of hybridity depends on the ambivalence of queerness. First, the demand that hybrid figures be disciplined—and eventually eliminated—does not depend on their presumably nonreproductive sexuality, but rather on the possibility that they might actually pass on their queer/hybrid genes to subsequent generations. That is, Bunge does not fear that these types will not reproduce, but that they actually might do so. Second, the disgust that he shows toward the Mulatto musician, the Mestizo politician, and the spinster Mulatress, belies the anxiety generated by racial hybridity and gender nonconformity, which is to say, inversely, the desire for aesthetic, ethnic, and performative congruence *in white criollo subjects*. Bunge's rejection of these figures is clearly aligned with turn-of-the-century positivist notions of racial degeneracy, but reading against the grain, we can also see that their presence reveals the limits of erotic (im)propriety by exceeding them, laying bare the desirability of fleshly abundance or sensual touch, a glance, a turn of phrase. While each of these figures performs both racial and gender hybridity, Bunge's rejection of them marks their bodies as dangerous and yet, enticing. They must be disciplined precisely because they might be desirable.

Bunge concludes, the Mulatto "es irritable y veleidoso como una mujer, y, como mujer, como degenerado, como el demonio mismo, 'fuerte de grado y débil por fuerza.' Sabe hacerse pequeño y dúctil, para luego erguirse y desafiaros mejor; sabe doblar su elástico espinazo, para después enderezarlo con soberbia de Luzbel. Porque, nuevo Luzbel, es el eterno Rebelado" ("is irritable and fickle as a woman, and, as a woman, as a degenerate, like the Devil himself, 'weak perforce and strong by choice.' He knows how to make himself small and ductile, to then straighten up and defy you better; he knows how to bend his elastic spine, to later rise with the arrogance of Lucifer. Because, the new Lucifer, he is the eternal Rebel"; 158). Strangely, his positivist denigration of gender and racial hybridity culminates with a quotation of a parable included in St. Ignatius of Loyola's *The Spiritual Exercises* (Rule 12 of The Rules for The Discernment of Spirits).[8] In this, Bunge's work evidences an ideological shift in the Argentine elite in which the fear of the growing workers movement led positivists to seek an alliance with the Catholic Church (Salessi 190). This alliance would provide the foundation for the Catholic nationalism that would dominate Argentina in the 1930s and '40s.[9] *Nuestra América* underscores the threat of racial decadence, but also changing gender roles, early feminism, and class and labor activism. In his simple equation Mulatto: Woman: Degenerate: Devil,

Bunge seeks to reposition white masculine authority as both spiritually ordained and scientifically incontrovertible. Notably, this same reference to St. Ignatius is also quoted in "La perfidia femenina" ("Femenine perfidy"), the final short story of Bunge's 1908 collection, *Viaje a través de la estirpe* ("A Trip through the Race"). Fiction and Science combine in the demonization of racial and gendered hybridity.

For Bunge the danger of the Mulatto lies in the incongruence between his outward appearance (strength) and inward nature (weakness). This *pose* is what Bunge fears.[10] In a tautological critique, Bunge claims the Mulatto is diabolic because he rejects his true, "elastic," nature, and because of this very nature he deserves to be rejected. As Jossianna Arroyo notes regarding Romantic novels of the late nineteenth century (in both Latin America and the United States), the Mulatto served an aesthetic and pedagogical function in early nationalist discourse (74-76). In the case of Brazilian literature, for example, the Mulatto character was portrayed as genetically and psychically divided and prone to emotional outbursts, "su sensibilidad artística, su espiritualidad y su fuerza ante el dolor hacen del mulato trágico una figura con una masculinidad cuestionada constantemente" ("his artistic sensibility, his spirituality and ability to endure pain make the tragic Mulatto a figure with a constantly questioned masculinity"; Arroyo 75). In contrast with the Brazilian case, however, for Bunge the Mulatto is not a figure prone to noble suffering, but rather ignoble deception. What remains constant regarding the figure of the racially hybrid Mulatto, however, is his portrayal as sensual and effete, irritable, and quarrelsome. The threat of the Mulatto's pose—his supposed tendency toward deception—reveals an ongoing debate around human nature and the civilizing possibilities of modernity in the early twentieth century. We should recall that "simulation" was a key object of study for turn of the century psychologists in Argentina, in particular for José Ingenieros, whose work proposed an evolutionary basis for the use of fraudulence, simulation, and deceit among the popular classes and ethnic minorities.[11] As ever keen to limit social disorder, Bunge does not simply demonize simulation, but he racializes and genders it is as well. In *Nuestra América*, the Mulatto is, like his hybrid blood, like the history that that blood bears, psychically unsettled and emotionally unstable.

For Bunge, the Mulatto is not dangerous simply because he is a degenerate subject, but for his capacity to arouse desire in, that is, to tempt morally upright men. If we can say that the Ignatian parable hinges on man's reaction to temptation (whatever its form), then the idealized white Christian man *must be* tempted by this Mulatto/Woman/Lucifer in order for the parable to function. The Christian must first feel the power of the Mulatto's sensual indeterminacy and then decide to reject this temptation through the spiritual exercise of faith. The fear that is at the heart of Bunge's critique is not of racial hybridity or gender variance alone, but the possibility of giving in to one's own proscribed desires. St. Ignatius concludes, "no wild animal on earth can be more fierce than the enemy of our human nature" (325). Clearly, for Bunge the enemy of progressive, modern, humanity is the degenerate hybrid, the disorderly amalgamation of genes and histories. And yet, we must also consider that even as the Mulatto represents a temporal, ethnic, and gendered aberration for Bunge, paradoxically, the exhortation to reject hybridity depends on him already existing in the field of desire. Gender and racial normativity operate in tandem, but only as the product of a successful rejection of hybridity's queerness, which, in the end, becomes the motor of subjective intelligibility in a rapidly shifting world. Bunge's depiction of racial and gendered hybridity reveals the constitutive role of queer desire in the ideological reformulation of a spiritually nationalist public.

## SPIRITUAL FEMINISM: DELFINA BUNGE'S *LAS MUJERES Y LA VOCACIÓN*

In her study of feminism in the Southern Cone, Asunción Lavrin describes how appealing to traditional values of domesticity and motherhood served feminists of varying ideological positions in the early decades of the twentieth century to enact social change. Her research points to diverging strands of feminist thought, however, around the role of the spirituality for women, when accusations of impropriety, masculinization, and disregard for the natural division of the sexes came from clergy and laymen alike (35–36). As the spiritual core of Argentina became a crucial battleground in the 1920s and '30s, cultural nationalists often derided feminists whose demands for labor protections, legal rights, and civic equality undermined what politicians saw as the urgent need to bolster traditional gender roles, paternal authority, and maternal abnegation. As we saw in chapter 3 regarding Julia's self-examination and Delfina's epistolary correspondence with Victoria Ocampo, marriage and motherhood were not static ideological constructs, but mobile and contingent, enticing and terrifying. Motherhood was, however, an unavoidable issue, and one that, as feminist scholar Marta Sierra argues, "was a key aspect of discourses on the modern identity of women, where traditional images of the patriotic mother of the nineteenth century were clashing with others that came from narratives of immigrant or lower-class women at the beginning of the twentieth century" (90). In this context, Delfina Bunge's essay *Las mujeres y la vocación*, published in 1922, represents a complex attempt to reconcile the momentum of modernization and the fear of modernity's effects on women, motherhood, and the national family. As Sierra is right to point out, *Las mujeres y la vocación* is a conservative text that promotes motherhood as the spiritual and moral compass that should orient all women. This orientation toward maternity is "naturalized" through positivist discourses around race, culture, and family, and bolstered by Catholic doctrine (Sierra 93). It is a text that attempts to reconcile two contradictory currents of thought: positivist science, which shows women's bodies are capable of entering the labor force, and Catholicism, which sees women as essentially defined by their mandate to bear children. Thus, while promoting the divine goodness of maternity, Bunge also advocates for the private development of women's intellectual and professional vocations—defining this term as a spiritual calling—and opens space for the public assertion of women's independence (still within certain limits). Her ambivalence toward the possibility of social change cannot be understood simply (or exclusively) as Catholic conservatism. Bunge's idea of womanhood was informed by Catholic doctrine, but also by liberal discourses of individual freedom, and even socialist notions of the collective good and mutual social accountability. Her ideas on "la cuestión femenina" are clearly tethered to the spiritual program of cultural nationalist thought, but her spiritual feminism constantly doubles back on itself, and is more nuanced than it might seem at first glance.

Toward the end of *Las mujeres y la vocación*, Delfina responds to her brother, Carlos Octavio (at least I would like to imagine that this was her intention) by taking up the same Ignatian parable cited in his *Nuestra América* and *Viaje a través de la estirpe*. She writes, with a just hint of sibling resentment: "Contrariamente a lo que se ha dicho que la mujer es 'fuerte de grado y débil por fuerza,' seamos débiles con agrado y fuertes por la fuerza. Dejemos al hombre sus derechos de Rey de la tierra, para que él respete los nuestros—aquellos a que nos hacen acreedoras nuestra debilidad y aquellos que nos hacen reinas en el reinado del Corazón" ("Contrary to what has been said, that women are 'weak perforce and strong by choice,' let us be willingly weak and firm by force. Let us leave to man his right of King of the earth, so that he respects our [rights]—those that make us believers in our weakness and those that make us queens of the kingdom of the Heart"; 93). This is a typical example of Delfina's intellectual enterprise in *Las mujeres y la vocación*. As she seeks to dismantle historical limitations placed on women, she does so by appealing to mutual and constitutive differences between men and women, proposing that the very weakness with which women have been characterized can actually become a source of empowerment. If man is divinely ordained to rule the world, she argues, then feminism should not attempt to undermine this order by claiming that women should be equal to men. Rather, by focusing on what she sees as the natural emotional capacity that all women possess, they can forge an individual path to self-fulfillment that maintains both domestic and national harmony. This point is key to understanding Delfina Bunge's spiritual feminism: accepting the divine order of things does not mean reducing women to mere adornment, servitude, or even motherhood. Rather, by accepting, even promoting women's unique gifts (here, emotional sensitivity) the common good is served more fully. Thus, she continues,

> Nuestros fines han de ser más nobles que el vano orgullo de *igualar al hombre*—cosa que no tiene ningún objeto—o que el insensato deseo de la preeminencia. Nuestras ambiciones de acción social, si las tenemos, deben responder principalmente *al deseo del bien común, o al imperioso mandato de una vocación determinada*; es decir, al anhelo del noble empleo de nuestras aptitudes personales.
>
> Our goals should be nobler than the vainglorious desire *to be equal to man*—which is pointless—or the foolish desire for preeminence. Our ambitions of social action, if we have them, should respond primarily *to the desire for the common good, or for the imperious mandate of a particular vocation*; that is, the longing for the noble exercise of our personal aptitudes. (94 emphasis in the original)

Discounting the possibility of gender equality as a spurious, futile effort, she proposes instead that the common good—understood as a society adhering to Catholic precepts of order and charity—benefits from the focused development of women's individual abilities. This argument abstracts the pursuit of any particular intellectual or professional endeavor such that the possibilities for women's engagement with the social sphere are not limited a priori, but rather are enacted as a consequence of the inclinations and spiritual calling (*vocación*) of each woman. In doing so, Delfina's essay depends on the definitional slippage carried by the term *vocación* to be at once spiritual and material, part of Catholic religiosity and modernity's narrative of expanding professional opportunities for women.

The freedom associated with the calling of a vocation is the most interesting part of Bunge's spiritual feminism. From the beginning of her essay she proposes that her goal is "invitar a todas las mujeres, de toda edad, a no oponer, como tenemos la costumbre de hacerlo, barreras de toda especie a nuestra propia acción presente o futura" ("to invite all women, of all ages, to not oppose, as we have been accustomed to doing, all sorts of barriers to our own actions in the present or the future"; 8). The search for women's freedom does not seek to displace men in an unquestioned social hierarchy. Rather, Bunge points to women, who, having internalized a conservative narrative of gendered possibilities apply pressure on other women to adhere to hegemonic beliefs. She repeatedly questions this type of self-undermining socialization. One notable example is her contention that women no longer be taught to see marriage as an obligatory "institución de beneficencia" ("charitable institution") (59-60). At least in this instance, Bunge is critiquing as antiquated the idea that any form of labor be proscribed for women, here particularly for middle- and upper-class women, such that marriage was seen as the only acceptable form of social and material advancement. The search for a vocation becomes a feminist project in that it opens up the possibilities for action, and for what counts as action, in private and public spheres, and across the differences of age (though, notably, not class or race). In seeking a vocation, Delfina maintains that two qualities are needed: "Primera, la humildad, que no mira con desprecio ninguna de las diferentes ocupaciones en que pudiéramos emplearnos, ni se obstina en buscar las que nos parece más elevadas. Y segunda, una cierta libertad de espíritu, para mirar sin prejuicios hacia todos los caminos" ("First, humility, to not look down at any of the different occupations that could employ us, or to obstinately seek those that seem to us the most elevated. And second, a certain freedom of spirit, to look without prejudice at all possible paths"; 25). While the overall sentiment is one of expanding the freedom to choose an individual path, it is clear that Bunge is directing herself to an audience that might need encouragement to do so. The working-class (likely immigrant) mother would not enjoy the luxury of obstinacy that Delfina criticizes. The middle- or even upper-class woman, in contrast, did, and it is to that woman that Bunge directs her advice. It is worth noting that the published essay *Las mujeres y la vocación* was originally given as two lectures, one at the Biblioteca Argentina del Rosario ("The Argentine Library of Rosario") and another at the Biblioteca del Consejo Nacional de Mujeres ("Library of the National Women's Council") in Buenos Aires. The audience that Delfina addresses, both in these lectures and in her essay, was a woman of means, a woman whose restriction to domestic life was beginning to ease as the expansion of leisure activities for the growing bourgeoisie meant that the possibility of a vocation *in addition to* a woman's domestic duties, became a subject worthy of debate.[12] Thus, when she advocates for a spiritual vocation it is first framed as a solution to women's "aburrimiento" ("boredom") and "materialismo" ("materialism") (15). In this, she charts a path for spiritual feminism that encourages women with the possibility of *choosing* to occupy themselves and their time with occupations beyond the domestic, that they do so in accordance with Catholic principles of charity, but also individual fulfillment and independence.

The freedom to choose a vocation is a central argument of Bunge's essay; one that seeks to dispel the notion that there are particular activities that women should not, or are not capable of exercising. She defines feminism in the following way: "El aceptar la multiplicidad de las vocaciones, y el respeto que debemos hacia las aptitudes y hacia la vocación particular de cada individuo, ya sea hombre o mujer" ("The acceptance of the multiplicity of vocations, and the respect that we owe the aptitudes and the unique vocation of each individual, for both men and women"; 28). Here, we see how Bunge's thought coincides with a more labor conscious strain of feminism. An almost identical sentiment is expressed in *El Obrero Textil* (*The Textile Worker*) in 1939: "Lo primero, pues, es asegurar en la sociedad igualdad de posibilidades para todos. No delimitar los campos de la acción femenina y de los de la acción masculina, sino dejar que sean las aptitudes de cada sexo y de cada persona las que determinen por sí mismas la realización práctica de esas posibilidades traducidas en aspiraciones" ("The first thing is, then, to ensure equal opportunity for all in society. Not to restrict the fields of feminine action and those of masculine action, but rather to let the aptitudes of each sex and of each person be what determines on their own the practical fulfillment of those possibilities translated in aspirations"; qtd. in Arnaiz & Chomnalez 33). This coincidence points to the role that the concept of individual freedom played in the development of a diverse feminist platform that nonetheless found access to professional vocations an essential component in promoting women's security. The expansion of women into the labor force was by no means a panacea for women's freedom, however. While working-class feminist leaders argued for the expansion of labor options, they also knew first-hand the precarious working conditions that prevailed in factories, mills, and domestic economies. On the other hand, the elite spiritual feminism espoused by Bunge, while advocating for what seems at first glance to be a more radical demand for particularity when judging a woman's ability to work, immediately attenuates that claim by embedding it within a tutelary model informed by Catholic doctrine. In a footnote to the original speech, Bunge adds the following:

> Si bien creo que no deben cerrarse a las mujeres ninguno de los caminos adonde su vocación personal las llame, como cristiana dejo sobreentendido que no han de arrogarse, en ninguna cosa, la Autoridad suprema entre las autoridades humanas, la cual, inconfundiblemente, puso Dios en manos del hombre. Me dirijo, pues no a las mujeres para que se rebelen contra la autoridad viril, sino más bien a los hombres para que no dificulten la acción de la mujer, sino que la alienten y dirijan como conviene.

> Even if I believe that none of the paths toward which a woman's individual vocation might call her should be foreclosed, as a Christian woman it should be understood that under no circumstances should [women] claim the supreme Authority among human authorities, which, incontrovertibly, God put in the hands of men. I am thus not addressing women so that they rebel against male [virile] authority, but rather men so that they do not make a woman's efforts more difficult, and instead encourage and guide her as needed. (29-30)

The mode of Bunge's intellectual intervention is one of expansion and contraction. At once proposing the freedom of thought and choice, the exercise of a liberty innate to all human beings and the couching of that freedom within a Catholic epistemology, Bunge's spiritual feminism constantly doubles back on itself. While no path of individual fulfillment should be proscribed to women, this right is also subject to the divine mandate that places the ultimate authority to determine that path in men. Thus, in expanding women's freedom, Delfina can only push so far, in the end appealing to men to exercise a more benevolent paternal authority in the modern era.

Perhaps the most innovative proposal to come from *Las mujeres y la vocación* is a model of shared labor by which single women (*solteras*) would help married women to manage the range of tasks required of daily domestic work. Delfina describes it as "un impuesto de trabajo a las solteras, en favor de las madres de familia" ("a labor tax on single women, to the benefit of mothers"; 49). This "tax" would function, she continues, "algo como un servicio militar, por el cual toda mujer sin hijos debía, durante un año, ayudar con dos horas de trabajo diario, a las más necesitadas de esta ayuda" ("something like a military service, for which every woman without children should, during one year, contribute two hours of daily labor, to those most in need of help"; 49-50). Her proposal is scant on details, but the general idea is in the absence of intergenerational kinship structures to pass down knowledge and to aid in maintaining a home, the state could be tasked with organizing and funding a sort of maternal "internship." Thus, nationalism and mutual cooperation combine in a proposal that depends on women sharing space and an orientation toward the home. While the proposal would serve married women by providing an extra set of hands, the implication is that by learning the skills required to successfully manage a home, unmarried women would in turn not only become better wives themselves, but would also gain a sense of commitment to the less fortunate. It is here that Delfina's own experience as a *niña* of the Porteño elite becomes evident. As we saw in her diaries, studied in chapter 3, Delfina was often dissatisfied with what she saw as the frivolity of her peers, young women more interested in ostentation than charity. Her proposal thus provides a corrective to the women of the upper class who should use their leisure time to serve others, rather than for their own personal enjoyment. As with her proposal to expand women's individual vocational options, this shared domestic labor at once opens possibilities for a women-centered cooperative environment, while it also limits that cooperation to the space of the home and at the service of the traditional family. As before, Delfina finds herself interested in a potentially radical alternative, yet returning to the domain of traditional kinship relations in the end. Women are in need of ways to occupy themselves, she seems to admit, but rather than advocate for the freedom of professional employment, she sees a less controversial alternative as more desirable for women's spiritual condition.

In Delfina's text this is redoubling is also evident with regard to marriage, which was of course a crucial issue for the early feminist movement in Argentina and across Latin America.[13] Keeping in mind the aforementioned tension between individual freedom and divine order, her thoughts on marriage once again reverberate between the individual and the collective. She writes,

> Una vez liberado nuestro espíritu de aquel sentimiento propio de la que ha nacido esclava, y cuya libertad limítase al derecho de elegir entre sus posibles dueños, ¡con cuánta mayor nobleza y desinterés miraremos el matrimonio! El hacerse esclava voluntaria, y por amor, del elegido, tendrá entonces otro valor. Y en esta generosa y libre esclavitud pondrá la mujer nobleza y majestad de reina.
>
> Once our spirit is freed of that self-feeling of which we were born a slave, and whose freedom is limited by the right to choose between possible masters, with how much more nobility and selflessness will we look at marriage! To become a voluntary slave, and for love, of one's chosen [husband], will thus have a different value. And in this generous and free enslavement women will add the nobility and majesty of a queen. (62)

Paradoxically hearkening Engels's inflammatory historical materialist conclusion that "the modern individual family is founded on the open or concealed domestic slavery of the wife" (105), Delfina at once broadens her critique of ongoing social unrest and proposes a Catholic solution to the apparent problem. Freedom comes with conditions. And yet, Bunge argues that these constraints should not be looked on with disdain; that women should not see their role in marriage as an inevitable choice to become one man's property or another. Rather, that in becoming an "esclava voluntaria" ("voluntary slave"), that is, in choosing to submit to man's authority in marriage, women should see themselves not only as fulfilling a divine mandate, but also exercising a fundamental right to dispose of their own bodies in the process. Thus, in willfully submitting to the husband, Delfina argues, a woman opens up the possibility of individual freedom. The term *voluntary slave* indicates that Delfina is choosing to identify the feminine condition with the privation of liberty and the institutional legacy of bondage in order to propose that it could be understood differently by those party to its structures. The contradiction here is between a discourse of liberal freedom, of individual liberty, and the collective social structure of Catholicism.

Early feminism often focused on expanding individual, personal freedom from within the institution of marriage, rather than questioning its validity (as would turn-of-the-century anarchists). The first years of the twentieth century saw feminists of different ideological stripes seek to modify marriage so that it became more agile, more able to negotiate the conflicts of modernity, while recognizing that this change remained the purview of men. If women's natural place was to be subordinate to men in marriage, and a successful marriage required the domain of men over their household and its inhabitants (*patria potestad*), then women's freedom could only be wielded within that institutional frame. It is important to note, briefly, that Argentina's 1868 Civil Code enshrined the patriarchal authority of men over women in matters including finances, patrimony, and legal contracts, and it was not until 1926 that the national Civil Code was reformed to allow women the freedom to testify in legal matters, dispose of their own income, receive an education, or choose a professional career.[14] The debates regarding voting rights and divorce were key for feminist groups in the 1920s, but so too was the legal standing required for women to exercise these types of rights within the Civil Code. Delfina Bunge is writing in the context of intense debate about what legal recourses women did and should have regarding the freedom to dispose of their own income, labor, and time, and thus, their bodies.

However, I want to consider in more detail the provocative question that Delfina asks: what is the value of submission in marriage? If it is unthinkable for a Catholic woman to question the institution of marriage or the submission of women to men within it, then the act of submitting *voluntarily* achieves something like a queer reimagining of power over one's own body. The queerness of this proposal is found in suspending the temporality of the body as an act of faith. The time of submission is both ongoing and momentary, perpetual and a process of constant negotiation. The "guise of consent" analyzed in chapter 1 returns here not as a proposition of desiring submission, but rather desiring to fulfill a spiritual mission while simultaneously negotiating the material needs of the modern economy. But to voluntarily submit to patriarchal authority is only voluntary in the sense that this submission forms the basis of a spiritual practice that takes as its foundation such a possibility. The ability to consent to submitting is the basis of Delfina's understanding of faith. A woman's "generous and free enslavement" is attenuated by her innate qualities of nobility, even majesty, and yet, also implies that it is only through engaging in an ongoing negotiation of intimacy, an offering and withholding of the spirit and the body, that a woman truly manages to establish herself as a man's equal. She can only give "generously" that which she has. Faith requires this negotiation, this will to believe that one's body and one's spirit are both singular and shared. And in sharing the material and the spiritual, the ontological and the cosmic, the social finds expression through and as faith.

As noted above, Delfina Bunge's spiritual feminism is aimed at the modern woman of means. On the one hand, she claims that women need the freedom to choose and develop a vocation, and on the other, they need to the freedom to choose to marry and submit to masculine authority. This juncture of cultural nationalism, spiritual fulfillment, and modern feminist thought finds expression in *Las mujeres y la vocación*, such that the enhancement of women's freedom (even within these limitations) is meant to make them better wives and mothers, and thus contribute to the moral and spiritual betterment of the nation. Delfina's silences are meaningful in this context as well. She does not deal with the possibility of abusive or absent husbands. This too, is a sort of privilege. This modern spiritual feminism coincides with the cultural nationalist vision of society organized through an unquestioned gender hierarchy that encourages women to develop individual talents at the service of the national cause, which, nevertheless depends on women's ability to choose to submit to that hierarchy. Bunge's thinking is aimed at improving the lives of women by increasing women's freedom, and in doing so increasing the ability of those women to have more and healthier children. Those children, in turn, will have a greater chance at becoming healthy and well-educated (and thus patriotic and moral) citizens. Her work intervenes in a moment of increasing uncertainty about women's roles in Argentina, and this uncertainty, she claims, can be alleviated by improving the ability that women have to develop individual talents and desires at the service of national unity and the common good. While the anxieties of the early twentieth century, in particular shifting gender roles, and the threat of declining birth rates, appear in Carlos Octavio's work as the fear of mixed-race degeneracy, and later, in Alejandro Bunge's alarmist view of the loss of white hegemony, in Delfina's text we see the fear of spiritual decline. The future is uncertain, and yet she turns to the past: "estas palabras han sonado a mis propios oídos como el eco de un tiempo ya pasado, y como disconformes con los días que corren, y que van más adelante que mis palabras..." ("These words have sounded to my own ears like the echo of a bygone era, and as dissatisfied with the present day, and as preceding my own words ..."; 97). Finally, Delfina reflects on the inevitability of social and economic change—on the need to propose alternatives in the present that draw on the past as they project into the future. She recognizes, in fact, that she is proposing a "futurism of the past," which returns to her ears as an echo of a lost era. This nostalgia, characteristic of the work of the elite in the early twentieth century, including *Las mujeres y la vocación*, proposes the inevitability of modernization, yet still yearns for a reprieve from the dissatisfying present by hearkening a social order that seems, now, a distant echo. But that echo would return, again and again in Argentine politics. And we can see a direct link between Delfina's dissatisfaction with the seemingly disorganized present and calls that would come over the following fifty years for order, religion, and hierarchy in Argentina. In the end, what she heard was both an echo and the siren song of authoritarian rule.

## THE PAST FUTURE OF WHITE NATIONALISM: ALEJANDRO BUNGE'S *UNA NUEVA ARGENTINA*

History, it bears repeating, has been at the center of the ideological conflicts in Argentina and across Latin America over the course of the modern era. The violent interruptions of democratic rule that characterize the second half of the twentieth century were consistently understood in terms of how they sought to redefine history. The threat of social upheaval has so often led those in power to erase or rewrite history, and Alejandro Bunge's *Una nueva argentina* (*A New Argentina*) is my final example of this nationalist melancholia.[15] It is a pessimistic essay of national diagnosis that spiritualizes and eroticizes Argentina's reproductive capacity as a nation of the past-future. *Una nueva argentina* stands out for its anachronism, perhaps published forty years too late, when the trend of diagnostic determinism had all but lost its luster. However, because of this context, it presents a forceful call for a "futurism of the past" that hearkens a return to the period in which the elite maintained uncontested hegemony over national politics, economics, and culture.

To be sure, *Una nueva argentina* does not mark the end of the predominance of the elite, or the final moment in which Argentina's past-future would serve as a rallying cry for the nation. But working-class, socialist, and anarchist organizing, the passage of universal male suffrage, the budding feminist movement, and the interwar period all brought into view the socioeconomic processes by which the elite had maintained its hegemony in the West. The pendulum of Argentine politics would swing between popular nationalist rule and right-wing military regimes from the first military coup d'état of 1930 until the final, genocidal dictatorship gave way to a new understanding of symbolic and biological kinship.[16] The military leaders of the 1976-1983 dictatorship would reprise appeals to a Catholic vision of family and order in justifying its "divine" mission (Rock, *Authoritarian* 222-31). The concept of family would never be the same after this genocide. And yet, as a series of tropological narratives, the family and the mutuality that it depends on, bears a constant process of evolution and (re)emergence. *Una nueva Argentina* exemplifies this contradiction: a text that at once depends on an imaginary of the nation as a family and instigates a queer refashioning of the familiar aimed at consolidating power in the hands of the elite.

Born in 1880, Alejandro Bunge would leave Argentina to be trained as an engineer in Germany, and eventually become a specialist in statistics and demography. Upon his return, he was named director of statistics for the Departamento Nacional de Trabajo (National Department of Labor) in 1910, and would lead the Departamento Nacional de Estadísticas (National Department of Statistics) from 1915 to 1925. In addition to his charge as a public official, he was affiliated with the Facultad de Ciencias Económicas (Department of Economics) at the Universidad de Buenos Aires, and in 1918 he would found the *Revista de Economía Argentina* (*Argentine Journal of Economics*) along with four of his colleagues.[17] His innovative use of statistics, political connections, family background, and economic ties made him an important figure in the 1920s and '30s. A deeply religious man, Alejandro would attempt to leverage his public position in the Argentine government, on the one hand, and his role as director of the country's most prominent economics journal, on the other, to advocate for a vision of the nation that coincided with his own understanding of what came to be known as "Social Catholicism." In 1912 he was elected president of the Círculos de Obreros Católicos (Circle of Catholic Workers), a syndicate intended to provide health care, mutual aid, and housing for working-class populations under the auspices of Catholic charity (Núñez 163). After its founding in late 1918, Bunge was also affiliated with the Liga Patriótica Argentina (Argentine Patriotic League), whose slogan "¡Salvemos el orden y la tradición nacional!" ("Let us Save National Order and Tradition!") combined a yearning for hierarchy and a view that moral reform could only be achieved through a return to traditional Catholic values (Rock, *Authoritarian* 67-68). Thus, the publication of *Una nueva argentina* in 1940—three years before his death—should be understood as a collection and synthesis of a lifetime of thought regarding the social and economic health of Argentina. And in Bunge's estimation, the outlook was dire.

Historians of Argentine economics are prone to identify Alejandro Bunge with his views that the nation's heavy dependence on foreign capital and support of international free trade policies meant the country was economically reliant on an agro-export model that was nearing exhaustion.[18] To be sure, his use of demographic trends was at the avant-garde of statistical methodology in Latin America. Bunge was the first to apply "index numbers" to track cost of living increases over time (Pantaleón 190). Likewise, his advocacy for diversified national industrial development and protectionist economics informed what would become the dominant economic philosophy in the region, import substitution industrialization (ISI), which in Argentina was led by one of his students and former colleagues, Raúl Prebisch.[19]

Of all the members of the Bunge family studied in this book, Alejandro is the one who has had the most significant impact on the daily lives of most Argentine citizens today. His influence extends into Peronist economic protectionism through Prebisch, an influence that would later give way to the huge national debt incurred during the military regime under Finance Minister (Ministro de Economía) José Alfredo Martínez de Hoz. This debt would later be restructured in the late 1980s under the tutelage of international lending organizations like the IMF, with disastrous consequences for the Argentine economy, leading to the hyperinflation, eventual default of sovereign debt, and widespread poverty that characterized the financial crisis of 1998-2001. The effects of this crisis linger, like the scent of carrion, while the central debate around economic protectionism and globalization rages on.[20] Thus, Alejandro Bunge's prognosis that the lack of national industrial development in Argentina was creating a false sense of economic security would prove clairvoyant. He was an innovative and diligent economist who aimed to link his observations to the social reality of the country, and to a certain extent, his diagnosis of Argentine economics—the threat of failing to diversify local economies—has yet to be fully reckoned with. This is a notable contribution. However, my focus in this section is not Bunge's understanding of political economy, but rather the sexual economy that is required in order to heed his warning. After all, his economic prognosis is linked to the availability of future workers and consumers, as informed by his use of demographics. When Bunge argues that the decline of Argentine industry is inevitably tied to its reproductive capacity *as a white nation* in Latin America, he is explicitly linking production to reproduction; labor to bodies. *Una nueva Argentina* is not just an economic tract, but a sex manual.

I want neither to over theorize nor trivialize this point. Insofar as Bunge aims to convince a specific population (elite white families) to reproduce more, his goal is sexual. Put another way, Bunge aims to recalibrate the social worth of procreative sexuality so that white hegemony can extend into the future. However, in order to carry out this shift in the cultural value of reproduction, Bunge must also attend to the material reality of economic development in Argentina. Production and reproduction share space in the ideology of the family, which is the central problem that Bunge addresses in *Una nueva Argentina*. According to his calculations, Argentina's white population, having reached a critical level of economic well-being, and in concert with comparative populations in other developing nations, was beginning an era of population decline (33). He calls this trend "*denatalidad*" ("denatality") among the "*raza blanca*" ("white race"), which, he claims, is caused by the relative economic success that they have enjoyed over the past several generations. According to scientists in Europe and the United States (and Bunge agrees), generally speaking, financial success leads to a decrease in fertility. Likewise, echoing the work of American biologist Raymond Pearl (1879-1940), Bunge claims that populations with fewer resources (this is obviously a racially charged descriptor) tend to reproduce at a higher rate than the economic elite (*Nueva* 37-39). If whiteness was understood as a sign of cultural and moral excellence, as Bunge believed, then these demographic trends signaled that in the near future Argentina would become overrun by culturally backward, intellectually deficient, morally corrupt, and racially inferior masses. Adopting a Darwinian metaphor, Alejandro Bunge calls this "la selección a la inversa" ("inverse selection") (49). The predominance of the unfit, the backward, *the inverted*, is what these demographic trends portend in Bunges view. They augur a degenerate future. Once again, if the history of Argentina is a history of its great families (its white criollo families), then a decline in birth rates of those families would represent a profound threat not just to the status quo, but to the survival of the nation itself.

Bunge's response is to encourage members of the elite to have more reproductive sex—to bear more children—within the confines of marriage. The burden of reproduction is a heavy one: "En este continente la conservación y la reproducción de la *élite* son esencialísimas; y lo es también que en sus manos siga la dirección política y cultural por arriba de las teorías. Los hombres superiores de toda América deben cumplir hasta heroicamente con la ley natural de la familia y con la misión directiva que para bien de su propio pueblo deben conservar" ("On this continent the conservation and reproduction of the elite are absolutely essential; as is it that in their hands remain the management of culture and politics, and not just in theory. Superior men across the Americas should fulfill even heroically the natural law of the family and the driving mission that for the good of their own people they should maintain"; 56). "Even heroically" Bunge describes, without irony, the sexual duty of the elite, whose men are narrated as part of an ongoing struggle, an epic, through which their phallic dominance is sacralized as part of a divine mission. In this, Bunge follows Eduardo Mallea's 1938 *Historia de una pasión argentina* in claiming a past history of white cultural dominance, a past of heroic nation builders enmeshed in a narrative of almost messianic progress. Cultural nationalists decried the direction of the country, its political and cultural leadership, as fraudulent, uncultured, and beholden to the whims of the masses, and proposed, like Bunge, that the destiny of the nation should be restricted to the elite. These twin proposals are crucial to Bunge's vision of the past-future nation: on the one hand, the elite must continue to govern, and in order for it to do so, on the other hand, it must increase in number. This antidemocratic position requires that elite men make sacrifices; that they find the will to continue to reproduce even at the expense of domestic comfort and security, "el deseo de vida cómoda, ambiciones triviales, libertad para los halagos" ("the desire for a comfortable life, trivial ambitions, freedom for flattery"; 41). The fate of the nation, of the race, thus depends on the reproductive will (*voluntad*) of white men, while white women must continue to serve as incubators for future generations.

As with most nationalists, Alejandro Bunge rejected earlier positivist thought as lacking moral and spiritual direction. The feeling of chaos derived from the modern world, the cosmopolitanism of Buenos Aires, and the threat of familial disintegration all led to a revision of tradition that brought Catholic thought closer to the budding nationalist movement.

Once more, the context of this shift matters, as Catholic nationalism in Argentina sought to undermine the past decades of liberal institution building, on the one hand, and the rising popularity of socialist and anarchist organizing at the turn of the century, on the other. Catholic nationalism, in Bunge's hands, was shaped according to the precepts of divine order, the natural division of human groups (class divisions), and the dominion of man over the earth (and thus of private property). His vision of a past-future draws on the emergence of a Catholic alternative to socialist class-consciousness. In particular, Bunge draws on an encyclical published in 1891 by Pope Leo XIII known as the *Rerum Novarum*, which offered a theological justification for class difference and a moral counterweight to the supposed laxity of liberalism and the radical immorality of socialism. The *Rerum Novarum* describes the rights of the individual in relation to human social structures; that is, to family and to the nation. At its core, the text aims to provide both spiritual and material justification for the working classes to turn to the Church rather than to socialism, and in doing so, it links the divine right to private property and the notion of an orderly society. This is a type of order that itself evokes a much older form of social welfare based on medieval workers guilds and confraternities (paragraphs 49-57). Still, the encyclical defends unionization, which at the time was a major break from the Church's previous position. And yet, it praises the right to association and the establishment of private societies as the most appropriate, that is, the most harmonious, form of collective action to the benefit of "body, soul, and property" (paragraph 57). This is collective action with a spiritual purpose within the framework of capitalism.

In establishing the sacred right to private property, the *Rerum Novarum* calls first on the unquestionable authority of man within natural law, "it is a most sacred law of nature that a father should provide food and all necessaries for those whom he has begotten," and then on the accumulative function of kinship, "and in no other way can a father effect this except by the ownership of productive property, which he can transmit to his children by inheritance" (paragraph 13). Thus, the transmission of property is seen as the only avenue by which a father can support his progeny; paternal authority as the vehicle through which this property is maintained and distributed; kinship as the hierarchical structure that, in accordance with natural law, facilitates this transmission of culture and property. What is more, the encyclical continues, "Paternal authority can neither be abolished nor absorbed by the State; for it has the same source as human life itself. 'The child belongs to the father,' and is, as it were, the continuation of the father's personality" (paragraph 14). If the child is a continuation of the personality of the father, then the extension of the family becomes a mechanism by which reproduction interfaces with economic production. In this way, Leo XIII calls on a logic of temporal continuity that is supported by capitalist tenets of labor and yet attenuated by Catholic notions of charity. The continuous, here, positions the child as an extension of the matter of blood. The social body is imagined as a collection of continuous reproductions of self through which the family, in turn, is justified as the primary unit of self-extension.

What is more, the shape of the family corresponds with that of the nation.

> Just as the symmetry of the human frame is the result of the suitable arrangement of the different parts of the body, so in a State it is ordained by nature that these two classes [labor and capital] should dwell in harmony and agreement, so as to maintain the balance of the body politic.... Mutual agreement results in the beauty of good order, while perpetual conflict necessarily produces confusion and savage barbarity. (Paragraph 19)

The beauty of the body follows an Aristotelian formalism, while the body's ugliness is likened to an Indigenous American wilderness. To be an efficient State is to be well proportioned, balanced, harmonious, contrapuntal, contained, but not necessarily (necessarily not) symmetrical in the conventional sense. The inequality of classes, working together to make a cohesive whole is what makes them both, together, beautiful, not that they occupy equal social or material space, or share the same amount of bodily matter. This constitutive inequality is at the heart not only of the Church's insistence on the divine nature of private property, but of the natural inequality of social classes. In this view, the nation, like the family, depends on each of its members understanding the role that has been assigned to them by God. This divine structuring of the social is arranged like a beautiful body that is like a family that is like a nation, a chain of symbolic equivalency that justifies the Church's intervention in socioeconomics as an effect of its harmonious mission.

To commemorate the fortieth anniversary of Pope Leo XIII's encyclical, in 1931 Pope Pius XI pronounced his *Quadragesimo Anno*, subtitled "On Reconstruction of the Social Order." This text extolled Leo's vision of social Catholicism, and expanded on the ideal form of labor relations after World War I. Pius was compelled, given the historical context, to take up the question of the corporatist economic model implemented in Italy under Mussolini's fascist regime. While the pope first praises "the new syndical and corporative order" for leading to a juncture in which "[t]he various classes work together peacefully, socialist organizations and their activities are repressed, and a special magistracy exercises a governing authority," he immediately curbs this enthusiasm, claiming that it "savors too much of an involved and political system of administration" (paragraph 95). While Mussolini's corporatist model produced clear and demarcated spheres of social interaction, it does so, according to the pontiff, at the expense of workers' individual freedom to join fraternal organizations independent of the state. In contrast, that inaugurated by António de Oliveira Salazar first as Finance Minister and later Prime Minister of Portugal under the banner of the Estado Novo, had been praised by Pius XI because of its efforts to bring Catholic social doctrine in line with that of the state. While Mussolini sought to reform through personality and bombast, Salazar concentrated power and encouraged a return to past glory through Catholic action.[21] Thus, forty years after Pope Leo's call to reinvigorate Catholic labor unions, Pope Pius echoes this sentiment but couches it within a new framing of "social justice" by which a stronger state, with the support of the Church, could enact the type of distributive economics that would do away with the class conflict that had plagued the world since the late nineteenth century. The ultimate goal, Pius states, is that "the conflict between the hostile classes be abolished and harmonious cooperation of the Industries and Professions be encouraged and promoted" (paragraph 81). The *Quadragesimo Anno* encouraged the state to intervene directly in economic matters, and would leave an important mark on nationalist social thought by legitimizing economic distribution through hierarchical and state-sponsored mediation between classes (Rock *Authoritarian* 120-21).

In summary, Alejandro Bunge's Catholic ideology adapted socioeconomic ideas from the *Rerum Novarum* and the *Quadragesimo Anno* and was influenced by fascist regimes in Europe, namely Salazar's Portugal, Franco's Spain, and Mussolini's Italy. In seeking to encourage the divine order of society, he rejected both laissez-faire and socialist economic platforms, preferring a vision of labor and capital in which the state provided spiritual guidance and mediation between corporatist associations. He notes, "[s]erá difícil el éxito si no surge un ideal esforzado, un concepto cristiano de la familia y una identificación vigorosa con los supremos intereses de la nación y de la raza" ("success will be difficult if an earnest ideal, a Christian concept of family and a vigorous identification with the supreme interests of the nation and of the race does not emerge"; 41-42). In seeking to spiritualize economics, he encouraged a nationalist revision of white supremacy that entrenched patriarchal authority as the necessary architecture of both intimate and public spheres. This vision, rooted in Catholic spiritual principles, was carried out to consolidate power in the hands of the rapidly dwindling white criollo elite, but also to encourage them to look at their own role in Argentine society as greater than themselves as a class. In shifting the discussion to the survival of the nation and the white race itself, he asks the elite to take pleasure not in their economic success, but in their contributions to national futurity.

Though he never states it directly, Bunge's nationalist revision of socioeconomics also revolves around the concept of pleasure. Pleasure is central to the monogamous, conjugal relationship—the pleasure of sex within marriage that is carnal, spiritual, and natural. Pleasure thus becomes proper to the realm of the nation, its futurity, and its racial ontology. In providing the nation with more elite white children, the thrust of Bunge's text demands an affective shift that transfers the love of the couple within marriage to love of the nation and its legitimacy through white racial dominance. As noted above, his insistence of the value of the white race, its longevity and cultural dominance, is only intelligible as part of a broader shift in value from the individual to the collective. Through this transfer, men's moral and patriotic duty is sexualized in a particular way: to provide children is thus to take pleasure in the future greatness of the nation. The nation, which demands these children, rewards reproductive sex between married, monogamous, white couples (both literally and symbolically) by dispensing benefits, such as housing subsidies and direct cash payments, but also social prestige (Biernat 198). The pleasure of material progress—of splendor—with all of the historical weight that that carries in Argentina, must be replaced by the spiritual pleasure of obeying God's will. Here pleasure hearkens back to a premodern Western ethics that depends on channeling a man's inner drives, his passions, his sexual conduct, through the contours of a practice of self by which he maintains social standing as part of the elite (Foucault, *History* 2: 25-32). Predictably, a woman's pleasure is unthinkable for Alejandro Bunge. Still, his quasi-eugenic platform is a national framework for a new regime of pleasure by which sex (the pleasure of sex) becomes crucial because it is offered to the state as tribute for the privileges, the power, the predominance, of a cultural apparatus that depends on producing and reproducing whiteness as the matter, the substance, of its longevity.[22] For the elite, however, offering one's children to the future of the nation becomes the greatest possible pleasure for a man and his family. It is a sexual model of integrating the psychic figure of authority and the material expression of erotics in a singular mode of feeling toward the ongoing perfection of the modern nation as expressed through the social value that whiteness accrues over time.

Alejandro Bunge's understanding of whiteness, and its relationship to national futurity, was not developed in isolation. The late-career work of José Ingenieros serves as an important contrast between the biotelluric determinism of men like José María Ramos Mejía, Francisco de Veyga, and Carlos Octavio Bunge of the turn of the century, and the past-future cultural nationalism of the 1920s and '30s espoused by Ricardo Rojas, Manuel Gálvez, Eduardo Mallea, and Alejandro Bunge. To be sure, all three visions (that of turn-of-the-century positivists, Ingenieros, and the cultural nationalists) depended on a racialized view of the Argentine *ser* (being), and all position whiteness as the pinnacle of racial and cultural development. However, as Fernando Degiovanni points out, "La formación de una raza argentina" ("The Formation of an Argentine Race"), an essay published by Ingenieros in 1915, inaugurates an anticriollo and anticolonial vision of the Argentine cultural tradition, which Ingenieros would fully develop through his editorial project La Cultura Argentina ("Argentine Culture") (244). The enterprise of consolidating Argentine nationalism carried on into the interwar period, when the technification of culture had reached its peak. While Ingenieros coincides with his contemporaries in seeing both race and the environment as important factors in the development of a national culture, he differs in claiming that it is the predominance of recent Latin immigrants to Argentina that led to the prosperous years of the turn of the century (Degiovanni 244). Still considered part of the "*raza blanca*," and thus endowed with an innate cultural advantage, immigrants of Spanish and Italian descent (such as Ingenieros himself) had been stigmatized by positivist scientists in Argentina as incapable of conforming to the traditional, criollo past on which the nation had been built. But in shifting the discursive frame from one of biological determinism to one of cultural heritage, Ingenieros was able to expand the definition of whiteness by minimizing the question of tradition and instead focusing on the shared white supremacy of both old and recent immigrants. Thus, entering the 1920s, Ingenieros advocated that it was the inherent superiority of the white settlers of and later immigrants (from both Northern and Southern Europe) to Argentina that led the "*la raza blanca*" to become the predominant ethnic and cultural group in the country. It was their whiteness, rather than their adaptation to the land, which made them the predominant ethnic group.

Ingenieros rejects the vision of Argentine nationalism that sees in its colonial heritage, in its feudal past, in its Catholic traditionalism, a new way forward. Rather, he proposes that it is only in eschewing dogmatic approaches to national culture, while foregrounding the implicit social compatibility of the white races, will the country manage to achieve the greatness to which it is, as the intellectual elite believed, Latin America's rightful heir. If the blood of the mixed-race population was indissolubly linked to degeneracy and cultural backwardness, then even those European immigrants who, as the elite feared at the turn of the century, were uneducable as loyal national citizens, could, by the 1920s be repurposed, reinvented, as a mass of white bodies, from which, according to Ingenieros, the *feeling* of nationalism must necessarily derive. With the environment no longer thought of as the essential factor in creating a sense of national belonging, it fell to the reproductive capacity of white men, or men now thought of as white, to take up that feeling, that duty, as members of the elite.

Bunge's *Una nueva Argentina* is an ethical critique buoyed by demographic trends and economic projections, but which maintains at its core the implication that the object of men's desire must be corrected. Bunge seeks a fundamental shift in the way desire functions in the family structure of the upper class. If capital accumulation, the growth and maintenance of a family's inheritance ("*la vida cómoda*") has led to the demographic crisis that threatens the future of the elite, then, Bunge proposes, the upper-class family can no longer operate exclusively as a system of material gain, but must put aside that historical endeavor in favor of one that serves the greater good of the nation: biological reproduction. In choosing nation over comfort, Bunge suggests the elite replace the desire for capital accumulation with the desire for whiteness itself. Thus, rather than an ethnic amalgam, Alejandro Bunge imagines nationalist kinship as a structure for the reproduction of sameness, a sameness that unfolds over time as racial homogeneity. This homogeneity, in turn, depends on the fear of racial diversity as the promise of racial degeneracy. If demographic trends continue, Bunge forecasts the collapse of Argentina as a white nation.

For Alejandro Bunge the family emerges in order to save the nation from itself, as the nation is called on to intervene in the decline of the white Catholic family. This proposed social hierarchy led to an anxious reevaluation of reproductive futurity. The future is bleak and time is running out, but a new time is possible. Family becomes the past-future rallying cry for the elite. A structure that can withstand the interventions of the military, economic collapse, and demographic change, it is a source of both history and destiny. For Bunge, the elite should not desire the accumulation of capital, but time. It is through the reproduction of more white children that the elite gains spiritual (rather than material) comfort, national predominance, and of course, more time as the dominant social group. The pleasure of capital accumulation is replaced by that of legacy; the immediate satisfaction of grandeur, by the delayed gratification of white supremacy.

To end this book with a text that directly calls for the expansion of white supremacist Catholic nationalism may seem strange. But as I have demonstrated throughout *Argentine Intimacies*, the inscription of kinship into the ongoing narrative of the nation owes to the discursive counterpoint of sameness and difference, belonging and alterity, normativity and queerness, as well as the material, lived enactment of the bonds that family depends on, those it rejects, and those it fears. In this case, the meaning of kinship is shaped by the refusal to acknowledge that the inevitable decline of the elite had already begun, the fact that no amount of reproductive nationalism could save the *oligarquía* from its own delirious desires for permanence and preeminence. By the 1940s, the social and political economies had become irreconcilable with the belief in the future grandiosity to which the elite believed it was destined, again and again. While the history of Argentina, its splendor and its failures, as well as its perseverance, is often described as the history of its great families, I hope this book shows that such a history is not as simple, not as straightforward as it is often taken to be. In the end, these disjunctures reveal the contingent and transitory imbrication of desires, a persistent contradiction that constantly undermines the viability of a singular accounting for what counts as family.

epilogue

# TOWARD A QUEER
# LATIN AMERICAN STUDIES

Instead of charting the alternatives to the normative family at the turn of the century in Argentina, this book has traced the intimate contradictions that make normative kinship queer. *Argentine Intimacies* has engaged with the familiar as an interface of relational dispositions, rather than a set of concrete norms, as it has provided a detailed analysis of the discourses, embodiments, and sensibilities that characterized the period of modernization in which positivist science and its promise of order and progress came to dominate the cultural imaginary of the elite. By highlighting the queer slippages that emerge in the writing of the Bunge family and in their enactments of daily life, this book has elaborated on the conceptual limits, political effects, and erotic ambiguities that gave family meaning in Argentina's age of splendor, a period of intense social change that saw the luster of upper-class hegemony begin to fade. This has required patience and care for the objects studied and the lives they link through time and space. Certainly, this care has to do with the material fragility of the archive. But it also responds to the modes of making kin that are revealed through the slow process of approaching the Bunge family itself as a dynamic site of study. In thinking through the queerness of diaries as they make and remake familiar relations; sepia photographs as they hold lingering reflections on and as kinship; essays, textbooks, and fiction that double back and *twist* forms of belonging, I have had to consider how the reverberations of conflicting desires mobilize bodies in relation and as related. Accounting for these complexities and for the epistemological context that informs them has been one of the central challenges of this book. In studying the Bunge family, I have not sought to romanticize family life *as it once was*, or to reject its normative momentum outright, but rather to take the normative family as a productive site of queer scholarship.

In a sense, one of the unstated goals of this book has been to show that we can better understand the conceptual bases of the new normativities of the twenty-first century by paying attention to the way that the modern family became sedimented as part of a contradictory Liberal ideology that first developed as the purview of science, politics, and the state in the late nineteenth and early twentieth centuries. Making the past matter in the present is often difficult, as it can undermine important distinctions between conceptual horizons and material realities, histories and lives, bodies and desires. New biopolitical regimes emerge, new technologies of control and of discipline, new approaches to old problems, old problems in new shapes and at new speeds. Nevertheless, this epilogue builds on the historical scope and methodological approach in this book to propose future directions for queer studies scholarship. Specifically, it suggests that the intersections of queer studies with Latin American studies and decoloniality can offer important lessons going forward for a hemispheric and transhistorical queer Latin American studies. Thus, this is not a field statement so much as a reflection on the possibilities of queer studies as it engages with multiple contexts.

If queer studies and Latin American studies scholarship are to engage with each other as interdisciplinary methodologies, they will need to address at least four crucial issues. First, following Kadji Amin, the development of queer studies in the US academe in the early 1990s needs to be historicized as a particularly situated methodological praxis rather than one that instigates a universalizing and thus infinitely mobile set of critical tools applicable to ontological realities of vastly different scope and tradition. Second, the embodied qualities of gender, sexuality, and race, as products of the colonial epistemology that gives meaning to normativity in the Americas, need to be understood as responding to practical and lived experiences in conjunction with aesthetic, performative, and theoretical interventions from queer studies, feminist studies, diasporic, and critical race studies as developed in local contexts. Third, queer studies must reckon with the critical shift harnessed under the rubric of decoloniality, and ask itself whether it can contribute to what Walter Mignolo calls "illuminat[ing] the darker side of modernity" and strive toward a different narrative and epistemological basis for contemporary social life than that instigated by the "colonial matrix of power" under which we are all living (111). In other words, queer studies will have to fundamentally question its development as a Western colonial ideology—despite its claims to radical antinormativity. Fourth, it must center the geopolitics of translation, circulation, and the privileging of certain queer studies texts and theorists in order to understand how distinct historical and material traditions in Latin America (and elsewhere) do not simply adapt "queer" to local contexts, but actively contest and rework the corporeal and epistemological horizons of queer critique. In doing so, it must revise how critique—the turning of practices, feelings, and histories into objects of critique—negotiates the intersection of queerness and coloniality, and open itself to what non-Western, nonwhite, and nonrepresentational methods bring to bear on the possibility of reimagining power as it could be in a future that might need for queer studies to be left behind. If these are the issues that must be addressed, a first step toward engaging with the operational possibilities of queerness across the Americas would require fully engaging with the many contradictions of hemispheric study. In doing so, we must ask how queerness attaches itself to discourses and bodies, but also, to feelings of critical praxis. Queer studies cannot be felt or enacted in the same way in different contexts. Finally, we must not stop at studying the effects of queerness, but instead bring queer's geotemporality to bear on the epistemological foundations of Western modernity, which are themselves currently being disrupted by the multiple framings of decoloniality that have emerged across the Americas since the 1970s. In the following sections, I develop what I see as an essential sketch of the stakes, the contradictions, and the promise of queer studies as it continues to grow and transform.

## QUEER'S HEMISPHERIC CONTRADICTIONS

When queerness is constantly framed as that against which the normative defines itself, then the institutions of family, the state, and capitalism that work together to inscribe the normative as natural do not have to confront the enduring violence that they enact. The family claims having always already achieved the idealized self-image on which it depends, a claim that nevertheless depends on feeling, even seeking out the proximity of queerness. Thus, the normative family pictures itself as having emerged fully fledged as part of an unbroken genealogy of families after families that have never been essentially different than they are now (or were then). The underlying premise of this reproductive futurity, paradoxically, is that the family in fact must have the ability to adapt to new sociopolitical realities. By understanding the dynamics of those adaptations, annexations, and incorporations, queer studies scholarship can make a case for divesting the normative family of its seemingly inherent and unquestionable hegemony in social, political, and affective domains.

As I have shown in this book, one strategy that queer studies can take is to denaturalize the self-evident value that the family garners as a normative institution, which is to work toward eroding the legitimacy it offers, tautologically, of and for itself, its configuration as self-evidently good for all. Another strategy is a politics that sees communal and reciprocal relationships, anticapitalist organizing, and political and erotic sovereignty as central to undermining the normative conceptions of gender and sexuality that uphold the longevity of the normative imaginary and enactment of the family. To take such a route, my book might have engaged with early socialist writing or the robust strain of anarchist thought that developed in the River Plate region at the turn of the century in order to demonstrate historical alternatives to normative family life. In this vein, Marcos Wasem's *El amor libre en Montevideo: Roberto de las Carreras y la irrupción del anarquismo erótico en el Novecientos* (2015) provides an impressive critique of the anticapitalist and nonmarital relations, as expressed in the published and unpublished writing of Roberto de las Carreras, among others. His focus on the eroticoaesthetic proposals of *modernismo* as they interface with shifting cultural norms and the contradictory "free love" movement is a good example of how densely archival work can gesture toward today's reconfigurations of queer embodiment, performativity, and desire. Another recent book, Matthew J. Edwards's *Queer Argentina: Movement towards the Closet in a Global Time* (2017), proposes to bring queer cultural production out of the "archival closet" in order to establish countergenealogies to heteronormativity (17). In doing so, Edwards posits a continuity between historical antecedents and recent queer writing, performance, and politics that has appealed to mainstream interests since the early 1980s in Argentina.

These recent publications—including my own work—provide evidence of the contested expansion of queer studies toward objects of study with epistemological and material realities that diverge from the original context out of which it developed in the US academe. Latin American populations have frequently been the object of critique for queer studies, and seldom taken as producers of (queer) knowledge themselves. However, the expansion of queer studies—as a consolidated field of study—has led academics, activists, and artists from Latin America to ask trenchant questions about its viability in local contexts, its translatability, and the power dynamics involved in queering Latin America. Indeed, the tendency to imagine queer studies as universalizing a set of conceptual tools with which to analyze the body and its practices, desire and its embodiments—this in spite queer's resistance to definitional fixity—has struck many as repeating an uncritical stance toward the coloniality of knowledge and of power. The question is often not whether, but how does queer studies repeat the epistemic coloniality of earlier methodological interventions such as structural anthropology, second-wave feminism, and deconstruction, through its valorization of particular forms of dissidence, bodies, histories, and feelings.

## QUEER FEELINGS: LOVE, FEAR, RESENTMENT, VULNERABILITY

*Love.* At present, there are a few queerly familiar junctures of discourse, affect, and politics that remind of the dialogic relationships that queerness establishes across time. While the affective logics of queer's enduring capaciousness owe to this seemingly ahistorical quality, the risk here is in presuming a universal (and thus colonial) norm against which queerness rebels in defiance. These junctures engage the queer feelings of relationality, how relating charges bodies with an affective history that is mobilized to do the political work of expressing difference. For example, Mario Pecheny elucidates how the rhetorical bases of LGBT activism in Argentina in the early 2000s regarding marriage equality had to do with accessing legal recognition by the state by valuing romantic love between committed couples, familiar love that was felt like it was in any other (normative) family, and thus formed the basis of a healthy relationship (247). The "love is love" argument, based on a disembodied ahistorical equivalence between romantic pairs, has allowed lesbian and gay couples to wield a legitimacy previously unavailable to them by virtue of the state's expansion of rights toward recognizable affective attachments. Queer's multifaceted, unpredictable desires become tethered to a singular object, a partner, and in that stability, that love, family becomes something familiar. The incitement to queerness that must be rejected in order for heteronormativity to function properly, as I describe in chapter 1, is transformed into an accommodating sense of love that makes certain feelings between bodies legible, certain relationships absorbed into the normative realm of the state. This argument hinged on expanding the purview of inalienable human rights in the wake of Argentina's last dictatorship (1976-1983), an argument that coincides with the liberal notion of equal justice under the law for all citizens. Pecheny points out that in addition to this liberal rhetoric, marriage equality advocates harnessed the positive value of love and family (or family as love), even though, as abundant feminist scholarship makes evident, marriage and the plot of romantic love have served the interests of patriarchal dominance and capitalist exploitation of women for centuries. Rather than undermine the structural bases of the sex/gender system, we see a new normativity. Queer studies helps us see that the violence expressed through the historical, material, and symbolic demand to adhere to sociocultural norms is not solved by asking those norms to become more inclusive.[1]

*Fear.* Since 2010, in addition to Argentina, several Latin American nations have passed marriage equality and gender identity laws. In response, conservative popular nationalist movements have expressed alarm and indignation, but most of all fear. They have channeled that fear with the support of evangelical denominations and the Catholic Church and organized in opposition. But this opposition is not only against gay marriage. Rather, it decries broader shift toward what they see as the imposition of a sexually permissive "*ideología de género*" ("gender ideology") in schools and public institutions. This conservative response is internationally organized and active on social media, and sees the mainstream acceptance of "gender" as a social construction, as opposed to biological or divinely ordained "sex," as undermining the family as an inherently good and timeless structure. Particularly in the Andean region, though not exclusively so, public protests and viral media campaigns have revolved around counterslogans such as "Con mis hijos no te metas" ("Don't mess with my children"), "Mis hijos me los educo yo" ("I educate my own children"), and, astonishingly, "Género Nunca Más" ("No More Gender"), a phrase that appropriates the mantra "Nunca Más" ("Never Again") widely adopted by several countries in Latin America as a promise to never forget or allow again the systematic violations of human rights that were characteristic of genocidal military regimes of the mid- and late-twentieth century.

The figure of the child and the rights of parents to educate *their* children take center stage in this debate that traffics in conspiratorial logics, possessiveness, and fear. These developments mark affective responses to shifting cultural norms and public policy decisions regarding the normative place of the family, the child, gender, and sexuality. Indeed, there is a distinctly familiar feeling that undergirds such proposals. The threat of economic decline, gender instability, and cultural disintegration, as I have shown throughout this book, position the family as the last bastion of stability, a haven, threatened by a world in flux. In 1910 and in 2010 and beyond, the anxieties over normativity's place, its enduring longevity, have not subsided.

"Gender ideology" is seen as a radicalization of feminism that no longer seeks to achieve gender equality, but the eradication of gender itself, and with it the basis of the family, and thus, society. Notably, it is portrayed as a culturally foreign imposition that is advanced and extended by the US, internationalist organizations like the European Union and the UN, and as such as repeating so many prior attempts to regulate colonized subjects from afar. (Catholicism, conveniently, does not enter this list as one of the imperial ideologies imposed by the metropole.) These popular movements connect "gender ideology" to a longer history of nationalist autonomist logics that fear the weakening of the national spirit and traditional morality, a debilitation of the soul of the nation that in turn exposes its people to extractivist economic logics that are facilitated by supposedly corrupt politicians who stand to gain by creating the conditions for a new social hegemony shaped in their image. These movements see the family unit as threatened by imperialist foes abroad and lax social mores at home. They pit the expansion of human rights by international organizations in the post–World War era against the right to national self-determination, embodied metonymically by parents' sacred obligation to supervise their children's education, and consequently, the future of normative gender, sexuality, and the family.

Curiously, however, both conservative movements on the extreme right and contemporary Latin American queer studies share a mistrust of queer theory's origin in the US and its expansion toward Latin America. In a sense, they agree that queer theory has not reckoned with Latin America's epistemological difference. However, they diverge regarding the effects of that difference. While conservative movements argue that "gender ideology" negates the natural and divine essence of the family, critiques from Latin American feminisms, gender and sexuality studies, and queer/cuir studies see US-based queer studies as incommensurable with the material realities of the body—of what the body means, how it moves, how it feels—in Latin America. This coincidence has to do with what I describe above as queer studies' lack of historical contextualization within the US academe and subsequent *pose* of universality. What it has led to, perhaps more than mistrust is a deep feeling of resentment.

*Resentment.* As Falconí Trávez, Castellanos, and Viteri suggest, "*resentimiento*," referring to both refeeling (to feel again) and resentment (to express pain, disappointment, even fear), has been a key feature of Latin American responses to the canonization of white, cisgendered queer theorists whose work dominates the academic landscape globally. As they put it, this resentment is meant to "interpela[r] a ambos circuitos académicos (el queer y el latinoamericanista), pues durante algún tiempo (quizá demasiado) han trabajado paralelamente y no se han ocupado sistemáticamente de un diálogo que sintonice (y desordene) las históricas discriminaciones en razón de sexualidad, etnia, clase social y situación poscolonial" ("interpolate both academic circuits [the queer and the Latin Americanist], because for a long time [perhaps too long] they have worked in parallel and have not endeavored to establish a systematic dialogue that could tune in to [and disorder] historical discriminations due to sexuality, ethnicity, social class, and postolonial condition"; 13). Resentment is a feeling that matters in this context for the historical depth that it approaches. Resentment of colonialism, of the theft of land and resources, of the systematic destruction of Native lifeways and languages, of US exceptionalism and interventionism, of the enduring imbalance of power in the hemisphere. And then, resentment of queer studies or of "gender ideology," imposed modes of relating to knowledge, history, bodies, land, and desire.

The "con mis hijos no te metas" movement has organized publicity campaigns that refer to "gender ideology" as part of an imperial legacy revived by the U.S. academe, and often cite Judith Butler's *Gender Trouble* as advocating that children should have the right to change gender at will. While this is a gross and willful misreading of Butler's work, it has nonetheless become a flashpoint in these discussions. Butler has become a shorthand for queer studies. This may be understandable for the impact and reach that her work has had on a global scale, an impact that owes to trends in publication and translation markets, academic celebrity, and other forms of institutionalization. However, this shorthand, while convenient, undermines the possibility of structural change for queer studies in a hemispheric context. I would even say that Bulter (Butler's celebrity) has become not just shorthand, but a caricature of queer theory for both the Christian right and for new intellectual and activist currents such as radical *disidencia sexual* (sexual dissidence) and the transfeminist left.[2] While these sex-positive, intersectional groups are asking vital questions about what queer studies can mean for and in Latin America, they often do so by characterizing North American queer studies as monolithic, devoid of the internal divisions or countergenealogies that have been produced by scholars and communities of color, including radical Black feminisms, Chicana/x and Latina/x feminisms, queer of color critique, and Indigenous queer studies, among others. What would a transnational queer studies look like if it took as its basis the work of Gloria Anzaldúa or Pedro Lemebel rather than Judith Butler? What mobilizations and critical contestations would such a shift make possible?

In the case of queer theory we need to recognize and reiterate that activists and academics *from within the US* were already speaking from their lived experiences, informed by their subjugation to colonial regimes of knowledge and power, as a form of queer critique before queer theory became legitimized as a field of study. This is not just a question of who published what first. It is imperative that queer theory, if it is going to be something worth fighting for, not be caricatured as only ever having been the white queer theory. Perhaps we should instead start to say queer theories, plural, because of the multiple trajectories that have informed what today is described as North American queer theory. Scholars and activists with immigrant backgrounds, immigrants themselves, people of color, with varying degrees of racialized history and/or colonial experience, challenged queer theory's epistemological positionality from the very beginning, and they continue to do so today.

Thus, the lived experiences of Black feminist activists and writers, as with the Combahee River Collective's "A Black Feminist Statement" (1977), demanded accountability from white feminism by centering "the multi-layered texture of Black women's lives" (Taylor 20). Similarly, in 1981 the publication of *This Bridge Called My Back* positioned the lived experiences of third world women of color as already speaking from a place of embodied and intersectional resistance. These publications and the activist work that they represent, are not simply a different point of origin for queer theory. Rather, they point to the contested origins of a field of study that would see in the poststructuralist turn a way of universalizing the experiences of gendered and sexed bodies, rather than taking the matter of the body, its flesh, as a site of theorization.

It is important to note that these early publications specifically position themselves as engaging in a politics of translation. The "bridge," the "border," the *"herida abierta"* ("the open wound") that sutures cultures together and bleeds. Translation has been at the center of negotiating embodied difference. In a way, the historical, critical, and political thought of early queer of color critique was essentially *about* translation. And I do not mean translation as a means of linguistic equivalency, but rather the reformulation of concepts, the speaking back and through the matrix of power in order to undermine its foundations and build solidarity. Today, the Anglo-centric origins of the term *queer* have become a stumbling block, one that leads to a well-founded critique of the possibility, indeed, the desirability of "translation" of just such a concept since it is tethered to the symbolic economy and epistemological history of the English-speaking world, and more precisely the US and Britain. But we should also recognize that "translation" has a long history in queer studies as a practice that evolved out of the writing of women of color whose multiple marginalizations demanded a conceptual dexterity that should not be erased in our contemporary discussions of queer's potential mobilities.

*Vulnerability.* This will require taking risks and becoming vulnerable. There will be failures and impasses and *malentendidos*. Vulnerability, Audre Lorde might say, is the antidote to fear (42). Or perhaps not the antidote, but the salve that makes bearable the opening of ourselves to the possibility of coming undone by the proximities of others whose languages, bodies, and histories point to shared flesh and shared pain. But also a shared humility. I write this from my own privileged vantage point as an Indigenous scholar who has institutional access to the spaces and repositories that makes such a claim possible. But if queer studies is going to reckon with its coloniality, and if it is to engage in a hemispheric critique, it seems to me that it cannot start with the version of queer theory that is now canonical. Rather, this vulnerable engagement must take as a point of departure the more nuanced and contested version of queer studies, the one that seeks erotic justice, Palestinian liberation, and an end to the prison industrial complex; the one that is diasporic; anti-ableist; anti white-supremacist and radically Black and Brown; anti-anthrocentric and in search of good relations with human and other-than-human kin, and the one that is trans and genderqueer; dissident and disidentifying; the one that is Indigenous and maroon; ancestral and untimely, rather than the one that begins and ends with gender performativity.

## QUEER STUDIES AND DECOLONIALITY

It would thus be a mistake to argue that Latin American studies is only now coming to articulate serious questions of the commensurability of queer studies with local contexts and epistemological and ontological materialities. Rather, from the very beginning of what eventually came to be understood as queer studies, its presumptions of universality were already being questioned from both within the US academe and from Latin America by scholars and activists attuned to the intersectional forces of racialization, colonialism, and patriarchal normativity.

For example, in 1992 activist and historian James Green organized a meeting during the annual Latin American Studies Association congress to discuss forming a gay and lesbian studies section. This is significant for the institutional status that it eventually provided "gay and lesbian studies" within the largest professional association in the world dedicated to Latin American studies. Gay and lesbian studies would have its own section starting in 1998, which allowed for sponsored panels to be presented at the annual congress, and its own track in 2001, which provided for presentations and panels from any discipline dealing with themes related to LGBT studies to be evaluated for inclusion in the congress. However, as José Quiroga and Laura Gutiérrez note in a fall 2002 report titled "The Present State of Latin American Gay and Lesbian Studies," even from these initial stages, questions of how queer activism from Latin America differed from that of the United States, as well as issues of identity politics and redemocratization in Latin America were sources of intense debate. As they write, "In the United States, 'lesbian and gay' are not at this point exclusively tied to radical politics, but may, in fact, proceed from a discourse that is completely linked to power itself" (14). Gay, lesbian, and (later) queer's institutionalization as a field of study in relation to Latin American studies revolved around questions of power, political positioning, asylum, and the radical left.[3] And while it is clear that professional associations like LASA operate according to market-based principles that structurally limit participation by activists, artists, and other marginalized groups, in the case of gay and lesbian studies, I want to emphasize, this structural imbalance was central to discussions from the beginning. Linking gender and sexuality studies, queer studies, and Latin American studies within the institutional framework of LASA in fact began as an attempt to share resources and strategies of resistance to social and political marginalization, but also, with suspicion of whether the process of institutionalization itself necessarily implied reinscribing imperial power dynamics and assumptions of North/South difference.

Academic publishing involved similar disputes. In 1995, the volume *¿Entiendes? Queer Readings, Hispanic Writings*, edited by Emilie L. Bergmann and Paul Julian Smith, brought together sixteen essays that would mark a collective act of thinking through the relationship between a nascent queer theory in the US and cultural and linguistic traditions that did not share the same relationships with identity or its politics in Latin America and Spain. The collection was published in English by Duke University Press, and all of the authors were either trained in or employed by universities in the United States. This highlights the institutional positioning of early gay and lesbian Latin American studies as emerging in relation to the US academe, though it also gestures toward a desire to question that emergence. In a pointed reflection, Bergmann and Smith note,

> [w]hile there has been much talk of respecting cultural difference in queer theory, there has as yet been little acknowledgment that the process of addressing national and linguistic borderlines requires a slow and patient labor of translation. Ironically, the social-constructionist bias now dominant in English-language queer theory has done little to right that wrong. [...] Of what value is this recent Anglo-American critique of identity (also visible in the explosion of categories of self-proclaimed deviants embracing the label "queer") for those cultures in which sexual preference has never been the basis for identity, in which no political or social community has been constructed around same-sex desire? (9-10)

The skepticism felt around the utility of gender as a social construction—presumed to function the same in all contexts—is one of the principal concerns of these scholars who identify queerness and the theory that emerges from it with an identity position that has no equivalent history or translation. Queer theory in this instance is specifically linked to identitarian claims that take same-sex desire as a point of departure. And these claims, the authors insinuate, may not make sense in places where same-sex desire has not undergone the same type of inscription into the domain of culture (science, art, politics) as in the US and England. We have yet to heed their call to envision the process of respecting difference as a process of translation that is necessarily slow, perhaps even painful. The patience that they call for flies in the face of the demand for academic productivity, the speed at which theory and practice diverge from each other, hurtling toward destinations unknown. It is a good reminder that even from this early example of Latin American queer studies, the issue of valuing time and labor, difference, and academic productivity, intersect with the more theoretical concerns of epistemological commensurability.

Another milestone is the 2008 special issue of *Revista Iberoamericana*, "Los estudios lésbico-gays y queer latinoamericanos," which traced the contested history of *queer* and its mobility in Latin American contexts and was published in Spanish. In an introductory essay to that volume, Luciano Martínez identifies two central concerns of queer's interface with Latin American Studies: (1) the question of importation and translation of "foreign" concepts to a Latin American context, and (2) the difference of "identity politics" between geopolitical contexts (862). These are questions that have to do with ongoing relations of power between disciplines, languages, and flows of intellectual and material bodies. They have to do with issues of editorial practice and field formation. The production of this knowledge follows the circuits of power long established by colonial epistemologies. In doing so, it enables the domination of conceptual forms and lived realities, understandings of life and the inhabiting of bodies, feelings, and discourses that have sedimented along with current nation-states and scientific and political institutions. The development of a particular methodology such as queer theory depends on and frames its intervention vis-à-vis academic practices that privilege Anglophone—and at times Francophone—intellectual labor, institutions, and departments. I say this not to bemoan the fact, but to state clearly that the economic differences between universities (and departments) in the US and those in Latin America matter a great deal to how knowledge is produced and consumed, what counts as knowledge, for and by whom. This economic disparity affects whose work circulates, whose airfare gets paid for, and who gets offered an honorarium to speak. Academic fields are not immune from global economic disparities; rather, they often help repeat them.

Over the past decade, innovative proposals such as Diego Falconí Trávez's *teoría cuir/cuyr*, serve not only to question the predominance of queer's linguistic context, but also its colonial foundations. In Brazil, Denilson Lopes has argued in favor of affect and artifice over "queer theory" as a way of approaching Black and Afro-diasporic subjectivities, while Larissa Pelúcio has developed *teoria cú* (anal theory) as a way of negotiating with enduring histories of colonial, patriarchal, and falogocentric violence.[4] In Chile, the Colectivo Universitario de Disidencia Sexual (CUDS) has argued in favor of a transfeminist approach to sexual dissidence, rather than an adaptation of "queer theory." In Colombia, Yecid Calderón/Pinina Flandes situates their performative and philosophical work, rather than decolonial, as "trans-colonial," emerging from an embodied form of nomadic, anthropophagous, and disidentificatory praxis of coquettish resistance (41-42). Intersections of sex work and trans and *travesti* epistemologies find expression in the monstrous reimaginings of Chilean Claudia Rodríguez and the "amor trava" of the late Lohana Berkins from Argentina.[5] These activists, writers, artists, and intellectuals have developed trenchant analyses of the interface of local cultural histories and the global reach of queer studies.[6] These interventions have sought to unearth and shed light on forms of being and belonging that preceded the invention and institutionalization of queer theory in the US Academe, or which undo or problematize queer theory, or simply do not see in it a way to approach the lived realities of Latin American social life. These proposals revisit the intellectual histories of Latin American feminisms, their interface with postcolonial and decolonial struggles, trauma and memory studies, Liberation Theology, as well as transfeminist and plurinational approaches in the region. Latin American queer/cuir/cuyr studies brings to bear its own particular struggles on the tools suggested by the Anglophone academe, and in doing so charts its own relationships to power and authoritarianism, economic and political interventionism, structural inequality, *mestizaje*, the African diaspora, and spirituality and religiosity. In translating and transforming, revising and reshaping, Latin American intellectuals, activists, artists, and other interested publics are creating new and diverse modes of engaging with, understanding, and disrupting normativity both in their own communities, and as part of the global circulation of academic production. We see in the catalogs of North American and European publishing houses how the marketability of queer theory privileges English-speaking theorists. But we also see this privilege extended through conference organizing and the politics of translation in the Global North *and* the Global South. While we may currently be in a stage where the contributions of Latin American activists and theorists are revising the Anglophone term (and its concomitant cultural baggage) and even rejecting it outright, we have yet to find the willingness to undermine the hegemony of English-language theorizations, and build new economic infrastructure to support intellectual production from currently underfunded and undervalued sites of critical inquiry.

If this is indeed the case, then what happens next? I can think of two possible paths: on the one hand, a reinscription of queer studies in the US Academe that takes into account the contributions of Latin American theorists (as with the case of third-wave feminism) through which the intersections of racial mixing, decoloniality, and locally situated political economies, adhere to and indeed modify previous formulations of queer theory's method of antinormative thinking, thus expanding and complicating its engagement with difference across various social markers (i.e., race, class, gender, ability, etc.). This might lead to greater fractioning of queer theory, that is, to an even greater array of ever-more-specific methods of critique that desire to be capacious enough to be read across geopolitical borders, but specific enough to not assume a singular middle-class white gay cisgendered subjectivity as hegemonic. This might be called something like Latin American Queer Studies, or Queer Latin American Studies. New courses would be devised, new jobs posted, departments rearranged. On the other hand, this current phase might also lead to a disjuncture, a rejection of Queer Theory's US origins, Anglophone bias, and institutional legacy as anathema to an autochthonous Latin American form of decolonial critique. In this version, the epistemological underpinnings of queer theory are too much to overcome, too engrained in colonial hierarchies and socioeconomic disparities.

An alternative and perhaps more optimistic iteration would see hemispheric dialogue as still possible, but not on the terms dictated by the North American academe. Not according to the demands of legibility only in English and for an American audience. Not by and for Anglophone readers or publishing houses. Not for "inclusion" or "diversity." Rather, it would require a form of ethical engagement across difference that necessarily involves a revision of the enshrinement of queer theory in the US Academe, its canon, and to work toward its own undoing. It would be to read Néstor Perlongher, Sylvia Molloy, Severo Sarduy, Nelly Richard, Ochy Curiel, and Marlene Wayar *in the North American academe*. It would be to revise citational practices to privilege Indigenous, Black, and Latin American theorists, artists, and activists; to reform curricular offerings in the academe to reflect this change; to demand *and fund* greater circulation and promotion of Latin American queer/cuir texts and scholars; to create digital publication platforms *in translation* that bypass traditional academic gatekeepers; to change the categories of tenure and promotion in US universities to account for collective and activist work as well as the work of translation. It would be to infiltrate and ruthlessly undermine the cultural biases that sustain the hegemony of North American queer theory. It would be to decolonize queer theory. And in doing so, find in the intersection of decoloniality and queer critique a project of embodied revision, recuperation, and renewal attuned to land-based, non-Cartesian epistemologies and Black and Brown ontologies that contests the viability of colonial biopolitical regimes.[7] It would be not simply to celebrate, but to actively privilege South-South dialogues and to collaborate in the creation of other frequencies of reciprocity and mutuality. Finally, this would mean that issues of translation and transformation, adaptation, and transculturation, would become central to an ethical engagement with and through transatlantic and hemispheric approaches. That is both the promise and the challenge of queer as a feeling, a practice, a lingering sense of what could become a more expansive, and yet historically situated and materially attuned form of critique. A queerness that resonates with bodies as they relate. Something different, and yet, familiar.

# NOTES

## INTRODUCTION

1. Unless otherwise noted, all translations are my own.
2. Though I discuss Delfina Bunge's literary ambitions in chapter 2, some of her first published works were the poetry collections *Simplement* (1911) and *La Nouvelle moisson* (1918), both written in French. For her part, in 1993 Delfina Tiscornia published a book of poems, *Equivocación del paisaje*, to critical acclaim in Argentina.
3. After years of struggle, Delfina Tiscornia took her own life on June 1, 1996. In the preface to *Ella camina sola* Lucía Gálvez writes, "En aquella mañana luminosa, Delfina voló con sus alas rotas. Crucificada en el asfalto, con los brazos abiertos, el hermoso pelo enrulado haciendo marco a su rostro fresco, como en un parto hacia otra Vida, Delfina se fue yendo en nuestros brazos" ("On that luminous morning, Delfina flew with her broken wings. Crucified on the asphalt, with her arms open, her beautiful curly hair framing her fresh visage, as if born into another Life, Delfina departed in our arms"; 9).
4. The entire generation of eight includes: Carlos Octavio (1875-1918), Augusto (1877-1943), Roberto (1878-1931), Alejandro (1880-1943), Julia Valentina (1880-1969), Delfina (1881-1952), Eduardo (1884-1968), and Jorge (1893-1961).
5. Mayra Navarro Gerassi defines the Argentine *oligarquía* in the following terms: "la oligarquía comprendía al pequeño grupo de terratenientes adinerados—no más de 300 familias—que había resultado más beneficiado por el desarrollo del país. La inmigración europea había significado mano de obra barata para sus estancias, y los pedidos europeos de carne argentina les habían significado firmes ingresos. Parte de las ganancias era reinvertida, aunque en poca cantidad; la mayor parte, sin embargo, era gastada en promover un 'modo de vida' oligarca simbolizado por el título de abogado, por el acceso a la Sociedad Rural, al Círculo de Armas y al Jockey Club, por uno o dos viajes a Europa y por lujosas mansiones construidas en Buenos Aires por arquitectos europeos y embellecidas con mobiliarios y obras de arte importadas" ("the Argentine oligarchy was comprised of the small group of wealthy landowners—no more than 300 families—who had

most benefitted from the development of the country. European immigration had resulted in cheap labor for their estates, and European orders for Argentine beef had resulted in a steady income. Part of their earnings was reinvested, though in small quantity; the majority, though, was spent promoting an oligarchical 'lifestyle' symbolized by a law degree, access to the Sociedad Rural, the Círculo de Armas and the Jockey Club, by one or two trips to Europe and by luxurious mansions constructed in Buenos Aires by European architects and adorned with imported furniture and art"; 25). This particular generation of Bunges was not as wealthy as other branches of the family, who did make fortunes in beef and grain exports. The now billion-dollar multinational corporation Bunge y Born is the most obvious example. For more about the development of the Argentine oligarchy as a class, see Sebreli *Apogeo y ocaso de los Anchorena*. For an excellent history of family politics in nineteenth-century Chile, see Chambers *Families in War and Peace*.

6   For a good overview of these interlocking class interests, see Balmori, Voss, and Wortman.

Throughout this book I use the term *criollo* rather than Creole to distinguish it from its usage in the United States and parts of the Anglophone and Francophone Caribbean. In Argentina and throughout most of Spanish America, *criollo* began as a term that identified the children of Spaniards born in the Americas, which came with specific legal rights and cultural privileges. Subsequently, it would refer to Spanish Americans with a predominantly European background and the culture derived from those people, though by the late nineteenth century in Argentina criollo referred to popular culture generally, and to the rural culture of the gaucho in particular. In his classic study *El discurso criollista en la formación de la Argentina moderna*, Adolfo Prieto describes three principle audiences who mobilized *criollismo*—the quality of being criollo or even exaggerating its qualities—according to their own interests: (1) rural communities displaced from the countryside to urban centers saw *criollismo* as an expression of nostalgia for their lost lifeways; (2) recent immigrants from Europe could demonstrate assimilation to Argentine nationalism by adopting elements of criollo culture; (3) the landed elite could mobilize *criollismo* to reaffirm their legitimacy as authentically Argentine in opposition to recent immigrants. Thus, *criollismo* was contested terrain in the late nineteenth and early twentieth century, as wealthy landowners sought to distinguish themselves from new immigrants who sought to prove their Argentine bona fides by *performing criollismo*.

7   The reference is to Weston *Families We Choose*.

8   Regarding the issue of normativity versus antinormativity in queer studies see Wiegman and Wilson "Introduction: Antinormativity's Queer Conventions." I would like to point out here that I coincide with their idea

that "antinormative stances project stability and immobility onto normativity" (13) through the exercise of queer theory and its attempts to undermine prescriptive identities, practices, and affects. I would add that throughout this book, I aim to describe the norm not as a prescriptive category, but rather one that accrues value and meaning though its negotiation with sexual, gender, and erotic differences.

9   I develop this idea below. See Butler "Is Kinship Always Already Heterosexual?"
10  For a general overview, see Stepan *"The Hour of Eugenics": Race, Gender, and Nation in Latin America*.
11  For more information, see Aronna *"Pueblos enfermos": The Discourse of Illness in the Turn-of-the-Century Spanish and Latin American Essay*.
12  This is drawn from Anderson *Imagined Communities* 3-8.
13  For example, see Edelman *No Future* 9-17 and Muñoz *Cruising Utopia* 91-95.
14  In addition to these monographic works, a number of important edited collections marked early interventions in Latin American gay, lesbian, and queer studies. See Bergmann and Smith *¿Entiendes? Queer Readings, Hispanic Writings*; Balderston and Guy *Sex and Sexuality in Latin America*, translated to Spanish as *Sexo y sexualidades en América Latina*; and Molloy and Irwin *Hispanisms and Homosexualities*. I elaborate on the juncture of queer studies and Latin American studies in the Epilogue.
15  As I describe in chapter 2, conspiracy is a key issue that I borrow from Bonnie Honig's *Antigone, Interrupted*. For more information about sisterhood and queer studies, see Stefani Engelstein, "Sibling Logic; or, Antigone Again."
16  For an excellent analysis of the relationship between queer studies and kinship studies, see Elizabeth Freeman "Queer Belongings: Kinship Theory and Queer Theory." As Freeman notes, technologies of visualization—in particular the family photograph—influenced how supposedly objective structural anthropology defined kinship over the course of the twentieth century. I expand on the relationship between photography and kinship in chapter 3.
17  I was tempted to include an analysis of *Mi amigo Luis* in this book. I decided against doing so because, as I note in chapter 1, I am invested in exploring how Bunge's fiction undermines normative imaginaries of heteroromance, rather than linking the autobiographical details of Bunge's life to his creative writing.
18  For example, there is a portrait of my brother, my cousin, and me on a shelf above the television in my parents' living room. We are wearing matching sweater vests that had been sewn by our grandmother, Mable, who likely insisted that the picture be made in the first place. She was prolific with needlework and belonged to a neighborhood quilting club, the "quilting lalies," as I once called them—not yet able to pronounce a hard *d*—a name now stuck permanently in family lore. They would sit around a table and

sew, gossip, and drink coffee (sometimes bourbon), working on a new quilt for each new grandchild, a Christmas stocking for a new spouse, a set of sweater vests for the boys. Mable had made us three boys matching vests and we were seated in an Olan Mills studio in the late 1980s, probably in the shopping mall at JCPenney, and we were arranged to display our kinship for posterity. There we were, related. And yet, so much goes on before that image, and after. The moment itself marks hours of Mable's labor, her hands stitching at a table with friends, whose own hands were making memories out of pieces of fabric to be given away and photographed, saved, stowed away. But the moment of the portrait in all its simplicity endures as a condensation of that labor and that love. We were then unaware then of what it meant to make us those vests, what knowledge and time went into their making, and now that Mable is gone, in the age of social media, the image circulates on Facebook and Instagram as new families are made, old relationships transformed, memories turned into algorithms. The temporality of kinship brings to bear these moments of recognition, the enduring middle-class desire for the memorialization of the relationships that make kinship matter in all their complications, and in their queerness. In posing for this photograph we position ourselves as part of the genealogy of family, but also the tradition of aristocratic portraiture that the Bunge family would also strive to emulate. How similar in motivation, and yet, how different, how unglamorous we were, there, in a shopping mall in Corpus Christi, Texas. Or at least that is how I remember it. The space of the professional studio moved to the quintessential suburban setting. Longing. Remembering. Projecting a future.

19  I write about this in "Adopted: Trace, Blood, and Native Authenticity."
20  For more information on the visceral and the archive, see Tortorici *Sins against Nature* 29–36.
21  Carlos Riobó's monograph *Sub-Versions of the Archive: Manuel Puig's and Severo Sarduy's Alternative Identities* has been useful to me here, especially chapter 2, "Raiding the Archive: An Analysis of an Archival Tradition and Its New Configurations."
22  Bunge writes this in *Mi amigo Luis*, which, as I note above, he published under a pseudonym (Hernán Prinz) when he was twenty years old.

### CHAPTER ONE

1  Founded in 1868, the Colegio del Salvador, a Jesuit school, was one of the principal centers of instruction of Argentina's elite at the turn of the century.
2  See Laureano Robles Carcedo "Cartas entre Unamuno y el argentino C. O. Bunge."
3  *Xarcas silenciario* was reviewed in the Spanish publication *Revista contemporánea* by Enrique Ferrer, who concludes with the following paragraph

that is illustrative of the contradictory effects of Bunge's place in the literary scene as well as his writing itself: "En suma, el ultimo libro de Bunge, cualquiera que sus deficiencias sean, es una obra de arte que en nada desmerece, sino más bien aumenta, la fama que en estos últimos tiempos se viene conquistando este eminente pensador y personalísimo artista en letras castellanas" ("In summary, Bunge's latest book, whatever its deficiencies may be, is a work of art that in no way detracts from, but in fact increases, the fame that in recent years this eminent thinker and extremely personal artist has achieved in Castilian letters"; 128). In this review Ferrer describes Bunge's writing as unique—at times clumsy at times melodic—and his growing fame deserved, intervening in an ongoing discussion of the "artistry" of this writer who from the very beginning of his career seems to divide opinions. I discuss the critical reception of Bunge's *La novela de la sangre* below.

4  A Porteño/a is a person from the port city of Buenos Aires. This denomination grew out of the particular qualities associated with the cosmopolitanism of Buenos Aires in the nineteenth century, and as a way to distinguish inhabitants of the port city from those of the countryside, often referred to as "el interior" (the interior).

5  See Salessi *Médicos maleantes y maricas* 187 and Cárdenas and Payá *La familia de Octavio Bunge* 270-72.

6  For a good overview, see Foster *The Argentine Generation of 1880*. Foster describes the liberal ideology implemented starting in 1880 as providing Argentina "with a basic national and sociocultural identity that, despite enormous subsequent political transformations, continues to characterize the nation's abiding self-image (at least from the optic of Buenos Aires) as a progressive, sophisticated, and essentially European people" (7).

7  For example, see Bletz *Immigration and Acculturation in Brazil and Argentina: 1890-1929*, especially 53-81.

8  The literature on race and racism in Argentina is extensive. For a comparative study of Argentina and Cuba in the nineteenth century, see Helg; for an intellectual history that bears in mind the role of positivist science on Argentine racism, see Hale; for an account of the relationship between liberalism and positivism, see Shumway *Historia personal de una pasión argentina* 111-211; for an excellent analysis of Bunge's contradictory position in the scientific milieu of the turn of the century, see Terán *Vida intelectual* 135-206.

9  This line of thinking follows Sylvia Molloy's "The Politics of Posing."

10 Rosas ruled Argentina as a dictator from 1835-1852. The literature on his influence is vast and contentious. For a concise history, see Rock *Argentina* 102-17 and Romero 79-88; for a good intellectual history, see Shumway *Invention* 116-22; for a balance of the intellectual debates regarding the historical revisionism of Rosas's figure, see Halperin Donghi *El revisionismo*.

11  Unless otherwise noted, all citations from the novel are taken from the 1903 edition. Likewise, since Bunge is prone to using ellipses in his writing, unless otherwise noted all ellipses are original.
12  For more information, see Navarro Gerassi *Los nacionalistas* and Cárdenas and Payá *El primer nacionalismo argentino en Manuel Gálvez y Ricardo Rojas*.
13  For a detailed analysis of *Ideas* and useful appendix detailing the bulk of its publication, see Delgado *El nacimiento de la literatura argentina en las revistas literarias (1896–1913)*.
14  The image is suggestive: *Columbus*, from the Latin, a pigeon; the kiss of the pigeons, euphemistically describing what today we might call the French kiss. I would like to thank my colleague Paul Firbas for pointing this out to me.
15  While Olivera and Gálvez write that *La novela de la sangre* was first published in Barcelona, the volume of Bunge's *Obras Completas* titled *Juicios sobre su personalidad y su obra* includes an annex confirming Madrid (with Daniel Jorro) as the original location. Bunge did, however, publish *Xarcas Silenciario* in Barcelona with Henrich y Cía in 1903.
16  The description of Pantuci as "de cutis terroso," literally translates to having "earthy" or "muddy" skin.
17  As Aline Helg argues, the nationalist ideas of this period involved a tension between cultural nationalism and xenophobia that does not easily map onto conceptualizations of *race* as deployed in the United States (44-47). Insofar as the overarching goal of the intellectual elite was to provide a model of sociality that took Southern European immigrants (in particular "southern" Italians and Spaniards) as biologically and not just culturally, inferior, Nouzeilles's idea of "somatic fictions" is worth emphasizing. In the case of *La novela de la sangre*, Pantuci is not simply portrayed as culturally foreign, but somatically deficient because of his ethnic makeup.
18  José María Ramos Mejía's *Las multitudes argentinas* brings European debates on eugenic thought and a stridently pessimistic view of racial mixing, particularly regarding Italians, to the fore in Argentina. See chapter 5 for a discussion of his work and its relation with positivist social science.
19  Muñoz's critique of Edelman reminds us of the need to consider race when discussing queer temporality. The figure of "*el nene*" speaks to this intersection, reinforcing—in a different context and era to be sure—that whiteness is a precondition of turn-of-the-century Argentine futurity.
20  The latter anticipates Enrique González Martínez's anti-*modernista* sonnet of 1909, "Tuércele el cuello al cisne."
21  "El Capitán Pérez" was adapted for film in 1946. According to Abel Posadas, Marta Speroni, and Mónica Landro, it was in fact the first literary text to be adapted as a cinematic comedy (10). Set in the 1920s, the film was directed by Enrique Cahen Salaberry and adapted by Manuel

Mujica Láinez. I can only speculate, but the fact that Mujica Láinez would have adapted the film is significant in that he was a key figure whose literature in the mid-twentieth century gave voice to homoerotic desires that had previously remained highly codified—as in Bunge's fiction. In fact, literary historians such as Adrián Melo and Jorge Luis Peralta place Mujica Láinez as one of the canonical queer writers of the mid-twentieth century in Argentina. While the bulk of his literary production would appear in the 1950s and '60s, I think we can say that Mujica Láinez saw in Bunge's short story a type of queerness—the queerness of melodrama, and of the idealized male figure (Pérez)—that demonstrates a sensibility that deserves further exploration. For more information see Melo 171-76 and Peralta 151-71.

22  Today Tandil is a popular tourist destination, but in the nineteenth century it remained a small provincial town that would expand rapidly after the arrival of the first railroad in 1883.

23  As David Viñas has argued, the history of the Argentine elite is dominated by *latifundistas* (large land holders) and military men. That is, power has consistently been concentrated in the hands of men engaged in military pursuits. In this, Bunge's narrative is not exceptional, though it is important to note that Ignacio does not enter the military with a high rank, but rather enrolls as a cadet, once again marking the family as having lost its economic and cultural capital. See Viñas *Indios, ejército y frontera* 207.

24  Coca or Chicoca are common nicknames for the youngest daughter in Latin American families, similar to calling the youngest son the Benjamín. Still, the phonetic similarity between Coca and *coqueta* (cocotte) is striking, and likely intentional.

25  Here I am thinking along with Honig's theorization of sororal conspiracy in *Antigone, Interrupted*. There are considerable differences between Classical tragedy and Bunge's naturalist melodrama, differences in form and intent, reception and politics, even if Honig seeks to question this facile difference of genre. Likewise, Bunge does not employ tragic, but rather dramatic irony. His is a titillating form of insinuation aimed at upholding social conventions. However, I would like to propose that this sororal conspiracy also opens up the possibility of undermining the commodification of women, their function as units of exchange, and the basis of patriarchal domination.

26  For a comprehensive overview, see Lavrin *Women, Feminism, & Social Change in Argentina, Chile, & Uruguay, 1890-1940*.

27  Since the publication of *Espíritu de la educación* in 1901, Bunge would revise, add, and edit the text for several years. The edition that I cite here, *La educación*, in three volumes, was published in 1920, two years after Bunge's death, as the final version. I also discuss this text in chapter 4.

28  For a historical account of the gaucho, see Slatta *Gauchos and the Vanishing Frontier*. An indispensable reference for literary and cultural representations

of the gaucho in Argentina is Ludmer *The Gaucho Genre: A Treatise on the Motherland*.

29  Bunge is referring to a survey conducted by the literary journal *Nosotros* between June and October of 1913 on the literary and cultural merits of *Martín Fierro*. Bunge, among other "men of letters" participated in the survey, which consolidated two distinct camps in Argentine literary criticism. On the one hand, the nationalist exaltation led by Lugones, Ricardo Rojas and Manuel Gálvez, on the other, less enthusiastic critics such as Bunge and Calixto Oyuela. The second group resisted qualifying the work as an epic based on what they saw as its formal and political shortcomings. See Albarracín-Sarmiento *Estructura del Martín Fierro* 3 and 304n3.

30  Susana Rotker's *Captive Women: Oblivion and Memory in Argentina* is a crucial and beautifully written account of the silences, omissions, and acts of forgetting that are at the heart of the captive tale in Argentina, with its ethnic and gendered dimensions bubbling at the surface.

31  Honoré de Balzac published *Les cent contes drolatiques* between 1832 and 1837, and Gustave Doré illustrated the stories in 1855. According to Fernando Sorrentino, there are at least three Spanish translations: Querubín de Ronda (Madrid, 1883), Joaquín García Bravo (Barcelona, 1902), and Eusebio Heras (Barcelona, date unknown). The first English translation was done in London by John Camden Hotten in 1874 and titled *Droll Stories*. See Sorrentino "El drolático *drolático*."

32  Bunge's use of macabre as an adverb does not have an adequate English translation. Though I have rendered it "dreadfully," I want to point out here his use of this very specific term, "*macabremente*," implies a history of celebrating the dead, the *danse macabre*.

33  "Ojos de ahorcado" would literally be translated as "the eyes of a hanged man." The notion is that Tucker is looking at them from beyond the grave.

34  Rosalind seems a reference to Shakespeare's *As You Like It*; Xanthippe to the wife of Socrates; Agrippina (the Younger) a Roman Empress (AD 15-AD 59); contrasting with the philanthropic St. Elizabeth of Hungary; and Our Lady of Sorrows, the Blessed Virgin Mary, *Mater Dolorosa*.

35  The concept of subjective impossibility borrows from Puar 195.

## CHAPTER TWO

1  *Heteroglossia* is taken from Bakhtin *The Dialogic Imagination*. In addition, Françoise Lionnet's term *métissage* invokes a braiding of voices in postcolonial texts. See her *Autobiographical Voices*. Nancy K. Miller and Paul John Eakin have expanded this notion to argue that all narratives are relational, involving a dialogic process that combines the assertion of individual autonomy and the recognition of intersubjective relations. See Miller "Representing Others" and Eakin *How Our Lives Become Stories* 43-98.

2   As Huff notes, after Adrienne Rich pronounced in her 1979 book *On Lies, Secrets, and Silence* that the diary was "that profoundly female, and feminist, genre," many scholars have taken the invitation to identify the diary as a touchstone for a revision of the literary canon and of women's writing in general, which for centuries has largely been excluded from the hegemonic, masculine public sphere.

3   In yet another citational maneuver, Julia opens her published diary, *Vida: época maravillosa, 1903-1911*, with an entry written by her sister, Delfina. Thus, the source for this quotation is Julia Bunge's *Vida*, rather than Lucía Gálvez's published version of Delfina Bunge's diaries, or Delfina's manuscripts themselves.

4   Though I am dealing with an autobiographical genre, the diary, I do not attempt to speak for all forms of autobiographical writing. Indispensable resources for the Argentine context include Molloy *At Face Value*; Prieto *La literatura autobiográfica argentina*; and Amícola *Autobiografía como autofiguración*.

5   This periodization creates an artificial break for the study of Delfina's diary writing. Still, my focus here is on the particular relationship between the social pressures of the Argentine elite at the turn of the century and the self-in-process that is staged by the diary of this era.

6   For more information on Monniot and her two-volume work, see Harrison *Romantic Catholics*.

7   The entire original quote reads: "—Stéphanie est chrétienne dans la plus large acception de ce mot divin, mon enfant. Jamais les vaines séductions de l'imagination, de vagues et dangereuses aspirations, ne la berceront dans le monde de rêves. Elle cherche, elle voit avant tout le devoir; la réalité pratique, agissante; la volonté de Dieu;—c'est te dire que, bien qu'une illusion quelconque puisse la troubler un instant; bien que la paix de son âme puisse être compromise quelquefois, la victoire lui restera toujours dans ces luttes intérieures. Elle sera toujours maîtresse d'elle-même" (—Stéphanie is Christian in the largest meaning of this divine word, my child. Never will the vain seduction of our imagination, the vague and dangerous aspiration, soothe her in the world of dreams. She thinks, she sees above all her duty; the practical and active reality; God's will;—this is to show you that, even though some illusion can trouble her for an instant; even though her soul's peace can sometimes be compromised, victory will always be one of her interior struggles. She will always have self-control; Monniot *A Vingt Ans*, 225).

8   For more context, see Berlanstein "Selling Modern Femininity: *Femina*, a Forgotten Feminist Publishing Success in Belle Epoque France."

9   According to Manuel Gálvez, the Buenos Aires newspaper *El Tiempo* revealed Delfina's identity even before the essay was published in Argentina by *Ideas* (*Recuerdos* 1: 117). Cárdenas and Payá are in fact paraphrasing Gálvez, ibid.

10 For more information, see Davidoff *Worlds Between* 206-26.
11 Lady Juana would publish four articles in the *Revista de Derecho, Historia y Letras* in 1903: two in the XV edition: " 'Season' en Mar del Plata," 219-27 and "La mujer en los salones," 382-86; and two in the XVI edition: "Palermo," 87-96, and "En la ópera"236-44. "A Marguerite" is from the XX edition, 106-10, 1904.
12 For more information, see Mizraje *Argentinas de Rosas a Perón* 171-88.
13 Lady Juana/Zeballos uses an interesting play on words here. To be an "*alma gemela*" is generally translated as "soul mate" or "twin flame" but literally means "soul twin." The question, then, is about the degree to which their souls can relate—again, this relation depends on a normative kinship imaginary—whether they can be "twins," and if not, then at least "friends." The difference between a soul mate—which implies a binary gendering that allows a man or a woman to find their "other half"—is curiously queered in translation here. Lady Juana might find her soul's "twin," while Zeballos might find his soul's "mate."
14 See Guy *Sex and Danger in Buenos Aires* 37-76.
15 Amazingly, Delfina's report card for her French classes at the Collége de le Sainte Union des Sacres Coeurs from 1894 to 96 still exists among the Bunge Family Archive. In almost all categories (*Conduite, Application, Politesse, Ordre,* and *Distinction*), she consistently received a grade of *Exemplaire* or *Trés Bien* (she seems to have been particularly polite).
16 July 9 celebrates the declaration of independence from the Spanish crown by the Provincias Unidas del Río de la Plata at the Congreso de Tucumán in 1816.
17 Ocampo's use of "*maricón*" might today be rendered as "faggot." The final line is referencing Jean de La Fontaine's fable "La laitière et le pot au lait" ("The Milkmaid and the Pot of Milk"). The idiomatic phrase is sometimes translated as "Don't count your chickens before they've hatched."
18 For more information see the winter 1984 special edition of *The Journal of Family History* devoted to spinsters, introduced by Susan Cotts Watkins, "Spinsters."

CHAPTER THREE

1 One exception, however, is Yeon-Soo Kim's *The Family Album: Histories, Subjectivities, and Immigration in Contemporary Spanish Culture* (2005), a text that describes the family album as a visual medium arranged in order to reconstruct in the present an idealized history, a past, which exists in "the interstices between experience and fictional memory" (21). Kim's work focuses on recent iterations of the family album in Spain and points out how it organizes gendered dynamics and intergenerational histories, immigration stories, and processes of racialization.

2. Geoffrey Batchen's *Forget Me Not: Photography & Remembrance* marks a notable contrast, offering an important critique of the relationship between memory and affect, especially regarding quotidian forms of photography.
3. The most prominent example of this research is John Tagg's *The Disciplinary Frame: Photographic Truths and the Capture of Meaning*. Regarding Latin American photography, Robert M. Levine writes in his *Images of History*, "Cultural norms imported from Catholic Europe to Hispanic America and subject to church scrutiny dominated official life as well as the broader social milieu. Catholicism required uniformity and refused to accept—at least in principle—dissenting or heterodox views. Homogeneity and cultural conformity prevailed, not pluralism. In turn, photographers obeyed the rules and rarely experimented with the ways they portrayed their subjects. Most of the surviving images of nineteenth- and early-twentieth-century Latin America reflect this circumstance. Visual images conformed visually to accepted social values. One result was that photographs did not differ very much from country to country. Elites wanted to look European, whether in Montevideo, Guayaquil, or Bogotá. Photographs revealing the underside of everyday life were considered curiosities and usually dismissed" (32).
4. For an excellent analysis of the *ángel del hogar* (angel of the house) trope, see Nancy LaGreca *Rewriting Womanhood*.
5. Repelling the unsanctioned British attacks on Buenos Aires led to an outcry of popular and patriotic support of local criollo defenders. As David Rock notes, this attack "shattered the Spanish administration" in Buenos Aires and led to a new order that would inspire subsequent cries for independence from Spanish rule, events that would come shortly, in May of 1810 (*Argentina* 71-78). See also, Johnson "The Military as Catalyst of Change in Late Colonial Buenos Aires."
6. Historian, photographer, and curator Sara Facio has played a major role in situating early photography in Argentina as part of a local tradition with its own specific visual vocabulary. Her work on the most important and longest-lasting photography studio in Argentina, the Estudio Witcomb, founded in 1880 by the English entrepreneur Alejandro S. Witcomb (1835-1905), provides evidence of the vast array of subjects and poses that came to mark a collective form of gestural identification at the turn of the century. As Facio puts it in her introduction to the 1991 publication, *Witcomb: Nuestro Ayer*, "Las fotografías de este volumen son, sin excepción, una continuidad de seres viviendo un momento histórico que imaginamos ideal" ("The photographs in this volume are, without exception, a continuity of beings living at a historical moment which we imagine to have been ideal" 8, translation Sara Gullco). While I do not have any indication that the Bunge family portraits I study in this book were in fact taken in the Witcomb Studio, it is certainly possible. What does seem clear, however, is that the type of familial gaze that Facio describes as continuous and ideal

was also sought by the Bunge family in their portraiture. The idealization of this past is also part of the reason why the Witcomb Collection became the basis of the visual archive of the Archivo General de la Nación in 1938. Facio curated the 2006 exhibition at the Museo de Bellas Artes, which was based on her earlier archival research and the publication of the aforementioned catalog and study of Witcomb's photographs. See, https://www.bellasartes.gob.ar/exhibiciones/estudio-witcomb.

7   For example, see Masotta "Representación e iconografía de dos tipos nacionales. El caso de las postales etnográficas en Argentina 1900-1930."

8   For example, see the caricature of Wilde in the satirical magazine *Punch* after his *Lady Windermere's Fan* opened at the St. James's Theatre on February 19, 1892.

9   As Michael J. Horswell documents in *Decolonizing the Sodomite*, the trope of the Indian as sexual deviant, in particular as "sodomite," has a long and complex history in Latin America, one that Barrantes Abascal seems to be insinuating in this caricature.

10  Mizraje details Argentina's philately as negotiating the presence and representation of women according to shifting political interests, especially in the late twentieth century. See her *Argentinas de Rosas a Perón* 85-86n28. For a general appraisal of Argentinean stamp production in the transition to democracy, see Hoyo Prohuber "Visiones encontradas: El V centenario en estampillas postales" 137-38.

11  I borrow this term from José Esteban Muñoz. See his *Disidentifications*.

CHAPTER FOUR

1   For an overview, see Szuchman "Childhood Education and Politics in Nineteenth-Century Argentina: The Case of Buenos Aires."

2   The Normal School or teaching college did not grant a baccalaureate degree, as did secondary schools, and thus did not permit graduates access to higher education.

3   A good example is the website and digital library *Memoria de la Educación Argentina*, which is maintained by the Biblioteca Nacional de Maestros. See http://www.bnm.me.gov.ar/e-recursos/medar/index.php. For an example how the analysis of the school textbook can help to understand broader trends in national identity and belonging, see Cucuzza *Yo Argentino: La construcción de la Nación en los libros escolares (1873-1930)*.

4   For an overview of the development of education over the course of the nineteenth century in Spanish America, see Newland "La educación elemental en Hispanoamérica."

5   For a good summary of the early-nineteenth-century controversies regarding the philosophies of education, see Kristal "Dialogues and Polemics: Sarmiento, Lastarria, and Bello."

6   For a concise and well documented analysis of Sarmiento's early engagement with women's education, see Garrels, "Sarmiento and the Woman Question: From 1839 to the Facundo."
7   Regarding turn-of-the-century wage differences in the Southern Cone, see Lavrin *Women, Feminism, and Social Change* 68-72.
8   As I note above, Julia and Delfina Bunge's *El Arca de Noé* was published in two volumes. In this chapter I focus on the second volume, for third-grade students, although the introductory note cited here was only included in the first volume (for second-grade students).
9   By the mid-nineteenth century, "Gallego" had become a common generic term for all Spanish immigrants, irrespective of regional ties or origin, and was often deployed in a dismissive or demeaning manner by the criollo elite. See Moya *Cousins and Strangers* 15-22.
10  As Samuel L. Baily notes, "Italian immigrants successfully participated in the organization of Argentine labor because there was a good fit between their experience in Italy and the kind of labor movement that emerged in Buenos Aires. Given the restricted nature of the Argentine political system, it is not surprising that the direct action of the anarchists and the revolutionary unionism of the syndicalists held greater appeal to the immigrants than the socialists' call to naturalize and change the system by participation in essentially meaningless elections" (201).
11  Baily writes: "The golondrinas—the Italians who like swallows went every year to Argentina to harvest the crops—numbered at least twenty thousand annually during the decade or so prior to World War I" (60).
12  See for example, Guy *Sex and Danger in Buenos Aires*.
13  These chapters, which are also subdivided into smaller lessons, include: "I. El hogar" ("The Home"), "II. La casa y la huerta" ("The House and Garden"), "III. El niño" ("The Child"), "IV. La Naturaleza" ("Nature"), "V. La Escuela" ("School"), "VI. La Conciencia" ("One's Conscience"), "VII. El campo" ("The Countryside"), "IX. La ciudad" ("The City"), and "X. La Nación" ("The Nation").
14  See Molloy *At Face Value* 97-107.
15  There are slight changes made between the 1909 article and the 1910 version published in *Nuestra Patria*. To facilitate easier reading I will quote the 1910 version in the text and, if the variant is significant, quote the 1909 text in a note. Here, Bunge includes the personal pronoun, "yo" in the 1909 version, "¿Soné yo la aventura?" (6), which is later deleted.
16  There is a significant change here. The 1909 article reads: "la impresión del frío del agua, mi terror, la rapidez con que fui pescado a tiempo" ("the impression of the cold of the water, my terror, the speed at which I was fished out in time"; 6). Thus, Bunge substitutes the speed of his rescue in the 1909 version for the impression left on his body by the net that was used to rescue him in that of 1910.

## CHAPTER FIVE

1 See the essays collected in Castro-Klarén and Chasteen *Beyond Imagined Communities: Reading and Writing the Nation in Nineteenth-Century Latin America*.
2 "Descamisados" literally means "shirtless people" and refers to the working-class sectors courted by Perón in the 1940s. Likewise, "cabecitas negras" (literally "little black heads"), refers to people with dark skin and black hair—a racialized marker for the working class.
3 I am drawing here on Jack Halberstam's theorization of temporality and/as queerness in his *In a Queer Time and Place: Transgender Bodies, Subcultural Lives*. However, in placing the queerness of time in the early twentieth century, rather than the twenty-first century's postmodern present, I am suggesting a historical continuity between modernity and postmodernity that is visible in these reformulations of kinship.
4 Bunge first published *Nuestra América* in 1903, and, as with most of his essays, would revise and edit the text throughout his life. I cite here from the 1926 edition published in his *Obras Completas*.
5 On Bunge's geographical determinism and his use of "Hispanoamérica" as opposed to "América Latina," see Fernández Bravo "Americanismo, biología e identidad: El cuerpo continental en Manoel Bomfim y Carlos Octavio Bunge."
6 The basis for this claim begins in the colonial period. For a good overview of the history of religion and sex in Latin America, see *Sexuality and Marriage in Colonial Latin America* (Ed. Asunción Lavrin).
7 The "mesita de tres pies" ("three legged table") refers to the practice of calling spirits collectively or through a medium, also known as table-turning, in which a group of people place their hands on a table and wait for it to move. Popular in mid-nineteenth-century England, it was salaciously "documented" as a new practice in Buenos Aires by *Caras y Caretas* in its August 27, 1904 edition. As Josefina Ludmer notes, the magazine published articles related to theosophy, occultism, and divination as part of an overarching investment in *modernista* antipositivism (*Corpus Delecti* 222-24). We see, then, how Bunge's derision of spiritism links to a broader debate about *what type* of spiritual future should govern Argentine social and literary life, an aesthetic-cosmology based on the occult or on Catholic doctrine.
8 The most common English translation of *The Spiritual Exercises* is by Louis J. Puhl (1951), and is now widely available. Puhl notes of the aphorism in question, "*He is a weakling before a show of force and a tyrant if he has his own will, 'en ser flaco por fuerza y fuerte de grado.'* We have tried to make the aphorism clear but have lost in brevity. We might retain the brevity by saying, 'Weak perforce and strong by choice.' But this would not be very clear. It means that Satan is of necessity weak if we courageously resist,

but would gladly tyrannize over us if we give him his way." See http://spex.ignatianspirituality.com/SpiritualExercises/Puhl#c21-1234.

9   For more information about Catholic Nationalism, see Sebreli *Crítica* 319-23.
10  Once again borrowing from Sylvia Molloy's "The politics of the pose."
11  See, for example, his *La simulación en la lucha por la vida*.
12  For a good overview of these changing public possibilities and the role of the woman writer in particular, see Unruh *Performing Women and Modern Literary Culture in Latin America*.
13  For a comprehensive overview of the period studied here, see Nari *Políticas de maternidad y maternalismo político*.
14  For a historical summary of women's claims for legal recognition, see Barrancos "Problematic Modernity."
15  David L. Eng's queer critique of affect and structural relationality, which borrows from Raymond Williams, has been useful to me here. See Eng *The Feeling of Kinship* 15-16.
16  Regarding the rearrangement and redefinition of kinship after the 1976-83 dictatorship, see *Lazos de familia: Herencias, cuerpos, ficciones* (Ed. Ana Amado and Nora Domínguez).
17  For a good overview of Alejandro Bunge's professional affiliations, in particular his work with the *Revista de Economía Argentina*, see Pantaleón "El surgimiento de la nueva economía argentina: el caso Bunge." For a detailed look at the breadth of his work, see De Imaz "Alejandro E. Bunge, economista y sociólogo (1880-1943)."
18  For example, see Araya "El sistema nacional de economía política (1840) para una nueva Argentina (1940). Friedrich List en Alejandro E. Bunge" and Llach "Alejandro Bunge, la *Revista de Economía Argentina* y los orígenes del estancamiento económico argentino."
19  Prebisch would go on to become a prominent figure in international economics. He was elected as executive director of the Economic Commission for Latin America (Comisión Económica para America Latina y el Caribe—CEPAL) in 1950 and in that same year published his most influential text, *The Economic Development of Latin America and Its Principal Problems*. He had studied under Alejandro Bunge at the National University of La Plata, where Bunge later helped Prebisch join the faculty. Prebisch would eventually find the socialist ideas of Augusto (rather than Alejandro) Bunge more convincing, at least in his early years. For more information on this period, see Dosman *The Life and Times of Raúl Prebisch 1901-1986* 30-38.
20  I take some poetic license here, but the central issue of Argentina's sovereign debt and its ability or willingness to pay back investors holding vulture funds (*fondos buitres*), marks a stark contrast between the respective presidencies of Cristina Fernández de Kirchner (2007-2015), who refused to pay back defaulted bonds, and Mauricio Macri (2015-), who has agreed to repay the bonds in full. For more information, see Guzman and Stiglitz.

21 For a good overview, see De Meneses *Salazar: A Political Biography*.
22 I say quasi-eugenic because, while Bunge feared the uneducated, largely mixed-race population having a higher birth rate than the elite, he did not advocate for intervening directly to terminate particular pregnancies, but rather to put pressure on the poor (through financial incentives) to reproduce less frequently.

## EPILOGUE

1 This is not to say that all marriages are essentially normative. Certainly, people across the globe are and have been utilizing same-sex marriage in creative and subversive ways, ways that do not see in marriage the consummation of an eternal love, but as a strategic form of undermining the legal apparatus by which it normalizes monogamy and romantic attachments.
2 Regarding "disidencia sexual." see the Colectivo Universitario de Disidencia Sexual virtual magazine: https://disidenciasexualcuds.wordpress.com/; regarding "transfeminism" see Garriga-López "Transfeminist Crossroads: Reimagining the Ecuadorian State."
3 I would add, from my own experience having served as both a section chair of the sexualities studies section (in 2013) and track chair of LGBT and sexuality studies (in 2017), that these issues remain as salient now as they were then.
4 See Lopes *O homem que amava rapazes e outros ensaios* and Pelúcio "Traduções e torções ou o que se quer dizer quandodizemos queer no Brasil?"
5 See Rodríguez *Dramas pobres* and Berkins "Si me querés, quereme trava." For more information on how gender nonconforming artists are using monstrosity as a form of resisting normalization, see my forthcoming essay, "I Monster: Embodying Trans and Travesti Resistance in Latin America."
6 Héctor Domínguez Ruvalcaba's *Translating the Queer: Body Politics and Transnational Conversations* provides a useful overview of many of these ongoing debates.
7 This borrows from Nelson Maldonado-Torres's conceptualization of the "decolonialidad del ser" ("decoloniality of being"), while also proposing a queer connection between the two forms of embodied relationality.

## WORKS CITED

Acree, William. "Hemispheric Travelers on the Rioplatense Stage." *Latin American Theatre Review* 47, no. 2 (Spring 2014): 5-24.
Ahmed, Sara. *Queer Phenomenology: Orientations, Objects, Others*. Durham, NC: Duke University Press, 2006.
Albarracín-Sarmiento, Carlos. *Estructura del Martín Fierro*. Purdue University Monographs in Romance Languages. Amsterdam: John Benjamins, 1981.
Amado, Ana, and Nora Domínguez, eds. *Lazos de familia: Herencias, cuerpos, ficciones*. Buenos Aires: Paidós, 2004.
Amícola, José. *Autobiografía como autofiguración: Estrategias discursivas del Yo y cuestiones de género*. Rosario, Argentina: Beatriz Viterbo, 2007.
Amin, Kadji. *Disturbing Attachments: Genet, Modern Pederasty, and Queer History*. Durham, NC: Duke University Press, 2017.
Anderson, Benedict. *Imagined Communities: Reflections on the Origin and Spread of Nationalism*. New York: Verso, 1991.
Araya, Diego Gastón. "El sistema nacional de economía política (1840) para una nueva Argentina (1940): Friedrich List en Alejandro E. Bunge." *Cuestiones de Sociología* 15 (2016): 1-21.
Area, Lelia. *Una biblioteca para leer la Nación: lecturas de la figura Juan Manuel de Rosas*. Rosario, Argentina: Beatriz Viterbo, 2006.
Arnaiz, María del Carmen, and Patricia Chomnalez. *Mujeres que trabajan (1930-1940)*. Buenos Aires: Centro Editor de América Latina, 1992.
Aronna, Michael. *"Pueblos enfermos": The Discourse of Illness in the Turn-of-the-Century Spanish and Latin American Essay*. Chapel Hill: University of North Carolina, Department of Romance Languages, 1999.
Arroyo, Jossianna. *Travestismos culturales: literatura y etnografía en Cuba y Brasil*. Pittsburgh, PA: Instituto Internacional de Literatura Iberoamericana, 2003.
Baily, Samuel L. *Immigrants in the Lands of Promise: Italians in Buenos Aires and New York City, 1870-1914*. Ithaca, NY: Cornell University Press, 1999.
Bakhtin, M. M. *The Dialogic Imagination: Four Essays*. Trans. Michael Holquist. Austin: University of Texas Press, 1981.

Balderston, Daniel, and Donna J. Guy, eds. *Sex and Sexuality in Latin America*. New York: NYU Press, 1997.
——, eds. *Sexo y sexualidades en América Latina*. Buenos Aires: Paidós, 1998.
Balmori, Diana, Stuart F. Voss, and Miles Wortman. *Notable Family Networks in Latin America*. Chicago and London: University of Chicago Press, 1984.
Barbero, María Inés, and Fernando Devoto. *Los nacionalistas (1910-1932)*. Buenos Aires: Centro Editor de América Latina, 1983.
Barrancos, Dora. "Problematic Modernity: Gender, Sexuality, and Reproduction in Twentieth-Century Argentina." *Journal of Women's History* 18, no. 2 (Summer 2006): 123-50.
Barthes, Roland. *Camera Lucida: Reflections on Photography*. Trans. Richard Howard. New York: Hill and Wang, 1981.
Batchen, Geoffrey. *Forget Me Not: Photography & Remembrance*. Amsterdam and New York: Van Gogh Museum and Princeton Architectural Press, 2004.
Bazán, Osvaldo. *Historia de la homosexualidad en la Argentina: de la conquista de América al siglo XXI*. Buenos Aires: Editorial Marea, 2004.
Benarós, León. *Paul Groussac en el Archivo General de la Nación*. Buenos Aires: Ediciones Archivo General de la Nación, 1998.
Bergmann, Emilie L., and Paul Julian Smith. "Introduction." In *¿Entiendes? Queer Readings, Hispanic Writings*. Eds. Bergmann, Emilie L. and Paul Julian Smith. Durham, NC: Duke University Press, 1995, 1-14.
Berkins, Lohana. "Si me querés, quereme trava." *Página 12. Soy*. September 11, 2015. https://www.pagina12.com.ar/diario/suplementos/soy/1-4173-2015-09-11.html. Accessed September 20, 2018.
Berlanstein, Lenard R. "Selling Modern Femininity: *Femina*, a Forgotten Feminist Publishing Success in Belle Epoque France." *French Historical Studies* 30, no. 5 (Fall 2007): 623-49.
Bersani, Leo. *Homos*. Cambridge, MA: Harvard University Press, 1995.
Biernat, Carolina. "Debates poblacionistas en la matriz de la política social argentina de entreguerras." *Anuario del Centro de Estudios Históricos "Prof. Carlos S. A. Segreti,"* no. 11 (2011): 189-208.
Bletz, May E. *Immigration and Acculturation in Brazil and Argentina: 1890-1929*. New York: Palgrave Macmillan, 2010.
Bourdieu, Pierre. *Masculine Domination*. Trans. Richard Nice. Stanford: Stanford University Press, 2001.
Brilliant, Richard. *Portraiture*. Cambridge, MA: Harvard University Press, 1991.
Bunge, Alejandro E. *Una nueva Argentina*. Madrid: Hyspamérica, (1940) 1984.
Bunge, Carlos Octavio [Hernán Prinz]. *Mi amigo Luis*. Buenos Aires: Editorial Elzeviriana, 1895.
Bunge, Carlos Octavio. *El derecho en la literatura gauchesca: discursos leídos ante la Academia de Filosofía y Letras de la Universidad de Buenos Aires en la recepción pública del Dr. C. O. Bunge, el día 22 de agosto de 1913*. Buenos Aires: Academia de Filosofía y Letras, 1913.

———. *La educación: tratado general de pedagogía*. *Obras Completas*. 16 vols. Madrid: Espasa-Calpe, 1928.
———. *El Espíritu de la Educación: Informe para la instrucción pública nacional*. Buenos Aires: Penitenciaría Nacional, 1901.
———. *Juicios sobre su obra y su personalidad*. *Obras Completas*. 16 vols. Madrid: Espasa-Calpe, 1928.
———. *La Novela de la Sangre*. Madrid: Daniel Jorro, 1903.
———. *La novela de la sangre*. Buenos Aires: Biblioteca de "La Nación," 1904.
———. "La novela de la sangre." *Ideas* 3, no. 13 (May 1904): 14–42.
———. *Nuestra América: Ensayo de psicología social*. *Obras Completas*. 16 vols. Madrid: Espasa-Calpe, (1903) 1926.
———. *Nuestra patria: Libro de lectura para la educación nacional*. 14th ed. Buenos Aires: Angel Estrada y Cía, 1910.
———. "Recuerdos de la infancia." *Monitor de la Educación Común* 29, no. 442 (1909): 5–30.
———. "Teoría de un libro de lectura escolar." *Monitor de la Educación Común* 29, no. 456 (1910): 571–83.
———. *Thespis (Novelas cortas y cuentos)*. Buenos Aires: Biblioteca de "La Nación," 1907.
Bunge de Gálvez, Delfina. *Las mujeres y la vocación*. Buenos Aires: Agencia de Librería y Publicaciones, 1922.
———. *Viaje alrededor de mi infancia*. Buenos Aires: Peuser, 1956.
Bunge, Delfina [Marguerite], "La jeune fille d'aujourd'hui est elle heureuse?" *Ideas* July (1904): 268–97.
Bunge, Julia, and Delfina Bunge. *El Arca de Noé. Libro de lectura para tercer grado*. 3rd ed. Buenos Aires: Cabaut y Cía, 1916.
Bunge, Julia Valentina. *Vida. Época maravillosa, 1903-1911*. Buenos Aires: Emecé Editores, 1965.
Butler, Judith. *Bodies that Matter: On the Discursive Limits of "Sex."* New York: Routledge, 1993.
———. *Gender Trouble: Feminism and the Subversion of Identity*. New York: Routledge, 1990.
———. "Is Kinship Always Already Heterosexual?" *differences: A Journal of Feminist Cultural Studies* 13, no. 1 (2002): 14–44.
———. *Giving an Account of Oneself*. New York: Fordham University Press, 2005.
Calderón, Yecid/Pinina Flandes. *Deviniendo Loca: Textualidades de una marica sureada*. Santiago, Chile: Los libros de la Mujer Rota, 2016.
Cárdenas, Eduardo José, and Carlos Manuel Payá. *El primer nacionalismo argentino en Manuel Gálvez y Ricardo Rojas*. Buenos Aires: A. Peña Lillo, 1978.
———. *La familia de Octavio Bunge*. Vol. 1. Buenos Aires: Sudamericana, 1995.
———. *La Argentina de los hermanos Bunge*. Vol. 2. Buenos Aires: Sudamericana, 1997.

Castro-Klarén, Sara, and John Charles Chasteen, eds. *Beyond Imagined Communities: Reading and Writing the Nation in Nineteenth-Century Latin America*. Washington, DC: Woodrow Wilson Center Press, 2003.

Chambers, Sarah C. *Families in War and Peace: Chile from Colony to Nation*. Durham, NC: Duke University Press, 2015.

Cirlot, J. E. *A Dictionary of Symbols*. Trans. Jack Sage. New York: Dover, (1971) 2002.

Cobrin, Pamela. "She's Old Enough to Be a Beautiful Young Boy: Sarah Bernhardt, Breeches Roles and the Poetics of Aging." *Women & Performance: a journal of feminist theory* 22, no. 1 (2012): 47-66.

Conlon, James. "Men Reading Women Reading: Interpreting Images of Women Readers." *Frontiers: A Journal of Women Studies* 26, no. 2 (2005): 37-58.

Cuarterolo, Miguel Angel. "Las primeras fotografías del país." *Los años del daguerrotipo: Primeras fotografías argentinas 1843-1870*. Buenos Aires: Fundación Antorchas, 1995, 15-19.

Cucuzza, Héctor Rubén. *Yo Argentino: La construcción de la Nación en los libros escolares (1873-1930)*. Buenos Aires: Miño y Dávila, 2007.

Davidoff, Leonore. *Worlds Between: Historical Perspectives on Gender and Class*. New York: Routledge, 1995.

De Meneses, Filipe Ribeiro. *Salazar: A Political Biography*. New York: Enigma Books, 2009.

Degiovanni, Fernando J. *Los textos de la patria: nacionalismo, políticas culturales y canon en Argentina*. Rosario, Argentina: Beatriz Viterbo, 2007.

DeLaney, Jeane H. "Imagining 'El Ser Argentino': Cultural Nationalism and Romantic Concepts of Nationhood in Early Twentieth-Century Argentina." *Journal of Latin American Studies* 34, no. 3 (August 2002): 625-58.

Deleuze, Gilles, and Félix Guattari. *A Thousand Plateaus: Capitalism and Schizophrenia*. Trans. Brian Massumi. Minneapolis: University of Minnesota Press, 1987.

Delgado, Verónica. *El nacimiento de la literatura argentina en las revistas literarias (1896-1913)*. La Plata, Argentina: Universidad Nacional de La Plata, 2009.

Domínguez-Ruvalcaba, Héctor. *La modernidad abyecta: Formación del discurso homosexual en Hispanoamérica*. Xalapa, Mexico: Universidad Veracruzana, 2001.

———. *Translating the Queer: Body Politics and Transnational Conversations*. London: Zed Books, 2016.

Dosman, Edgar J. *The Life and Times of Raúl Prebisch, 1901-1986*. Montreal: McGill-Queen's University Press, 2008.

Eakin, Paul John. *How Our Lives Become Stories: Making Selves*. Ithaca, NY: Cornell University Press, 1999.

Edelman, Lee. *No Future: Queer Theory and the Death Drive*. Durham, NC: Duke University Press, 2004.

Edwards, Matthew J. *Queer Argentina: Movement towards the Closet in a Global Time*. New York: Palgrave Macmillan, 2017.

Eljaiek-Rodríguez, Gabriel. "Semillas de maldad: Early Latin American Gothic." *Studies in Gothic Fiction* 3, no. 2 (2014): 13-23.

Eng, David L. *The Feeling of Kinship: Queer Liberalism and the Racialization of Intimacy*. Durham, NC and London: Duke University Press, 2010.

Engels, Friedrich. *The Origin of the Family, Private Property and the State*. London: Penguin, (1884) 2010.

Engelstein, Stefani. "Sibling Logic; or, Antigone Again." *PMLA* 126, no. 1 (2011): 38-54.

Facio, Sara. *Witcomb: Nuestro Ayer*. Trans. Sara Gullco. Buenos Aires: La Azotea, 1991.

Falconí Trávez, Diego. *De las cenizas al texto: Literaturas andinas de las disidencias sexuales en el siglo XX*. La Habana, Cuba: Casa de las Américas, 2016.

Falconí Trávez, Diego, Santiago Castellanos, and María Amelia Viteri. "Resentir lo queer en América Latina: diálogos desde/con el Sur." *Resentir lo queer en América Latina: diálogos desde/con el Sur*. Eds. Diego Falconí Trávez, Santiago Castellanos, and María Amelia Viteri. Barcelona: Egales, 2014, 9-18.

Fernández Bravo, Álvaro. "Americanismo, biología e identidad: El cuerpo continental en Manoel Bomfim y Carlos Octavio Bunge." *Hispamérica* 31, no. 92 (2002): 61-74.

Ferrer, Enrique. "Xarcas silenciario, novela, por Carlos Octavio Bunge—1903." *Revista Contemporánea* 29, no. 127 (July-December 1903): 126-28.

Fiol-Matta, Licia. *A Queer Mother for the Nation: The State and Gabriela Mistral*. Minneapolis: University of Minnesota Press, 2002.

Foster, David William. *The Argentine Generation of 1880: Ideology and Cultural Texts*. Columbia and London: University of Missouri Press, 1990.

———. *Sexual Textualities: Essays on Queer/ing Latin American Writing*. Austin: University of Texas Press, 1997.

Foucault, Michel. *The History of Sexuality: An Introduction*. Trans. Robert Hurley. Vol. 1. 3 vols. New York: Vintage Books, 1990.

———. *The History of Sexuality*. Trans. Robert Hurley. Vol. 2. 3 vols. New York: Vintage, 1990.

Foucault, Michel. *Technologies of the Self: A Seminar with Michel Foucault*. Eds. Luther H. Martin, Huck Gutman, and Patrick H. Hutton. Amherst: University of Massachusetts Press, 1988.

Freeman, Elizabeth. "Queer Belongings: Kinship Theory and Queer Theory." *A Companion to Lesbian, Gay, Bisexual, Transgender, and Queer Studies*. Eds. George E. Haggerty and Molly McGarry. Oxford: Blackwell, 2007, 295-314.

Freud, Sigmund. *The Freud Reader*. Ed. Peter Gay. New York: Norton, 1989.

Gálvez, Lucía. *Delfina Bunge: Diarios íntimos de una época brillante*. Buenos Aires: Planeta, 2000.

Gálvez, Manuel. *El diario de Gabriel Quiroga: opiniones sobre la vida argentina.* Buenos Aires: Taurus, (1910) 2001.

———. *Recuerdos de la vida literaria.* Vol. 1. 2 vols. Buenos Aires: Taurus, 2002.

———. " 'La Novela de la Sangre' por Carlos Octavio Bunge." *Ideas* 3, no. 9 (January 1904): 75-85.

Garrels, Elizabeth. "Sarmiento and the Woman Question: From 1839 to the *Facundo*." *Sarmiento: Author of a Nation.* Eds. Tulio Halperín Donghi, Iván Jaksić, Gwen Kirkpatrick, and Francine Masiello. Berkeley: University of California Press, 1994, 272-93.

Garriga-López, Claudia Sofía. "Transfeminist Crossroads: Reimagining the Ecuadorian State." *TSQ: Transgender Studies Quarterly* 3, no. 1-2 (May 2016): 104-19.

Giorgi, Gabriel. *Sueños de exterminio: Homosexualidad y representación en la literatura argentina contemporánea.* Rosario, Argentina: Beatriz Viterbo, 2004.

Guy, Donna J. *Sex and Danger in Buenos Aires: Prostitution, Family, and Nation in Argentina.* Lincoln: University of Nebraska Press, 1991.

Guzman, Martin, and Joseph E. Stiglitz. "How Hedge Funds Held Argentina for Ransom." *New York Times* (April 1, 2016), A25. https://www.nytimes.com/2016/04/01/opinion/how-hedge-funds-held-argentina-for-ransom.html. Accessed September 20, 2018.

Haggerty, George E. *Queer Gothic.* Urbana: University of Illinois Press, 2006.

Halberstam, Jack. *In a Queer Time & Place: Transgender Bodies, Subcultural Lives.* New York: NYU Press, 2005.

Hale, Charles A. "Political Ideas and Ideologies in Latin America, 1870-1930." In *Ideas and Ideologies in Twentieth Century Latin America.* Ed. Leslie Bethell. New York: Cambridge University Press, 1996, 133-205.

Halperin Donghi, Tulio. *El revisionismo histórico argentino como visión decadentista de la historia nacional.* Buenos Aires: Siglo XXI, 2005.

Harrison, Carol E. *Romantic Catholics: France's Postrevolutionary Generation in Search of a Modern Faith.* Ithaca, NY: Cornell University Press, 2014.

Helg, Aline. "Race in Argentina and Cuba, 1880-1930: Theory, Policies, and Popular Reaction." In *The Idea of Race in Latin America, 1870-1940.* Ed. Richard Graham. Austin: University of Texas Press, 1990, 37-69.

Hirsch, Marianne. *Family Frames: Photography, Narrative, and Postmemory.* Cambridge, MA: Harvard University Press, 1997.

Honig, Bonnie. *Antigone, Interrupted.* Cambridge, UK: Cambridge University Press, 2013.

Horswell, Michael J. *Decolonizing the Sodomite: Queer Tropes of Sexuality in Colonial Andean Culture.* Austin: University of Texas Press, 2005.

Hoyo Prohuber, Henio. "Visiones encontradas: El V centenario en estampillas postales." In *Autorretratos del Estado.* Ed. Guillermo Navarro Oltra. Vol. 3.

3 vols. Madrid: Universidad de Cantabria and Universidad de Castilla-La Mancha, 2015, 126-49.

Huff, Cynthia. " 'That Profoundly Female, and Feminist Genre': The Diary as Feminist Practice." *Women's Studies Quarterly* 17, no. 3/4 (Fall-Winter 1989): 6-14.

De Imaz, José Luis. "Alejandro E. Bunge, economista y sociólogo (1880-1943)." *Desarrollo Económico* 14, no. 55 (October-December 1974): 545-67.

Ingenieros, José. *La psicopatología en el arte*. Buenos Aires: Losada, 1961.

Johnson, Lyman L. "The Military as Catalyst of Change in Late Colonial Buenos Aires." *Revolution and Restoration: The Rearrangement of Power in Argentina, 1776-1860*. Eds. Mark D. Szuchman and Jonathan C. Brown. Lincoln: University of Nebraska Press, 1994, 27-53.

Kim, Yeon-Soo. *The Family Album: Histories, Subjectivities, and Immigration in Contemporary Spanish Culture*. Lewisburg: Bucknell University Press, 2005.

Klein, Melanie. *The Selected Melanie Klein*. Ed. Juliet Mitchell. New York: The Free Press, 1987.

Kristal, Efraín. "Dialogues and Polemics: Sarmiento, Lastarria, and Bello." In *Sarmiento and His Argentina*. Ed. Joseph T. Criscenti. Boulder, CO: Lynne Rienner, 1993, 61-70.

De Kurth, Gilberta S. "El Arca de Noé por Julia y Delfina Bunge." *Monitor de la Educación Común* 31, no. 482 (1913): 122-24.

Lacan, Jacques. *The Four Fundamental Concepts of Psychoanalysis*. Trans. Alan Sheridan. New York: Norton, 1981.

LaGreca, Nancy. *Rewriting Womanhood: Feminism, Subjectivity, and the Angel of the House in the Latin American Novel, 1887-1903*. University Park: Pennsylvania State University Press, 2009.

Lavrin, Asunción, ed. *Sexuality and Marriage in Colonial Latin America*. Lincoln: University of Nebraska Press, 1989.

———. *Women, Feminism, and Social Change in Argentina, Chile, and Uruguay, 1890-1940*. Lincoln: University of Nebraska Press, 1998.

Lejeune, Philippe. *On Diary*. Trans. Katherine Durnin. Eds. Jeremy D. Popkin and Julie Rak. Honolulu: The Center for Biographical Research of the University of Hawai'i at Manoa and University of Hawai'i Press, 2009.

Leo XIII. "Rerum Novarum." May 15, 1891. *The Holy See*, http://w2.vatican.va/content/leo-xiii/en/encyclicals/documents/hf_l-xiii_enc_15051891_rerum-novarum.html. Accessed October 10, 2018.

Lévi-Strauss, Claude. *The Elementary Structures of Kinship*. Trans. James Harle Bell and John Richard von Sturmer. Ed. Rodney Needham. Boston: Beacon Press, (1949) 1969.

Levine, Robert M. *Images of History: Nineteenth and Early Twentieth Century Latin American Photographs as Documents*. Durham, NC: Duke University Press, 1989.

Lionnet, Françoise. *Autobiographical Voices: Race, Gender, Self-Portraiture.* Ithaca, NY: Cornell University Press, 1989.

Llach, Juan José. "Alejandro Bunge, la Revista de Economía Argentina y los orígenes del estancamiento económico argentino." *Valores en la Sociedad Industrial* 22, no. 59 (2004): 51-65.

Lorde, Audre. *Sister Outsider.* 1984. Berkeley: Crossing Press, 2007.

Lopes, Denilson. *O homem que amava rapazes e outros ensaios.* Rio de Janeiro: Aeroplano, 2002.

Losada, Leandro. *Historia de las elites en la Argentina: Desde la Conquista hasta el surgimiento del peronismo.* Buenos Aires: Sudamericana, 2009.

Ludmer, Josefina. *The Gaucho Genre.* Trans. Molly Weigel. Durham, NC: Duke University Press, 2002.

———. *The Corpus Delicti: A Manual of Argentine Fictions.* Trans. Glen S. Close. Pittsburgh, PA: University of Pittsburgh Press, 2004.

Maldonado-Torres, Nelson. "Sobre la colonialidad del ser: contribuciones al desarrollo de un concepto." *El giro decolonial. Reflexiones para una diversidad epistémica más allá del capitalismo global.* Eds. Santiago Castro-Gómez and Ramón Grosfoguel. Bogotá: IESCO/Siglo del Hombre/ Pontificia Universidad Javeriana, 2007, 127-67.

Marcus, Sharon. "Salomé!! Sarah Bernhardt, Oscar Wilde, and the Drama of Celebrity." *PMLA* 124, no. 4 (2011): 999-1021.

Martínez, Luciano. "Transformación y renovación: los estudios lésbico-gays y queer latinoamericanos." *Revista Iberoamericana* 74, no. 225 (October-December 2008): 861-76.

Masiello, Francine. *Between Civilization & Barbarism: Women, Nation, and Literary Culture in Modern Argentina.* Lincoln: University of Nebraska Press, 1992.

Masotta, Carlos. "Representación e iconografía de dos tipos nacionales. El caso de las postales etnográficas en Argentina 1900-1930." *Arte y antropología en la Argentina.* Buenos Aires: Fundación Espigas and FIAAR, 2005, 65-114.

Melo, Adrián. *Historia de la literatura gay en Argentina: Representaciones sociales de la homosexualidad masculina en la ficción literaria.* Buenos Aires: Ediciones Lea, 2011.

Micale, Mark S. *Approaching Hysteria: Disease and Its Interpretations.* Princeton, NJ: Princeton University Press, 1995.

———. *Hysterical Men: The Hidden History of Male Nervous Illness.* Cambridge, MA: Harvard University Press, 2008.

Michie, Helena. *Sororophobia: Differences among Women in Literature and Culture.* New York and Oxford: Oxford University Press, 1992.

Mignolo, Walter, and Catherine E. Walsh. *On Decoloniality: Concepts, Analytics, and Praxis.* Durham, NC: Duke University Press, 2018.

Miguel, Adriana de. "Escenas de lectura escolar: La intervención normalista en la formación de la cultura letrada moderna." *Para una historia de la enseñanza de la lectura y la escritura en Argentina: Del catecismo colonial a la Razón de mi Vida*. Eds. Cucuzza, Héctor and Pablo Pineau. Madrid: Miño Dávila, 2002, 109-46.

Miller, Nancy K. "Representing Others: Gender and the Subjects of Autobiography." *differences: A Journal of Feminist Cultural Studies* 6, no. 1 (Spring 1994): 1-27.

Mitchell, Juliet. *Siblings: Sex and Violence*. Cambridge, UK and Malden, MA: Polity Press, 2003.

Mizraje, María Gabriela. *Argentinas de Rosas a Perón*. Buenos Aires: Biblos, 1999.

Molloy, Sylvia. *At Face Value: Autobiographical Writing in Spanish America*. Cambridge, UK: Cambridge University Press, 1991.

———. "Too Wilde for Comfort." *Social Text* 31/32 (1992): 187-201.

———. "The Politics of Posing." *Hispanisms and Homosexualities*. Eds. Sylvia Molloy and Robert McKee Irwin. Durham, NC: Duke University Press, 1998, 141-60.

Molloy, Sylvia, and Robert McKee Irwin, eds. *Hispanisms and Homosexualities*. Durham, NC: Duke University Press, 1998.

Monniot, Victorine. *Marguerite à vingt ans: suite et fin du Journal de Marguerite*, 1879, https://gallica.bnf.fr/ark:/12148/bpt6k6570542d. Accessed August 10, 2018.

Montaldo, Graciela. *La sensibilidad amenazada: Fin de siglo y modernismo*. Rosario, Argentina: Beatriz Viterbo, 1994.

———. "Mass and Multitude: Bastardised Iconographies of the Modern Order." *Images of Power: Iconography, Culture and the State in Latin America*. Eds. Jens Andermann and William Rowe. New York and Oxford: Berghahn Books, 2005, 217-38.

———. "Hombres de la multitud y hombres de genio en el *fin-de-siècle*." *Entre hombres: Masculinidades del siglo XIX en América Latina*. Eds. Anna Peluffo and Ignacio M. Sánchez Prado. Madrid: Iberoamericana and Veuvert, 2010, 123-44.

Montero, Oscar. "Modernismo y homofobia. Darío y Rodó." *Sexo y sexualidades en América Latina*. Eds. Daniel Balderston and Donna J. Guy. Buenos Aires: Paidós, 1998, 163-84.

Moya, Jose C. *Cousins and Strangers: Spanish Immigrants in Buenos Aires, 1850-1930*. Berkeley: University of California Press, 1998.

Muñoz, José Esteban. *Disidentifications: Queers of Color and the Performance of Politics*. Minneapolis: University of Minnesota Press, 1999.

———. *Cruising Utopia: The Then and There of Queer Futurity*. New York: NYU Press, 2009.

Musser, Amber J. *Sensational Flesh: Race, Power, and Masochism*. New York: New York University Press, 2014.

Nari, Marcela. *Políticas de la maternidad y maternalismo político: Buenos Aires (1890-1940)*. Buenos Aires: Biblos, 2004.

Navarro Gerassi, Maryssa. *Los nacionalistas*. Trans. Alberto Ciria. Buenos Aires: Jorge Álvarez, 1968.

Newland, Carlos. "La educación elemental en Hispanoamérica: desde la Independencia hasta la centralización de los sistemas educativos nacionales." *Hispanic American Historical Review* 71, no. 2 (1991): 335-64.

Nouzeilles, Gabriela. *Ficciones somáticas: naturalismo, nacionalismo y políticas médicas del cuerpo (Argentina 1880-1910)*. Rosario, Argentina: Beatriz Viterbo, 2000.

Ocampo, Victoria. *Autobiografía*. Vol. II, *El Imperio Insular*. Buenos Aires: SUR, 1980.

Olivera, Ricardo. "La Novela de la Sangre." *Ideas* 3, nos. 11 and 12 (March-April 1904): 299-306.

Ossenbach, Gabriela. "Manuales escolares y patrimonio histórico-educativo." *Educatio Siglo XXI* 28, no. 2 (2010): 115-32.

Palmer, Steven, and Gladys Rojas Chaves. "Educating Señorita: Teacher Training, Social Mobility and the Birth of Costa Rican Feminism, 1885-1925." *Hispanic American Historical Review* 78, no. 1 (1998): 45-82.

Pantaleón, Jorge F. "El surgimiento de la nueva economía argentina: el caso Bunge." *Intelectuales y expertos: la constitución del conocimiento social en la Argentina*. Eds. Federico Neiburg and Mariano Plotkin. Buenos Aires: Paidós, 2004, 175-201.

Pecheny, Mario. "El papel del amor en el discurso político reivindicativo en sexualidad." In *Políticas del amor: Derechos sexuales y escrituras disidentes en el Cono Sur*. Eds. Fernando A. Blanco, Mario Pecheny, and Joseph M. Pierce. Santiago, Chile: Cuarto Propio, 2018, 245-60.

Pelúcio, Larissa. "Traduções e torções ou o que se quer dizer quando dizemos queer no Brasil?" *Periódicus* 1, no. 1 (2014): 68-91.

Peralta, Jorge Luis. *Paisaje de varones: Genealogías del homoerotismo en la literatura argentina*. Barcelona: Icaria, 2017.

Pierce, Joseph M. "Adopted: Trace, Blood, and Native Authenticity." *Critical Ethnic Studies* 3, no. 2 (Fall 2017): 57-76.

——. "I Monster: Embodying *Trans* and *Travesti* Resistance in Latin America."*Latin American Research Review*, forthcoming.

——. "Regulating Queer Desire in Carlos O. Bunge's *La novela de la sangre*." *Revista Hispánica Moderna* 69, no. 1 (June 2016): 55-71.

——. " 'Usted no es hombre para esas cosas': masculinidad y renegación en la obra de Carlos O. Bunge." *Taller de Letras* 58 (September 2016): 127-39.

Pius XI. "Quadragesimo Anno." May 15, 1931. The Holy See, http://w2.vatican.va/content/pius-xi/en/encyclicals/documents/hf_p-xi_enc_19310515_quadragesimo-anno.html. Accessed October 10, 2018.

Posadas, Abel, Marta Speroni, and Mónica Landro. *Cine y Novela: Imágenes argentinas del siglo XX*. Vol. 3. 3 vols. Buenos Aires: Argus-a, 2015.

Prebisch, Raúl. "The Economic Development of Latin America and Its Principal Problems." Economic Commission for Latin America. Lake Success, NY: United Nations Department of Economic Affairs, 1950.

Príamo, Luis. "Fotografía y vida privada (1870-1930)." *Historia de la vida privada en la Argentina*. Eds. Fernando Devoto and Marta Madero. Vol. 2. 3 vols. Buenos Aires: Taurus, 1999, 270-310.

Prieto, Adolfo. *La literatura autobiográfica argentina*. Buenos Aires: Jorge Álvarez, 1966.

———. *El discurso criollista en la formación de la Argentina moderna*. Buenos Aires: Sudamericana, 1988.

Puar, Jasbir K. *Terrorist Assemblages: Homonationalism in Queer Times*. Durham, NC: Duke University Press, 2007.

Quiroga, José. *Tropics of Desire: Interventions from Queer Latino America*. New York: NYU Press, 2000.

Quiroga, José, and Laura Gutiérrez. "The Present State of Latin American Gay and Lesbian Studies." *LASA Forum* 33, no. 2 (Fall 2002): 14-15.

Rama, Ángel. *La ciudad letrada*. Montevideo, Uruguay: Arca, 1998.

Ramos Mejía, José María. *Las multitudes argentinas: estudio de psicología colectiva*. Buenos Aires: Editorial de Belgrano, (1899) 1977.

Renan, Ernest. "What Is a nation?" Trans. Martin Thom. In *Nation and Narration*. Ed. Homi K. Bhabha. New York: Routledge, 1990, 8-22.

Riobó, Carlos. *Sub-versions of the Archive: Manuel Puig's and Severo Sarduy's Alternative Identities*. Lewisburg, PA: Bucknell University Press, 2011.

Robles Carcedo, Laureano. "Cartas entre Unamuno y el argentino C. O. Bunge." *Cuadernos de la Cátedra Miguel de Unamuno* 29 (1994): 251-97.

Rock, David. *Argentina, 1516-1987: From Spanish Colonization to Alfonsín*. Berkeley: University of California Press, 1987.

———. *Authoritarian Argentina: The Nationalist Movement, Its History, and Its Impact*. Berkeley: University of California Press, 1993.

Rodríguez, Claudia. *Dramas pobres*. Santiago de Chile: Ediciones del Intersticio, 2016.

Rodríguez, Juana María. *Sexual Futures, Queer Gestures, and Other Latina Longings*. New York: NYU Press, 2014.

Rodríguez, Richard T. *Next of Kin: The Family in Chicano/a Cultural Politics*. Durham, NC: Duke University Press, 2009.

Romero, José Luis. *Breve historia de la Argentina*. Buenos Aires: Fondo de Cultura Económica, 1996.

Rotker, Susana. *Captive Women: Oblivion and Memory in Argentina*. Trans. Jennifer French. Minneapolis: University of Minnesota Press, 2002.

Rubin, Gayle. "The Traffic in Women: Notes toward a Political Economy of

Sex." In *Toward an Anthropology of Women*. Ed. Rayna Reiter. New York: Monthly Review Press, 1975, 157-210.

Salessi, Jorge. *Médicos maleantes y maricas: Higiene, criminología y homosexualidad en la construcción de la nación Argentina (Buenos Aires, 1871-1914)*. Rosario, Argentina: Beatriz Viterbo, 1995.

Sebreli, Juan José. *Apogeo y ocaso de los Anchorena*. Buenos Aires: Siglo Veinte, 1972.

———. *Crítica de las ideas políticas argentinas: los orígenes de la crisis*. Buenos Aires: Sudamericana, 2002.

Sedgwick, Eve Kosofsky. *Between Men: English Literature and Male Homosocial Desire*. New York: Columbia University Press, 1985.

Shumway, Nicolas. *Historia personal de una pasión argentina*. Buenos Aires: Emecé, 2011.

———. *The Invention of Argentina*. Berkeley: University of California Press, 1991.

Sierra, Marta. "Scripts for Modern Mothers: Representations of Motherhood in Delfina Bunge and Alfonsina Storni." *Revista de Estudios Hispánicos* 45, no. 1 (2011): 89-106.

Sifuentes-Jáuregui, Ben. *The Avowal of Difference: Queer Latino American Narratives*. Albany, NY: SUNY Press, 2014.

Slatta, Richard W. *Gauchos and the Vanishing Frontier*. Lincoln: University of Nebraska Press, 1983.

Solberg, Carl E. *Immigration and Nationalism: Argentina and Chile, 1890-1914*. Austin: University of Texas Press, 1970.

Soler, Ricaurte. *El positivismo argentino: Pensamiento filosófico y sociológico*. Buenos Aires: Paidós, 1968.

Sommer, Doris. *Foundational Fictions: The National Romances of Latin America*. Berkeley, Los Angeles, London: University of California Press, 1991.

Sontag, Susan. *On Photography*. New York: Farrar, Straus and Giroux, 1977.

Sorrentino, Fernando. "El drolático *drolático*." *El Trujamán: Revista diaria de traducción* (July 24, 2003). https://cvc.cervantes.es/trujaman/anteriores/julio_03/24072003.htm. Accessed May 3, 2015.

Spicer-Escalante, J. P. *Visiones patológicas nacionales: Lucio Vicente López, Eugenio Cambaceres y Julián Martel ante la distopía argentina finisecular*. College Park, MD: Hispamérica, 2006.

Stepan, Nancy Leys. *"The Hour of Eugenics": Race, Gender, and Nation in Latin America*. Ithaca, NY: Cornell University Press, 1991.

Szuchman, Mark D. "Childhood Education and Politics in Nineteenth-Century Argentina: The Case of Buenos Aires." *Hispanic American Historical Review* 70, no. 1 (February 1990): 109-38.

Tagg, John. *The Disciplinary Frame: Photographic Truths and the Capture of Meaning*. Minneapolis: University of Minnesota Press, 2009.

Taylor, Keeanga-Yamahtta, ed. *How We Get Free: Black Feminism and the Combahee River Collective*. Chicago: Haymarket Books, 2017.

Tedesco, Juan Carlos. *Educación y sociedad en la Argentina (1880-1900)*. Buenos Aires: Pannedille, 1970.

Terán, Oscar. *Vida intelectual en el Buenos Aires fin-de-siglo (1880-1910): Derivas de la "cultura científica."* Buenos Aires: Fondo de Cultura Económica, 2000.

———. *Historia de las ideas en la Argentina: Diez lecciones iniciales, 1810-1980*. Buenos Aires: Siglo Veintiuno, 2010.

Tiscornia, Delfina. *Ella camina sola*. Buenos Aires: Olmo, 2006.

Torrado, Susana. *Historia de la familia en la Argentina moderna (1870-2000)*. Buenos Aires: Ediciones de la Flor, 2003.

Tortorici, Zeb. *Sins against Nature: Sex and Archives in Colonial New Spain*. Durham, NC: Duke University Press, 2018.

Unruh, Vicky. *Performing Women and Modern Literary Culture in Latin America: Intervening Acts*. Austin: University of Texas Press, 2006.

Viñas, David. *Apogeo de la oligarquía*. Buenos Aires: Ediciones Siglo Veinte, 1975.

———. *Indios, ejército y frontera*. Buenos Aires: Santiago Arcos Editor, 1982.

Wasem, Marcos. *El amor libre en Montevideo: Roberto de las Carreras y la irrupción del anarquismo erótico en el Novecientos*. Montevideo, Uruguay: Banda Oriental, 2015.

Watkins, Susan Cotts. "Spinsters." *Journal of Family History* 9 (Winter 1984): 310-25.

Wiegman, Robyn, and Elizabeth A. Wilson. "Introduction: Antinormativity's Queer Conventions." *differences: A Journal of Feminist Cultural Studies* 26, no. 1 (2015): 1-25.

Weston, Kath. *Families We Choose: Lesbians, Gays, Kinship*. New York: Columbia University Press, 1991.

Willey, Angela. *Undoing Monogamy: The Politics of Science and the Possibilities of Biology*. Durham, NC: Duke University Press, 2016.

Yeager, Gertrude M. "Elite Education in Nineteenth-Century Chile." *Hispanic American Historical Review* 71, no. 1 (February 1991): 73-105.

Zeballos, Estanislao [Lady Juana]. "Palermo." *Revista de Derecho, Historia y Letras* 6, no. 16 (1903): 88-96.

———. "A Marguerite." *Revista de Derecho, Historia y Letras* 7, no. 20 (1904): 106-10.

# INDEX

Note: page numbers followed by *f* indicate figures

Alberdi, Juan Bautista, 152, 205
Álvarez Boero, Horacio, 169, 171*f*
*Amalia* (Mármol), 9, 39, 44, 47
Amin, Kadji, 18, 268
anarchism, 193, 210, 255, 260, 270
anarchists, 33, 60, 129, 205, 235, 253, 295n96
antipositivism, 242, 296n109. *See also* positivism
*El Arca de Noé* (Bunge, Delfina and Julia), 21–22, 26, 190, 192, 198–204, 206, 208, 211, 214, 229, 295n94. *See also* textbooks
Areco, Felisa, 175, 185
Argentine centennial, 26, 71, 101, 128–31, 190, 218
*argentinidad* (Argentineness), 31, 40, 54, 86, 204
archive, 286n20; Carlos Octavio Bunge's narratives as, 35, 38; Delfina Bunge's diaries as, 95–97, 100–101; diary as, 91–92, 94; family album as, 138–39, 142–43, 171, 181, 187; material fragility of, 267; photography and, 141, 178; queer, 27; queer materiality of, 94; queerness of, 19; visual, 26, 294n81. *See also* Bunge family archive
authoritarianism, 38, 43, 232, 234, 255, 280
authority, 28, 92–93, 201, 262, 264; of the military, 229; nationalist, 43; paternal, 245, 250, 260; patriarchal, 60, 67, 75–77, 92, 143, 244, 250, 252–54, 263 (*see also* family: patriarchal; normativity: patriarchal; patriarchy); queer undoings of, 93; of the state, 73, 190–92
Area, Lelia, 43, 47

Balzac, Honoré de, 77, 290n53
Barrantes Abascal, F., 153–54, 294n84
Barthes, Roland, 2, 26, 140–41, 182, 187
Bazán, Osvaldo, 31–32
Becher, Emilio, 112, 218
Benjamin, Walter, 140–41, 182
Bernhardt, Sarah, 115, 161–65
*blanqueamiento* (racial whitening), 34, 54
bodies, 6, 8, 10, 12, 14, 16–17, 30, 82–83, 93–94, 274, 276; disciplining of, 35, 142, 192, 242; family album and, 143;

313

bodies *(cont'd)*
  gendered, 120; labor and, 258; masculine, 225; material, 237–38, 279; nonnormative, 7, 34, 193; other, 2; of people of color, 239; photography and, 138–40, 182; queerness and, 269, 282; in relation, 138, 168, 173–74, 178, 181, 186, 202, 225, 268, 271–72, 282; sexual reproduction and, 86; social, 209; unruly, 71; white, 265; women's, 181, 246, 252–53
Bunge, Alejandro, 3, 27, 233, 235, 254–59, 262–66, 283n4, 297n119, 297n121; *Una nueva Argentina*, 27, 233, 255–59, 262–63, 265–66
Bunge, Carlos Octavio: "El Capitán Pérez," 57–70, 89, 224, 288n43; caricatures of, 147, 151–57, 160, 228 (*see also* Barrantes Abascal, F.); "El Chucro," 57, 70–77, 89; as a dandy, 31, 153, 155, 158–59; *El espíritu de la educación*, 30, 147, 152; homosexuality of (purported), 20, 25, 32–33, 84, 159; *Mi amigo Luis*, 20, 285n17, 286n22; "Pesadilla Drolática," 57, 77–89; physical presence of, 31–32, 147, 153; portraiture of, 147–51, 157–60; queerness of, 29, 32, 37, 47, 54, 56–58, 60, 69, 75, 78, 89, 147, 155, 157, 159; *Thespis*, 25, 33, 56–57, 71, 77; *Viaje a través de la estirpe*, 244, 246. See also Cané, Miguel; *La novela de la sangre*; *Nuestra América: Ensayo de psicología social*; *Nuestra Patria: Libro de lectura para la educación nacional*
Bunge, Delfina: "el caso Delfina," 110–19, 166 (*see also* Monniot, Victorine); commemorative stamp, 169–70, 294n85 (*see also* Álvarez Boero, Horacio); *cuadernos-copia* (journal copies), 97–98, 100–101, 103, 121, 167; diaries of, 4, 20, 23, 25, 28, 89, 92–103, 108, 110–11, 115, 121–22, 133–35, 160, 167, 251, 291n60; essay in *Femina* (magazine), 103, 110, 115–18, 121, 124, 132, 165–66; marriage to Manuel Gálvez, 101, 122, 126, 129, 132–34, 169–70, 175, 204–205; portraiture of, 160, 166–68; *Viaje alrededor de me infancia*, 137–38, 185. See also *El Arca de Noé*; Areco, Felisa; Gálvez, Manuel; Monniot, Victorine; Ocampo, Victoria
Bunge, Delfina Tiscornia, 2–3, 21, 28, 95–96, 141–42, 283nn2–3
Bunge, Julia Valentina: diary of, 4, 20, 25, 89, 92–95, 96–97, 104–106, 108, 110–11, 115, 117–19, 128–32, 135, 160; portraiture of, 160–64 (*see also* Bernhardt, Sarah); self-image of, 164–65. See also *El Arca de Noé*; Uranga, Ignacio
Bunge Arteaga, María Luisa, 4, 168, 182, 184
Bunge family album, 21–22, 135, 138, 142–43, 157–59, 170–72, 180–81, 186–88; archiving of, 24; political value of, 146; queer relationality and, 26; self-imaging and, 165, 168; sibling relatedness and, 175, 178. See also Bunge, Carlos Octavio: portraits of
Bunge family archive, 4, 11, 16, 19–24, 27, 103, 138, 141, 145–46, 159, 185, 230, 292n72
Butler, Judith, 7, 15, 17–18, 86, 93–94, 274–75

Cambaceres, Eugenio, 9–10, 34
Cané, Miguel, 153, 219
captive tale, 73, 76, 290n52
*Caras y Caretas* (magazine), 114–15, 119, 155–57, 296n109
Cárdenas, Eduardo José, 6, 20, 84, 110, 158–59, 291n66
Catholicism, 170, 179, 233, 246, 252, 273, 293n78; social, 256, 262. *See also* nationalism: Catholic
celebrity, 101, 161; academic, 275; Julia Bunge and, 164–66 (*see also* Bernhardt, Sarah); queer, 168
charity, 203, 247, 249, 251, 256, 261
childhood, 138, 144; of the Bunge siblings, 200, 202, 215, 218–20, 226; creativity, 223; development, 225; education, 190–91, 200, 220; memories, 220, 222; sexuality, 201, 203
class, 3, 9, 65, 123, 138–39, 248, 281; activism, 243; alliance, 94; anxiety, 20, 218; Argentine oligarchy as a, 284n5; belonging, 36, 103, 144, 197; conflict, 30, 262; conventions, 164; distinctions, 14; divisions, 260; expectations, 119; hierarchy, 235; identification, 150; interests, 284n6; inversion, 7, 139, 218; markers of, 125; performance of, 147; privilege, 86, 103, 121, 199; queerness and, 25; relations, 214; structures, 115, 189; subjectivity, 143
consent, 76, 231, 253. *See also* submission
cosmopolitanism, 33, 37, 43, 86, 259, 287n26
criollo, 218–19, 221, 284n6, 293n80; elite, 4, 11, 130, 263, 295n95; family, 33, 258;

man, 39, 216; past, 264; subject, 154, 161, 243; values, 115
cultural nationalism, 28, 41, 43, 54, 89, 139, 190–92, 200, 204, 207, 210, 212–13, 215, 229, 233, 288n39; Argentine, 235–36, 245–46, 254, 259, 264
cultural studies, 6, 8, 13, 199; Latin American, 80

death drive, 38, 108
decoloniality, 268–69, 280–82; of being, 298n131
Delgado, Verónica, 40–41
desire, 5, 8–10, 14, 15, 17–19, 21, 33, 35–37, 49–51, 54–58, 60, 63–66, 68–70, 75, 76, 78, 84, 87–89, 106, 107, 116, 121, 128, 141, 143, 150, 157, 168, 193, 200, 201, 204, 207, 220, 232, 244, 245, 265, 270, 271, 274, 278, 279; heteronormative, 8, 56, 60, 63–64, 69; heterosexual, 55–56, 65; homosocial, 68; social critique of, 64. *See also* queer desire
diary/diaries: as archive, 91; genre of, 91–92, 94–96, 106, 115, 291n59, 291n61; as palimpsest, 24, 100, 102, 167; as a practice, 93–97, 103–104, 106; as queer genre, 91–92; queerness of, 92, 110, 267; shared, 108; subversiveness of, 93; as technologies of self, 93–94, 103–104, 106, 110, 135. *See also* Bunge, Delfina: diaries of; Bunge, Julia Valentina: diary of
domesticity, 7, 35, 122, 124, 127–28, 202, 233, 245; female, 211; normative, 188; queer, 187

Echeverría, Esteban, 42, 74
Edelman, Lee, 38, 54, 288n41
education, 3, 30, 190–92, 194–99, 203, 206, 208, 211, 216–17, 219, 228, 230, 236, 253; childhood, 191, 220, 273; higher, 294n88; intellectual, 40; in nineteenth-century Spanish America, 294nn90–91; primary, 192, 226; right to, 33; secondary, 192, 194; women's, 62, 295n92; youth, 189. *See also* pedagogy
Eng, David L., 15, 86, 297n117
erotic excess, 37, 144, 147
eroticism, 50, 58, 66, 228; between men, 66 (*see also* homoeroticism); queer, 79
Escuelas Normales (Normal Schools/teaching colleges), 189, 194, 196, 294n88
Estrada, Ángel de, 112, 153
eugenics, 6, 10, 34, 44, 65, 89, 237, 288n40; aesthetic (Vasconcelos), 195; Bunge, Alejandro and, 263, 298n124; photography and, 151; Spencerian, 154

familial gaze/look, 2, 141–42, 144, 146, 172, 176, 178, 181–82, 184–86, 293n81; queer, 158, 161, 168
family album, 139–42, 160, 292n76; technology of, 188. *See also* Bunge family album
fascism, 232, 262
femininity, 46, 62, 74, 83, 211
feminism, 14, 62, 89, 92–93, 96, 107, 231, 235, 275; Alejandro Bunge on, 241–42; Delfina Bunge's, 116, 170, 233, 246–50, 254; early, 120, 196, 243, 251, 253, 255; intersectional, 197; Latin American, 274, 280; radicalization of, 273; second-wave, 271; in the Southern Cone, 245–46; third-wave, 281. *See also* transfeminism
filiation, 16, 35, 80, 83, 107, 124
*fin de siglo*, 161; Argentina's, 2, 44–45, 62, 71, 157; criticism, 37
Foster, David William, 13, 287n28
Foucault, Michel, 8, 16, 25, 87, 93–94, 203, 209
Freud, Sigmund, 45–46, 49–50, 64–65, 108, 220. *See also* Oedipal socialization; psychoanalysis
future, the: of Argentina, 35, 48, 189–90, 192, 195, 200, 203–205, 218, 229–30, 237, 241, 258, 263–64, 296n109; diaries and, 91–94, 96–97, 99–100, 105; of the elite, 232–33, 265–66; nationalism and, 54, 234, 236; photography and, 139, 144–45, 150, 175, 178, 181, 187
futurity, 2, 35, 55, 151, 154, 185; of the archive, 21–22; Argentine, 288n41; of diaries, 91–92; of the family album, 139; of kinship, 11; national, 11, 25, 35–37, 218, 236–37, 263–64; reproductive, 36, 54–55, 266, 270

Gálvez, Lucía, 2–3, 20–21, 24, 28, 95, 99, 146, 283n3, 288n37, 291n60
Gálvez, Manuel, 21, 31, 40–41, 43–44, 51, 55, 100, 110–12, 114–15, 122, 127, 216, 235, 291n66; cultural nationalism of, 207, 264, 290n51; *El diario de Gabriel Quiroga* (*The Diary of Gabriel Quiroga*), 205–206; marriage to Delfina Bunge, 101, 126, 129, 132–34, 169–70, 175, 204–205; photographs of, 182–85. *See also* Bunge, Delfina; Gálvez, Lucía

gaucho, the, 35, 71–73, 76, 233, 284n6, 289–90n50
gender and sexuality studies, 8, 15, 274, 278, 298n127
gender equality, 247, 273
gender performance/performativity, 4, 15, 32, 37, 277
genre, 7–8, 25, 42, 168, 289n47; of *carte de visite*, 163; of the diary, 91–92, 94–96, 106, 115, 291n59, 291n61; family album as, 139, 146; Gothic, 80; of memoir, 138
Gerassi, Navarro, 234, 283n5
Groussac, Cornelia ("Taita"), 178–81, 185
Guy, Donna, 34, 115

Hale, Charles A., 6, 287n30
Hernández, José, 70–71
heteronormativity, 24, 33, 41, 56, 64, 124, 193, 201, 272; countergenealogies to, 270; demands of, 89, 160; patriarchal, 7. *See also* desire: heteronormative
Hirsch, Marianne, 2, 26, 140–42, 182
homoeroticism, 20, 229. *See also* eroticism: queer
homophobia, 32, 64, 127
homosocial rivalry, 64, 66, 70, 127
Huff, Cynthia, 92, 96, 291n59
hybridity, 238, 241, 243–45
hysteria, 45–47, 52, 56

*Ideas* (magazine), 40–42, 50–51, 54, 111–12, 114–15, 117, 124, 151, 156–57, 288n35
Igon, J.B., 192–93
incest, 16, 46, 79, 84–88
Indigenous populations, 154, 195–96, 237, 240

Ingenieros, José, 48–49, 64–65, 153, 216, 244, 264–65
intimacy, 3, 38, 70, 101, 111, 124, 128, 141, 254; of the archive, 20, 24; the Bunge family and, 19, 143, 159–60, 169, 171, 180–81, 185–86; disciplining of, 139; of the family, 22, 215; kinship and, 21, 35; limits of, 138; masculine, 20; performance of, 7; sexual, 56. *See also* celebrity; domesticity; privacy; publicity

kinship, 2–3, 5–8, 11–17, 21–22, 27, 32, 53, 79, 81–82, 84–85, 92, 100, 103, 107, 130, 138–42, 168, 172, 188, 190–91, 193, 198, 214, 230–33, 251, 256, 260, 265–66, 286n18; as always already heterosexual, 86; bonds, 46, 208; Bunge, Carlos Octavio and, 55; Bunge, Delfina and, 99; futurity of, 11; horizontality and, 16, 26, 124; ideologies of, 207; imaginary, 200, 235; impossibility of, 59; memorializing, 171, 178; normative, 8, 12, 24, 35–36, 76–77, 86–87, 89, 122, 128, 141, 143, 181, 267, 292n70; Oedipal primacy of, 221; paradoxes of, 2–3; queer critiques of, 15–16; queerness and, 13–14, 25; reformations of, 296n105, 297n118; rhetoric of, 53, 130; studies, 285n16; structural basis of, 14. *See also* familiar relations; family; queer kinship
Krafft-Ebing, Richard von, 49, 239

Latin American studies, 6–8, 10–12, 277–78; queer, 27, 268, 278–79, 281; queer studies/theory and, 5, 285n14

Lavrin, Asunción, 211, 245
Le Bon, Gustave, 221, 236
Lejeune, Philip, 91, 104
Lévi-Strauss, Claude, 14, 67
liberalism, 230, 234, 240, 260, 287n30
literary criticism, 37–38, 40–41, 54, 72; Argentine, 290n51
love, 3, 63–67, 75–76, 88, 108, 200, 202–203, 214, 230–31, 252, 271–72, 298n125; of country, 190, 192–93, 201, 209, 213–14, 218, 263; familiar, 229; free, 270; heterosexual, 8; ideal, 9; maternal, 107; romantic, 144
Lugones, Leopoldo, 71, 206–207, 290n51

Mansilla, Eduarda, 4, 74
Mármol, José, 9, 39, 42–43
marriage, 9, 14, 26, 101, 113, 245, 298n125; Alejandro Bunge on, 259, 263; in "El Capitán Pérez," 60, 65–66, 70; in "El Chucro," 76; Delfina Bunge on, 125–26, 128, 133–35, 248, 251–53; elite hegemony and, 160; equality, 271–72; gay, 17; heterosexual/heteronormative, 8, 62; in *La novela de la sangre*, 38, 46–47, 51, 56; in "Pesadilla Drolática," 82, 86; rejection of, 124; strategic, 4, 130; Victoria Ocampo on, 132–34
Martel, Julián, 34, 59
Martí, José, 37, 237
masculinity, 57, 73; Bunge, Carlos Octavio and, 150–51; failed, 60; idealized, 204; martial/militarism and, 144, 206–207, 225; the Mulatto and, 244; national, 45; patriotism and, 206; performance of, 147, 207; violent, 43, 76–77, 223, 229

memory, 21, 128, 137, 219–25; the Bunge siblings and, 193, 198; childhood and, 191, 215, 219–20, 223; the family and, 140–41, 159, 200; fictional, 292n76; historical, 89; kinship and, 2; in *Nuestra Patria*, 26; photography and, 138, 159, 175, 185, 188, 293n77; studies, 280; trauma and, 46
Mestizo, 35, 195–96, 237, 240–43. *See also* miscegenation
Micale, Mark S., 46–47
Michie, Helena, 106–107
miscegenation, 57, 195, 233, 236–38, 240, 242. *See also* Mestizo
Mistral, Gabriela, 195, 197–98
Mitchell, Juliet, 16, 46, 107–108
Mizraje, María Gabriela, 111, 294n58
modernity, 3–5, 9, 12, 45, 88–89, 139, 164, 242; abject, 69; Argentine, 35–36; Bunge, Carlos Octavio and, 149–50, 153–54, 215; of the Bunge family, 146; civilized, 195–96; civilizing possibilities of, 244; conflicts of, 253; crisis of, 34; European, 165, 168; kinship and, 296n105; political dynamics of, 199; positivist, 228; queerness and, 147, 165, 170; technological, 186; technologies of, 23; Western, 15, 269; women and, 161, 246, 248
Molloy, Sylvia, 37, 164, 219, 282, 267n31
monogamy, 238–40, 263, 298n125
Monniot, Victorine, 102–103, 110, 291n63. *See also* Bunge, Delfina: "el caso Delfina"
motherhood, 76, 134, 197, 245–47; national, 196; normative, 75
*Las mujeres y la vocación* (Bunge, Delfina), 27, 233, 246–52, 254–55

Muñoz, José Esteban, 54, 92, 288n41

nation, the, 11–12, 22, 34, 139, 189–194, 197–200, 231, 273; future of, 20, 25, 35, 189, 238, 264; heteronormative desire and, 8, 35; love of, 8; promise of, 55; romance of, 89. See also *patria* (homeland)
national belonging, 33, 36, 51, 94, 198–99, 203, 265
nationalism, 3, 7, 27, 35, 190, 194, 231, 235; Argentine, 36, 43, 101, 130, 232, 234, 264–65, 284n6; Catholic, 243, 260, 265, 297n111; Delfina Bunge on, 251; as familiar, 26; Lugones on, 206; Manuel Gálvez on, 205; public demonstrations of, 11. See also cultural nationalism
national novel, 7, 49
national romance, 9, 36, 39
nationhood, 26, 231
Naturalism, 9–11, 34, 43, 45, 80, 139; Bunge, Carlos Octavio and, 37, 289n47
nonnormativity, 7, 13, 19, 34, 142
Normal Schools. See Escuelas Normales
normative, the, 4–6, 13–14, 18–19, 27, 87, 121, 269. See also family: normative; heteronormativity; normativity; queer, the
normative sex/gender system, 46, 75–77
normativity, 5–8, 12–19, 23, 36, 86, 89, 111, 121, 143, 145, 197, 225, 245, 266; in the Americas, 268, 280; gendered, 119; new, 272; patriarchal, 4, 124, 277; queerness and, 3, 14, 58, 266; in queer studies, 284–85n8; state, 193; temporal logics of, 236; threat to, 242; violence of, 77. See also heteronormativity; normative, the; queer, the; queerness
normative kinship, 12, 15, 24, 35–36, 79–77, 86–87, 89, 122, 128, 292n70; Bunge family album and, 143; ideology of, 8, 141; patterns, 181; queering of, 85, 267
nostalgia, 149, 185, 199, 220, 235, 255, 284n6
Nouzeilles, Gabriela, 9–10, 34, 39, 288n39. See also somatic fictions
*La novela de la sangre* (Bunge, Carlos Octavio), 10, 25, 30, 33, 36–39, 41–43, 46–47, 49–56, 58, 72, 78, 84, 87, 89, 287n25, 288n37, 288n39; queerness of, 37, 44, 47, 54, 56
*Nuestra América: Ensayo de psicología social* (Bunge, Carlos Octavio), 27, 30, 151, 153, 233, 236–46, 296n106
*Nuestra Patria: Libro de lectura para la educación nacional* (Bunges, Carlos Octavio), 26, 144, 190, 192, 198–200, 209, 215–29, 295n101

Ocampo, Victoria, 4, 119–21, 132–34, 161, 245, 292n74
Oedipal socialization, 15–16, 46, 55
Olivera, Ricardo, 36, 40–46, 51, 55, 288n37. See also *Ideas* (magazine)

*patria* (homeland), 26, 134, 192, 204, 206, 208–209, 213–17, 223–24; *postestad*, 124, 253. See also nation, the
patriarchy, 10, 63, 73, 75–77, 82, 85; hetero-, 23
patriotism, 7, 35, 72, 189–90, 193, 196, 201, 203, 206, 213–14

Payá, Carlos Manuel, 6, 20, 84, 110, 291n66
Pecheny, Mario, 271–72
pedagogy, 22, 26, 30, 190, 195–99, 217, 229; collective, 110, 201, 208; national, 22, 192, 194, 196, 242; nostalgic, 219; patriotic, 218, 230; public, 196, 209, 215; queer, 190–91
Perón, Juan Domingo, 95, 296n104
Peronism, 232, 257
photography, 26, 138–41, 293n77; in Argentina, 145–46, 293n81; Bunge siblings and, 170–71, 185; captions, 151–52, 155–56, 179, 187; eugenic, 151; family, 146; glamour, 161; kinship and, 285n16; Latin American, 293n78; memorialized quality of, 188
polygamy, 238–40
positivism, 7, 11–12, 34, 56–57, 139, 195, 216–17, 228–29, 233–35, 246, 267, 287n30; Bunge, Alejandro and, 259, 264; Bunge, Carlos Octavio and, 6, 30, 62, 236, 243; the Mulatta and, 242; Ramos Mejía and, 288n40
Prebisch, Raúl, 257, 297n121
privacy, 20, 22, 24, 101, 115, 121, 135, 138, 170. *See also* celebrity; domesticity; intimacy; publicity
psychoanalysis, 46, 86, 225; Lacanian, 15
publicity, 22, 101, 110–12, 121, 135, 138–39, 160, 171; campaigns, 274; sibling, 168. *See also* celebrity; domesticity; intimacy; privacy

queer desire, 18, 25, 57–58, 60, 64–66, 68–69, 78, 85, 89, 227–28, 245

queer home, 124, 126–28, 187
queer kinship, 2, 15–16, 18–19, 21–22, 27, 106
queerness, 3, 5–7, 9, 12–14, 16–19, 24–25, 33, 44, 47, 64, 85–86, 92, 110–112, 121, 142–43, 145, 164, 197–201, 229, 266, 269–272, 282, 286n18; ambivalence of, 243; in Argentina, 138; education and, 191–193; of familial proximity, 22; of hybridity, 245; of kinship, 25, 27; of melodrama, 289n43; modernity and, 147, 165, 168, 170; objects and, 223; queer theory and, 278; repression of, 203; of Sarah Bernhardt, 161, 165; of the spinster, 126; temporality as, 296n105
queer studies, 5–6, 12, 18, 76, 199, 268–72, 274–78, 280–81, 284n8, 285nn14–16; formation of, 79; future of, 27, 268; Latin American, 197, 273, 279, 281; utopianism and, 92
queer temporality, 1, 185, 288n41
queer theory, 5, 8, 15–16, 18, 275–76, 278–82, 285n8; Anglo-American, 13; incest taboo and, 86; Latin American studies and, 5; origins, 273, 276
Quiroga, José, 13, 277

race, 3, 25, 35, 139, 151, 195, 228, 232, 237–38, 242, 268, 281; in Argentina, 287n30; Argentine, 207; mixed-, 35, 52, 54, 173, 238, 254, 265, 298n124; the nation and, 259, 263–64; positivist discourse on, 246; queer temporality and, 288n41; in the United States, 288n39; white, 258, 263. *See also* Mestizo

racism, 27, 35, 92; in Argentina, 287n30; of Bunge, Carlos Octavio, 35, 219, 237, 242; scientific, 35, 236
Ramos Mejía, José María, 191, 216–17, 221, 264
*Rerum Novarum* (Leo XIII), 260–62
Rock, David, 129, 210, 233, 293n80
Rodríguez, Juana María, 76–77
Rojas, Ricardo, 218, 235, 264, 290n51
romantical friendship, 30, 147, 150
Rosas, Juan Manuel de, 38–39, 42–48, 50, 53–56, 152, 221, 287n32
Rubin, Gayle, 15, 60, 70

Salessi, Jorge, 6–7, 13
Sarmiento, Domingo, 42–43, 152, 191, 194–95, 217, 237, 295n92
Sedgwick, Eve Kosofsky, 15, 66
sexuality, 4, 7–8, 15, 17, 32, 56, 121, 164, 180, 198, 268; in Argentina, 103, 122–23; Carlos Octavio Bunge on, 62–63, 237; childhood, 201, 203; discourses of, 35, 190–91; enactment of, 144; *fin de siglo*, 45–46, 103; Foucault on, 201; heteronormative, 63, 79, 236; incestuous, 86, 88; in Latin America, 3, 13; nonreproductive, 233; normative, 33, 193, 232, 270, 273; pregenital, 50; principles of, 63; procreative, 56, 258; regime of, 209; reproductive, 86, 108; sibling, 108; women's, 62–64. *See also* gender and sexuality studies
Shumway, Nicolas, 6, 216
sibling bonds, 107–108, 175
siblinghood, 16, 108; queer possibility of, 124

Sierras Hotel and Casino, 145, 171–78, 182–84
sisterhood, 26, 106–107, 112, 132, 138, 285n15
social hygiene, 7, 35, 56
socialism, 206, 232, 246, 255, 260, 262, 267, 297n121
socialists, 33, 60, 129, 235, 295n96
*soltera* (single woman), 61, 111, 123, 125–26, 251
*solterona* (spinster), 122, 125–26, 241
somatic fictions, 39, 78, 288n39
Sommer, Doris, 8–9, 34, 39
Sontag, Susan, 139–40
sororal conspiracy, 58, 62, 65, 70, 289n47
sororal relations, 25, 178
Spicer-Escalante, J.P., 10–11
structural anthropology, 86, 271, 285n16
subjectivity, 12, 14, 79, 107; ethnic, 143; familial, 141; multiple, 116; mutual, 110, 112
submission, 49, 76, 85, 253; to men, 63; to patriarchal authority, 60, 201; to order, 71. *See also* consent

technologies of self (Foucault), 16, 25, 93–94, 103–104, 106, 110, 135. *See also* diary/diaries
Terán, Oscar, 6, 217
textbooks, 7, 25, 189, 191–92, 197–98, 214, 218, 294n89; by the Bunge siblings, 4, 21–22, 24, 26, 190–91, 193, 198, 200–201, 230, 267 (see also *El Arca de Noé*; *Nuestra Patria*)
transculturation, 80, 238, 282
transfeminism, 275, 280, 298n126

translation, 13, 40, 269, 275–76, 278–79, 281–82

*Una nueva Argentina* (Bunge, Alejandro), 27, 233, 255, 258–59, 262–65
Uranga, Ignacio, 129, 176, 177f, 182–84

Vasconcelos, José, 195, 238
Viñas, David, 40–41, 289n45

whiteness, 52, 166, 228, 237, 239, 258, 264–65, 288n41; Argentine, 27, 233. See also *blanqueamiento*; Bunge, Alejandro; *raza blanca*
white supremacy, 6–7, 23, 35, 237, 263, 265–66, 277. See also Bunge, Carlos Octavio; racism
Wilde, Oscar, 37, 79, 153, 294n83
women, 69–70, 83, 89, 113, 161, 196, 246–47, 294n85; Bunge, Carlos Octavio on, 62–64, 241–42; Bunge, Delfina on, 247–52, 254; of color, 275–76; commodification of, 289n47; diaries written by, 93; as domestic angels, 143; exchange of, 15, 60, 67, 70; identification with other, 107; marriage and, 14, 126–27; masochism and, 49; patriarchal authority and, 75, 253, 272; in the public sphere, 33, 103; reading (as trope), 179–81; role of, 52, 103, 111, 116, 189, 194–97, 211; spirituality and, 245; white, 259; working, 115 (*see also* women's labor); writers, 111, 119–21 (*see also* women's writing)
women's labor, 26–27, 180, 211, 248–50
women's writing, 113, 119–21, 291n59

*Xarcas Silenciario* (Bunge, Carlos Octavio), 30, 286n25, 288n37

Zeballos, Estanislao, 112–13, 292n70

www.ingramcontent.com/pod-product-compliance
Lightning Source LLC
Chambersburg PA
CBHW030009240426
43672CB00007B/879